Disgaea® 2 Volume 1

Eng
Tra ... nashita
Eng
Touc
Cove ... Dougall

Editor: ... Seto
Sales Manager: Ardith D. Santiago
Managing Editor: Shizuki Yamashita
Publisher: Kaname Tezuka

Email: editor@broccolibooks.com
Website: www.broccolibooks.com

A BROCCOLI BOOKS Broccoli Books Manga
Broccoli Books is a division of Broccoli International USA, Inc.
1728 S. La Cienega Blvd. Los Angeles, CA 90035

ISBN-13: 978-1-5974-1113-4
ISBN-10: 1-59741-113-2

Published by Broccoli International USA, Inc.
Second printing, August 2007
First printing, December 2006

All illustrations by Hekaton unless otherwise noted.
Cover illustration by Takehito Harada.
Special thanks to Hiroko Nelson and NIS America, Inc.

Distributed by Publishers Group West

ANIME GAMERS

BROCCOLI INTERNATIONAL USA
www.bro-usa.com

10 9 8 7 6 5 4 3 2
Printed in Canada

TABLE OF CONTENTS

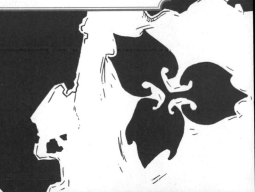

DISGAEA 1 CHARACTERS

PRINNIES

Impure Souls

Beings who have committed grievous sins are brought back to life as Prinnies, and must atone for their sins until reincarnated.

FLONNE

Fallen Angel

An angel trainee and a love freak. She came to the Netherworld to assassinate the overlord, but she failed.

ETNA

Loyal Vassal

Laharl's vassal who worships the previous overlord. She's very ambitious.

LAHARL

Resident Overlord

An overlord who took the throne after the death of his father. He's a natural born brawler.

DISGAEA 2 CHARACTERS

The Story of Disgaea

The death of the great King Krichevskoy, who maintained peace in the Netherworld, brings an age of war. With the help of his vassal Etna and the Celestian assassin Flonne, Krichevskoy's son, Laharl, stabilizes the conflict and becomes the overlord of the Netherworld. For a moment, it seems as if peace has returned.

ROZALIN

Loving Daughter

The only daughter of Overlord Zenon. She loves her father, and he adores her.

ADELL

Only Human

The only human left in Veldime. A passionate boy with a strong sense of justice.

ADELL'S FAMILY

From the left: Taro, Mom, Dad, Hanako

They are a family of demons. Adell's mother is a former summoner.

AXEL

Washed up Dark Hero

He is a shadow of his former self. His current profession is "travel show host."

DISGAEA 2
Cursed Memories

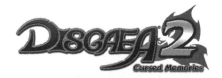

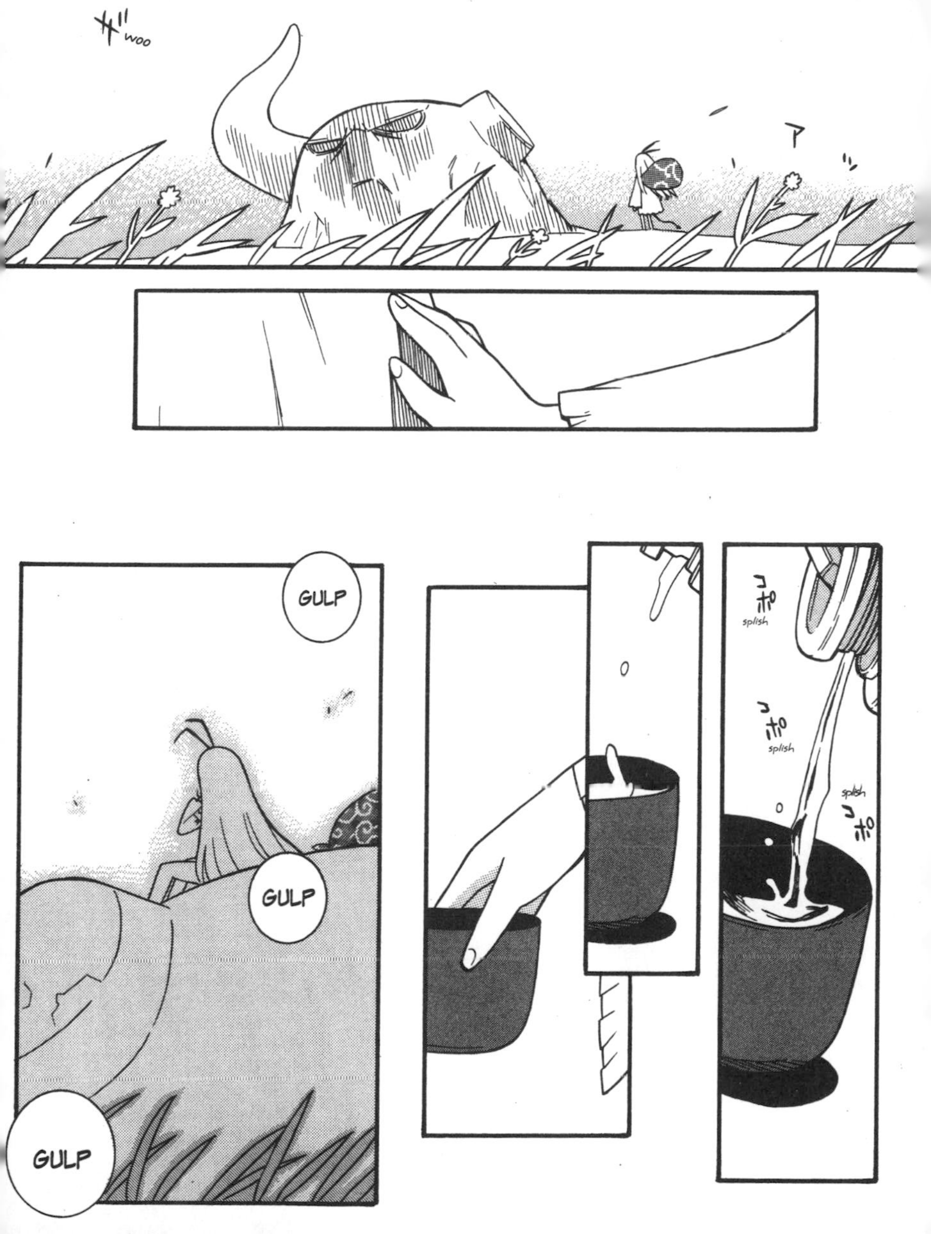
woo
splish
splish
splish
GULP
GULP
GULP

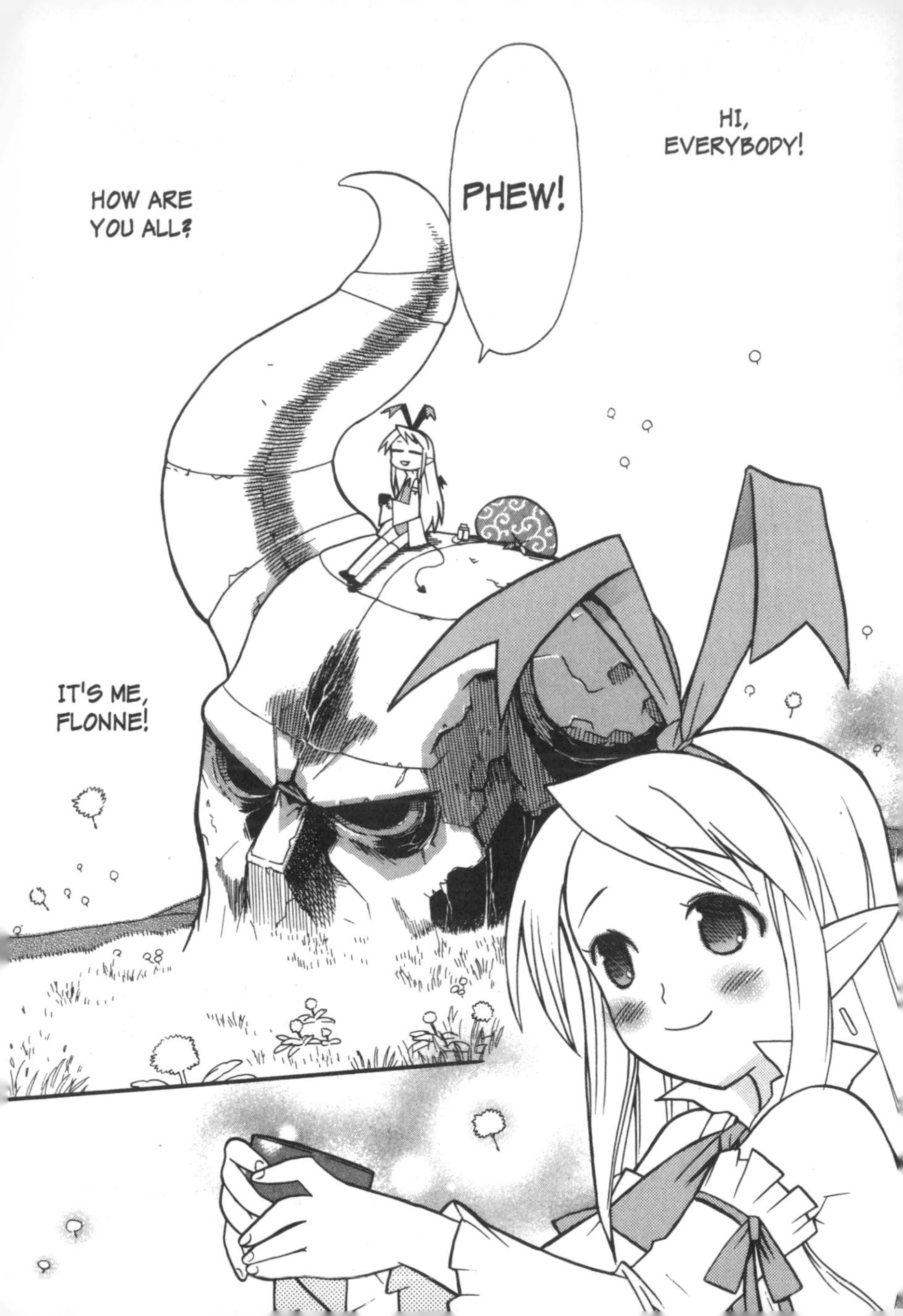
HI, EVERYBODY!
PHEW!
HOW ARE YOU ALL?
IT'S ME, FLONNE!

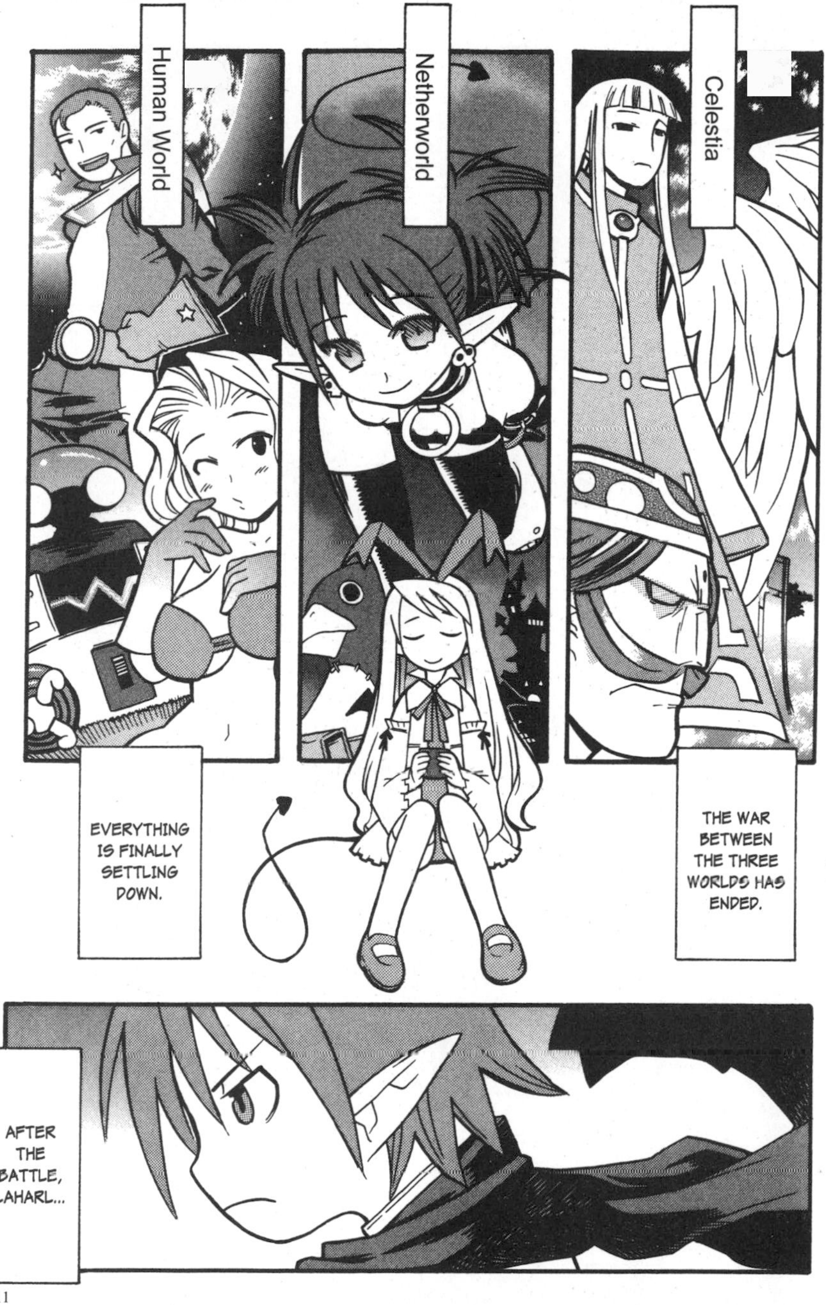
Celestia
Netherworld
Human World
THE WAR BETWEEN THE THREE WORLDS HAS ENDED.
EVERYTHING IS FINALLY SETTLING DOWN.
AFTER THE BATTLE, LAHARL...

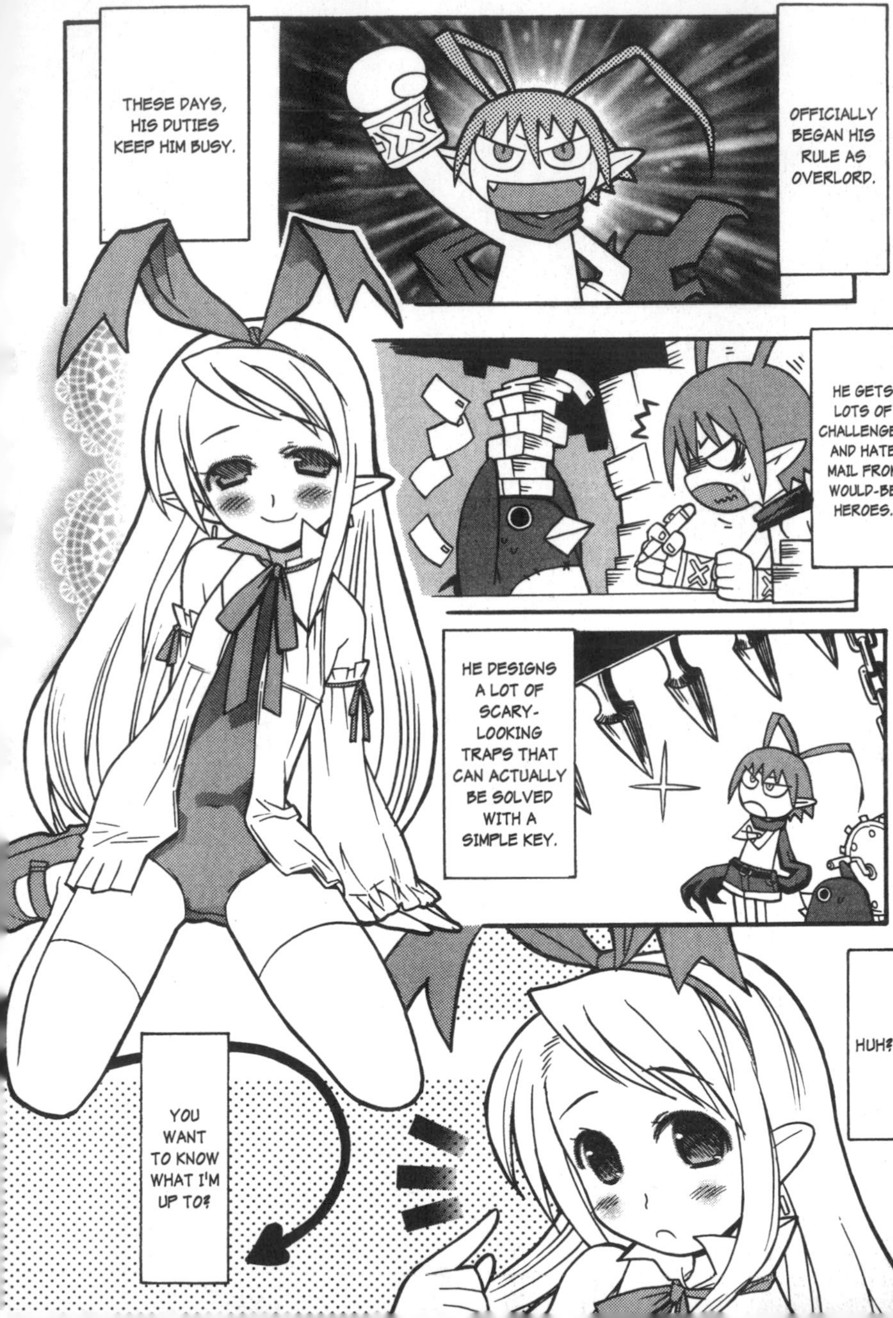
OFFICIALLY BEGAN HIS RULE AS OVERLORD.
THESE DAYS, HIS DUTIES KEEP HIM BUSY.
HE GETS LOTS OF CHALLENGES AND HATE MAIL FROM WOULD-BE HEROES.
HE DESIGNS A LOT OF SCARY-LOOKING TRAPS THAT CAN ACTUALLY BE SOLVED WITH A SIMPLE KEY.
HUH?
YOU WANT TO KNOW WHAT I'M UP TO?

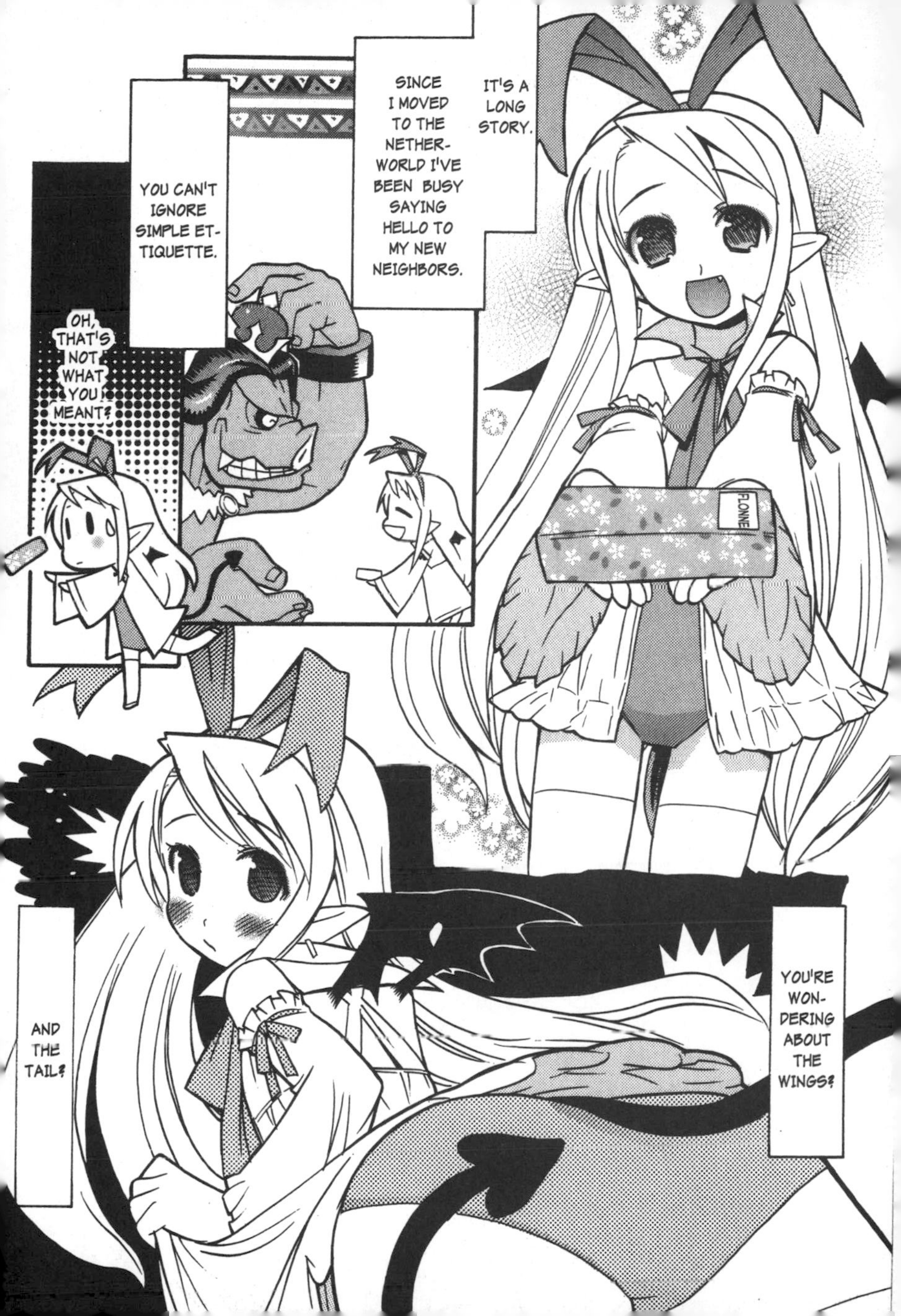
IT'S A LONG STORY.
SINCE I MOVED TO THE NETHER-WORLD I'VE BEEN BUSY SAYING HELLO TO MY NEW NEIGHBORS.
FLONNE
YOU CAN'T IGNORE SIMPLE ET-TIQUETTE.
OH, THAT'S NOT WHAT YOU MEANT?
YOU'RE WON-DERING ABOUT THE WINGS?
AND THE TAIL?

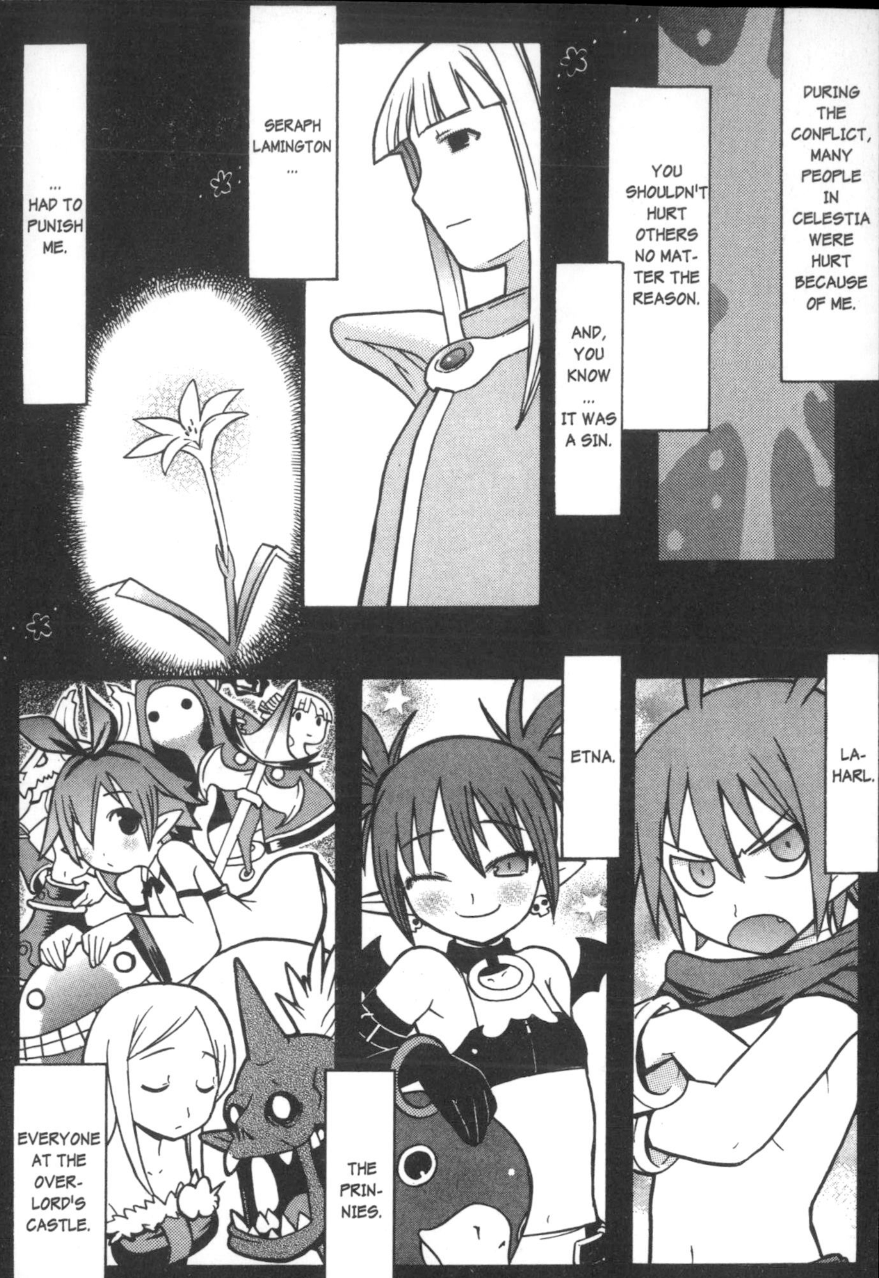
DURING THE CONFLICT, MANY PEOPLE IN CELESTIA WERE HURT BECAUSE OF ME.
YOU SHOULDN'T HURT OTHERS NO MATTER THE REASON.
AND, YOU KNOW ... IT WAS A SIN.
SERAPH LAMINGTON ...
... HAD TO PUNISH ME.
LA-HARL.
ETNA.
THE PRIN-NIES.
EVERYONE AT THE OVER-LORD'S CASTLE.

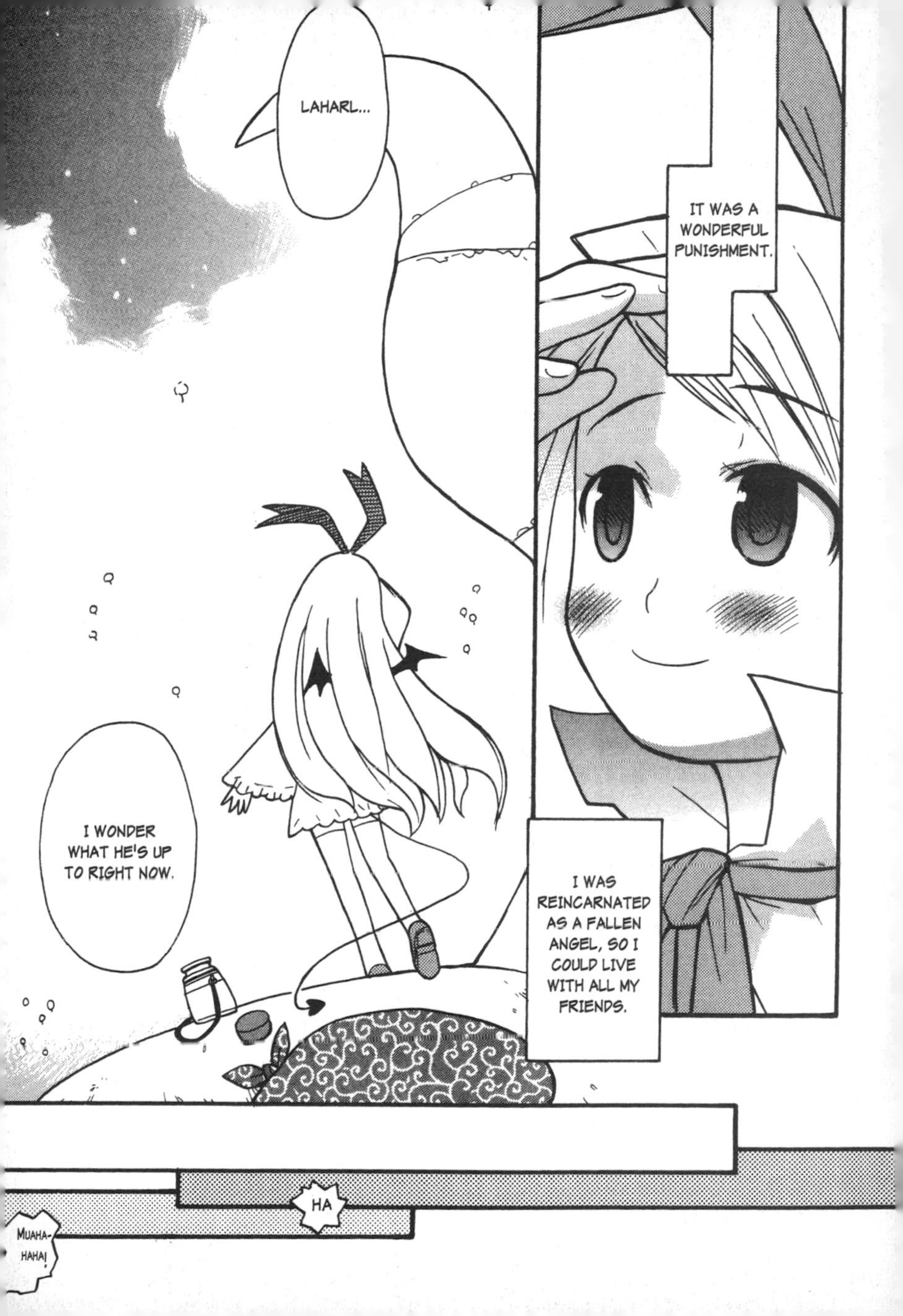
IT WAS A WONDERFUL PUNISHMENT.
I WAS REINCARNATED AS A FALLEN ANGEL, SO I COULD LIVE WITH ALL MY FRIENDS.
LAHARL...
I WONDER WHAT HE'S UP TO RIGHT NOW.
HA
MUAHA-HAHA!

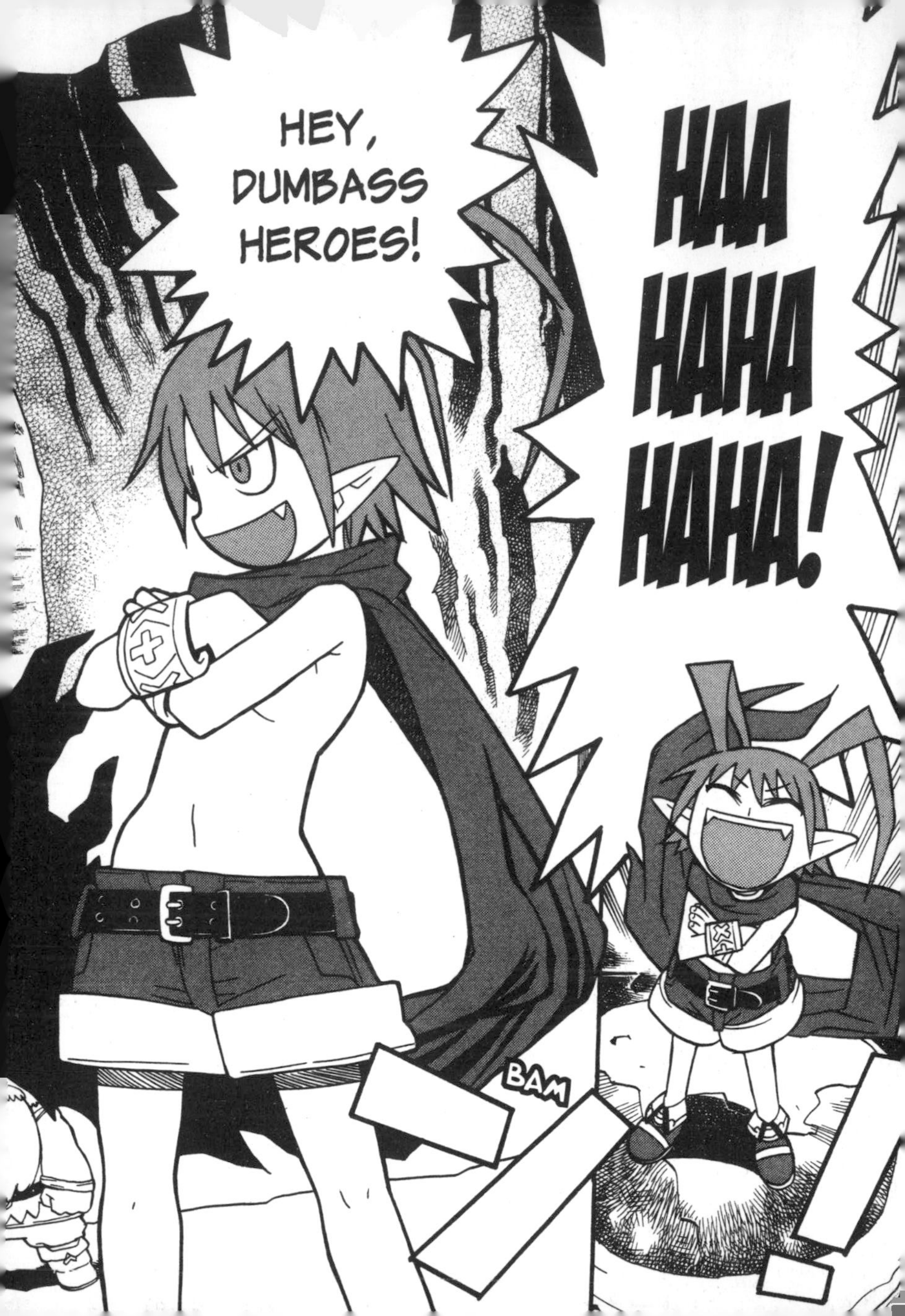
HAA HAHA HAHA!
HEY, DUMBASS HEROES!
BAM

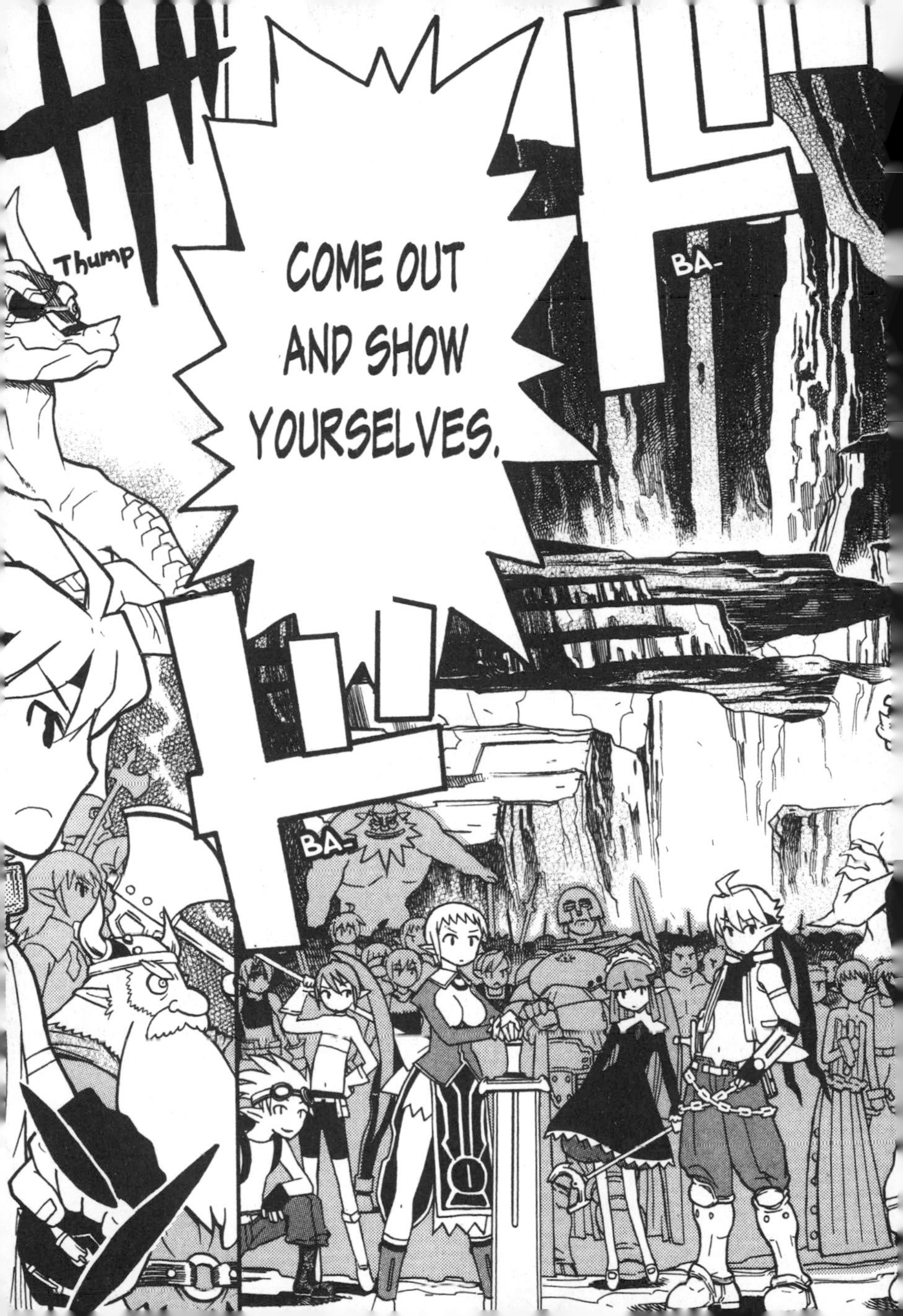
BA-
COME OUT AND SHOW YOURSELVES.
Thump
BA-

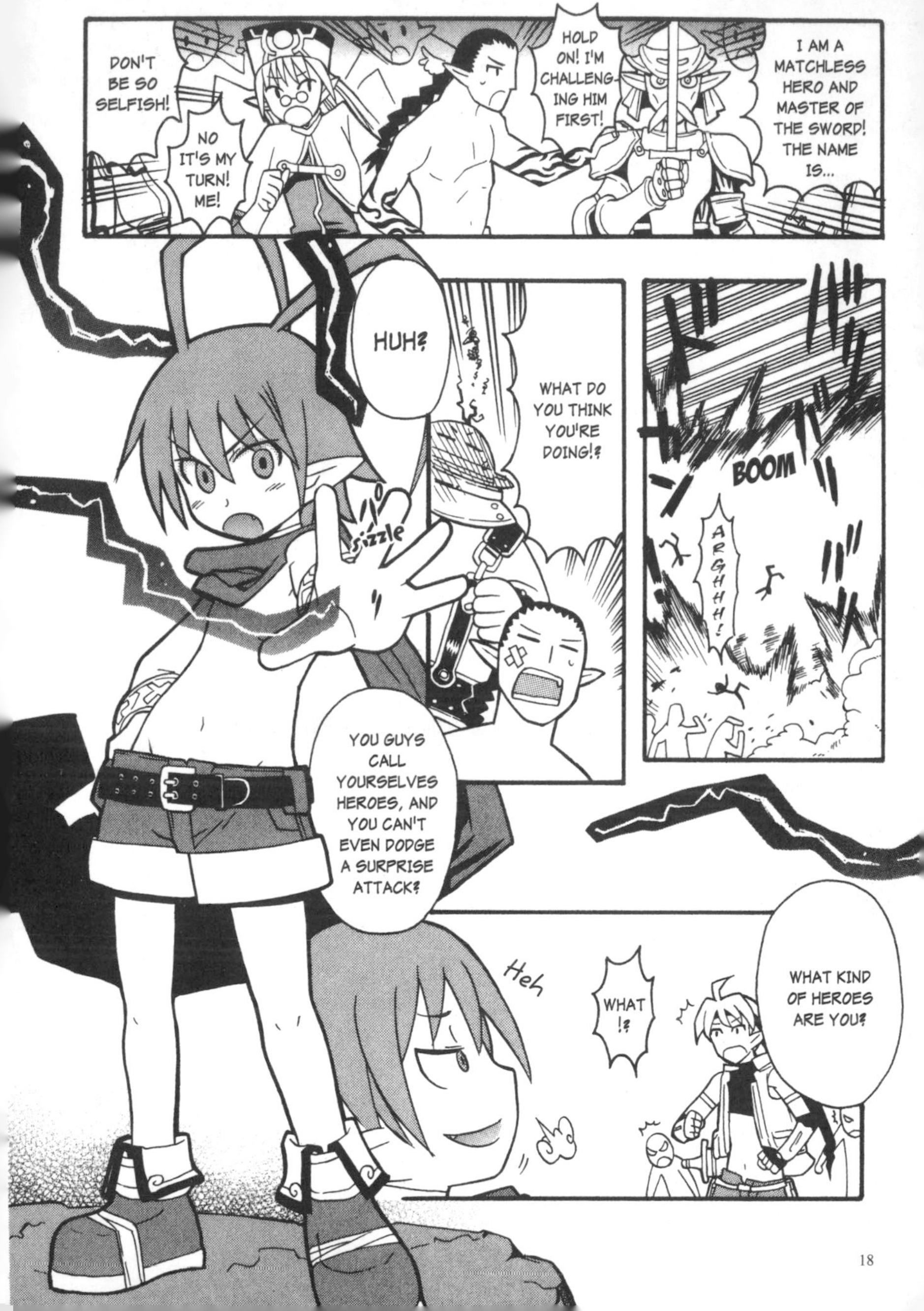
I AM A MATCHLESS HERO AND MASTER OF THE SWORD! THE NAME IS...
HOLD ON! I'M CHALLENG-ING HIM FIRST!
DON'T BE SO SELFISH!
NO IT'S MY TURN! ME!
BOOM
ARGHHH!
WHAT DO YOU THINK YOU'RE DOING!?
sizzle
HUH?
YOU GUYS CALL YOURSELVES HEROES, AND YOU CAN'T EVEN DODGE A SURPRISE ATTACK?
WHAT KIND OF HEROES ARE YOU?
WHAT !?
Heh

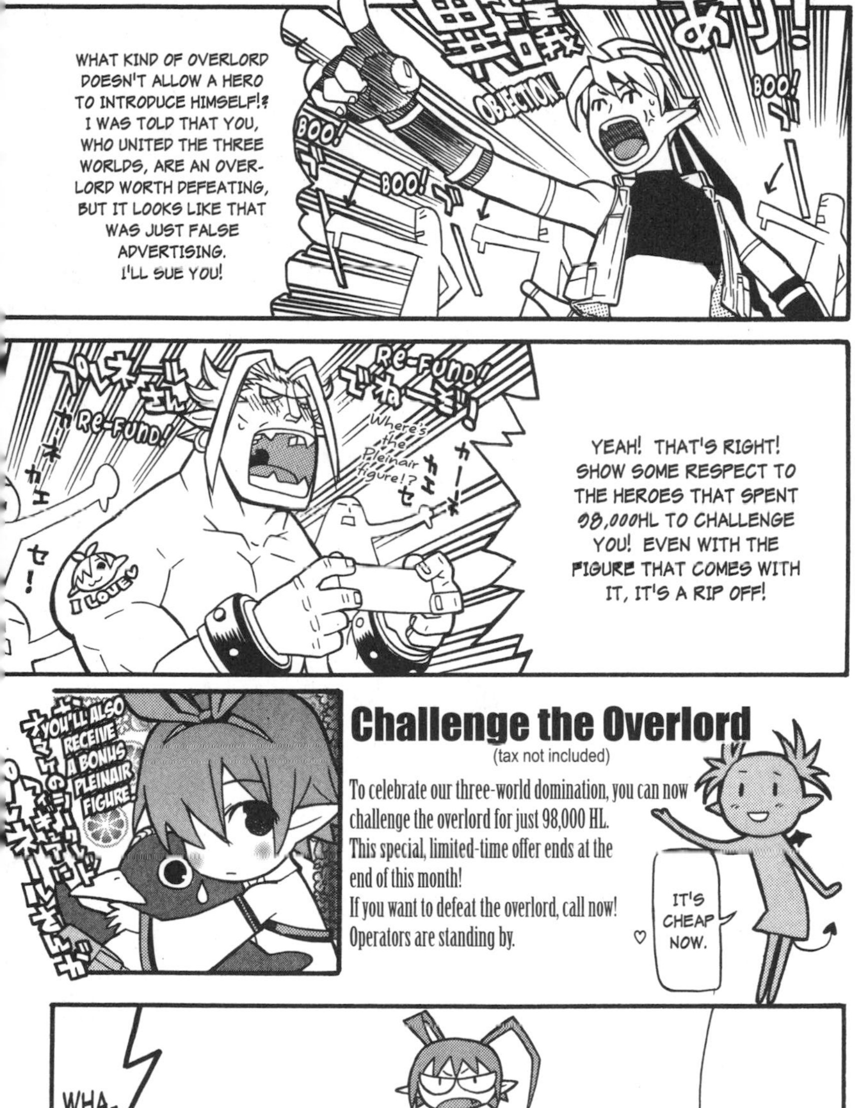

異議あり!
OBJECTION!
BOO!
BOO!
BOO!
WHAT KIND OF OVERLORD DOESN'T ALLOW A HERO TO INTRODUCE HIMSELF!? I WAS TOLD THAT YOU, WHO UNITED THE THREE WORLDS, ARE AN OVER-LORD WORTH DEFEATING, BUT IT LOOKS LIKE THAT WAS JUST FALSE ADVERTISING. I'LL SUE YOU!
YEAH! THAT'S RIGHT! SHOW SOME RESPECT TO THE HEROES THAT SPENT 98,000HL TO CHALLENGE YOU! EVEN WITH THE FIGURE THAT COMES WITH IT, IT'S A RIP OFF!
RE-FUND!
Where's the Pleinair figure!?
RE-FUND!
I LOVE
Challenge the Overlord
(tax not included)
To celebrate our three-world domination, you can now challenge the overlord for just 98,000 HL.
This special, limited-time offer ends at the end of this month!
If you want to defeat the overlord, call now!
Operators are standing by.
IT'S CHEAP NOW.
YOU'LL ALSO RECEIVE A BONUS PLEINAIR FIGURE!
IDIOTS.
WHA-!?

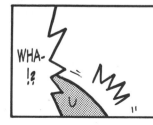

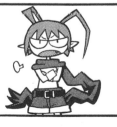

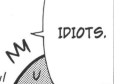

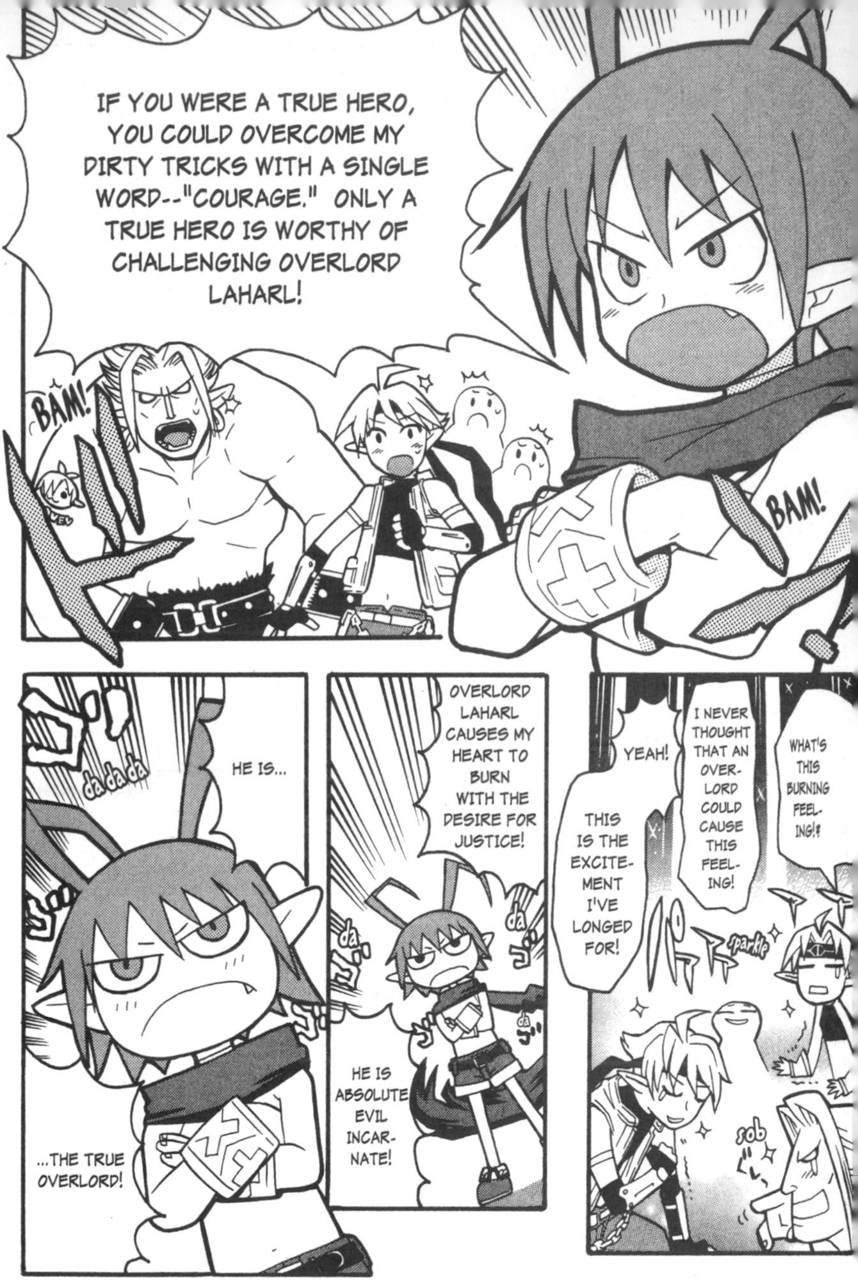
IF YOU WERE A TRUE HERO, YOU COULD OVERCOME MY DIRTY TRICKS WITH A SINGLE WORD--"COURAGE." ONLY A TRUE HERO IS WORTHY OF CHALLENGING OVERLORD LAHARL!
BAM!
BAM!
WHAT'S THIS BURNING FEEL-ING!?
I NEVER THOUGHT THAT AN OVER-LORD COULD CAUSE THIS FEEL-ING!
YEAH!
THIS IS THE EXCITE-MENT I'VE LONGED FOR!
sparkle
sob
OVERLORD LAHARL CAUSES MY HEART TO BURN WITH THE DESIRE FOR JUSTICE!
da
da
da
HE IS ABSOLUTE EVIL INCAR-NATE!
da da da
HE IS...
...THE TRUE OVERLORD!

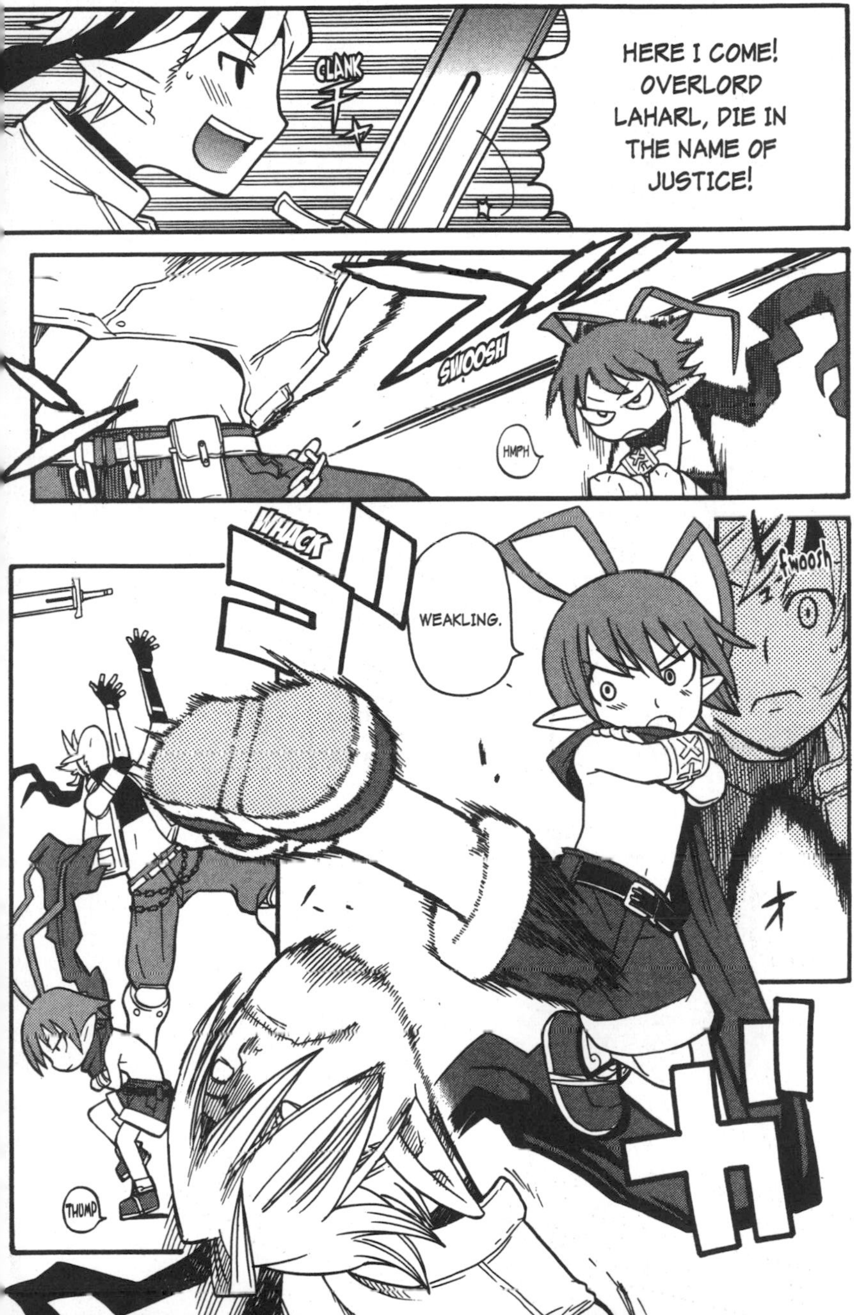
HERE I COME! OVERLORD LAHARL, DIE IN THE NAME OF JUSTICE!
CLANK
HMPH
SWOOSH
fwoosh
WEAKLING.
WHACK
THUMP

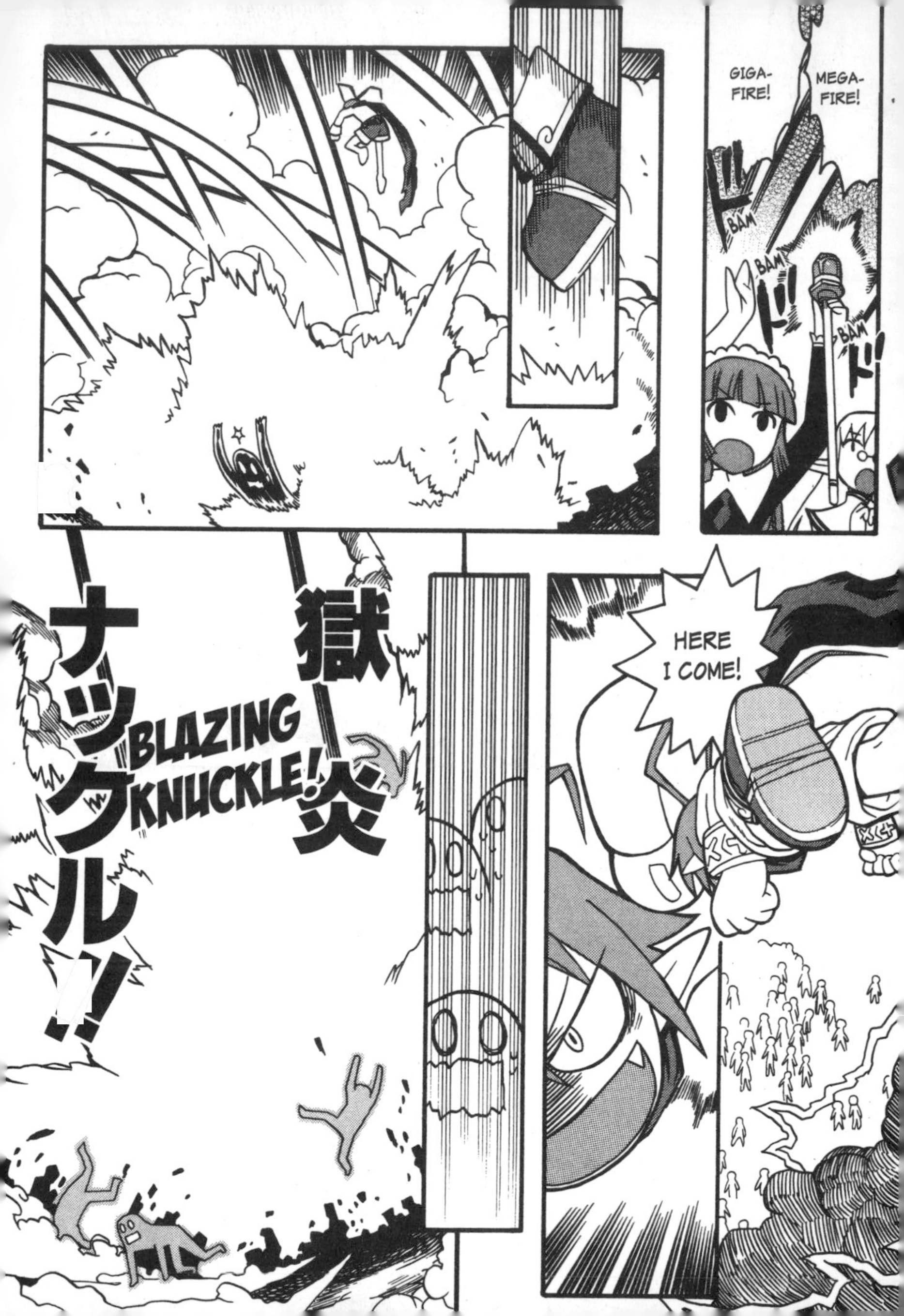
MEGA-FIRE!
GIGA-FIRE!
ドド
BAM
BAM
ドド
BAM
ドド
HERE I COME!
獄炎ナックル!!
BLAZING KNUCKLE!

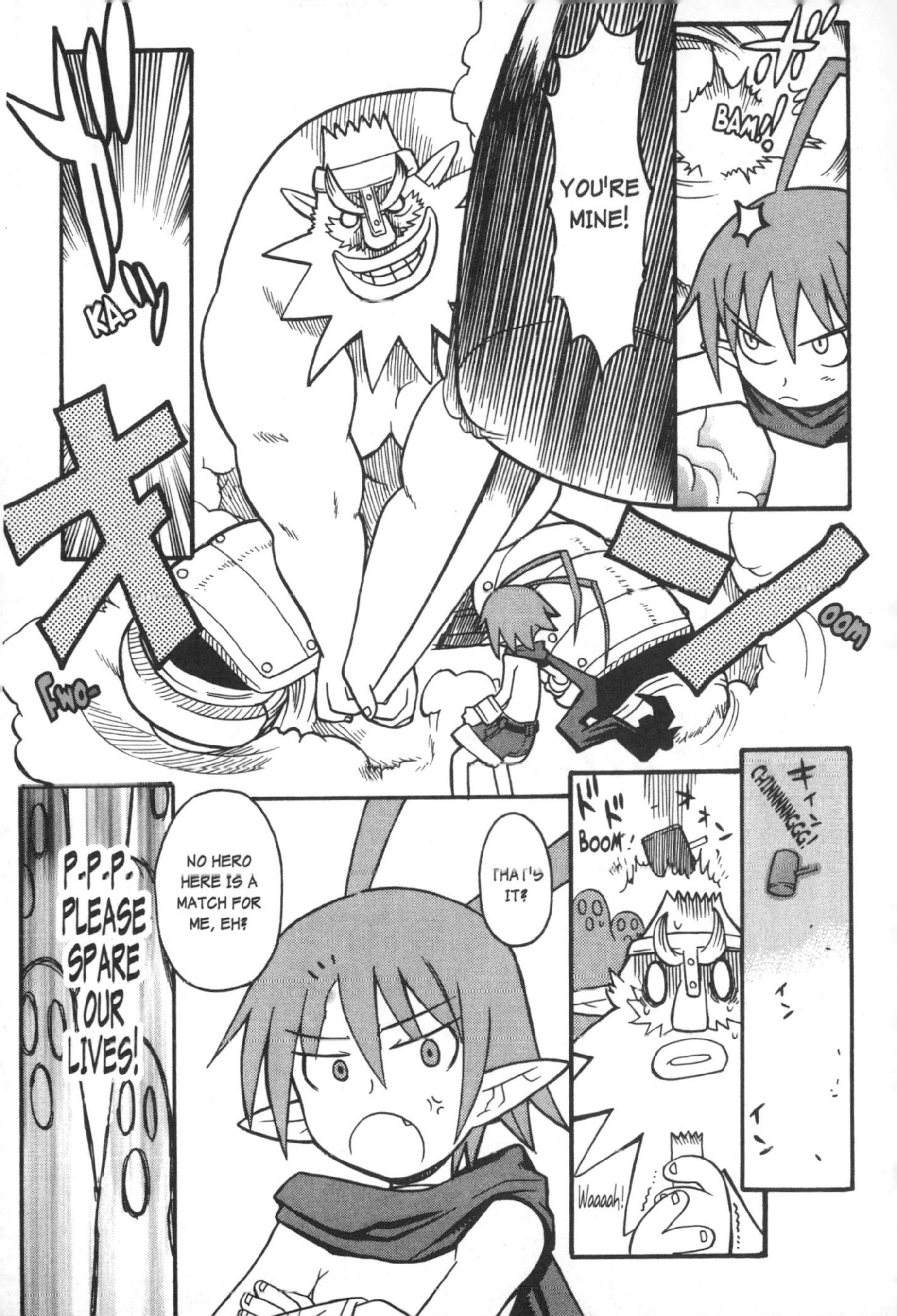
BAM!!
YOU'RE MINE!
KA-
FWO-
OOM
CHINNNNGGG!
BOOM!
Waaaah!
THAT'S IT?
NO HERO HERE IS A MATCH FOR ME, EH?
P-P-P-PLEASE SPARE YOUR LIVES!

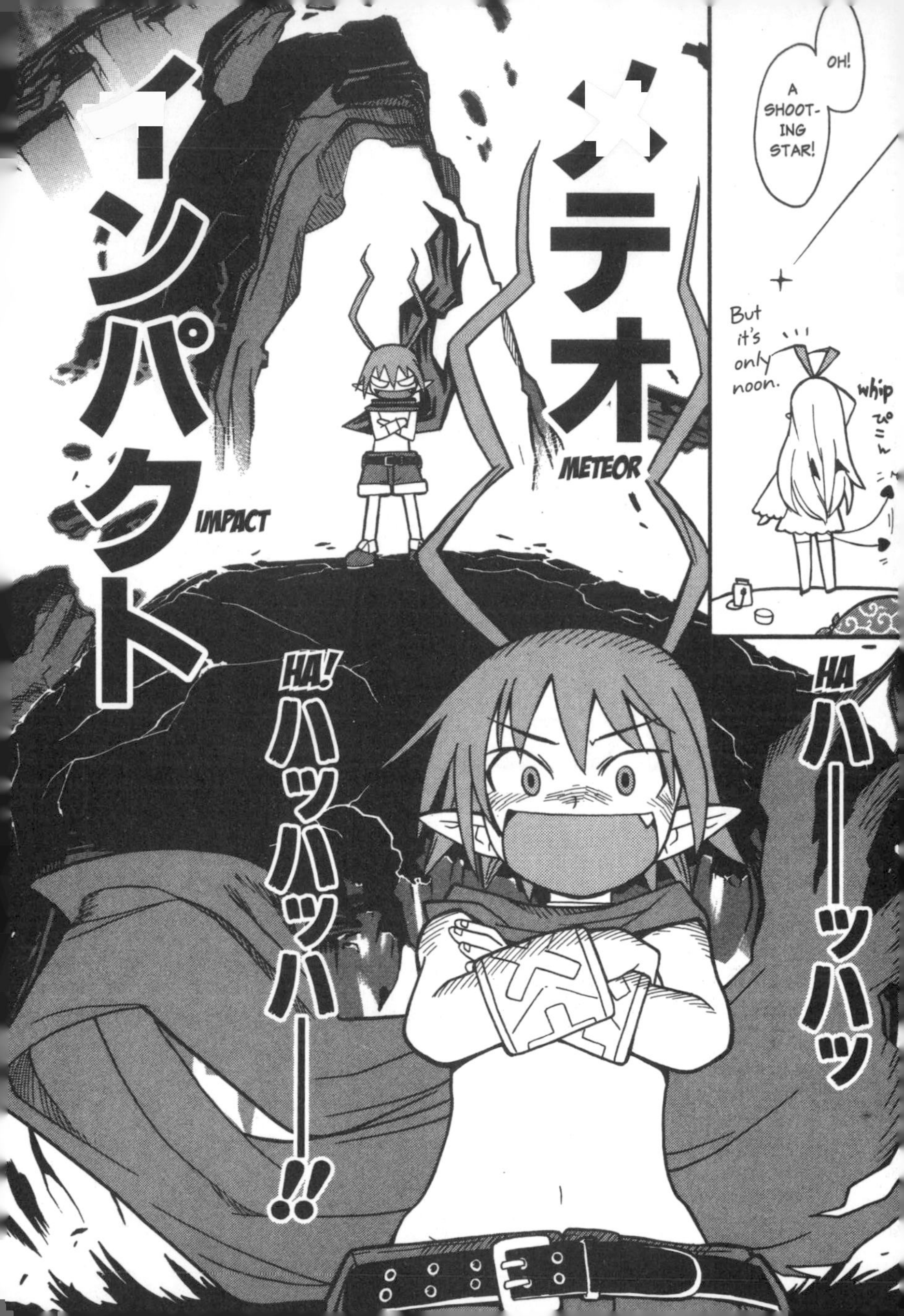
OH! A SHOOTING STAR!
But it's only noon.
whip
ぴこん
メテオ
METEOR
インパクト
IMPACT
ハーッハッ
HA
ハッハッハーー!!
HA!

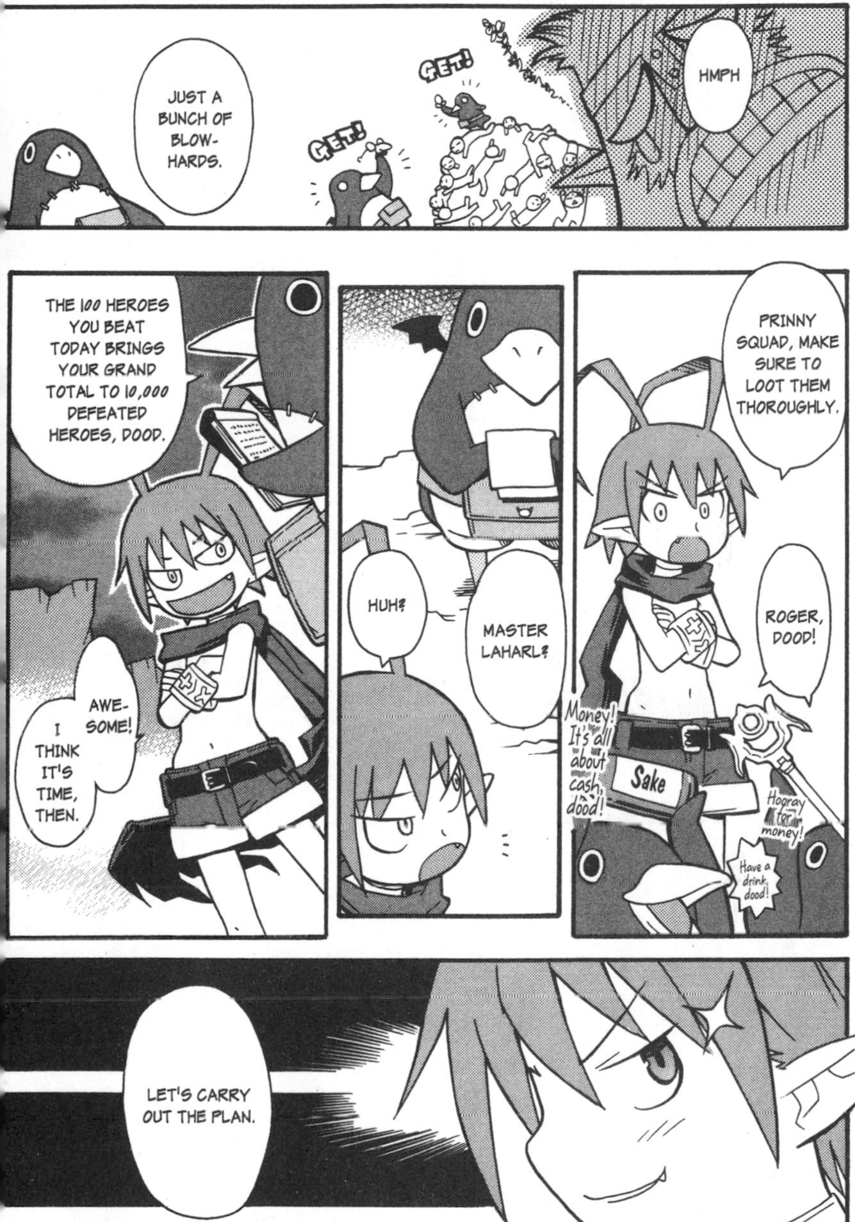
HMPH
GET!
GET!
JUST A BUNCH OF BLOW-HARDS.
PRINNY SQUAD, MAKE SURE TO LOOT THEM THOROUGHLY.
ROGER, DOOD!
Money! It's all about cash, dood!
Sake
Hooray for money!
Have a drink, dood!
MASTER LAHARL?
HUH?
THE 100 HEROES YOU BEAT TODAY BRINGS YOUR GRAND TOTAL TO 10,000 DEFEATED HEROES, DOOD.
AWE-SOME!
I THINK IT'S TIME, THEN.
LET'S CARRY OUT THE PLAN.

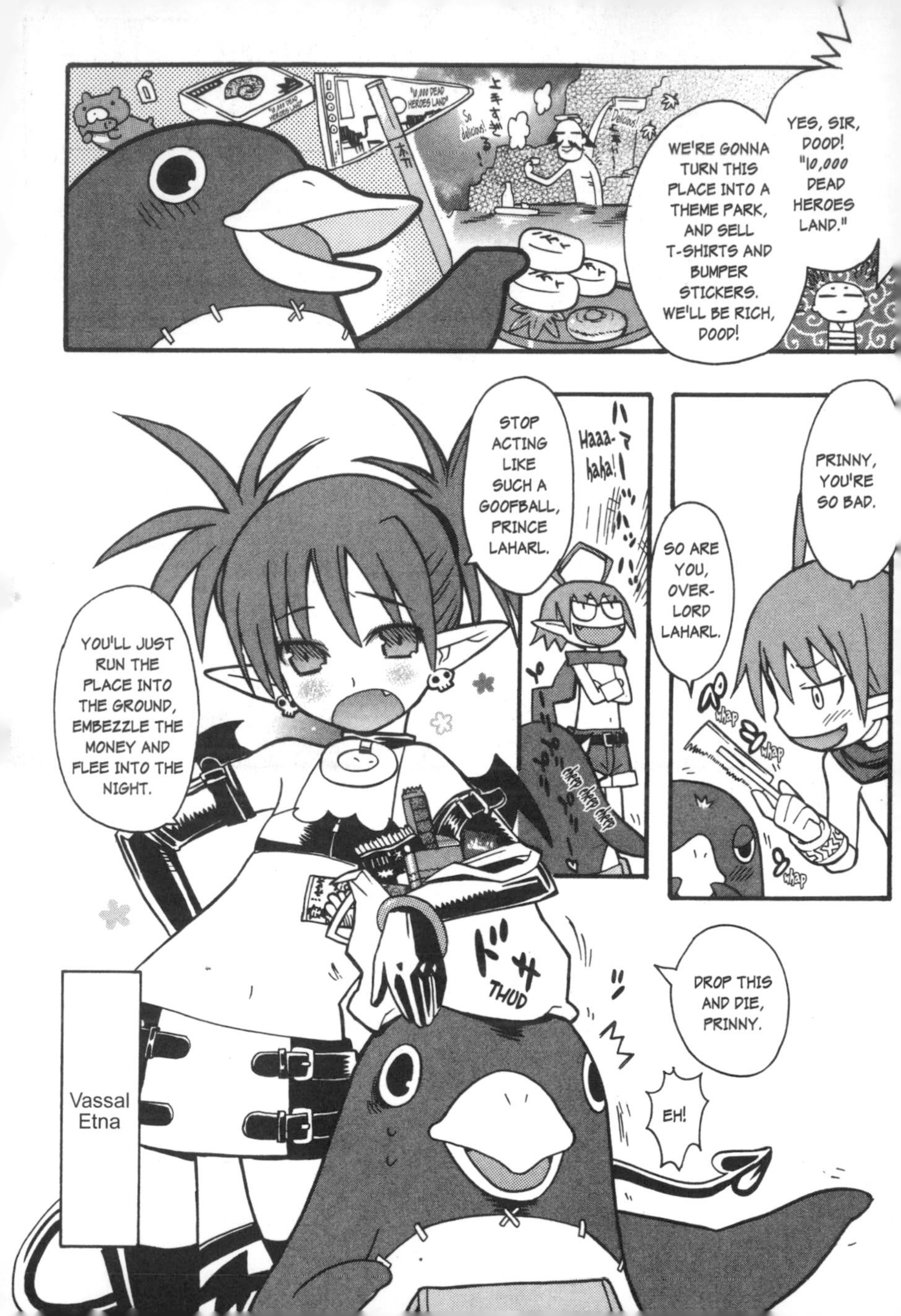
YES, SIR, DOOD! "10,000 DEAD HEROES LAND."
WE'RE GONNA TURN THIS PLACE INTO A THEME PARK, AND SELL T-SHIRTS AND BUMPER STICKERS. WE'LL BE RICH, DOOD!
Delicious!
So delicious!
"10,000 DEAD HEROES LAND"
PRINNY, YOU'RE SO BAD.
SO ARE YOU, OVER-LORD LAHARL.
whap
whap
whap
whap
STOP ACTING LIKE SUCH A GOOFBALL, PRINCE LAHARL.
Haaa-haha!
cheep cheep cheep cheep
YOU'LL JUST RUN THE PLACE INTO THE GROUND, EMBEZZLE THE MONEY AND FLEE INTO THE NIGHT.
THUD
DROP THIS AND DIE, PRINNY.
EH!
Vassal Etna

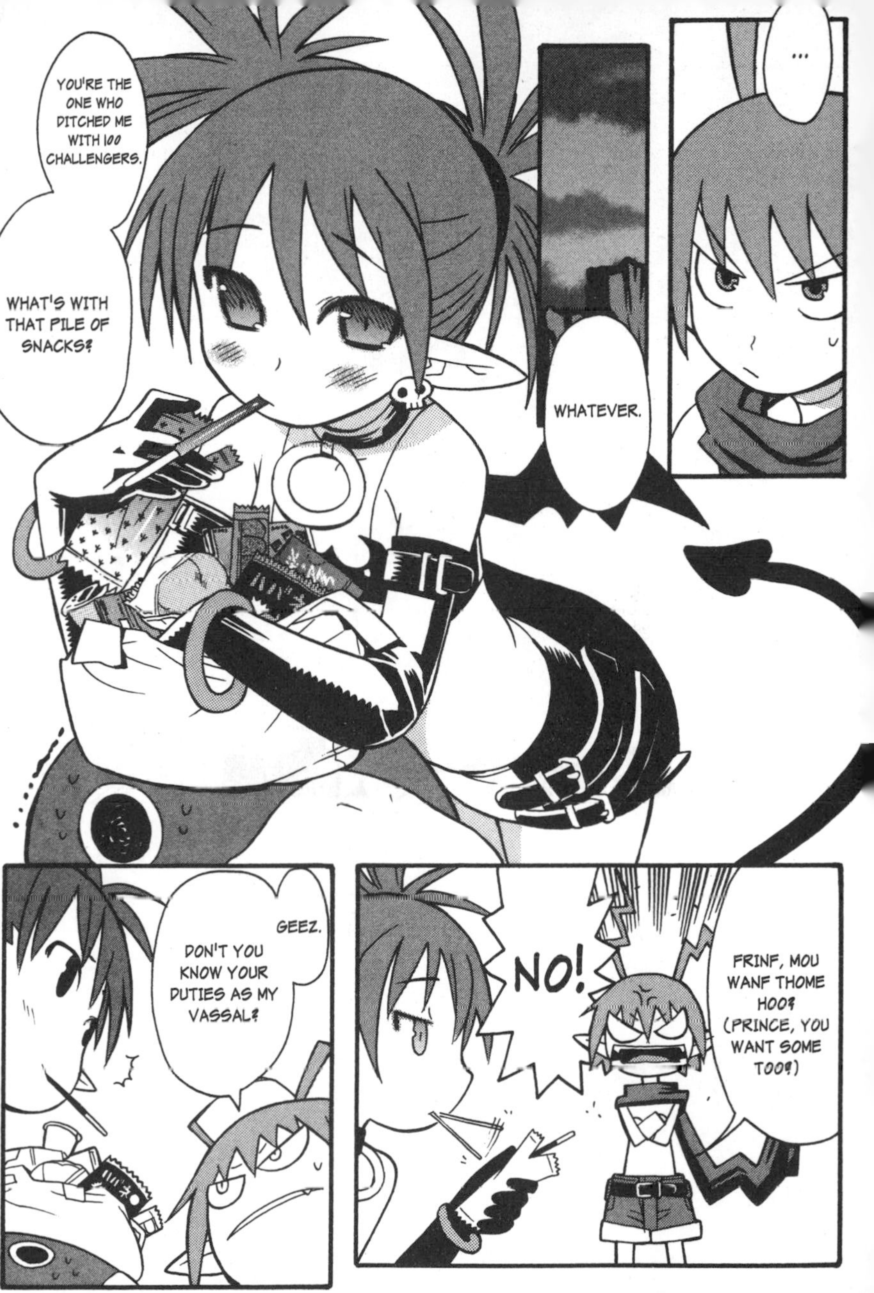
...
WHATEVER.
YOU'RE THE ONE WHO DITCHED ME WITH 100 CHALLENGERS.
WHAT'S WITH THAT PILE OF SNACKS?
FRINF, MOU WANF THOME HOO? (PRINCE, YOU WANT SOME TOO?)
NO!
GEEZ.
DON'T YOU KNOW YOUR DUTIES AS MY VASSAL?

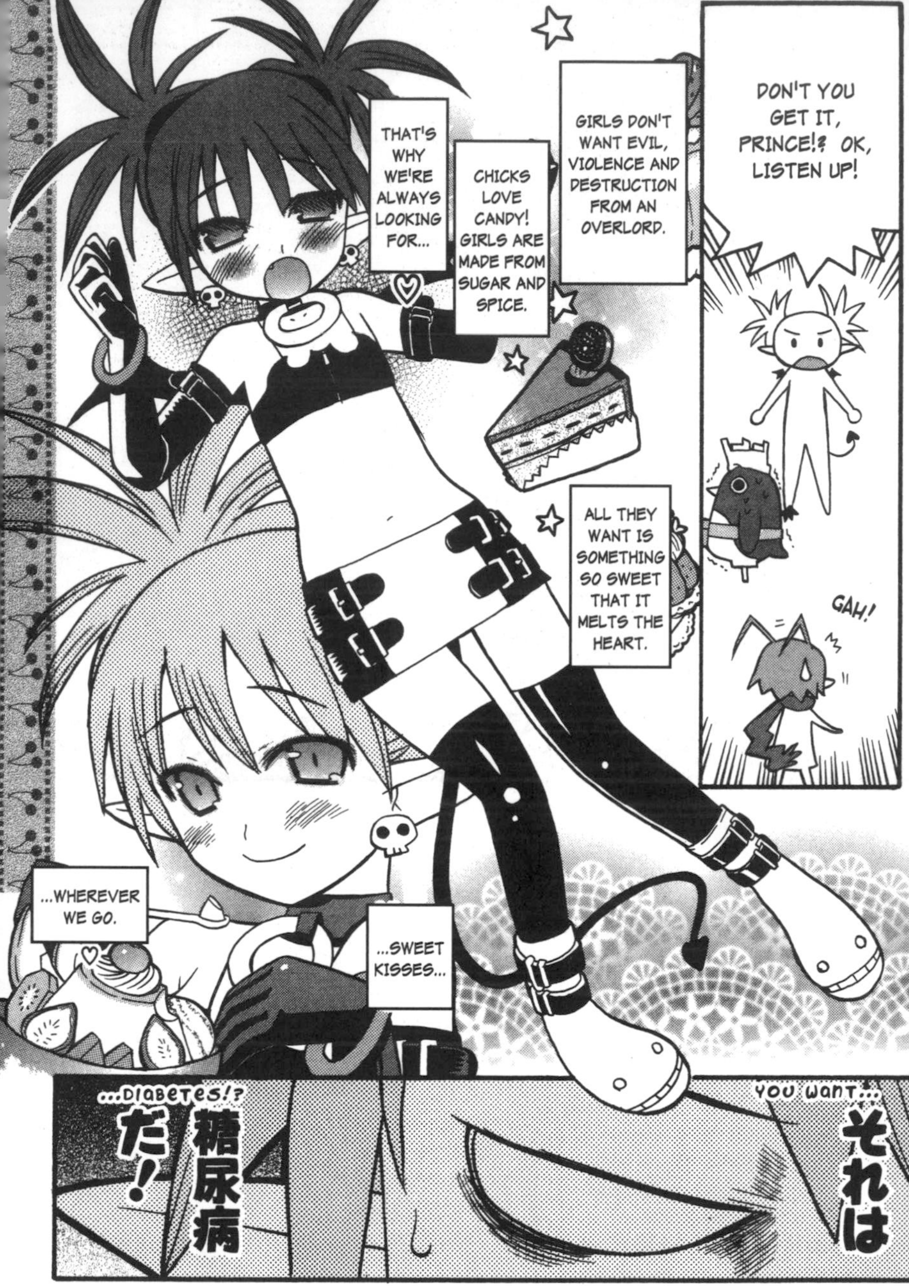
DON'T YOU GET IT, PRINCE!? OK, LISTEN UP!
GAH!
GIRLS DON'T WANT EVIL, VIOLENCE AND DESTRUCTION FROM AN OVERLORD.
CHICKS LOVE CANDY! GIRLS ARE MADE FROM SUGAR AND SPICE.
THAT'S WHY WE'RE ALWAYS LOOKING FOR...
ALL THEY WANT IS SOMETHING SO SWEET THAT IT MELTS THE HEART.
...SWEET KISSES...
...WHEREVER WE GO.
YOU WANT...
それは
...DIABETES!?
糖尿病だ!

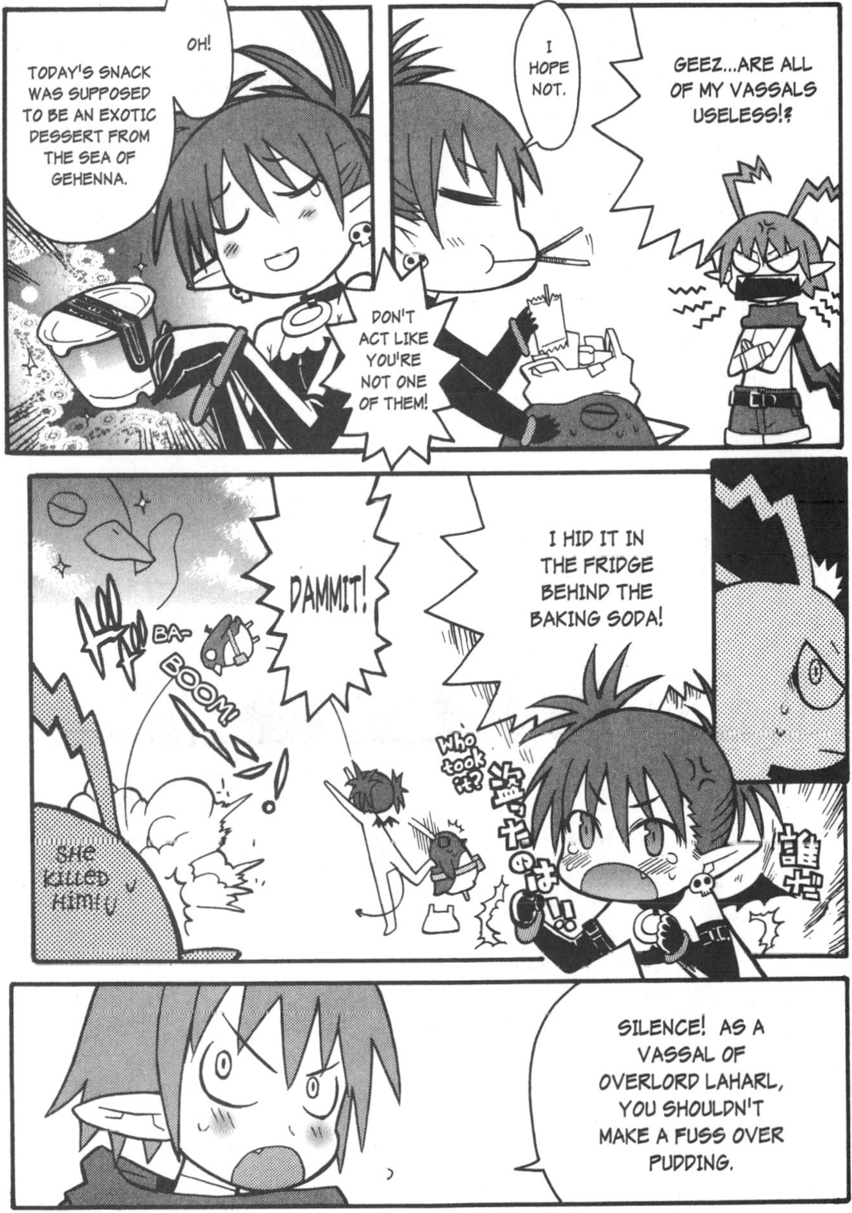
GEEZ...ARE ALL OF MY VASSALS USELESS!?
I HOPE NOT.
DON'T ACT LIKE YOU'RE NOT ONE OF THEM!
OH!
TODAY'S SNACK WAS SUPPOSED TO BE AN EXOTIC DESSERT FROM THE SEA OF GEHENNA.
I HID IT IN THE FRIDGE BEHIND THE BAKING SODA!
誰だ
盗ったのは!!
Who took it?
DAMMIT!
BA-BOOM!
SHE KILLED HIM!
SILENCE! AS A VASSAL OF OVERLORD LAHARL, YOU SHOULDN'T MAKE A FUSS OVER PUDDING.

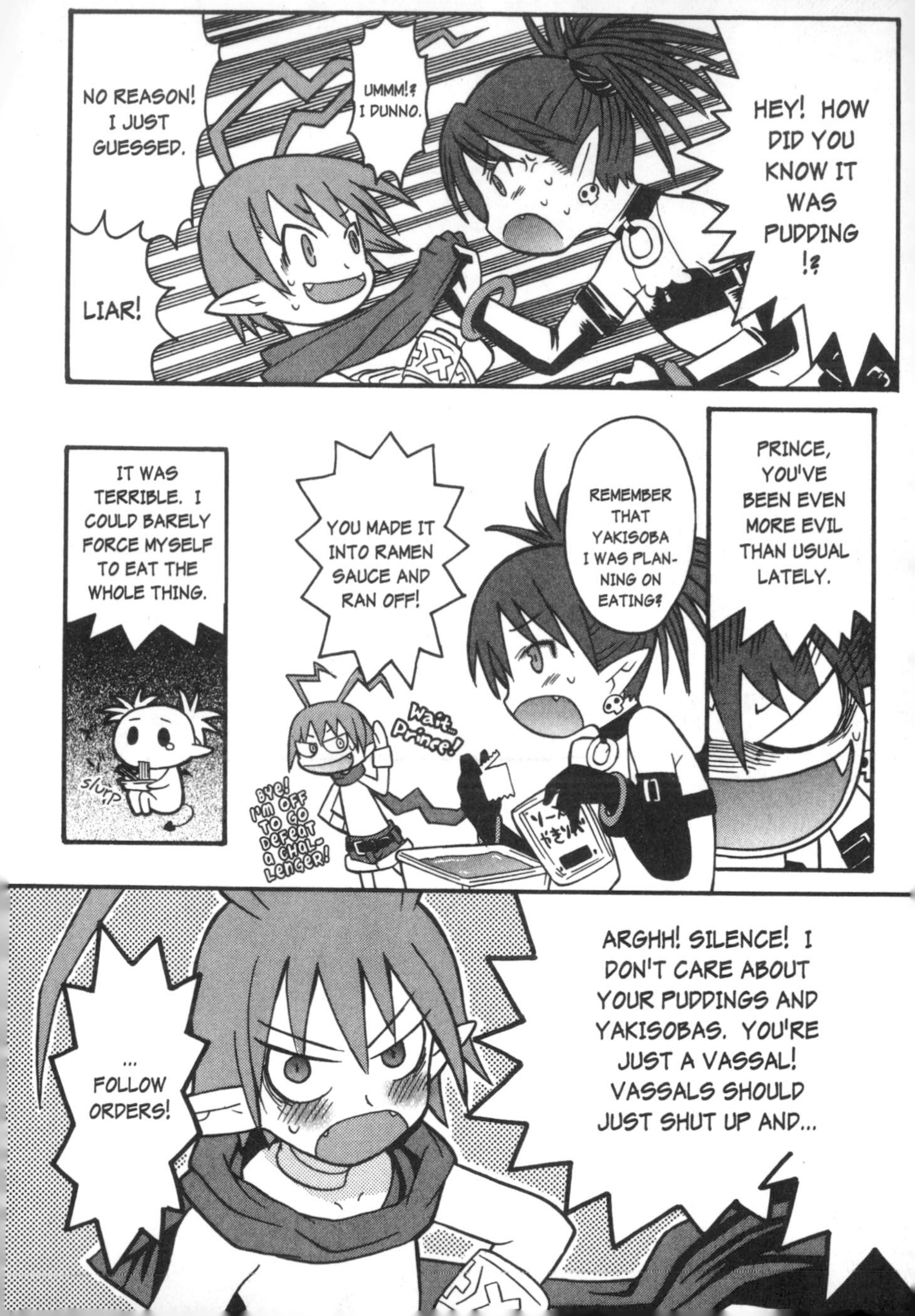
HEY! HOW DID YOU KNOW IT WAS PUDDING !?
UMMM!? I DUNNO.
NO REASON! I JUST GUESSED.
LIAR!
PRINCE, YOU'VE BEEN EVEN MORE EVIL THAN USUAL LATELY.
REMEMBER THAT YAKISOBA I WAS PLAN-NING ON EATING?
YOU MADE IT INTO RAMEN SAUCE AND RAN OFF!
Wait... Prince!
Bye! I'm off to go defeat a chal-lenger!
IT WAS TERRIBLE. I COULD BARELY FORCE MYSELF TO EAT THE WHOLE THING.
slurp
ARGHH! SILENCE! I DON'T CARE ABOUT YOUR PUDDINGS AND YAKISOBAS. YOU'RE JUST A VASSAL! VASSALS SHOULD JUST SHUT UP AND...
... FOLLOW ORDERS!

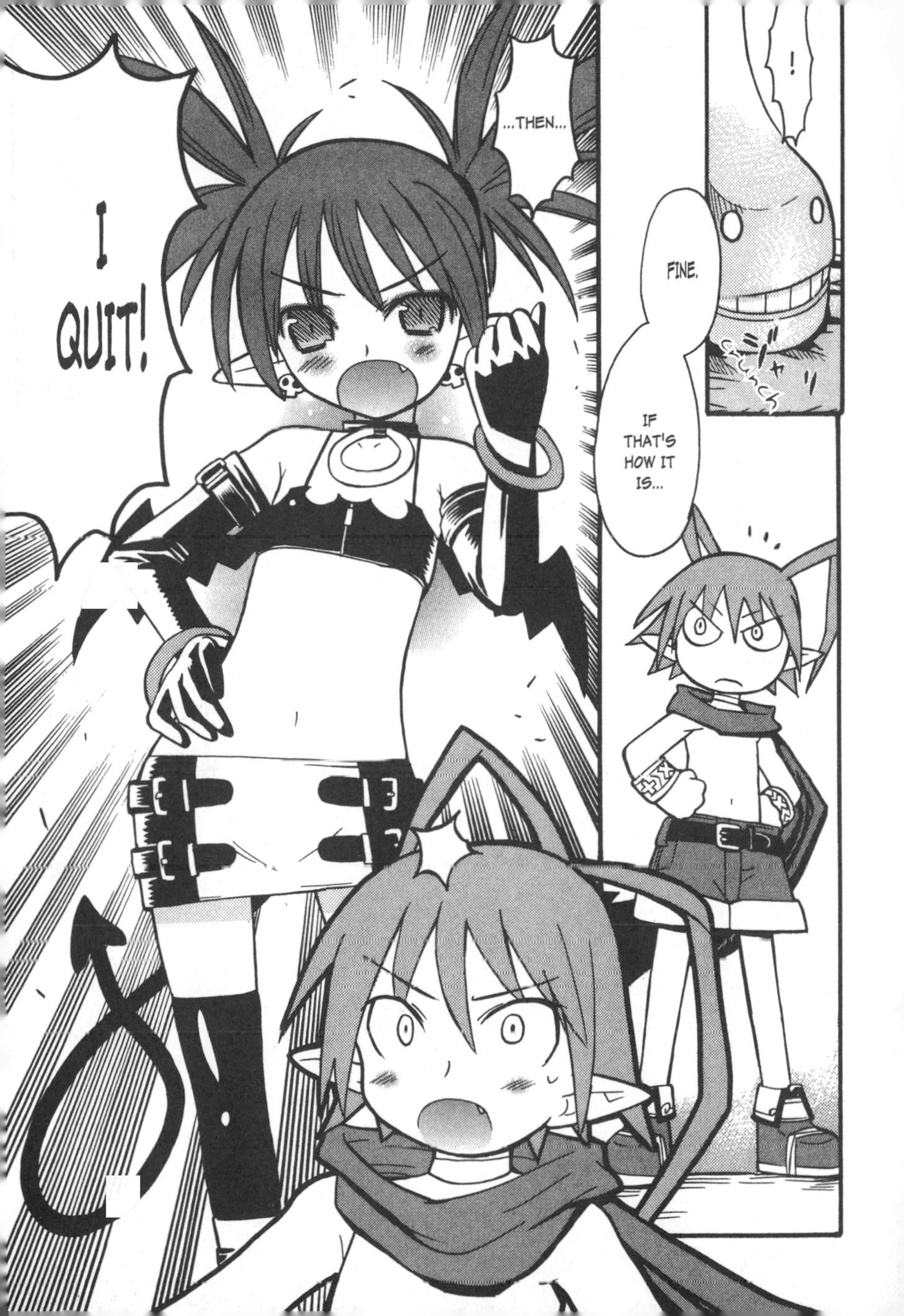
!
CRUNCH
FINE.
IF THAT'S HOW IT IS...
...THEN...
I QUIT!

EPISODE PREVIEW

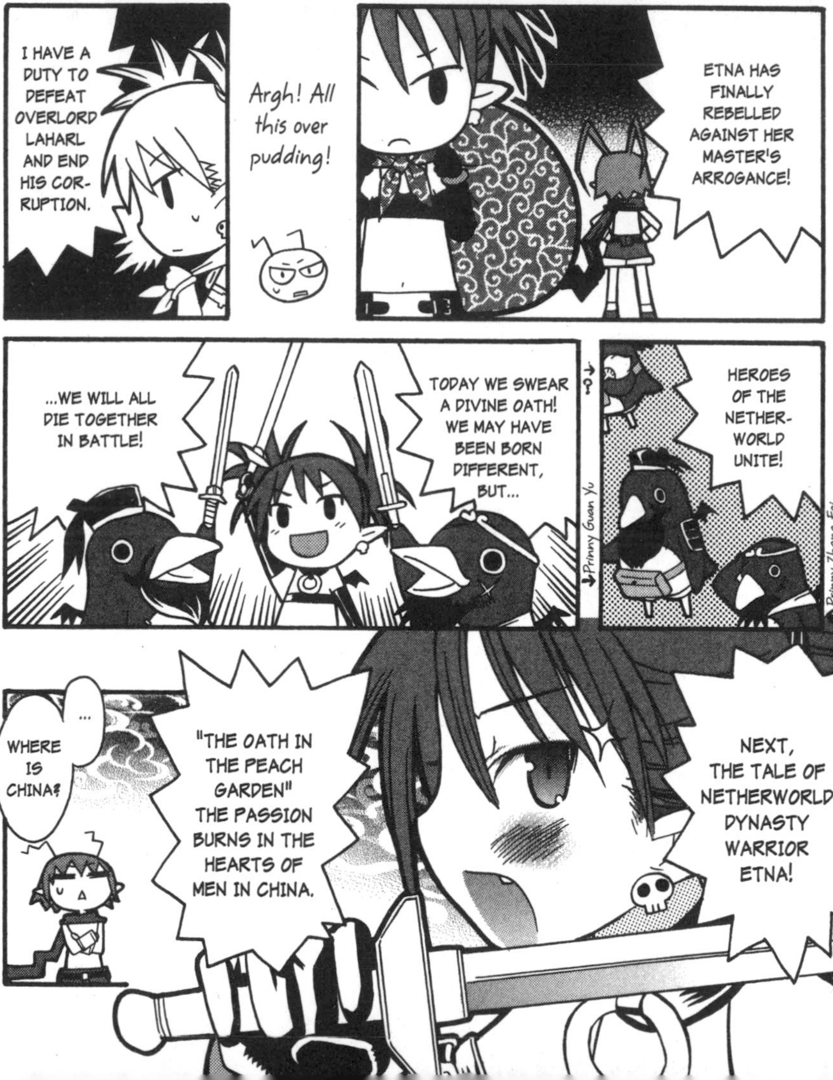
ETNA HAS FINALLY REBELLED AGAINST HER MASTER'S ARROGANCE!
I HAVE A DUTY TO DEFEAT OVERLORD LAHARL AND END HIS COR-RUPTION.
Argh! All this over pudding!
HEROES OF THE NETHER-WORLD UNITE!
Prinny Zhang Fei
Prinny Guan Yu
TODAY WE SWEAR A DIVINE OATH! WE MAY HAVE BEEN BORN DIFFERENT, BUT...
...WE WILL ALL DIE TOGETHER IN BATTLE!
NEXT, THE TALE OF NETHERWORLD DYNASTY WARRIOR ETNA!
"THE OATH IN THE PEACH GARDEN" THE PASSION BURNS IN THE HEARTS OF MEN IN CHINA.
...
WHERE IS CHINA?

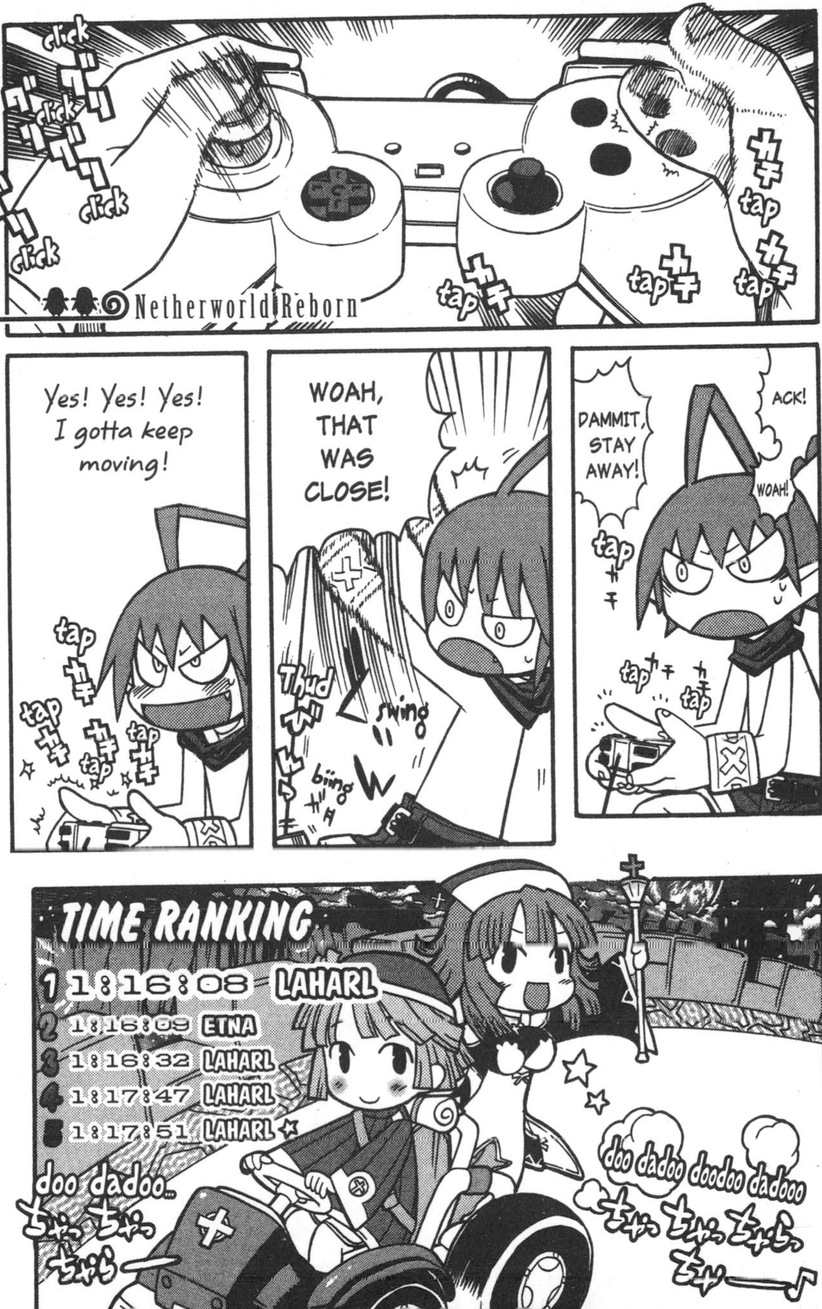
click
click
click
click
tap
tap
tap
tap
Netherworld Reborn
ACK!
DAMMIT, STAY AWAY!
WOAH!
tap
tap
tap
WOAH, THAT WAS CLOSE!
Thud
swing
biing
Yes! Yes! Yes! I gotta keep moving!
tap
tap
tap
tap
TIME RANKING
1 1:16:08 LAHARL
2 1:16:09 ETNA
3 1:16:32 LAHARL
4 1:17:47 LAHARL
5 1:17:51 LAHARL
doo dadoo doodoo dadooo
doo dadoo..

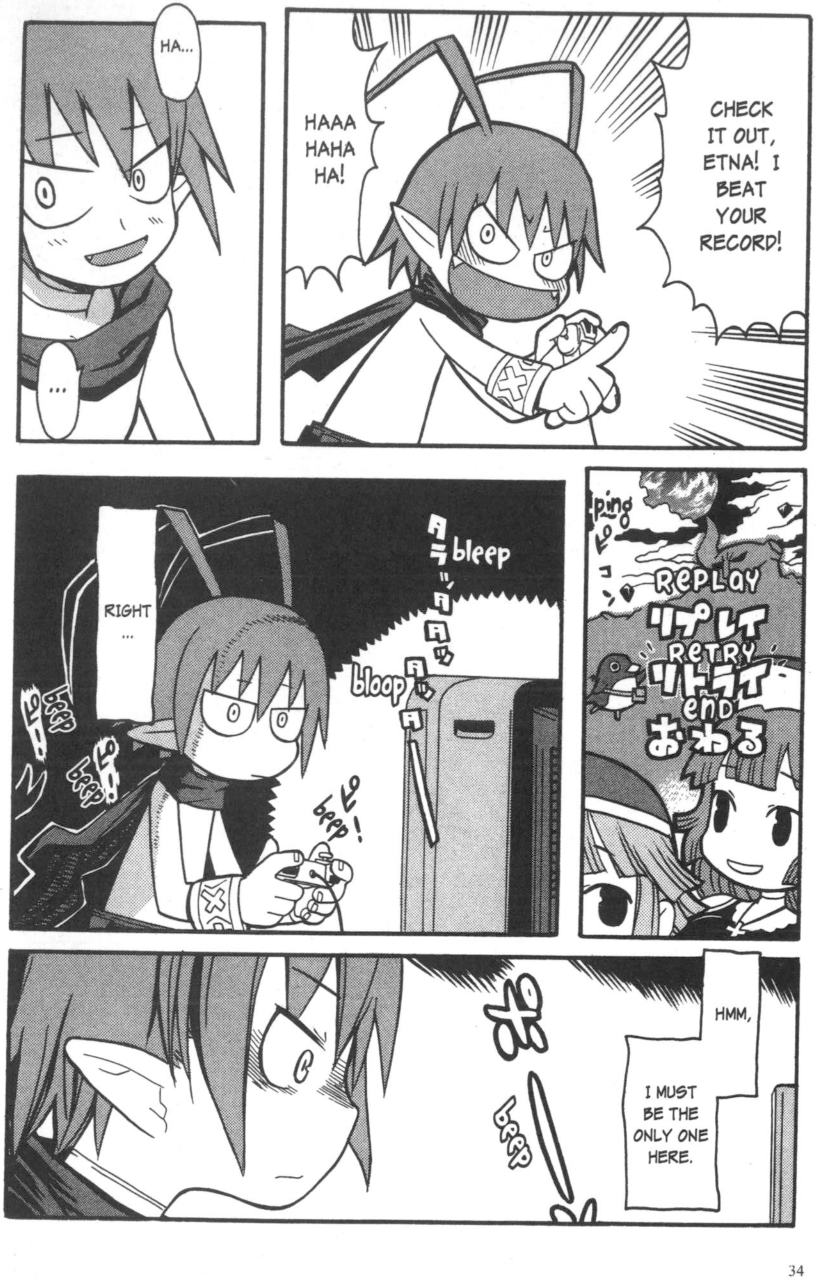

CHECK IT OUT, ETNA! I BEAT YOUR RECORD!
HAAA HAHA HA!
HA...
...
ping
REPLAY
リプレイ
RETRY
リトライ
end
おわる
bleep
bloop
RIGHT ...
beep
beep
beep!
beep
HMM,
I MUST BE THE ONLY ONE HERE.

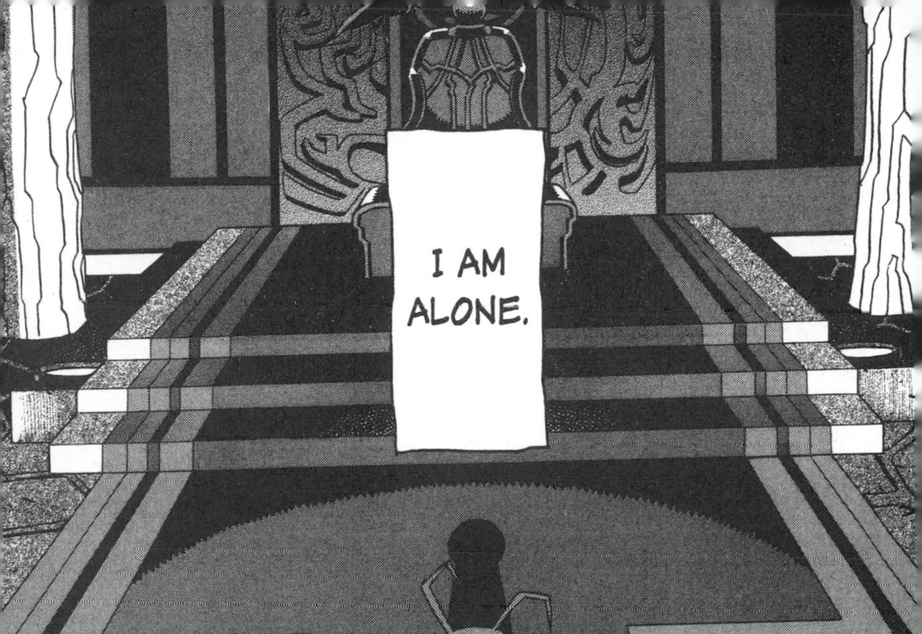
I AM ALONE.

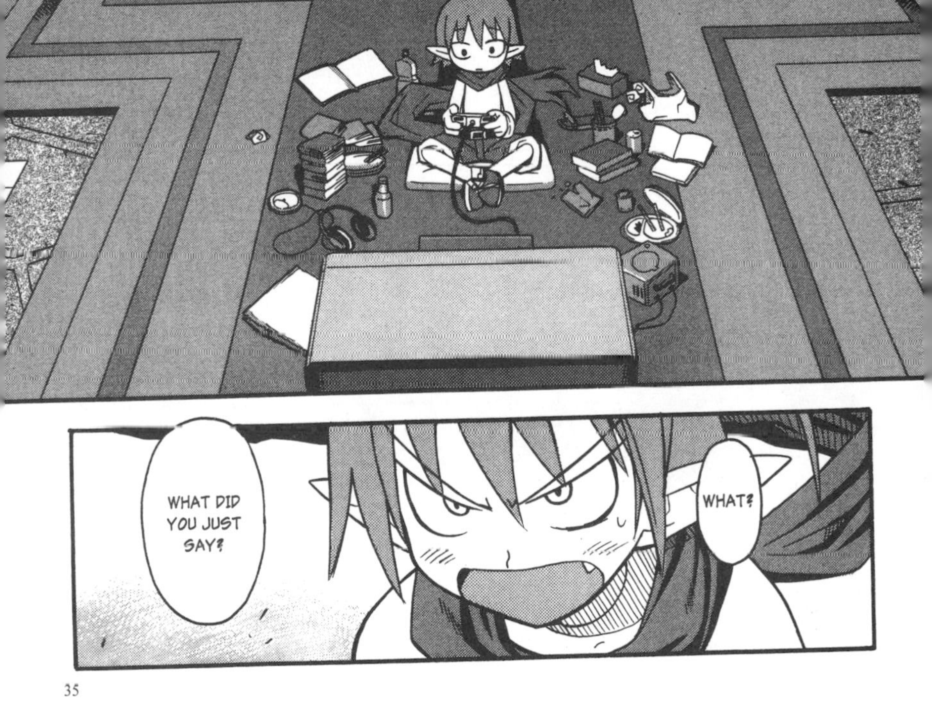
WHAT?
WHAT DID YOU JUST SAY?

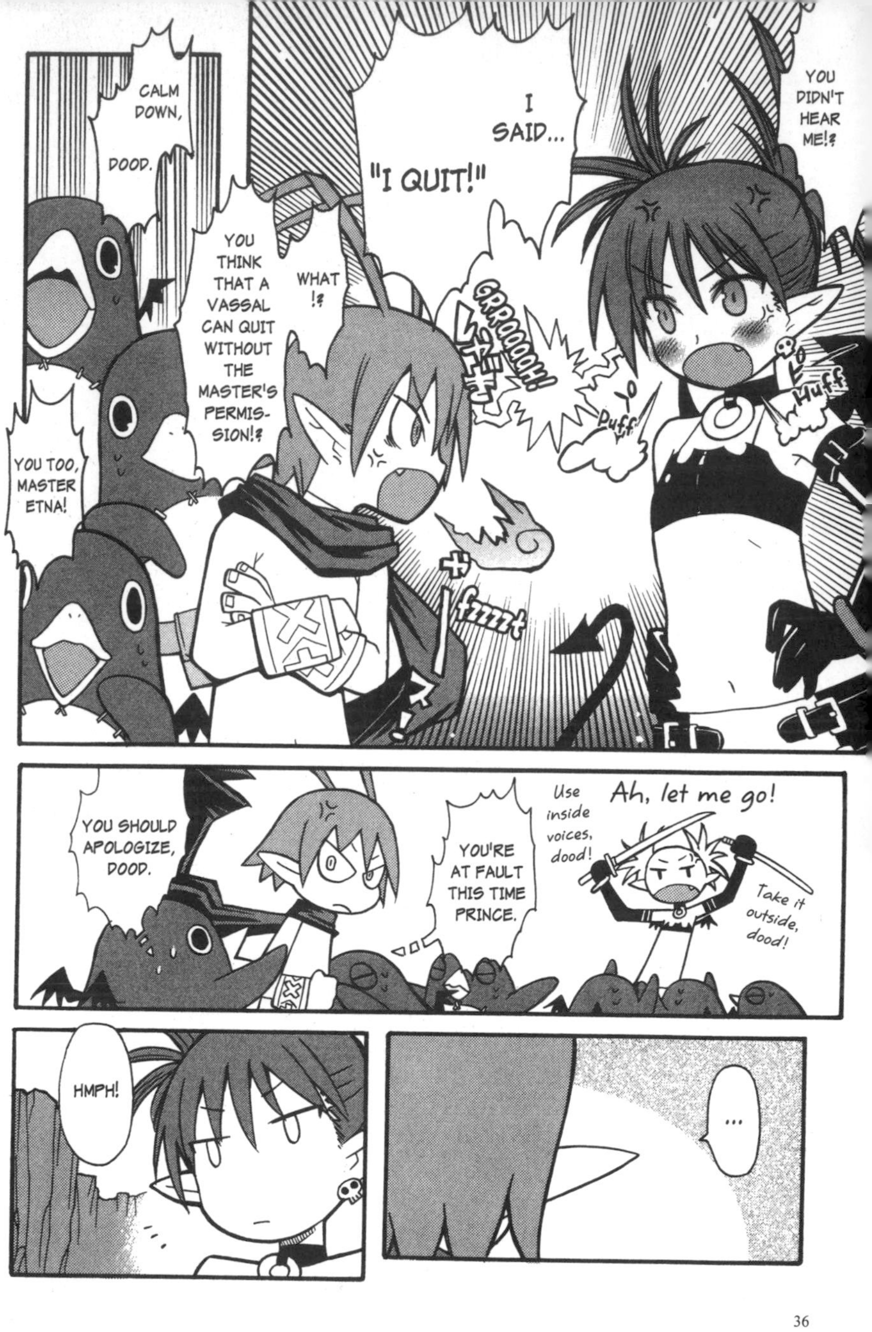
YOU DIDN'T HEAR ME!?
I SAID...
"I QUIT!"
GRRAAAAH!
Huff
Puff
CALM DOWN, DOOD.
WHAT!?
YOU THINK THAT A VASSAL CAN QUIT WITHOUT THE MASTER'S PERMISSION!?
YOU TOO, MASTER ETNA!
fzzzzt
Ah, let me go!
Use inside voices, dood!
Take it outside, dood!
YOU'RE AT FAULT THIS TIME PRINCE.
YOU SHOULD APOLOGIZE, DOOD.
...
HMPH!

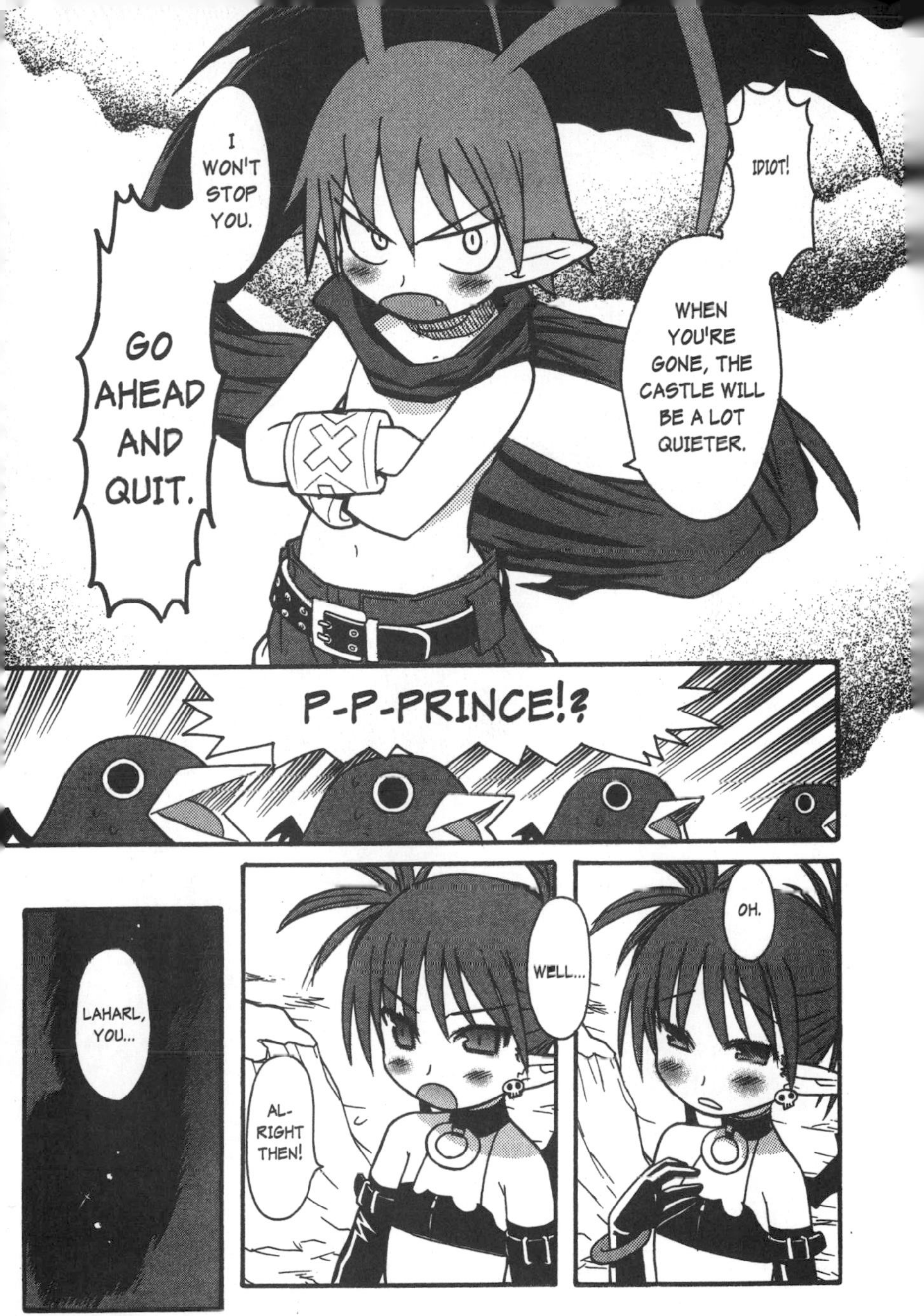
IDIOT!
WHEN YOU'RE GONE, THE CASTLE WILL BE A LOT QUIETER.
I WON'T STOP YOU.
GO AHEAD AND QUIT.
P-P-PRINCE!?
OH.
WELL...
AL-RIGHT THEN!
LAHARL, YOU...

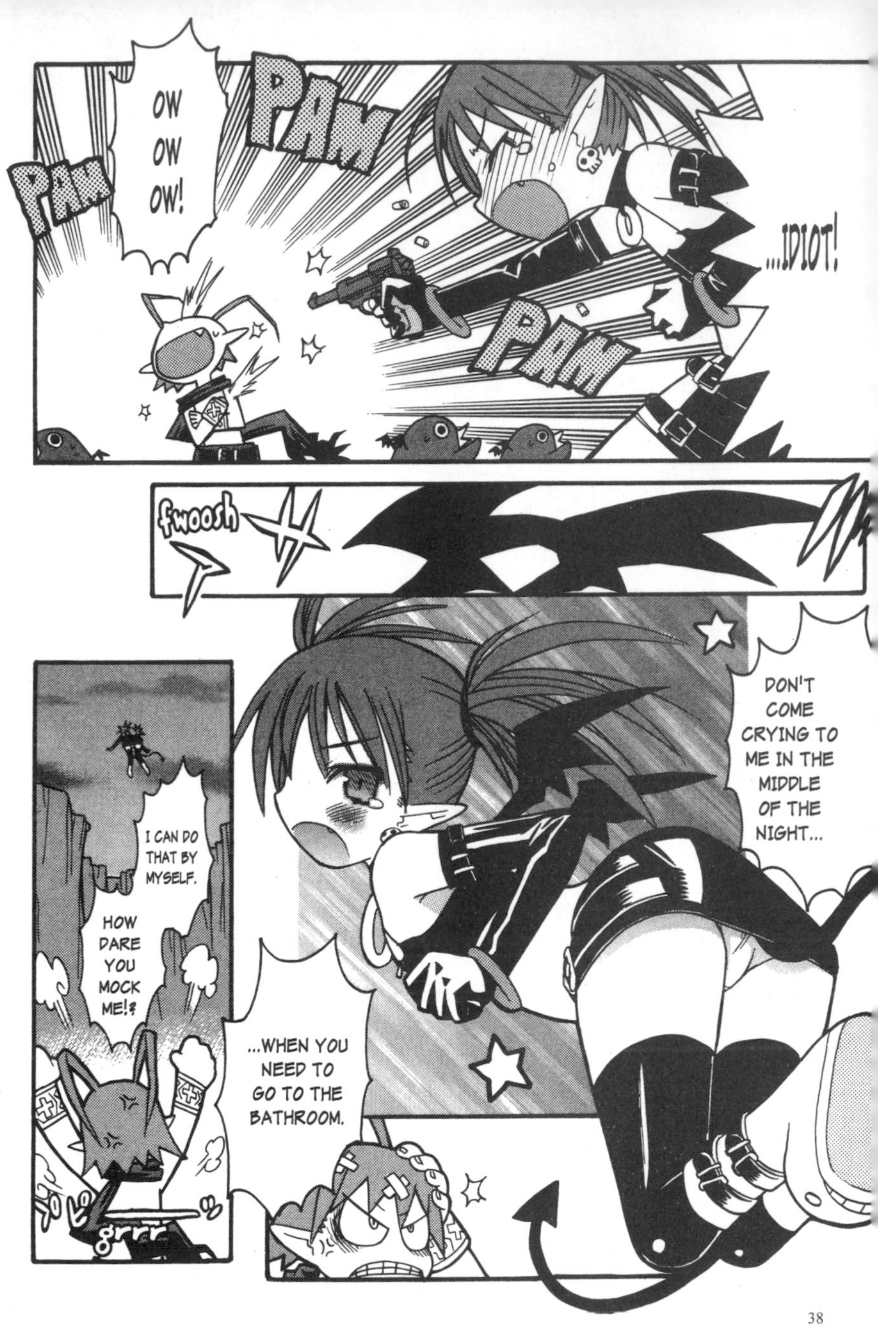
PAM
...IDIOT!
OW OW OW!
PAM
PAM
fwoosh
DON'T COME CRYING TO ME IN THE MIDDLE OF THE NIGHT...
...WHEN YOU NEED TO GO TO THE BATHROOM.
I CAN DO THAT BY MYSELF.
HOW DARE YOU MOCK ME!?
grrr

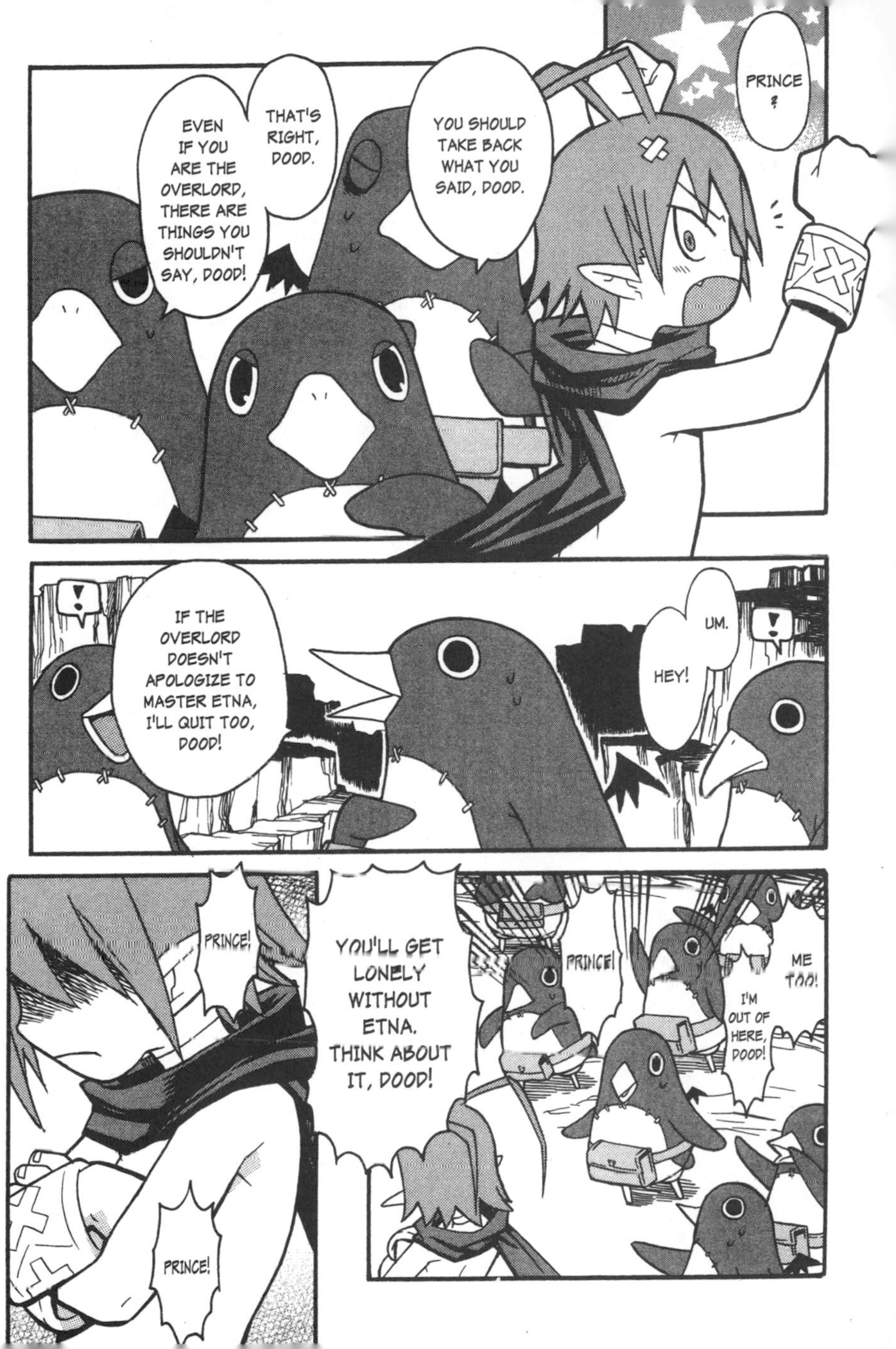
PRINCE?
YOU SHOULD TAKE BACK WHAT YOU SAID, DOOD.
THAT'S RIGHT, DOOD.
EVEN IF YOU ARE THE OVERLORD, THERE ARE THINGS YOU SHOULDN'T SAY, DOOD!
UM.
HEY!
IF THE OVERLORD DOESN'T APOLOGIZE TO MASTER ETNA, I'LL QUIT TOO, DOOD!
ME TOO!
I'M OUT OF HERE, DOOD!
PRINCE!
YOU'LL GET LONELY WITHOUT ETNA. THINK ABOUT IT, DOOD!
PRINCE!
PRINCE!

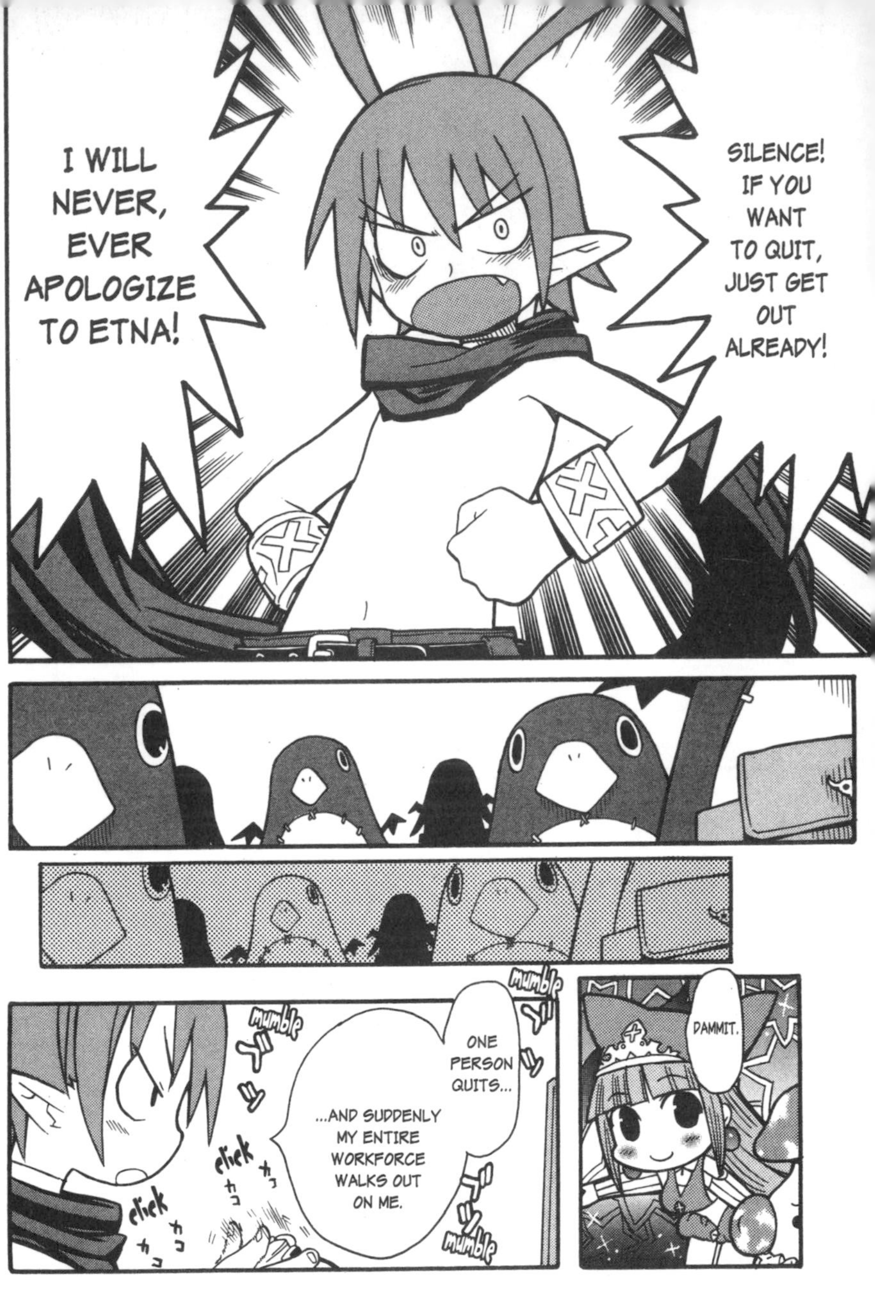
SILENCE! IF YOU WANT TO QUIT, JUST GET OUT ALREADY!
I WILL NEVER, EVER APOLOGIZE TO ETNA!
DAMMIT.
mumble
ONE PERSON QUITS...
mumble
...AND SUDDENLY MY ENTIRE WORKFORCE WALKS OUT ON ME.
click
click
mumble

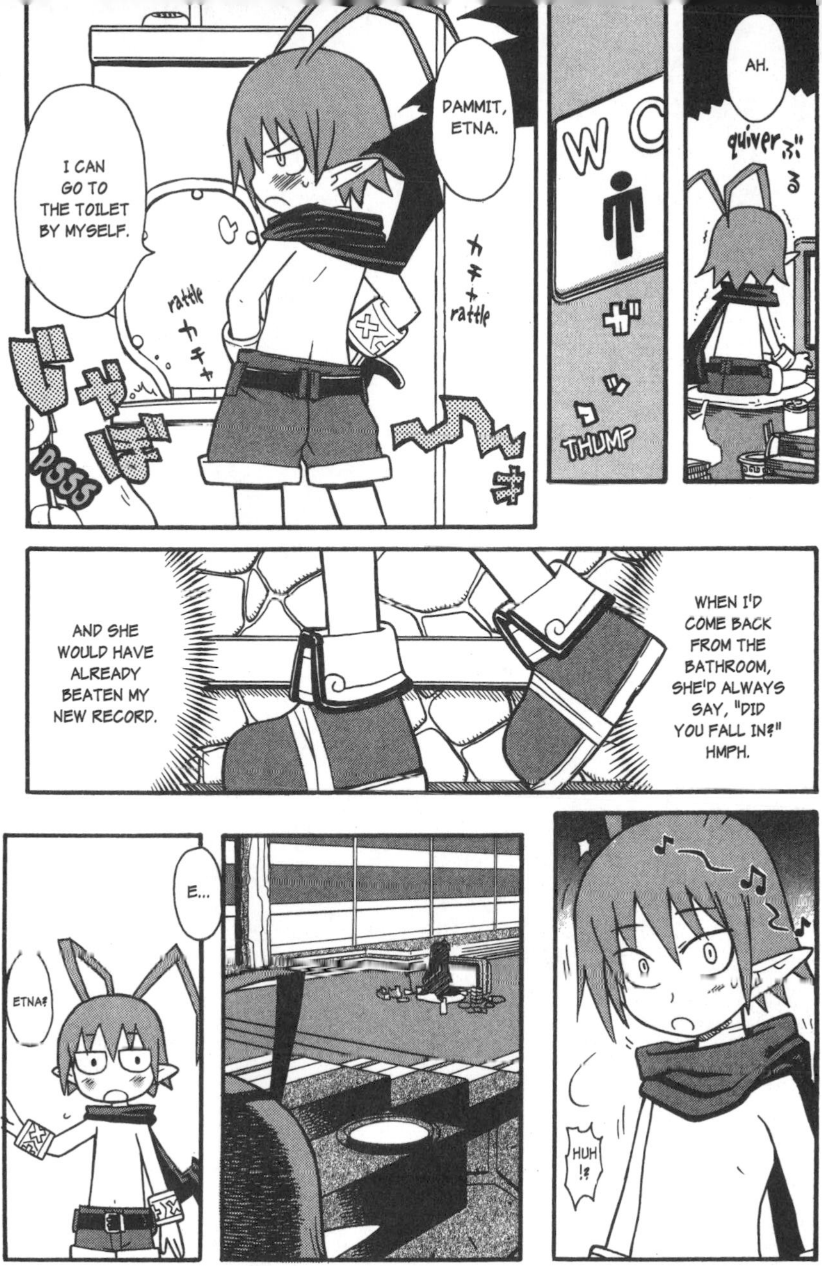
AH.
quiver ぶる
ガッ
THUMP
DAMMIT, ETNA.
I CAN GO TO THE TOILET BY MYSELF.
rattle
rattle
PSSS
WHEN I'D COME BACK FROM THE BATHROOM, SHE'D ALWAYS SAY, "DID YOU FALL IN?" HMPH.
AND SHE WOULD HAVE ALREADY BEATEN MY NEW RECORD.
HUH!?
E...
ETNA?

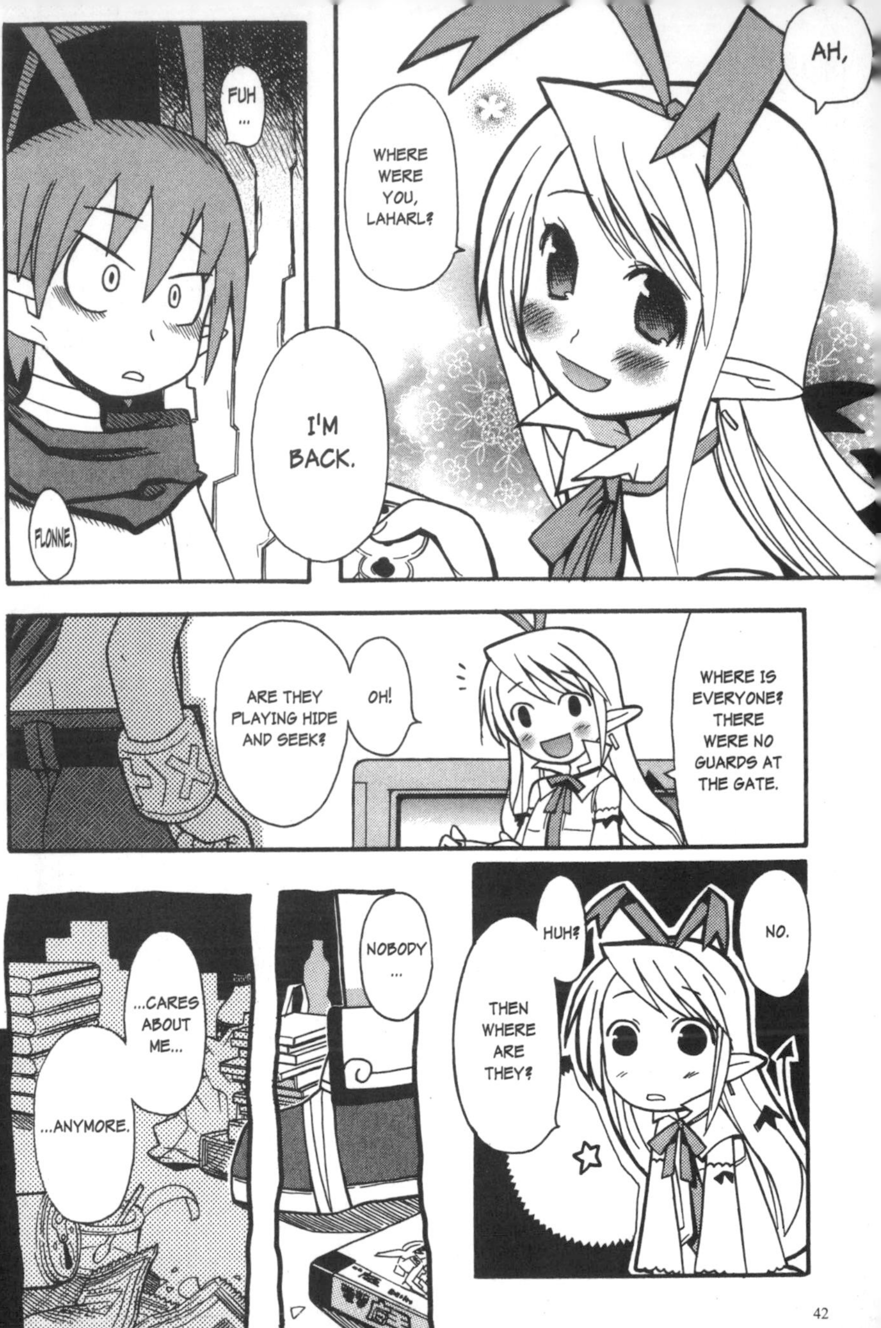
AH,
WHERE WERE YOU, LAHARL?
FUH ...
I'M BACK.
FLONNE.
WHERE IS EVERYONE? THERE WERE NO GUARDS AT THE GATE.
OH!
ARE THEY PLAYING HIDE AND SEEK?
NO.
HUH?
THEN WHERE ARE THEY?
NOBODY ...
...CARES ABOUT ME...
...ANYMORE.

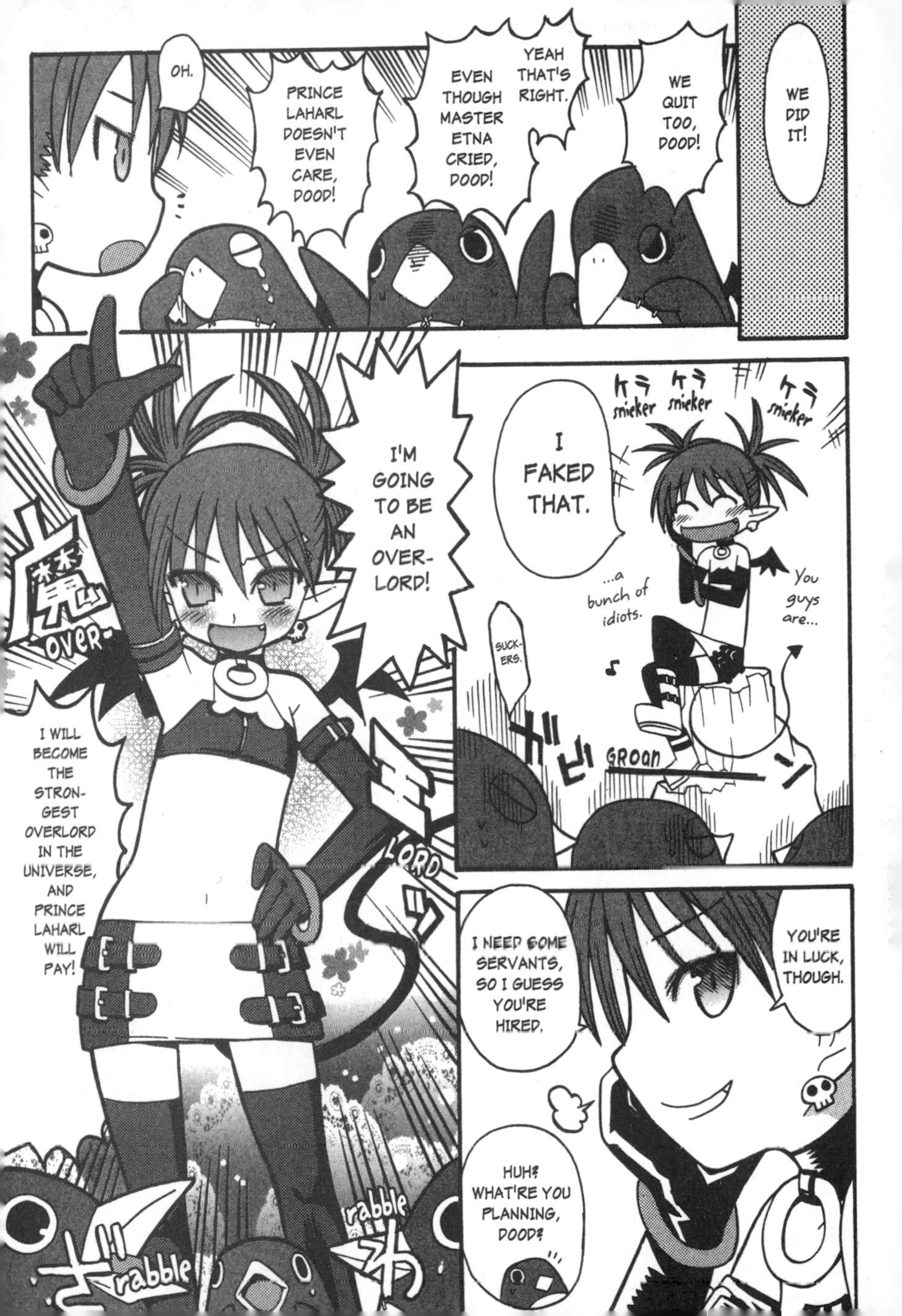
WE DID IT!
WE QUIT TOO, DOOD!
YEAH THAT'S RIGHT.
EVEN THOUGH MASTER ETNA CRIED, DOOD!
PRINCE LAHARL DOESN'T EVEN CARE, DOOD!
OH.
snicker snicker snicker
I FAKED THAT.
You guys are...
...a bunch of idiots.
SUCKERS.
GROAN
YOU'RE IN LUCK, THOUGH.
I NEED SOME SERVANTS, SO I GUESS YOU'RE HIRED.
HUH? WHAT'RE YOU PLANNING, DOOD?
I'M GOING TO BE AN OVERLORD!
OVER-
LORD
I WILL BECOME THE STRONGEST OVERLORD IN THE UNIVERSE, AND PRINCE LAHARL WILL PAY!
rabble
rabble

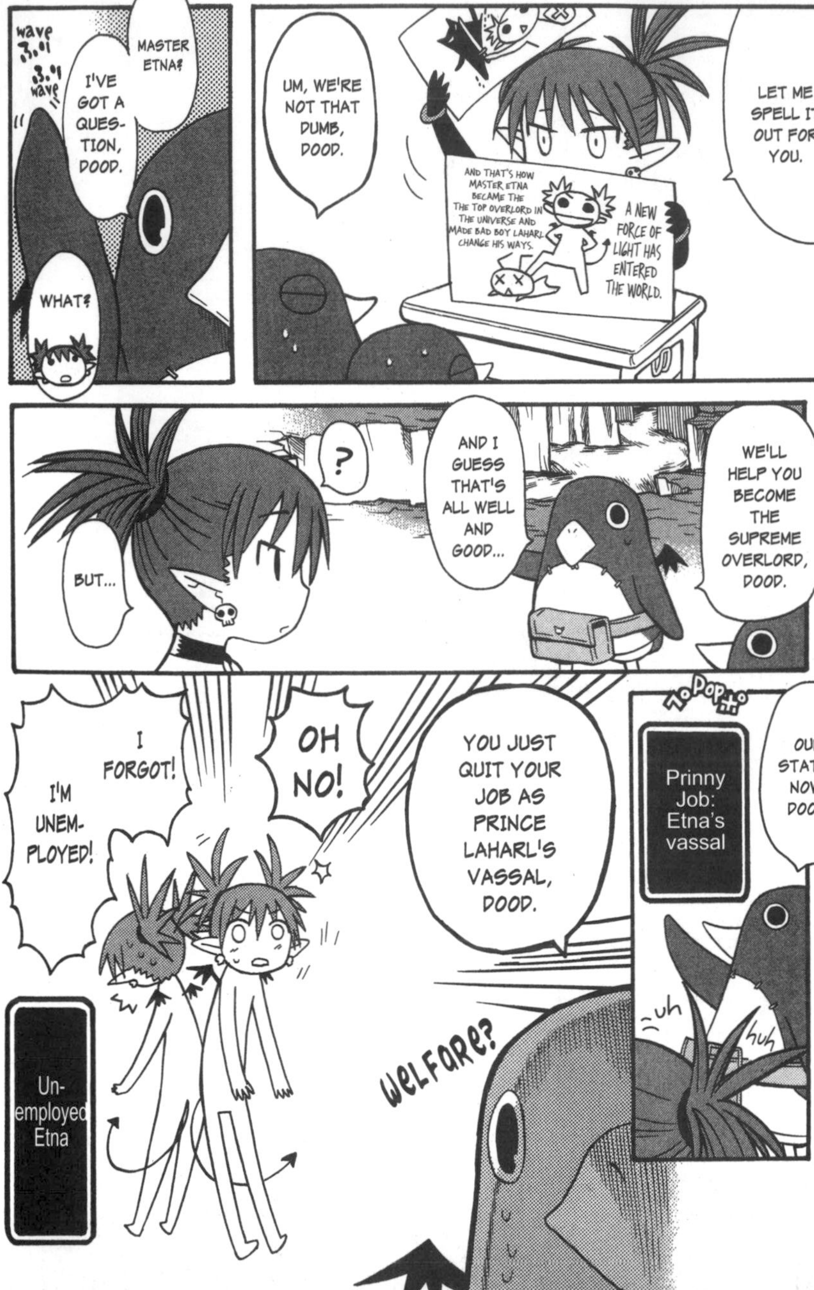
LET ME SPELL IT OUT FOR YOU.
AND THAT'S HOW MASTER ETNA BECAME THE THE TOP OVERLORD IN THE UNIVERSE AND MADE BAD BOY LAHARL CHANGE HIS WAYS.
A NEW FORCE OF LIGHT HAS ENTERED THE WORLD.
UM, WE'RE NOT THAT DUMB, DOOD.
MASTER ETNA?
I'VE GOT A QUES-TION, DOOD.
wave
wave
WHAT?
WE'LL HELP YOU BECOME THE SUPREME OVERLORD, DOOD.
AND I GUESS THAT'S ALL WELL AND GOOD...
?
BUT...
Pop
OUR STATUS NOW, DOOD.
Prinny Job: Etna's vassal
uh
huh
YOU JUST QUIT YOUR JOB AS PRINCE LAHARL'S VASSAL, DOOD.
OH NO!
I FORGOT!
I'M UNEM-PLOYED!
Un-employed Etna
WELFARE?

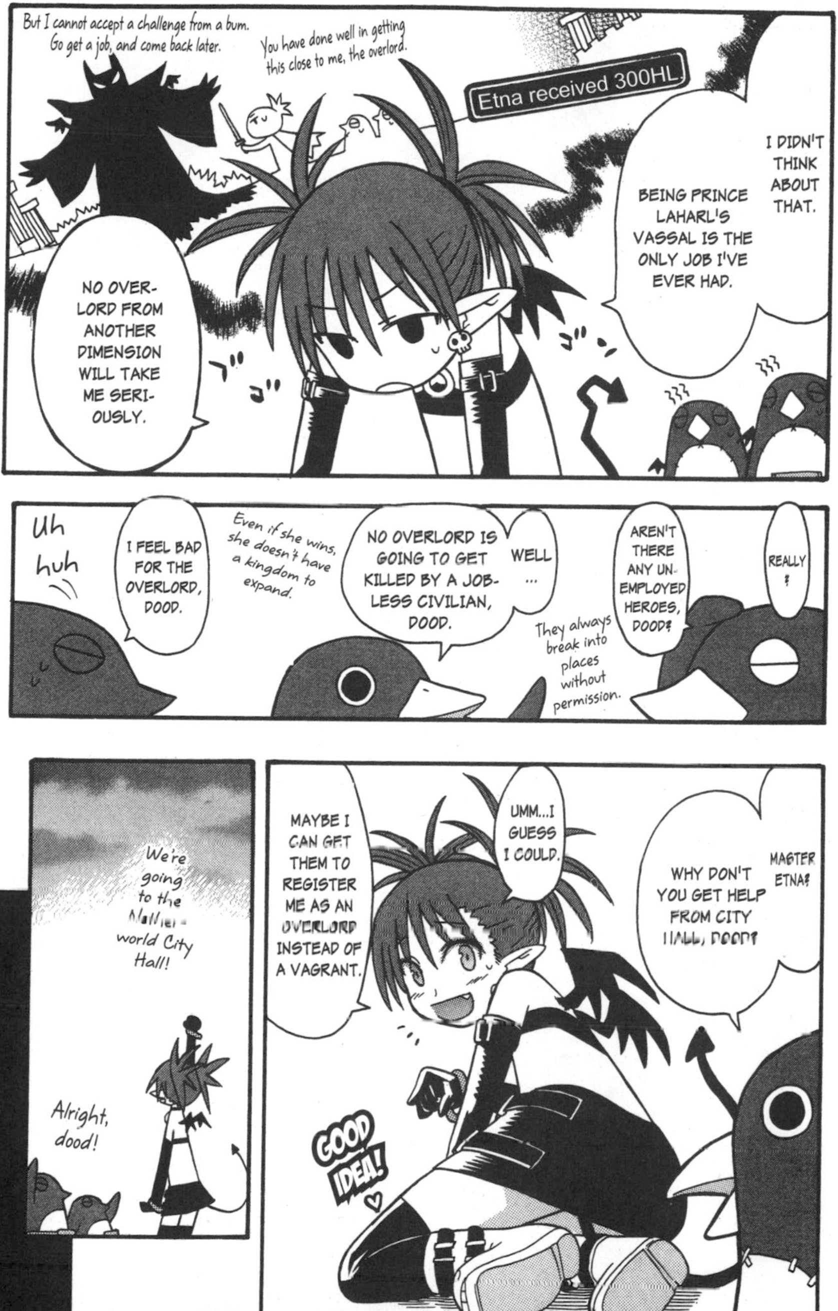
I DIDN'T THINK ABOUT THAT.
BEING PRINCE LAHARL'S VASSAL IS THE ONLY JOB I'VE EVER HAD.
Etna received 300HL.
You have done well in getting this close to me, the overlord.
But I cannot accept a challenge from a bum. Go get a job, and come back later.
NO OVER-LORD FROM ANOTHER DIMENSION WILL TAKE ME SERI-OUSLY.
REALLY?
AREN'T THERE ANY UN-EMPLOYED HEROES, DOOD?
They always break into places without permission.
WELL...
NO OVERLORD IS GOING TO GET KILLED BY A JOB-LESS CIVILIAN, DOOD.
Even if she wins, she doesn't have a kingdom to expand.
I FEEL BAD FOR THE OVERLORD, DOOD.
Uh huh
MASTER ETNA?
WHY DON'T YOU GET HELP FROM CITY HALL, DOOD?
UMM...I GUESS I COULD.
MAYBE I CAN GET THEM TO REGISTER ME AS AN OVERLORD INSTEAD OF A VAGRANT.
GOOD IDEA! ♥
We're going to the
world City Hall!
Alright, dood!

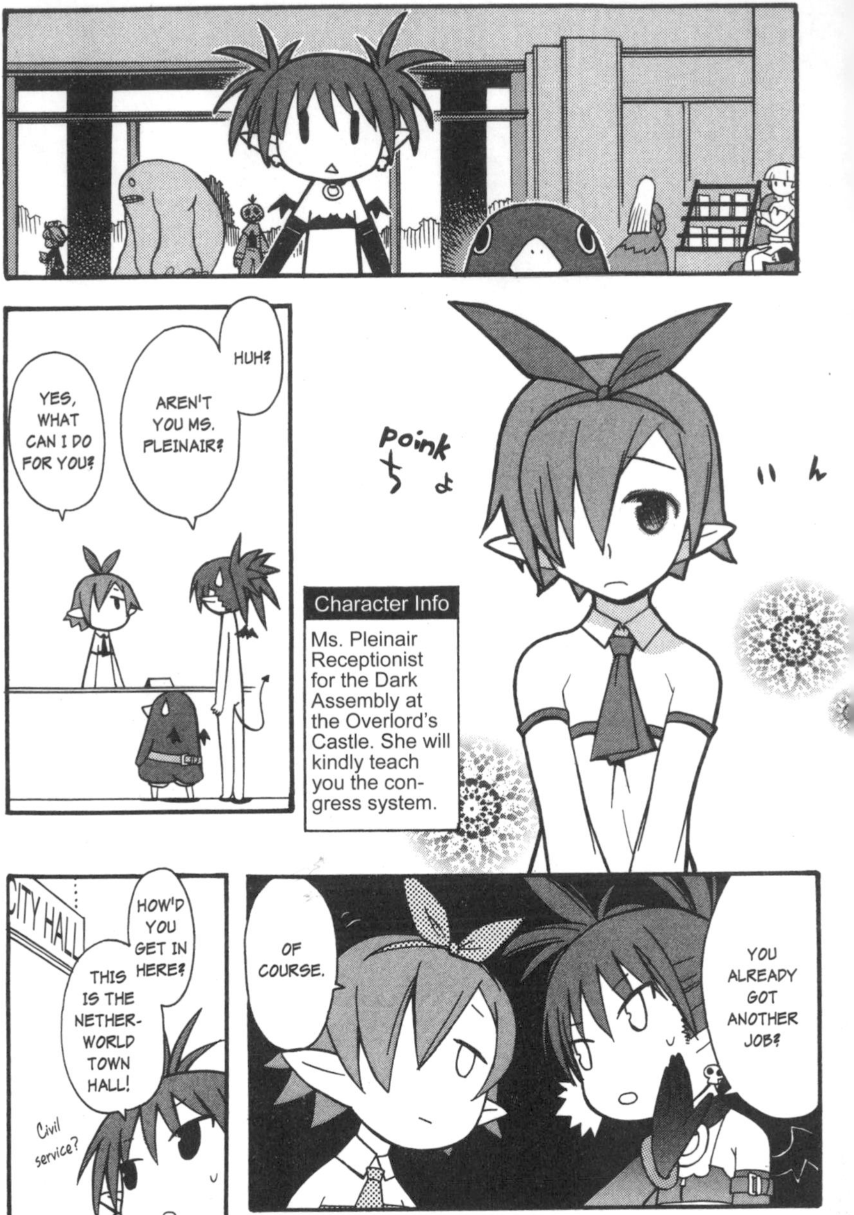
poink
ちょ
いん
Character Info
Ms. Pleinair Receptionist for the Dark Assembly at the Overlord's Castle. She will kindly teach you the congress system.
HUH?
AREN'T YOU MS. PLEINAIR?
YES, WHAT CAN I DO FOR YOU?
YOU ALREADY GOT ANOTHER JOB?
OF COURSE.
HOW'D YOU GET IN HERE?
THIS IS THE NETHER-WORLD TOWN HALL!
CITY HALL
Civil service?

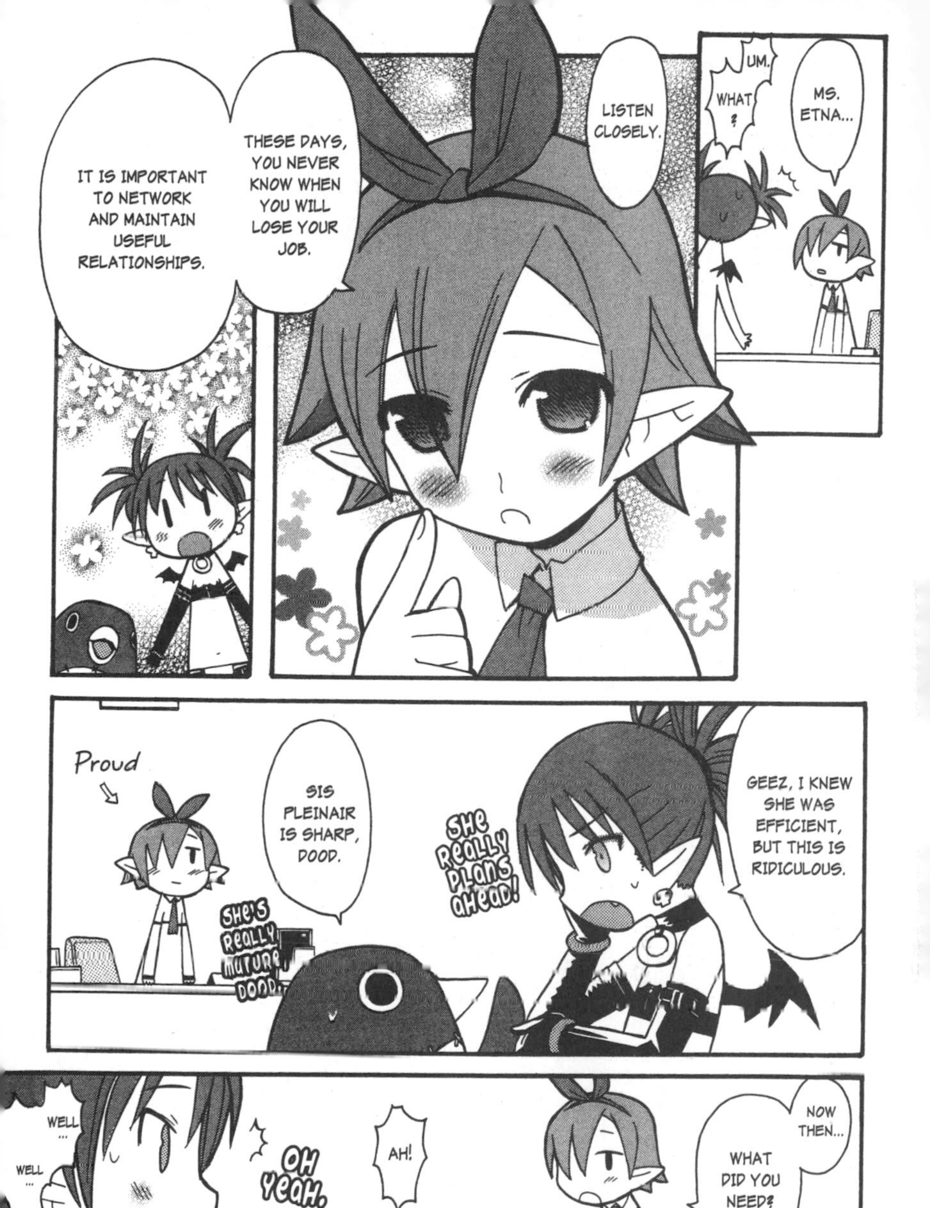
MS. ETNA...
UM. WHAT?
LISTEN CLOSELY.
THESE DAYS, YOU NEVER KNOW WHEN YOU WILL LOSE YOUR JOB.
IT IS IMPORTANT TO NETWORK AND MAINTAIN USEFUL RELATIONSHIPS.
GEEZ, I KNEW SHE WAS EFFICIENT, BUT THIS IS RIDICULOUS.
SHE REALLY PLANS AHEAD!
SIS PLEINAIR IS SHARP, DOOD.
SHE'S REALLY MATURE, DOOD!
Proud
NOW THEN... WHAT DID YOU NEED?
AH!
OH YEAH.
WELL...
WELL...

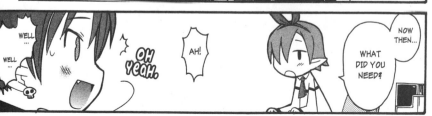

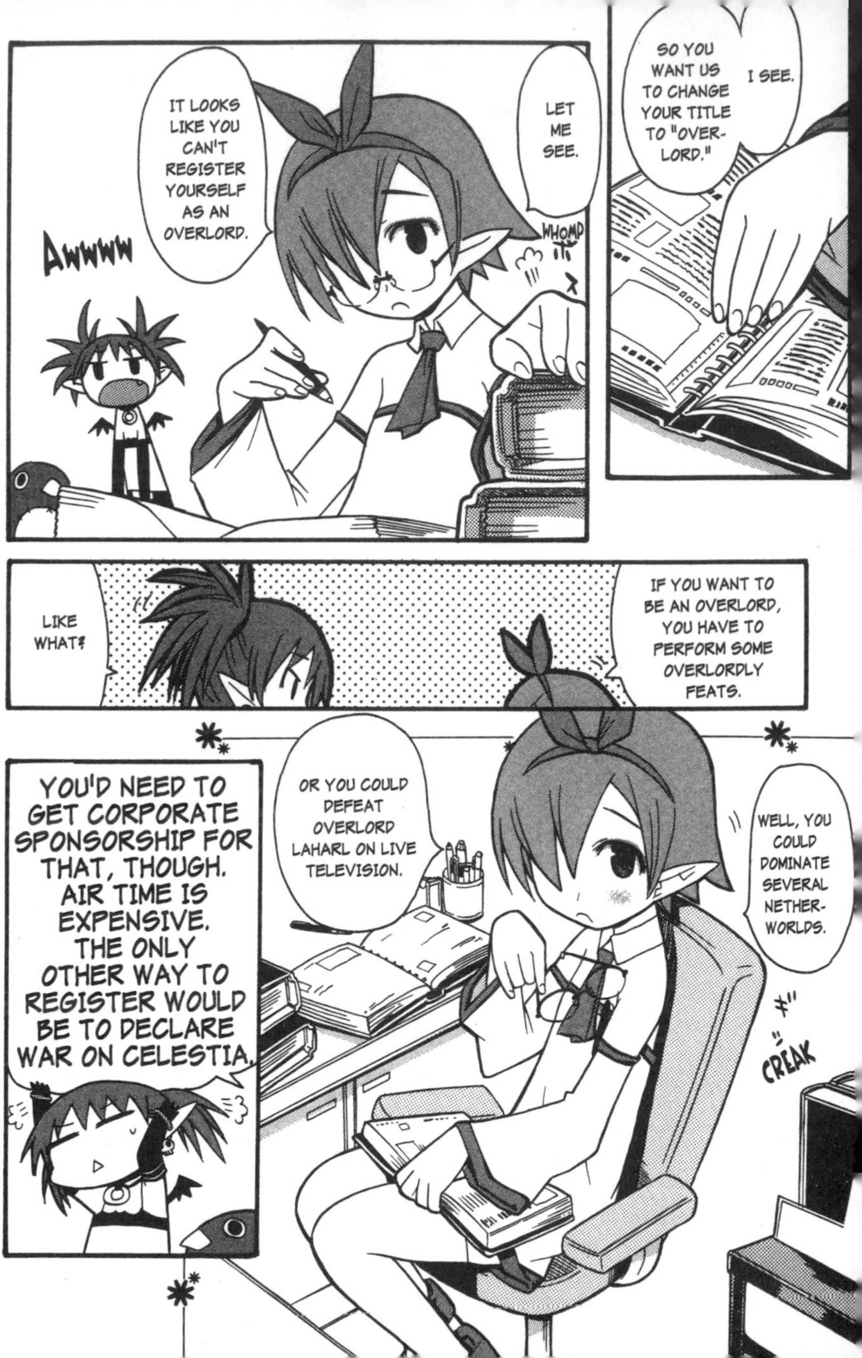
I SEE.
SO YOU WANT US TO CHANGE YOUR TITLE TO "OVER-LORD."
LET ME SEE.
IT LOOKS LIKE YOU CAN'T REGISTER YOURSELF AS AN OVERLORD.
WHOMP
AWWWW
IF YOU WANT TO BE AN OVERLORD, YOU HAVE TO PERFORM SOME OVERLORDLY FEATS.
LIKE WHAT?
WELL, YOU COULD DOMINATE SEVERAL NETHER-WORLDS.
CREAK
OR YOU COULD DEFEAT OVERLORD LAHARL ON LIVE TELEVISION.
YOU'D NEED TO GET CORPORATE SPONSORSHIP FOR THAT, THOUGH. AIR TIME IS EXPENSIVE. THE ONLY OTHER WAY TO REGISTER WOULD BE TO DECLARE WAR ON CELESTIA.

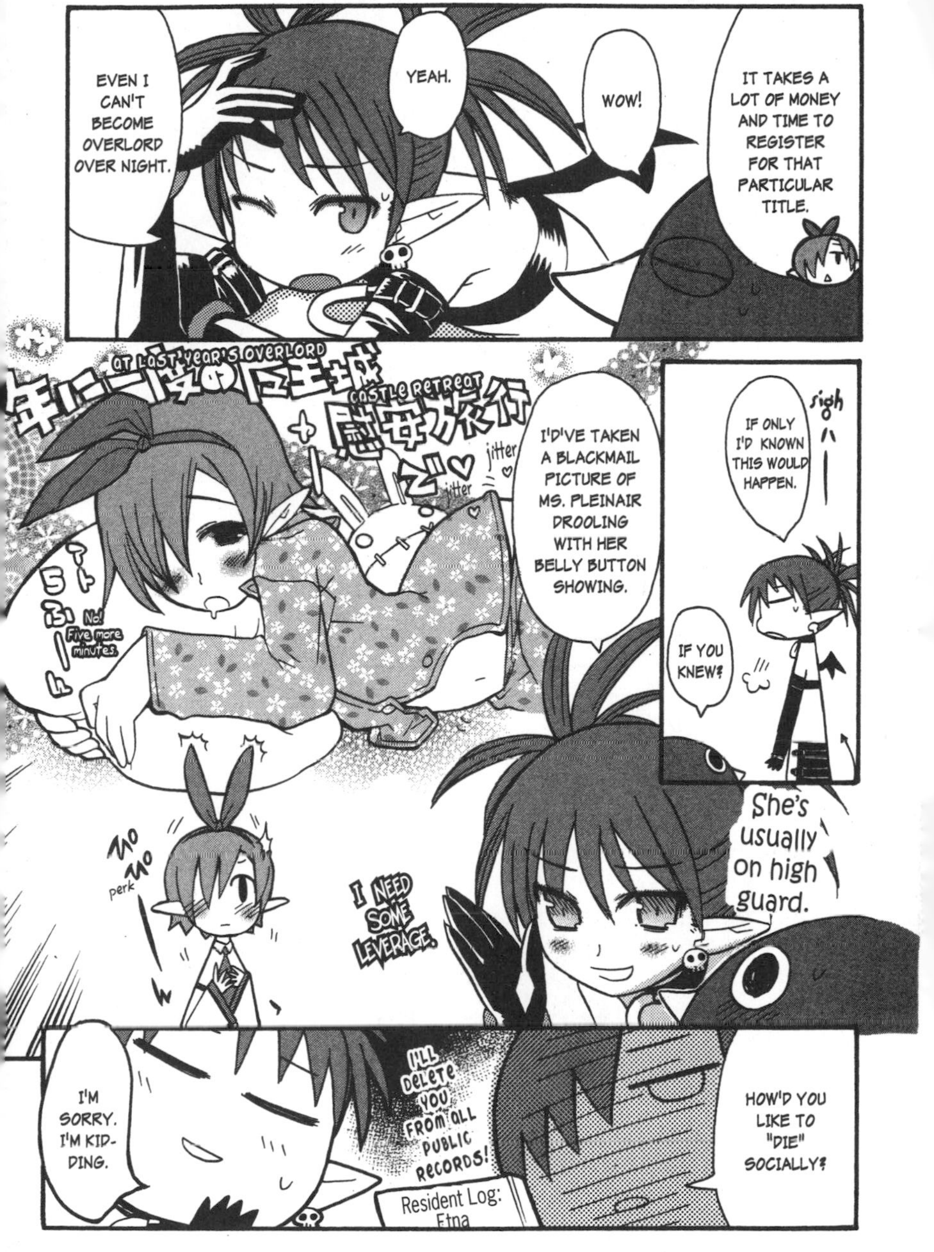
IT TAKES A LOT OF MONEY AND TIME TO REGISTER FOR THAT PARTICULAR TITLE.
WOW!
YEAH.
EVEN I CAN'T BECOME OVERLORD OVER NIGHT.
sigh
IF ONLY I'D KNOWN THIS WOULD HAPPEN.
IF YOU KNEW?
AT LAST YEAR'S OVERLORD
CASTLE RETREAT
I'D'VE TAKEN A BLACKMAIL PICTURE OF MS. PLEINAIR DROOLING WITH HER BELLY BUTTON SHOWING.
jitter
jitter
No! Five more minutes.
She's usually on high guard.
I NEED SOME LEVERAGE.
perk
HOW'D YOU LIKE TO "DIE" SOCIALLY?
I'LL DELETE YOU FROM ALL PUBLIC RECORDS!
Resident Log: Etna
I'M SORRY. I'M KID-DING.

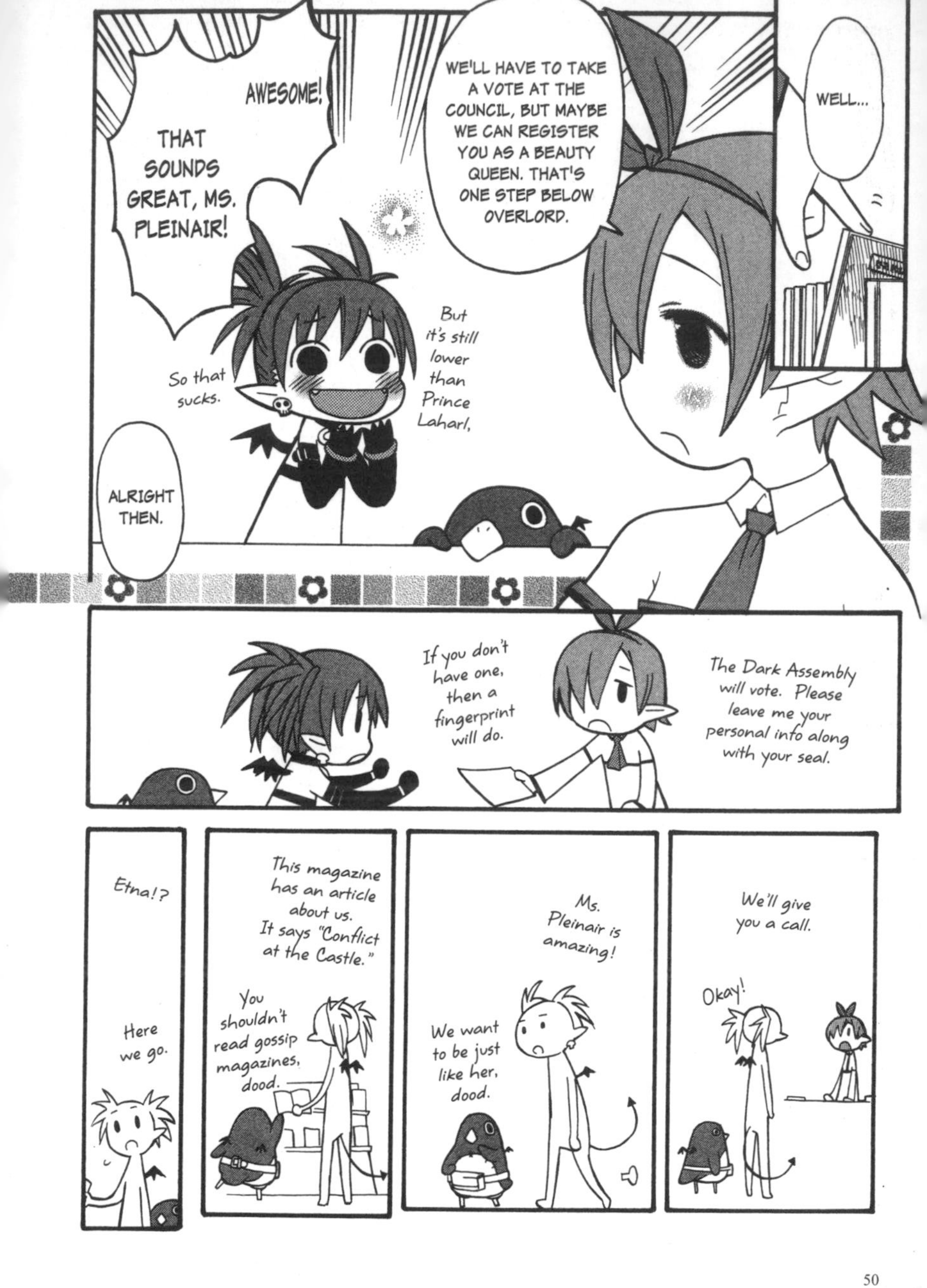
WELL...
WE'LL HAVE TO TAKE A VOTE AT THE COUNCIL, BUT MAYBE WE CAN REGISTER YOU AS A BEAUTY QUEEN. THAT'S ONE STEP BELOW OVERLORD.
AWESOME!
THAT SOUNDS GREAT, MS. PLEINAIR!
But it's still lower than Prince Laharl,
So that sucks.
ALRIGHT THEN.
The Dark Assembly will vote. Please leave me your personal info along with your seal.
If you don't have one, then a fingerprint will do.
We'll give you a call.
Okay!
Ms. Pleinair is amazing!
We want to be just like her, dood.
This magazine has an article about us. It says "Conflict at the Castle."
You shouldn't read gossip magazines, dood.
Etna!?
Here we go.

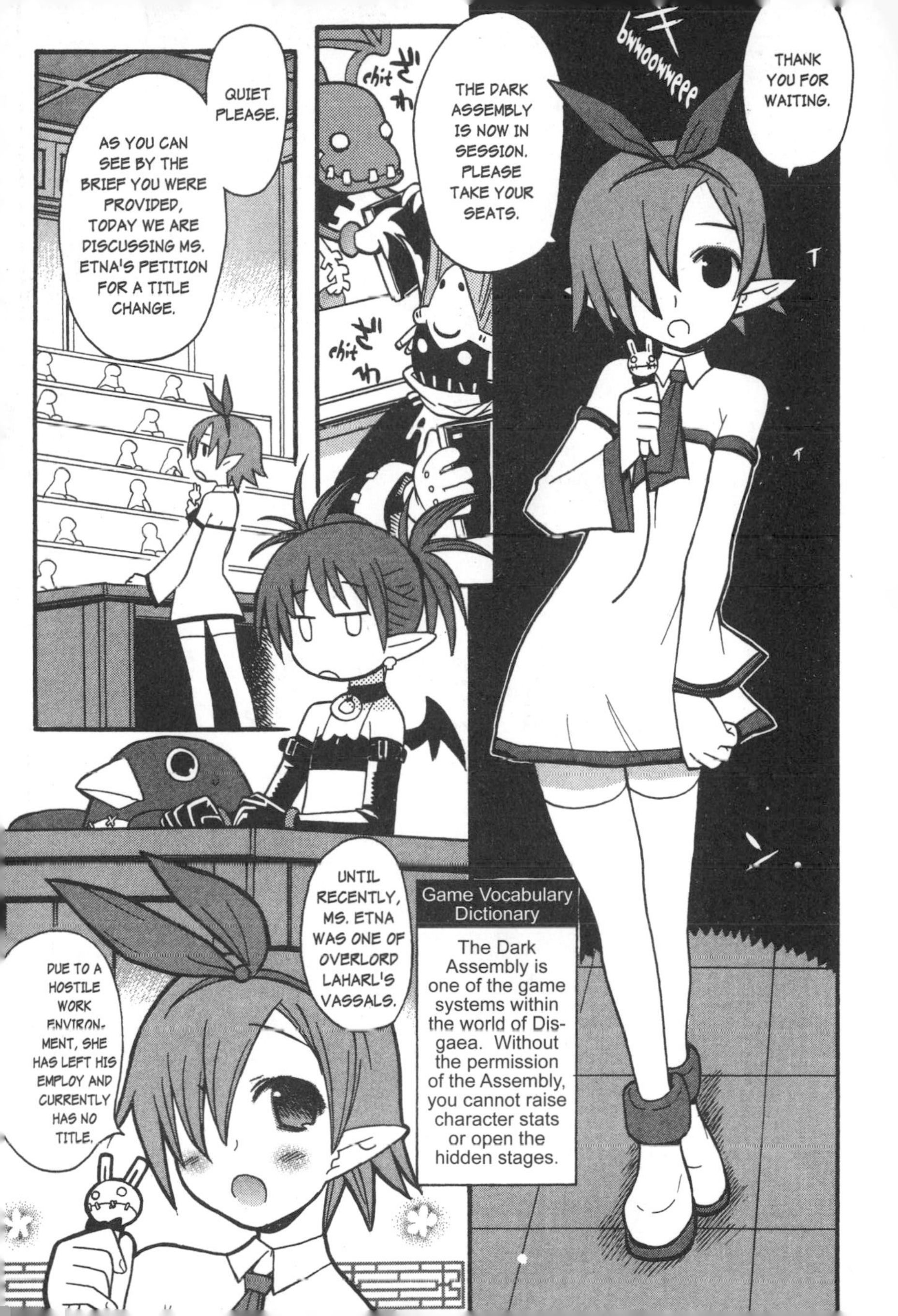
bwwoowweee
THANK YOU FOR WAITING.
THE DARK ASSEMBLY IS NOW IN SESSION. PLEASE TAKE YOUR SEATS.
chit
chit
QUIET PLEASE.
AS YOU CAN SEE BY THE BRIEF YOU WERE PROVIDED, TODAY WE ARE DISCUSSING MS. ETNA'S PETITION FOR A TITLE CHANGE.
UNTIL RECENTLY, MS. ETNA WAS ONE OF OVERLORD LAHARL'S VASSALS.
DUE TO A HOSTILE WORK ENVIRON-MENT, SHE HAS LEFT HIS EMPLOY AND CURRENTLY HAS NO TITLE.
Game Vocabulary Dictionary
The Dark Assembly is one of the game systems within the world of Disgaea. Without the permission of the Assembly, you cannot raise character stats or open the hidden stages.

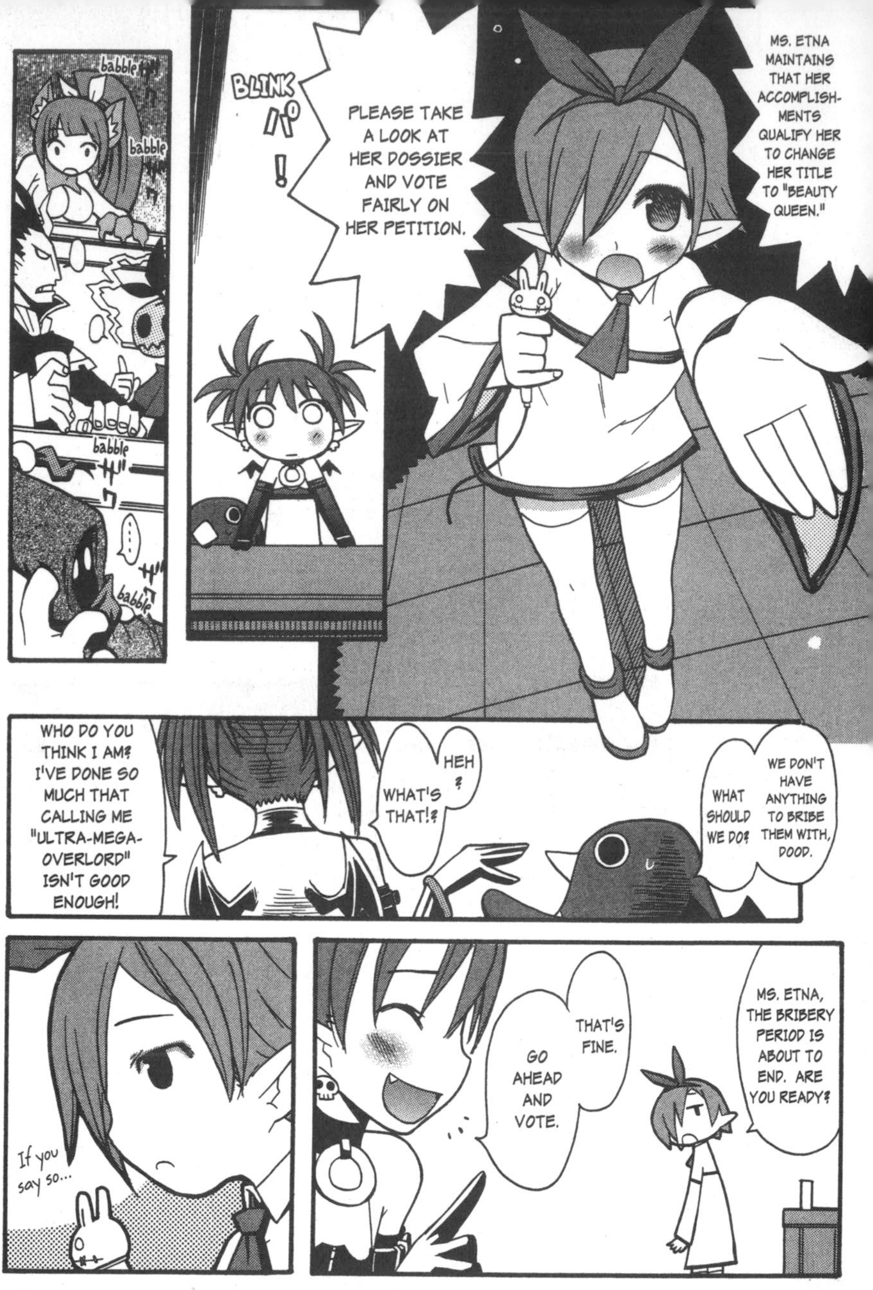
MS. ETNA MAINTAINS THAT HER ACCOMPLISH-MENTS QUALIFY HER TO CHANGE HER TITLE TO "BEAUTY QUEEN."
PLEASE TAKE A LOOK AT HER DOSSIER AND VOTE FAIRLY ON HER PETITION.
BLINK
!
babble
babble
babble
...
babble
WE DON'T HAVE ANYTHING TO BRIBE THEM WITH, DOOD.
WHAT SHOULD WE DO?
HEH?
WHAT'S THAT!?
WHO DO YOU THINK I AM? I'VE DONE SO MUCH THAT CALLING ME "ULTRA-MEGA-OVERLORD" ISN'T GOOD ENOUGH!
MS. ETNA, THE BRIBERY PERIOD IS ABOUT TO END. ARE YOU READY?
THAT'S FINE.
GO AHEAD AND VOTE.
...
If you say so...

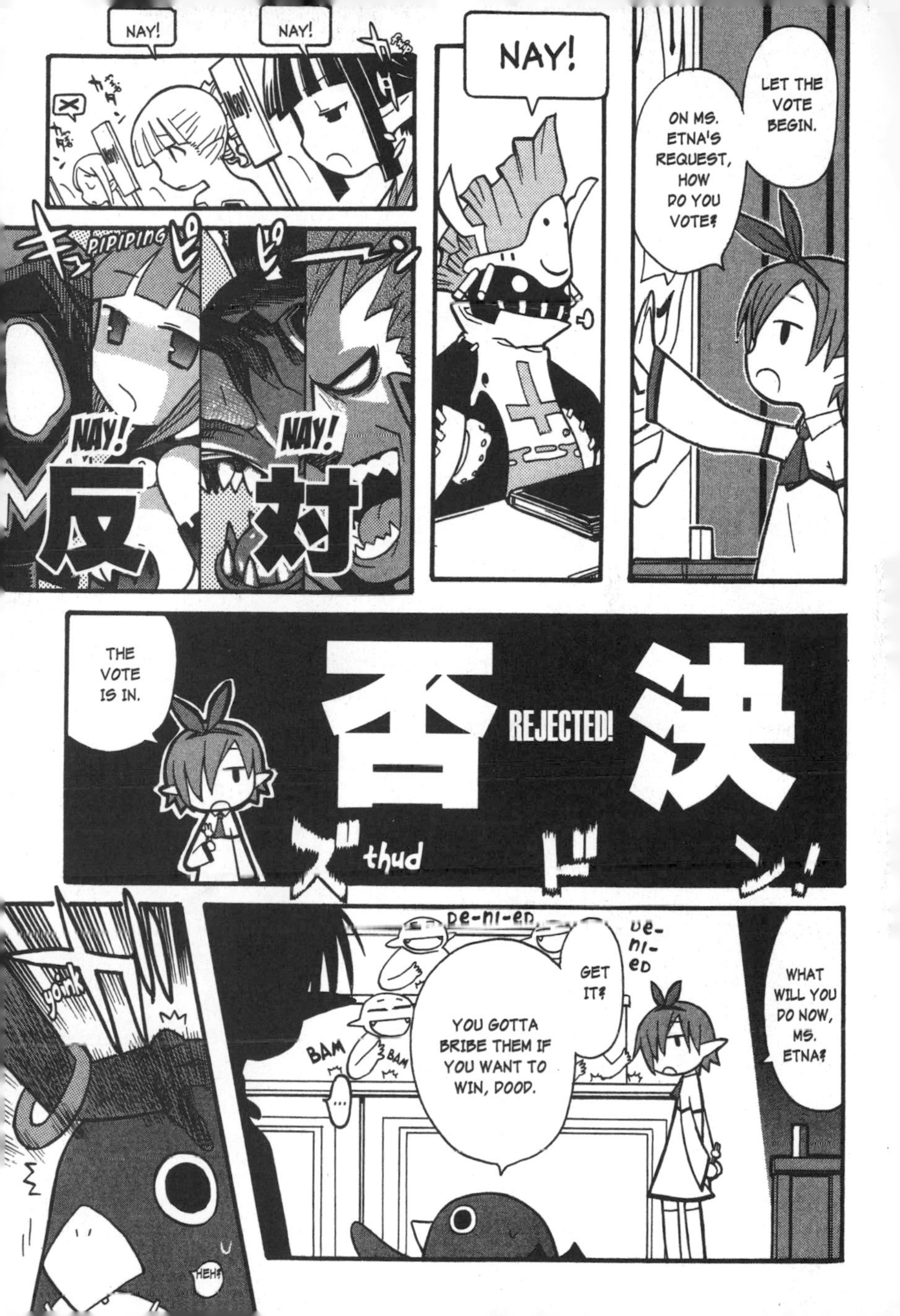
LET THE VOTE BEGIN.
ON MS. ETNA'S REQUEST, HOW DO YOU VOTE?
NAY!
NAY!
NAY!
fwip
Nay!
Nay!
PIPIPING
NAY!
NAY!
反対
THE VOTE IS IN.
否決
REJECTED!
thud
WHAT WILL YOU DO NOW, MS. ETNA?
de-ni-ed
de-ni-ed
GET IT?
YOU GOTTA BRIBE THEM IF YOU WANT TO WIN, DOOD.
BAM
BAM
...
yoink
HEH?

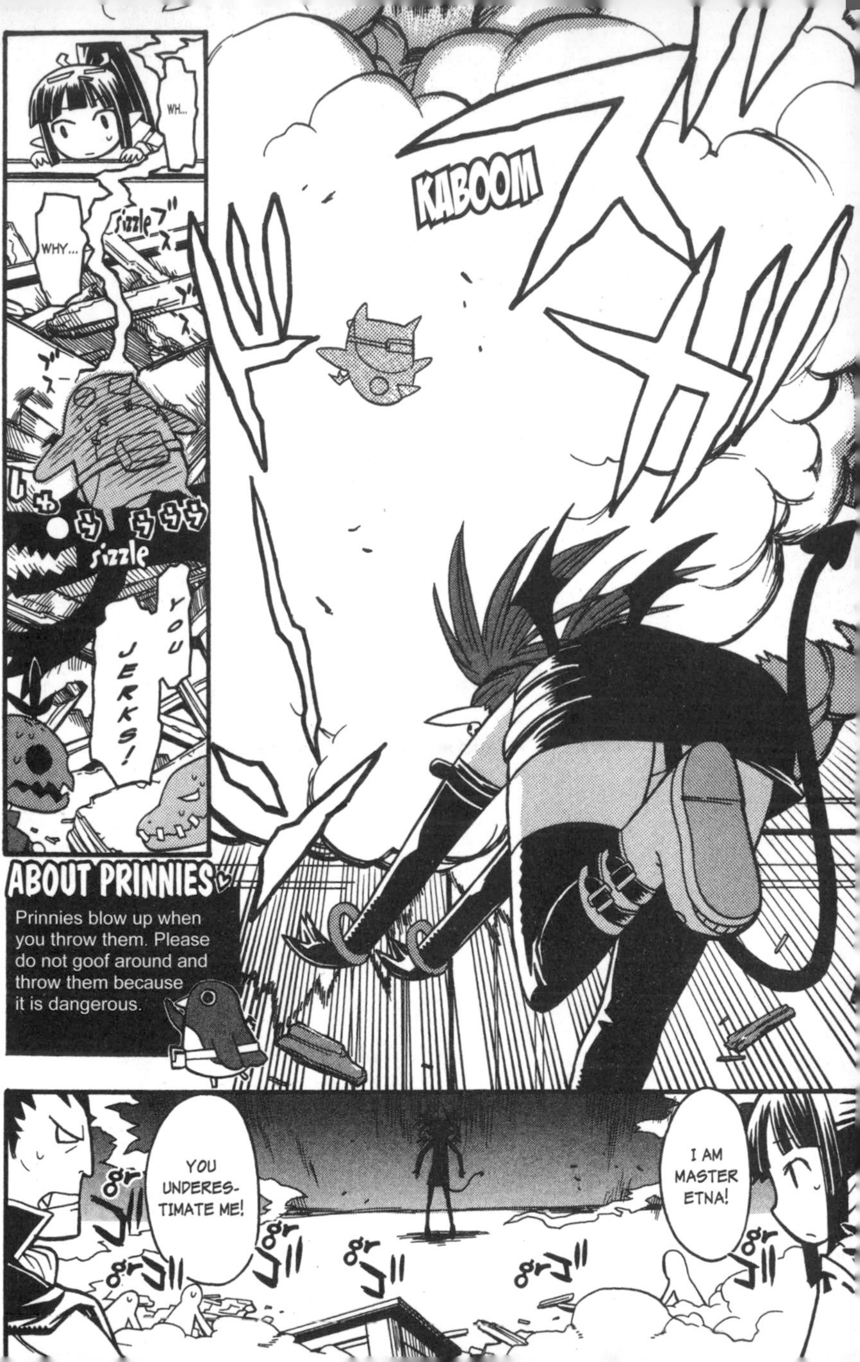
KABOOM
WH...
WHY...
sizzle
sizzle
YOU JERKS!
ABOUT PRINNIES
Prinnies blow up when you throw them. Please do not goof around and throw them because it is dangerous.
I AM MASTER ETNA!
YOU UNDERES-TIMATE ME!
gr
gr
gr
gr
gr
gr

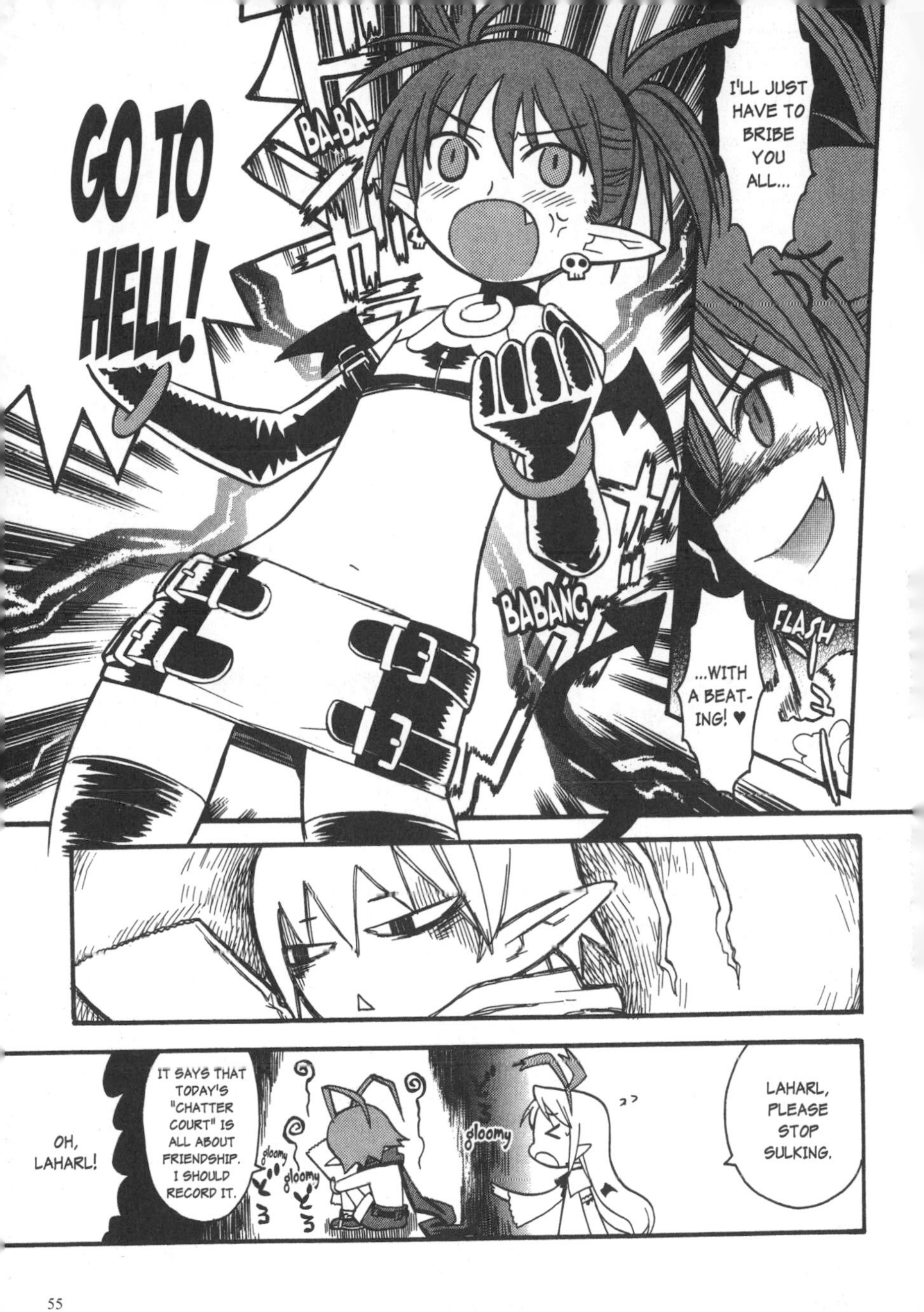
I'LL JUST HAVE TO BRIBE YOU ALL...
FLASH
...WITH A BEATING! ♥
BABANG
BA-BA-
GO TO HELL!
LAHARL, PLEASE STOP SULKING.
gloomy
gloomy
gloomy
IT SAYS THAT TODAY'S "CHATTER COURT" IS ALL ABOUT FRIENDSHIP. I SHOULD RECORD IT.
OH, LAHARL!

EPISODE PREVIEW

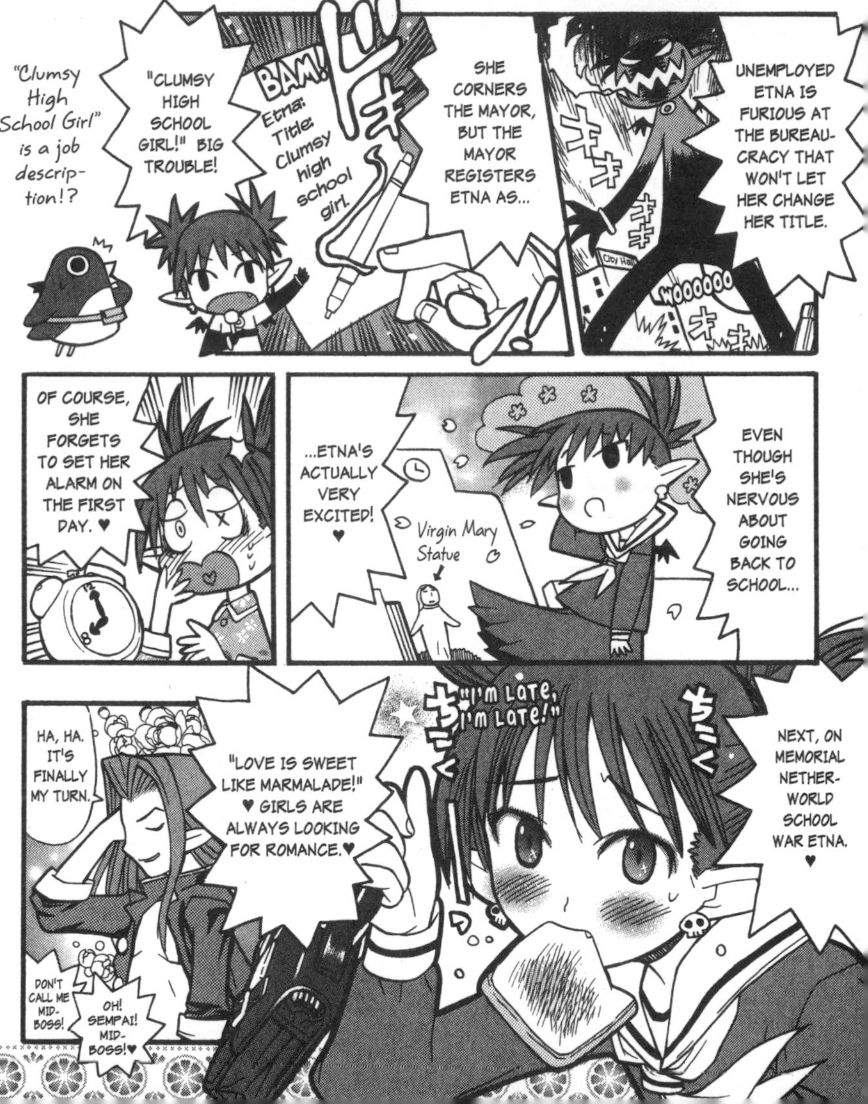
UNEMPLOYED ETNA IS FURIOUS AT THE BUREAUCRACY THAT WON'T LET HER CHANGE HER TITLE.
City Hall
WOOOOOO
SHE CORNERS THE MAYOR, BUT THE MAYOR REGISTERS ETNA AS...
BAM!
Etna: Title: Clumsy high school girl.
"CLUMSY HIGH SCHOOL GIRL!" BIG TROUBLE!
"Clumsy High School Girl" is a job description!?
EVEN THOUGH SHE'S NERVOUS ABOUT GOING BACK TO SCHOOL...
...ETNA'S ACTUALLY VERY EXCITED! ♥
Virgin Mary Statue
OF COURSE, SHE FORGETS TO SET HER ALARM ON THE FIRST DAY. ♥
NEXT, ON MEMORIAL NETHER-WORLD SCHOOL WAR ETNA. ♥
"I'M LATE, I'M LATE!"
"LOVE IS SWEET LIKE MARMALADE!" ♥ GIRLS ARE ALWAYS LOOKING FOR ROMANCE.♥
HA, HA. IT'S FINALLY MY TURN.
OH! SEMPAI! MID-BOSS!♥
DON'T CALL ME MID-BOSS!

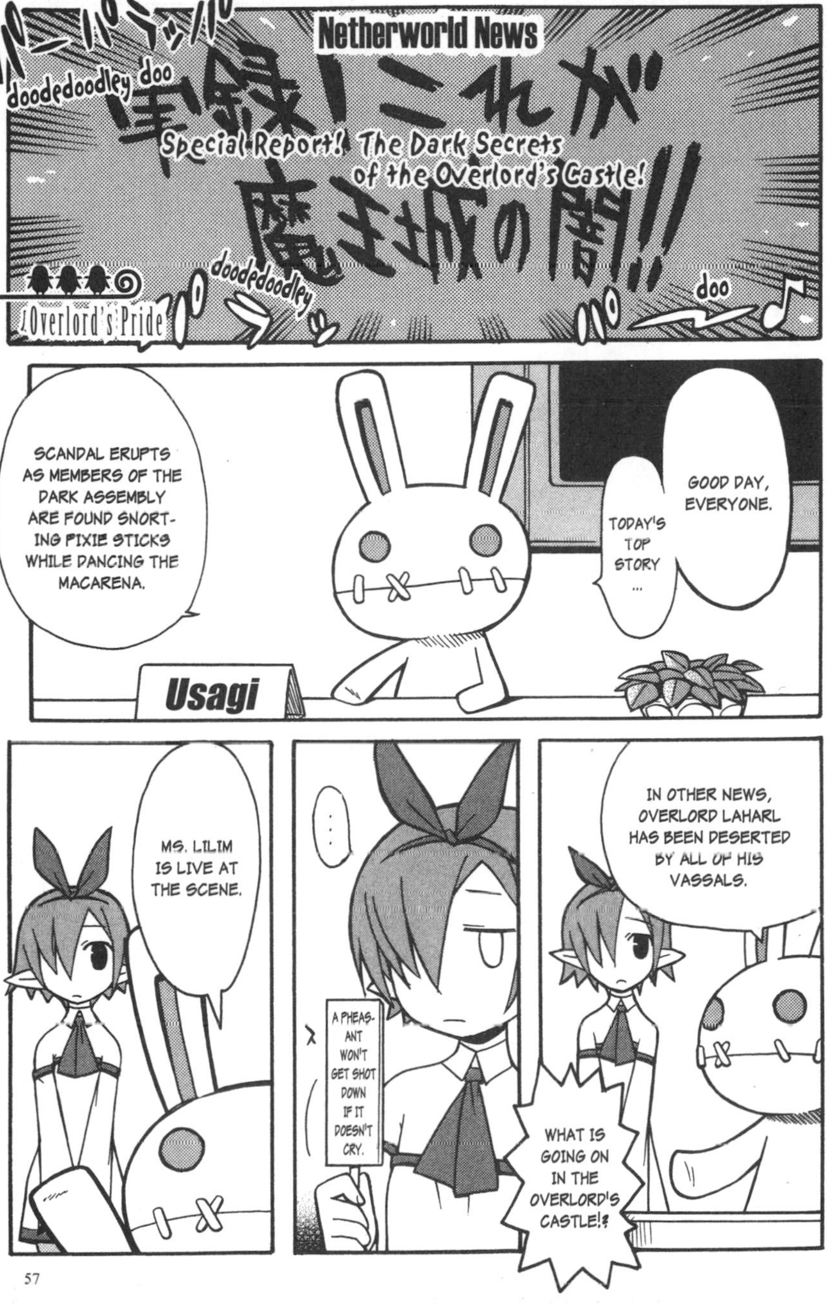
Netherworld News
doodedoodley doo
実録！これが魔王城の闇!!
Special Report! The Dark Secrets of the Overlord's Castle!
doodedoodley
doo
Overlord's Pride
GOOD DAY, EVERYONE.
TODAY'S TOP STORY ...
SCANDAL ERUPTS AS MEMBERS OF THE DARK ASSEMBLY ARE FOUND SNORT-ING PIXIE STICKS WHILE DANCING THE MACARENA.
Usagi
IN OTHER NEWS, OVERLORD LAHARL HAS BEEN DESERTED BY ALL OF HIS VASSALS.
WHAT IS GOING ON IN THE OVERLORD'S CASTLE!?
. . .
A PHEAS-ANT WON'T GET SHOT DOWN IF IT DOESN'T CRY.
MS. LILIM IS LIVE AT THE SCENE.

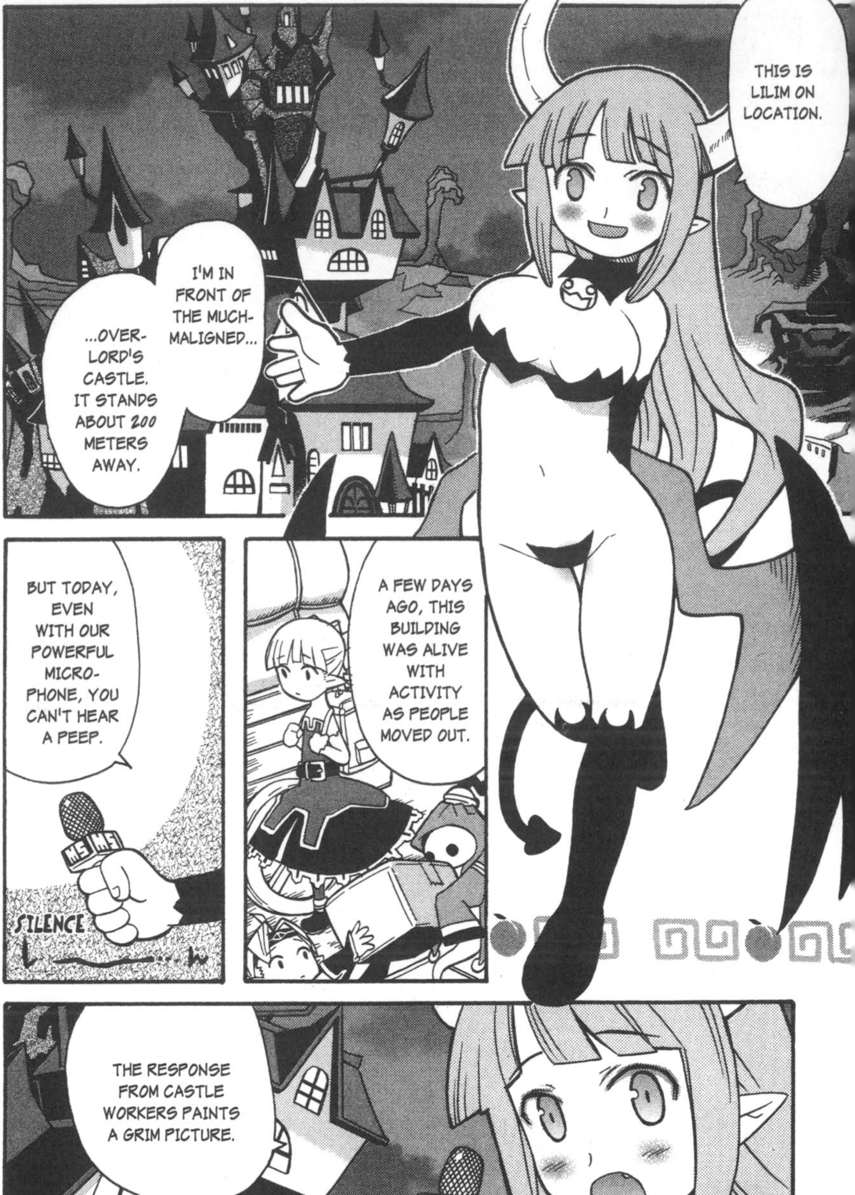
THIS IS LILIM ON LOCATION.
I'M IN FRONT OF THE MUCH-MALIGNED...
...OVER-LORD'S CASTLE. IT STANDS ABOUT 200 METERS AWAY.
A FEW DAYS AGO, THIS BUILDING WAS ALIVE WITH ACTIVITY AS PEOPLE MOVED OUT.
BUT TODAY, EVEN WITH OUR POWERFUL MICRO-PHONE, YOU CAN'T HEAR A PEEP.
MS MS
SILENCE
THE RESPONSE FROM CASTLE WORKERS PAINTS A GRIM PICTURE.
MS MS

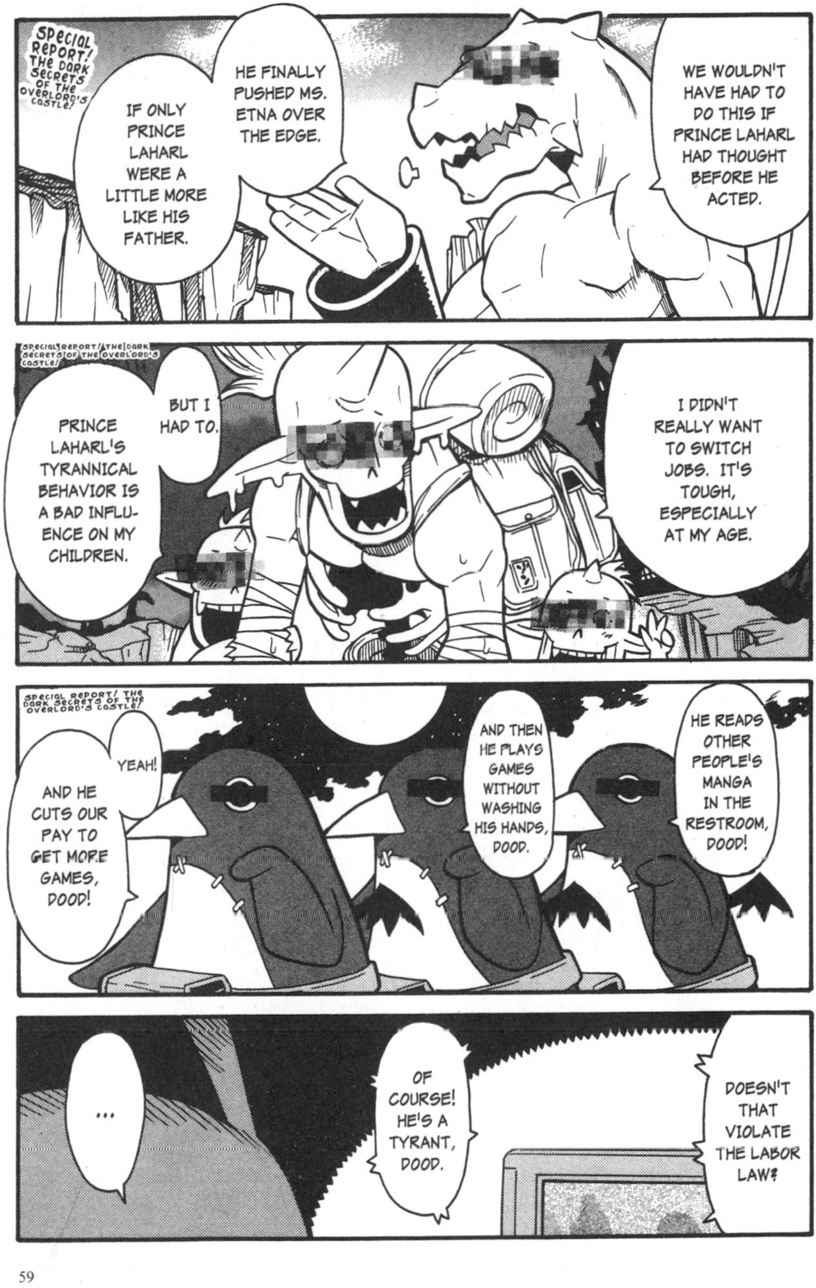
SPECIAL REPORT! THE DARK SECRETS OF THE OVERLORD'S CASTLE!
WE WOULDN'T HAVE HAD TO DO THIS IF PRINCE LAHARL HAD THOUGHT BEFORE HE ACTED.
HE FINALLY PUSHED MS. ETNA OVER THE EDGE.
IF ONLY PRINCE LAHARL WERE A LITTLE MORE LIKE HIS FATHER.
SPECIAL REPORT! THE DARK SECRETS OF THE OVERLORD'S CASTLE!
I DIDN'T REALLY WANT TO SWITCH JOBS. IT'S TOUGH, ESPECIALLY AT MY AGE.
BUT I HAD TO.
PRINCE LAHARL'S TYRANNICAL BEHAVIOR IS A BAD INFLU-ENCE ON MY CHILDREN.
SPECIAL REPORT! THE DARK SECRETS OF THE OVERLORD'S CASTLE!
HE READS OTHER PEOPLE'S MANGA IN THE RESTROOM, DOOD!
AND THEN HE PLAYS GAMES WITHOUT WASHING HIS HANDS, DOOD.
YEAH!
AND HE CUTS OUR PAY TO GET MORE GAMES, DOOD!
DOESN'T THAT VIOLATE THE LABOR LAW?
OF COURSE! HE'S A TYRANT, DOOD.
...

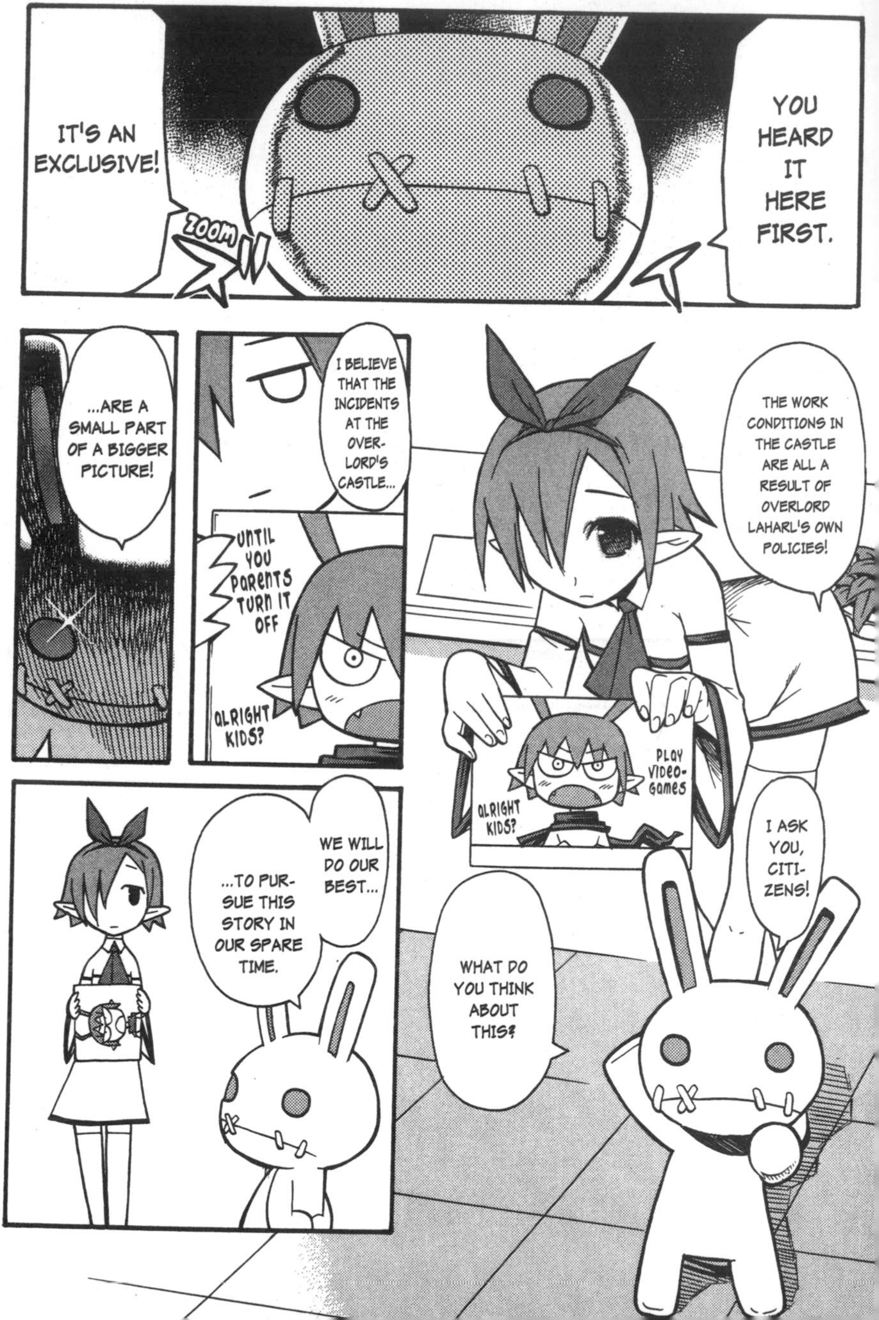
YOU HEARD IT HERE FIRST.
IT'S AN EXCLUSIVE!
ZOOM
THE WORK CONDITIONS IN THE CASTLE ARE ALL A RESULT OF OVERLORD LAHARL'S OWN POLICIES!
PLAY VIDEO-GAMES
ALRIGHT KIDS?
I ASK YOU, CITIZENS!
WHAT DO YOU THINK ABOUT THIS?
I BELIEVE THAT THE INCIDENTS AT THE OVER-LORD'S CASTLE...
UNTIL YOU PARENTS TURN IT OFF
ALRIGHT KIDS?
...ARE A SMALL PART OF A BIGGER PICTURE!
WE WILL DO OUR BEST...
...TO PURSUE THIS STORY IN OUR SPARE TIME.

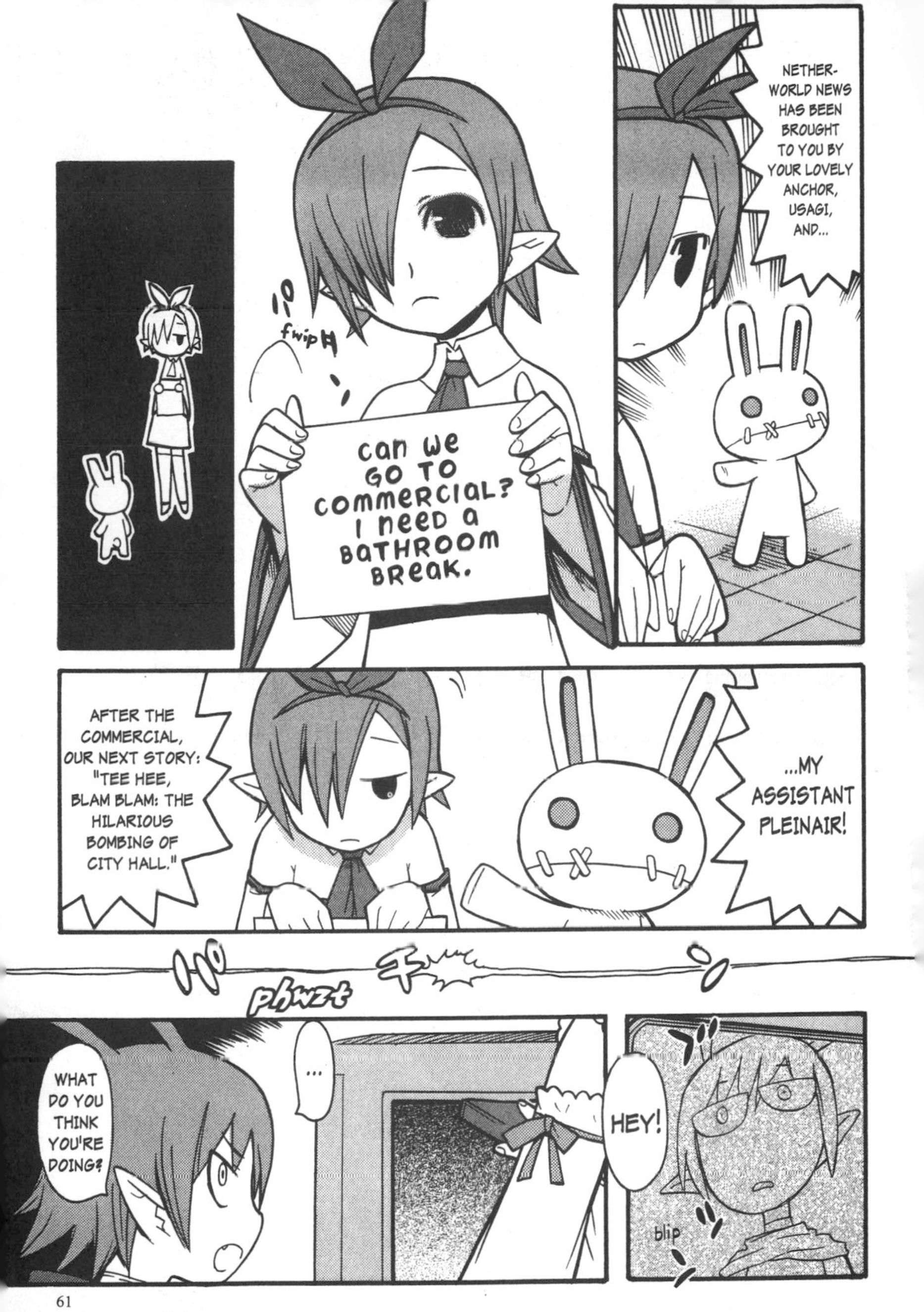
NETHER-WORLD NEWS HAS BEEN BROUGHT TO YOU BY YOUR LOVELY ANCHOR, USAGI, AND...
fwip
can we GO TO commercial? I need a BATHROOM BREAK.
...MY ASSISTANT PLEINAIR!
AFTER THE COMMERCIAL, OUR NEXT STORY: "TEE HEE, BLAM BLAM: THE HILARIOUS BOMBING OF CITY HALL."
phwzt
HEY!
blip
...
WHAT DO YOU THINK YOU'RE DOING?

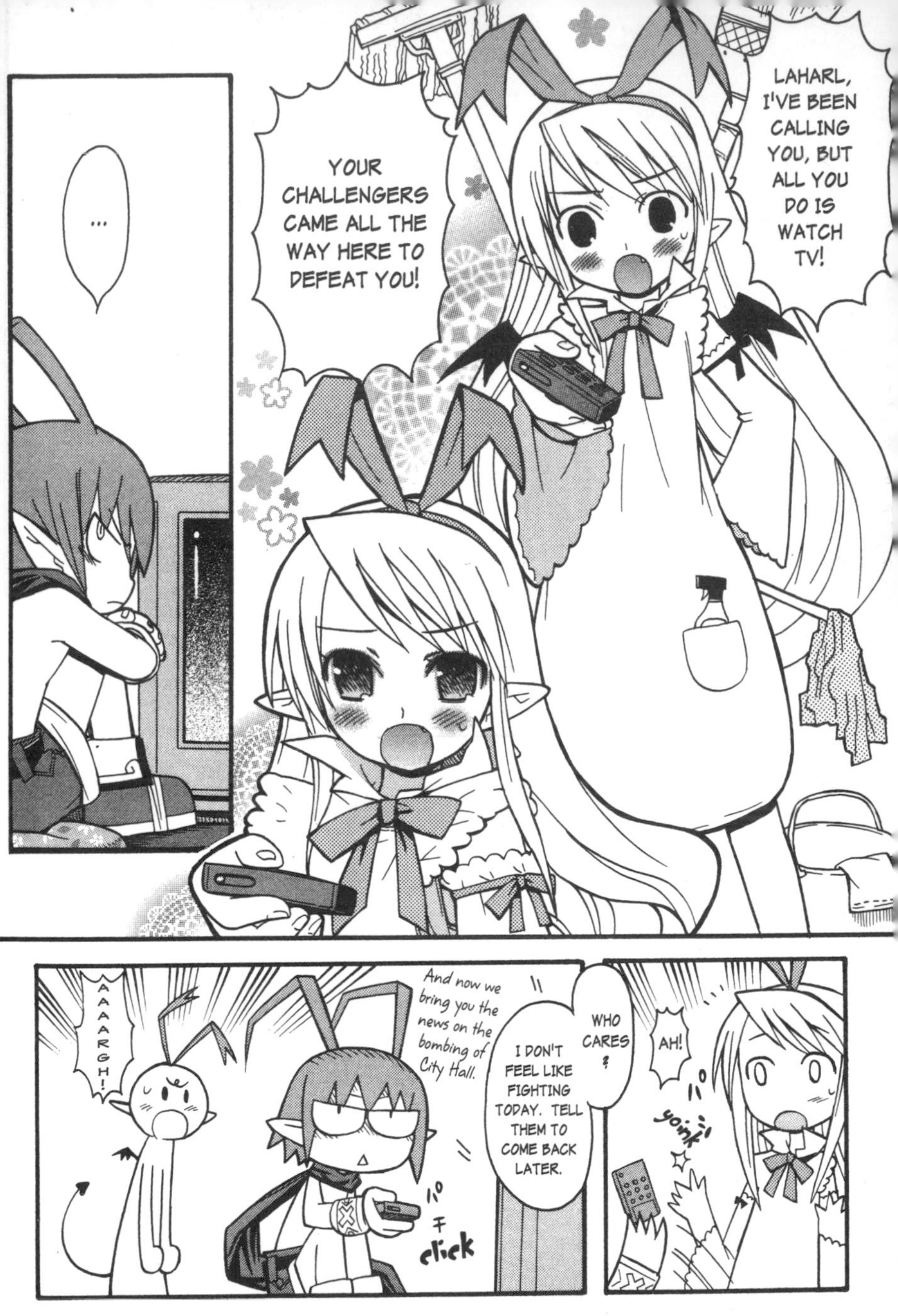
LAHARL, I'VE BEEN CALLING YOU, BUT ALL YOU DO IS WATCH TV!
YOUR CHALLENGERS CAME ALL THE WAY HERE TO DEFEAT YOU!
...
AH!
yoink
WHO CARES?
I DON'T FEEL LIKE FIGHTING TODAY. TELL THEM TO COME BACK LATER.
And now we bring you the news on the bombing of City Hall.
click
AAAARGH!

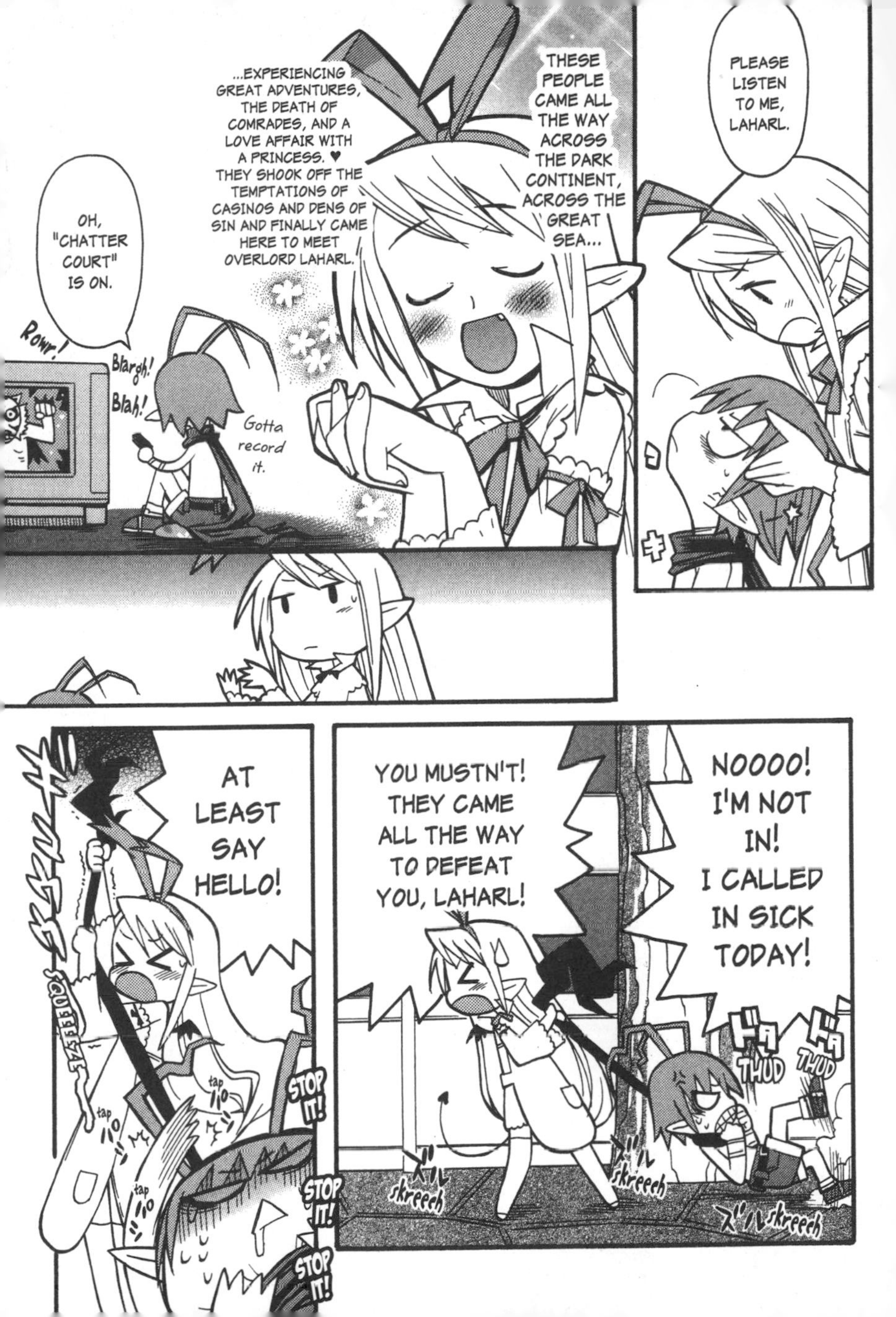
PLEASE LISTEN TO ME, LAHARL.
THESE PEOPLE CAME ALL THE WAY ACROSS THE DARK CONTINENT, ACROSS THE GREAT SEA...
...EXPERIENCING GREAT ADVENTURES, THE DEATH OF COMRADES, AND A LOVE AFFAIR WITH A PRINCESS. ♥ THEY SHOOK OFF THE TEMPTATIONS OF CASINOS AND DENS OF SIN AND FINALLY CAME HERE TO MEET OVERLORD LAHARL.
OH, "CHATTER COURT" IS ON.
Rowr!
Blargh!
Blah!
Gotta record it.
NOOOO! I'M NOT IN! I CALLED IN SICK TODAY!
YOU MUSTN'T! THEY CAME ALL THE WAY TO DEFEAT YOU, LAHARL!
THUD
THUD
skreech
skreech
skreech
AT LEAST SAY HELLO!
SQUEEEEZE
tap
tap
tap
STOP IT!
STOP IT!
STOP IT!

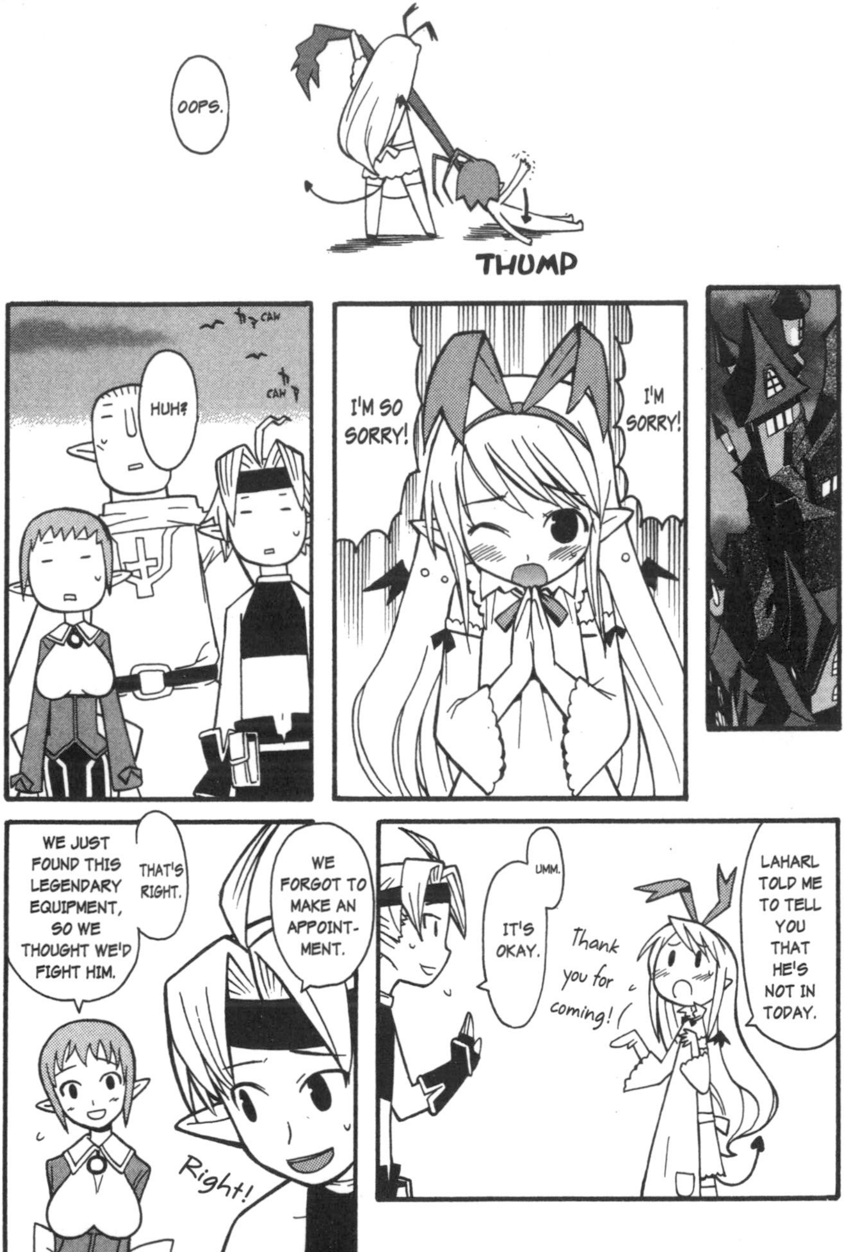
OOPS.
THUMP
I'M SORRY!
I'M SO SORRY!
CAW
HUH?
CAW
LAHARL TOLD ME TO TELL YOU THAT HE'S NOT IN TODAY.
Thank you for coming!
UMM.
IT'S OKAY.
WE FORGOT TO MAKE AN APPOINTMENT.
THAT'S RIGHT.
WE JUST FOUND THIS LEGENDARY EQUIPMENT, SO WE THOUGHT WE'D FIGHT HIM.
Right!

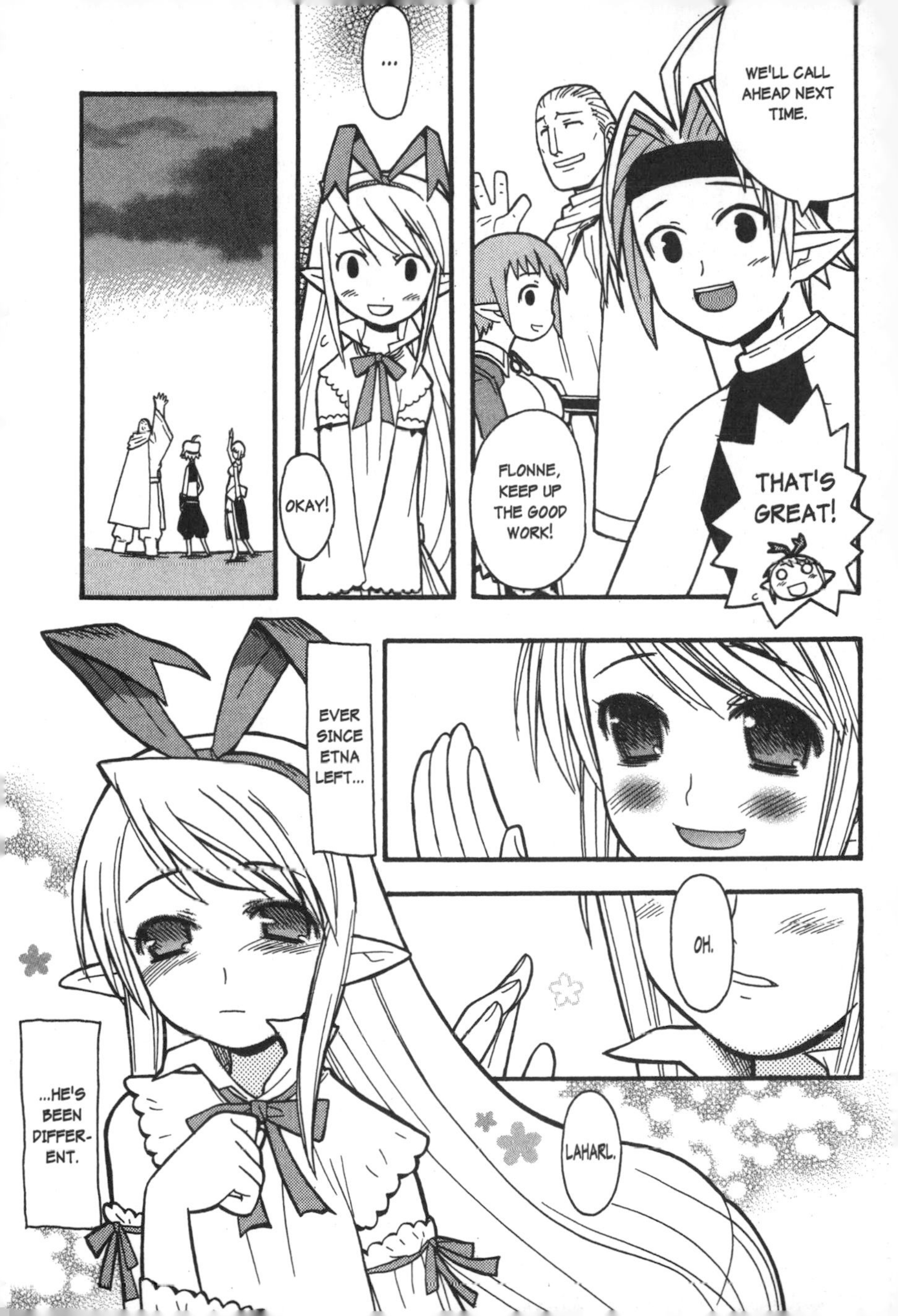
WE'LL CALL AHEAD NEXT TIME.
THAT'S GREAT!
FLONNE, KEEP UP THE GOOD WORK!
...
OKAY!
EVER SINCE ETNA LEFT...
OH.
LAHARL.
...HE'S BEEN DIFFER-ENT.

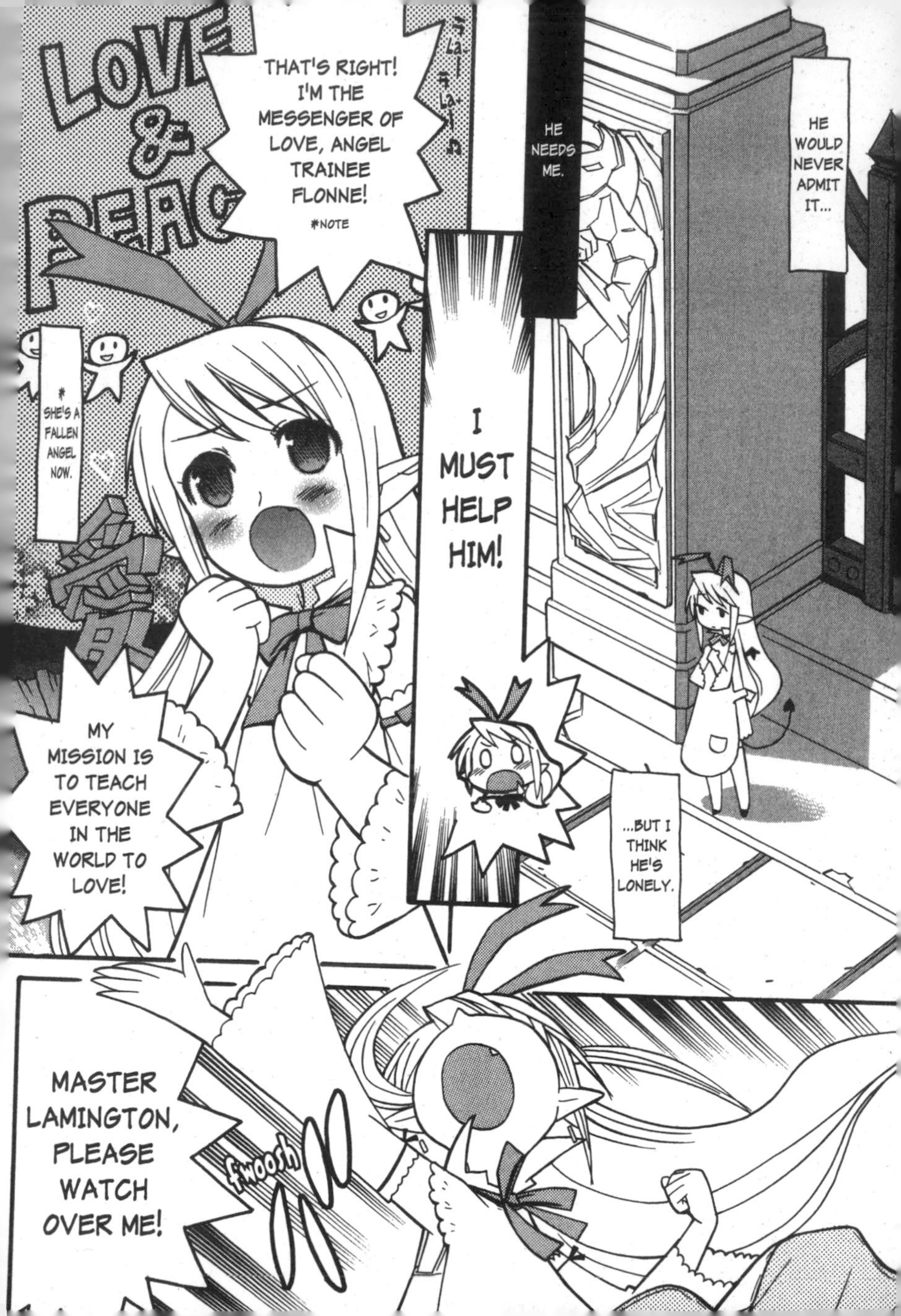
HE WOULD NEVER ADMIT IT...
...BUT I THINK HE'S LONELY.
HE NEEDS ME.
I MUST HELP HIM!
LOVE & PEAC
La~ La~ ♪
THAT'S RIGHT! I'M THE MESSENGER OF LOVE, ANGEL TRAINEE FLONNE!
*NOTE
* SHE'S A FALLEN ANGEL NOW.
MY MISSION IS TO TEACH EVERYONE IN THE WORLD TO LOVE!
MASTER LAMINGTON, PLEASE WATCH OVER ME!
fwoosh

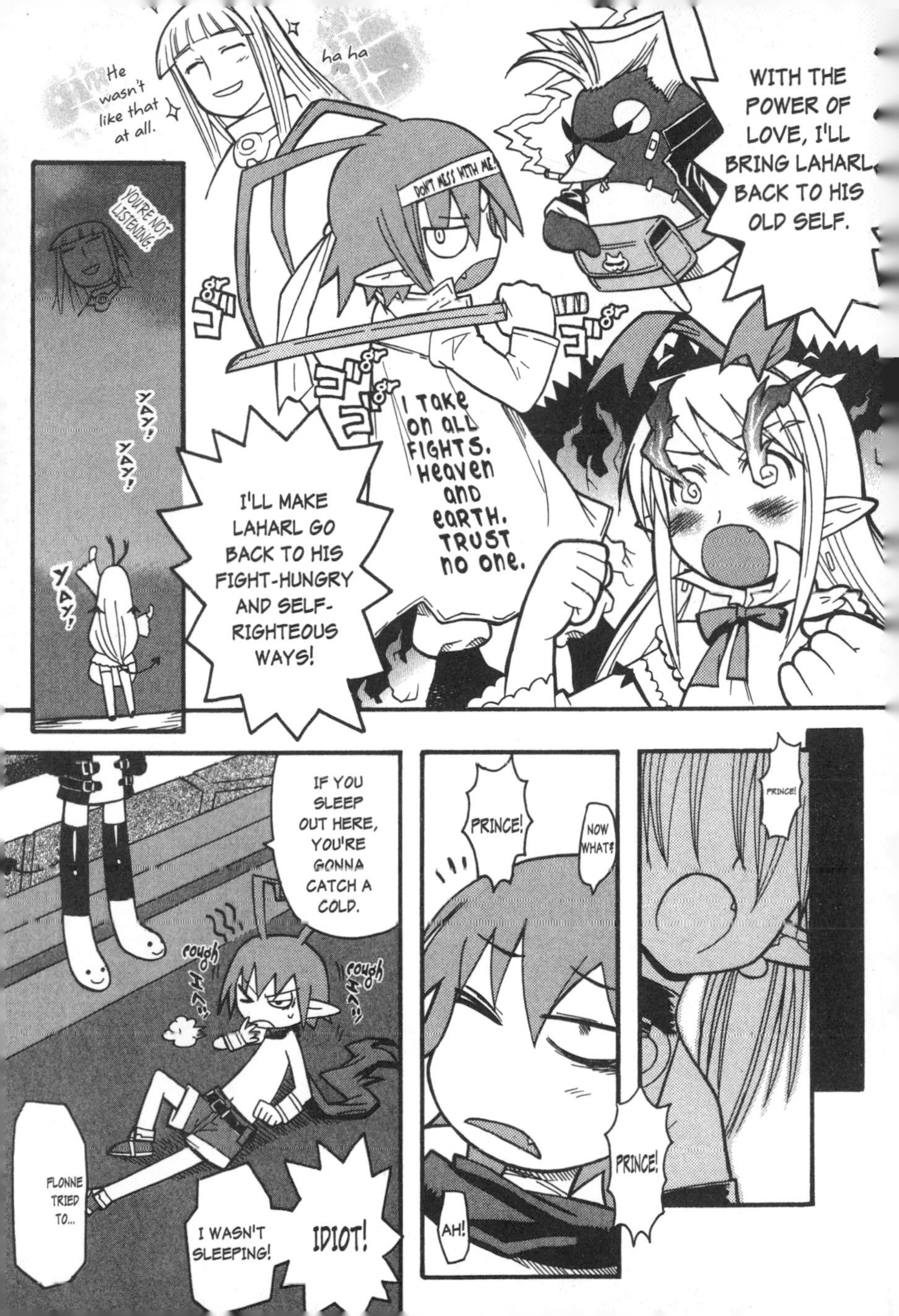
WITH THE POWER OF LOVE, I'LL BRING LAHARL BACK TO HIS OLD SELF.
ha ha
He wasn't like that at all.
DON'T MESS WITH ME!
gor
gor
gor
gor
I take on all FIGHTS. Heaven and earth. TRUST no one.
I'LL MAKE LAHARL GO BACK TO HIS FIGHT-HUNGRY AND SELF-RIGHTEOUS WAYS!
YOU'RE NOT LISTENING.
YAY!
YAY!
YAY!
PRINCE!
PRINCE!
NOW WHAT?
PRINCE!
AH!
IF YOU SLEEP OUT HERE, YOU'RE GONNA CATCH A COLD.
cough
cough
I WASN'T SLEEPING!
IDIOT!
FLONNE TRIED TO...

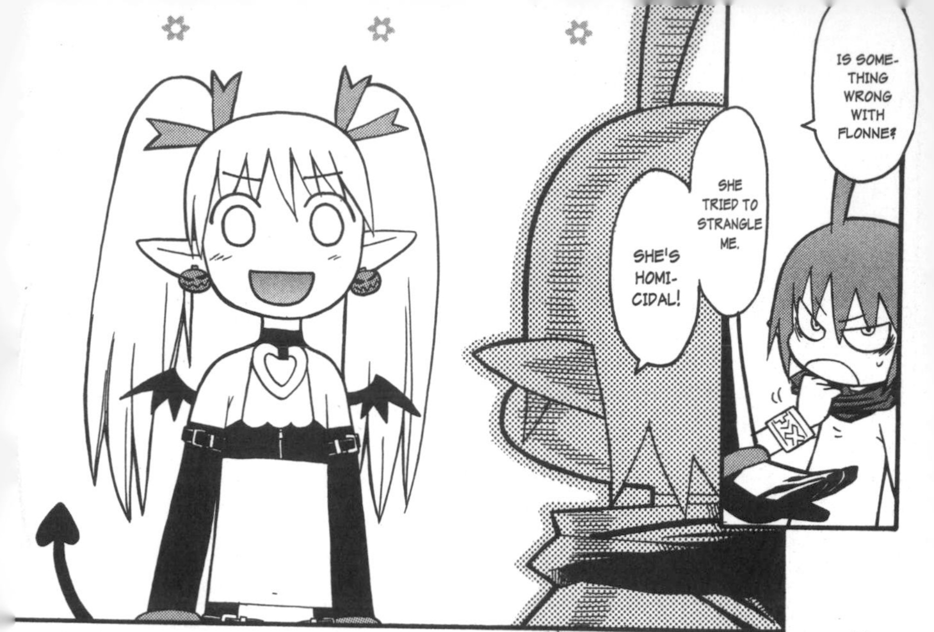
IS SOME-THING WRONG WITH FLONNE?
SHE TRIED TO STRANGLE ME.
SHE'S HOMI-CIDAL!

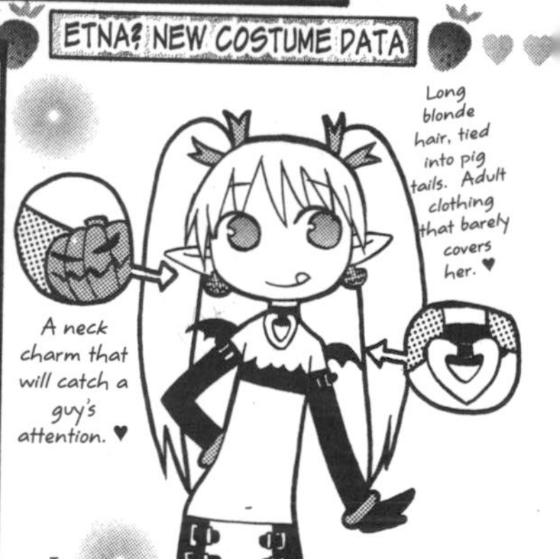
ETNA? NEW COSTUME DATA
Long blonde hair, tied into pig tails. Adult clothing that barely covers her. ♥
A neck charm that will catch a guy's attention. ♥
Instead of skulls, she has jack-o-lanterns. Much more stylish.
Drawings on the boots for a personal touch. ♥
Point
ACCESSORIES ARE THE SECRET TO CUTENESS.♥ DO IT RIGHT, AND YOU'LL LOOK BETTER THAN YOUR FRIENDS.♥

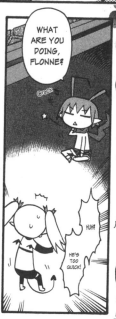

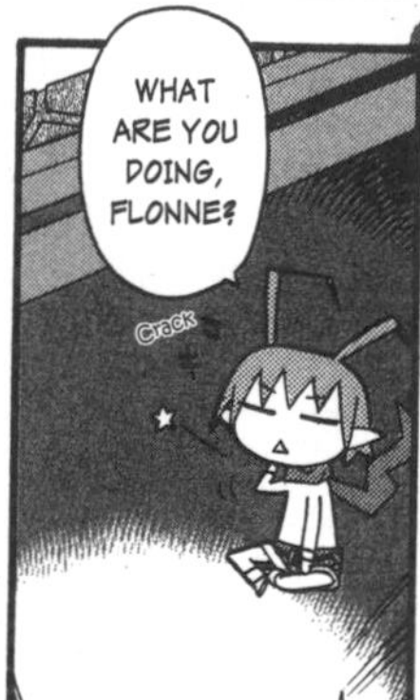
WHAT ARE YOU DOING, FLONNE?
Crack
HUH?
HE'S TOO QUICK!

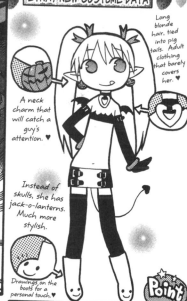

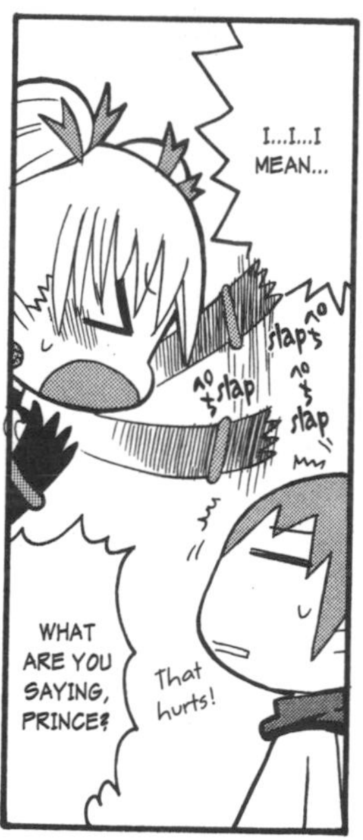
I...I...I MEAN...
slap
slap
slap
WHAT ARE YOU SAYING, PRINCE?
That hurts!

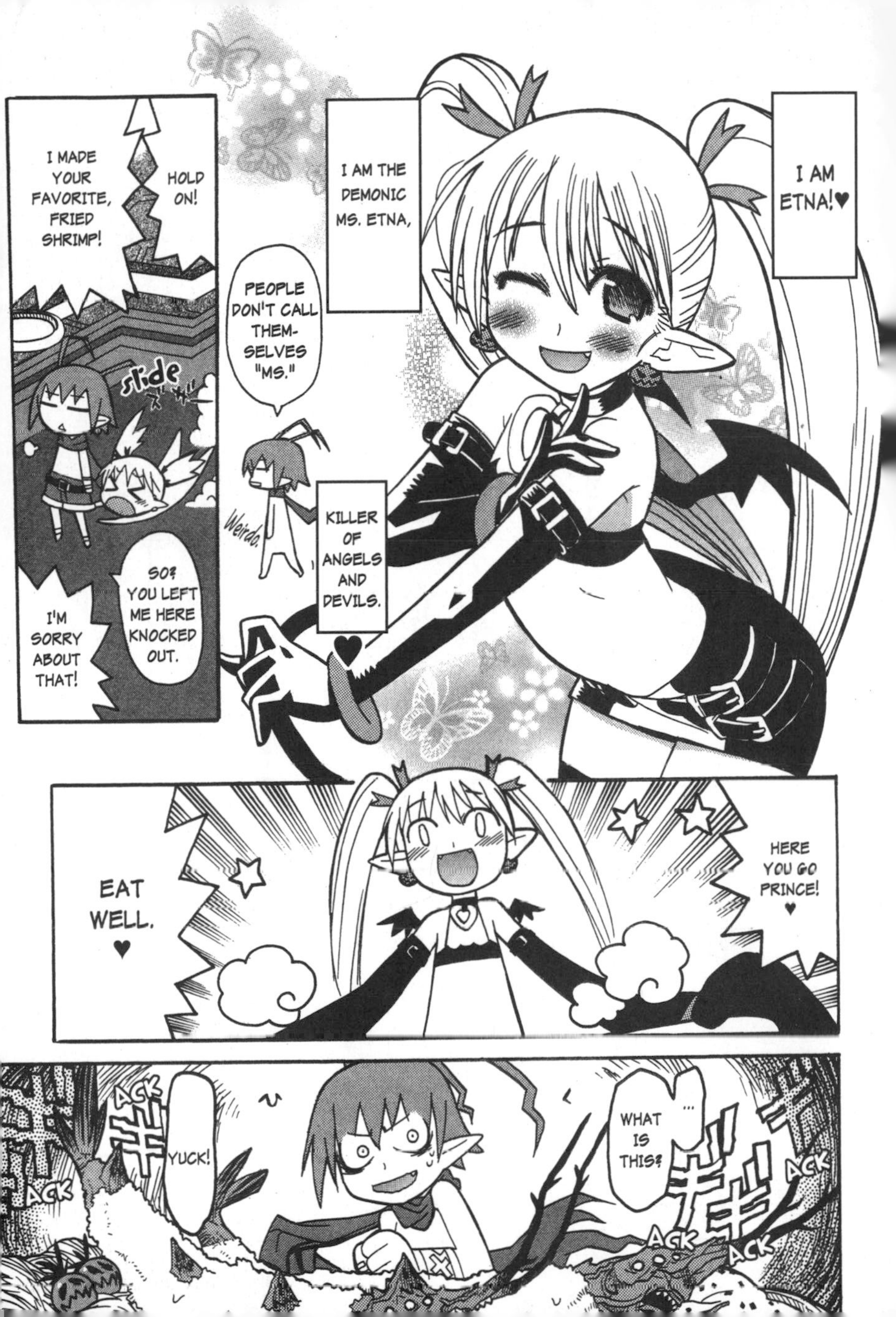
I AM ETNA!♥
I AM THE DEMONIC MS. ETNA,
KILLER OF ANGELS AND DEVILS.
PEOPLE DON'T CALL THEM-SELVES "MS."
Weirdo.
HOLD ON!
I MADE YOUR FAVORITE, FRIED SHRIMP!
slide
SO? YOU LEFT ME HERE KNOCKED OUT.
I'M SORRY ABOUT THAT!
HERE YOU GO PRINCE! ♥
EAT WELL. ♥
ACK
ACK
ACK
ACK
... WHAT IS THIS?
YUCK!
ACK
ACK

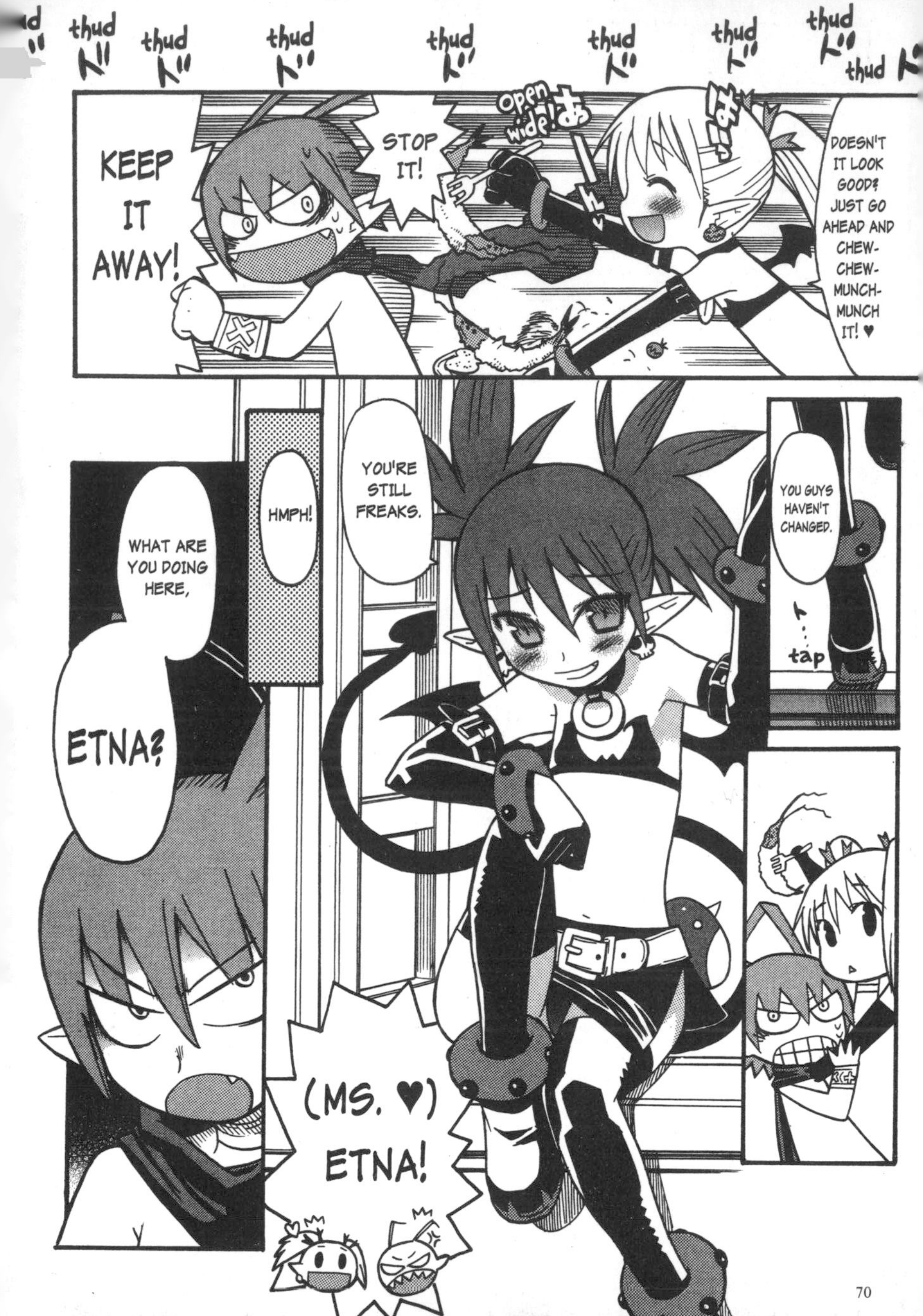
thud
thud
thud
thud
thud
thud
thud
thud
DOESN'T IT LOOK GOOD? JUST GO AHEAD AND CHEW-CHEW-MUNCH-MUNCH IT! ♥
open wide!
STOP IT!
KEEP IT AWAY!
YOU GUYS HAVEN'T CHANGED.
tap
YOU'RE STILL FREAKS.
HMPH!
WHAT ARE YOU DOING HERE,
ETNA?
(MS. ♥) ETNA!

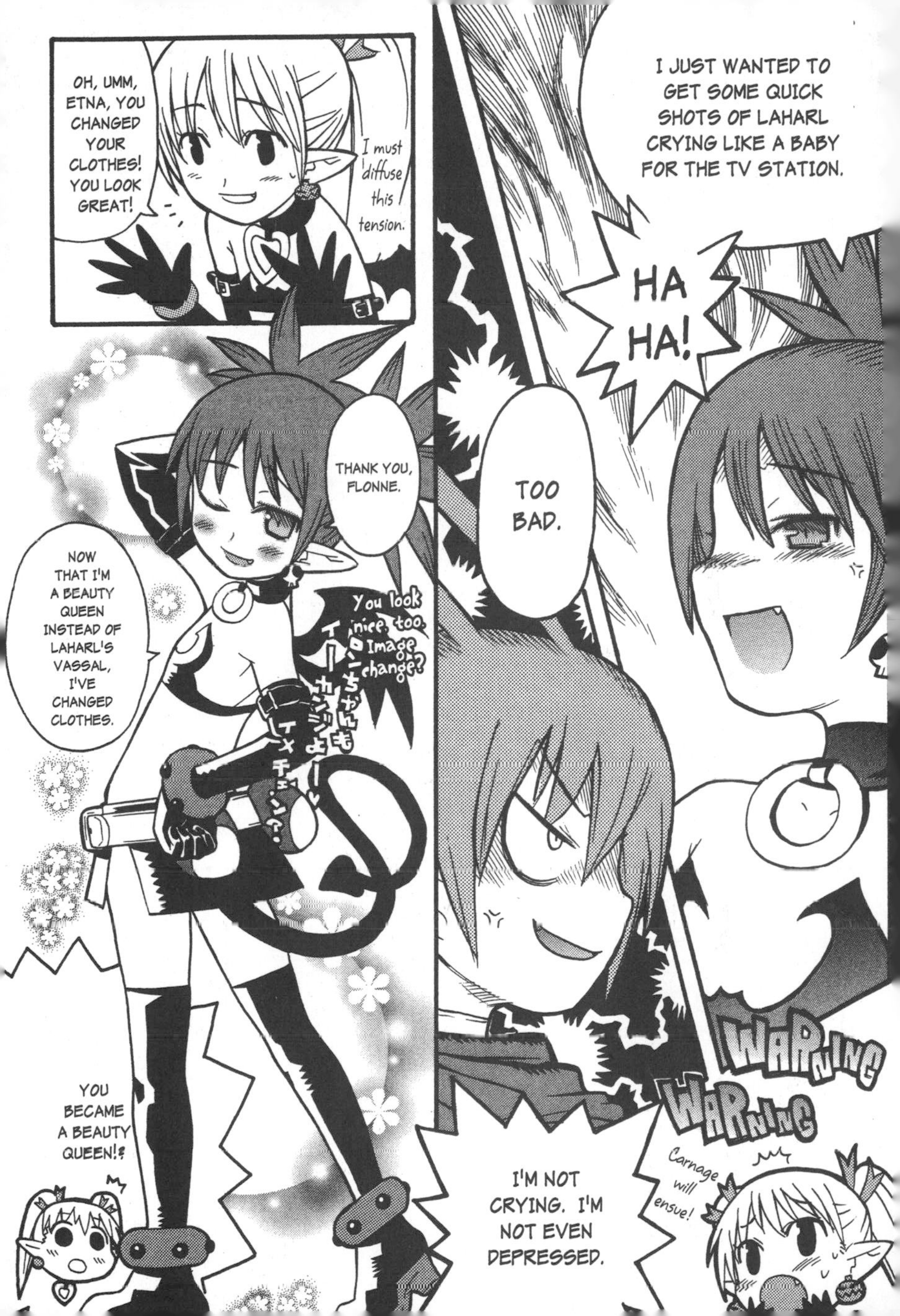
I JUST WANTED TO GET SOME QUICK SHOTS OF LAHARL CRYING LIKE A BABY FOR THE TV STATION.
HA HA!
TOO BAD.
WARNING
WARNING
Carnage will ensue!
I'M NOT CRYING. I'M NOT EVEN DEPRESSED.
I must diffuse this tension.
OH, UMM, ETNA, YOU CHANGED YOUR CLOTHES! YOU LOOK GREAT!
THANK YOU, FLONNE.
ロンちゃんも
イーカンジよー♥
イメチェン…?
You look nice, too. Image change?
NOW THAT I'M A BEAUTY QUEEN INSTEAD OF LAHARL'S VASSAL, I'VE CHANGED CLOTHES.
YOU BECAME A BEAUTY QUEEN!?

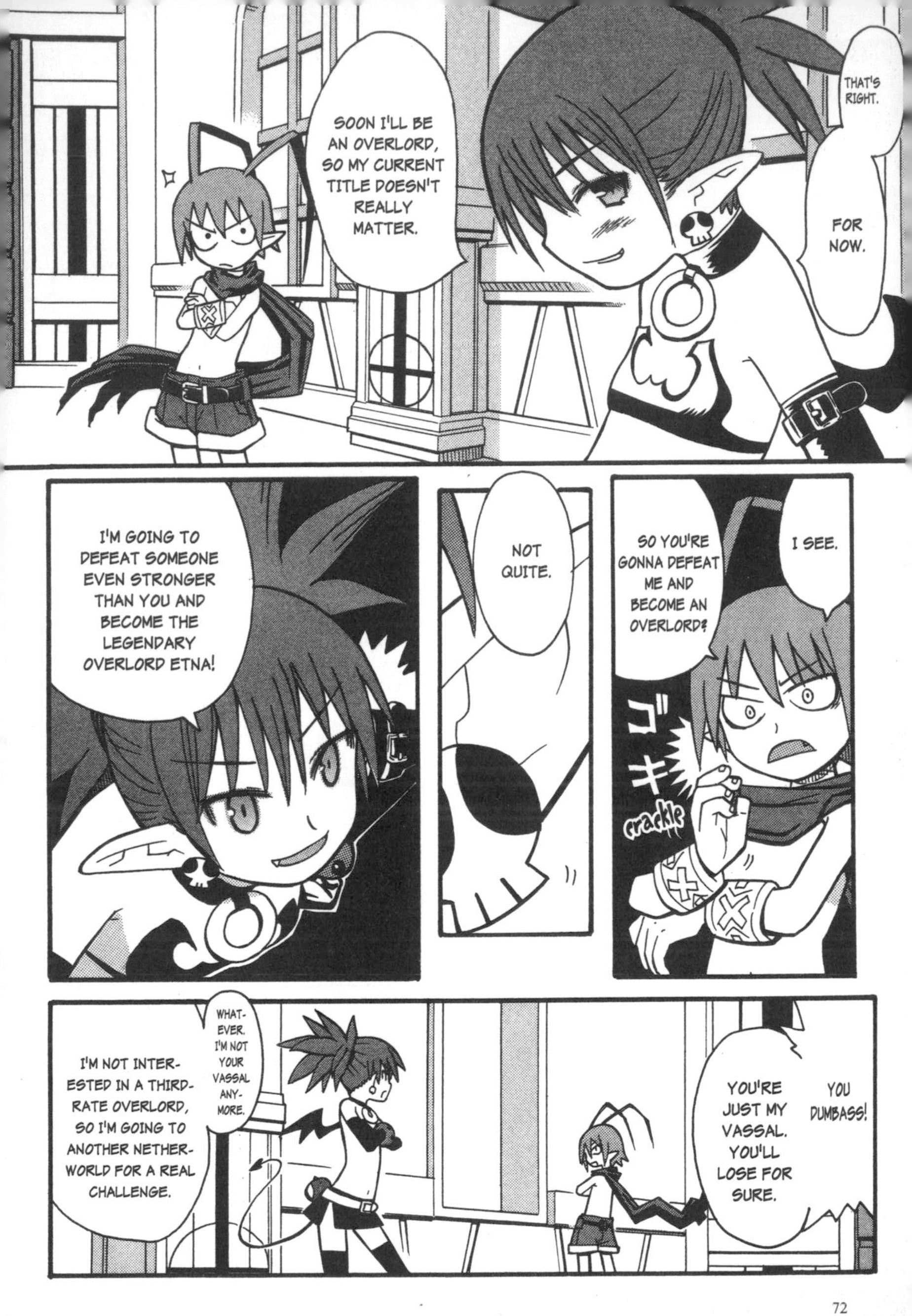
THAT'S RIGHT.
FOR NOW.
SOON I'LL BE AN OVERLORD, SO MY CURRENT TITLE DOESN'T REALLY MATTER.
I SEE.
SO YOU'RE GONNA DEFEAT ME AND BECOME AN OVERLORD?
ゴキ
crackle
NOT QUITE.
I'M GOING TO DEFEAT SOMEONE EVEN STRONGER THAN YOU AND BECOME THE LEGENDARY OVERLORD ETNA!
YOU DUMBASS!
YOU'RE JUST MY VASSAL. YOU'LL LOSE FOR SURE.
WHAT-EVER. I'M NOT YOUR VASSAL ANY-MORE.
I'M NOT INTER-ESTED IN A THIRD-RATE OVERLORD, SO I'M GOING TO ANOTHER NETHER-WORLD FOR A REAL CHALLENGE.

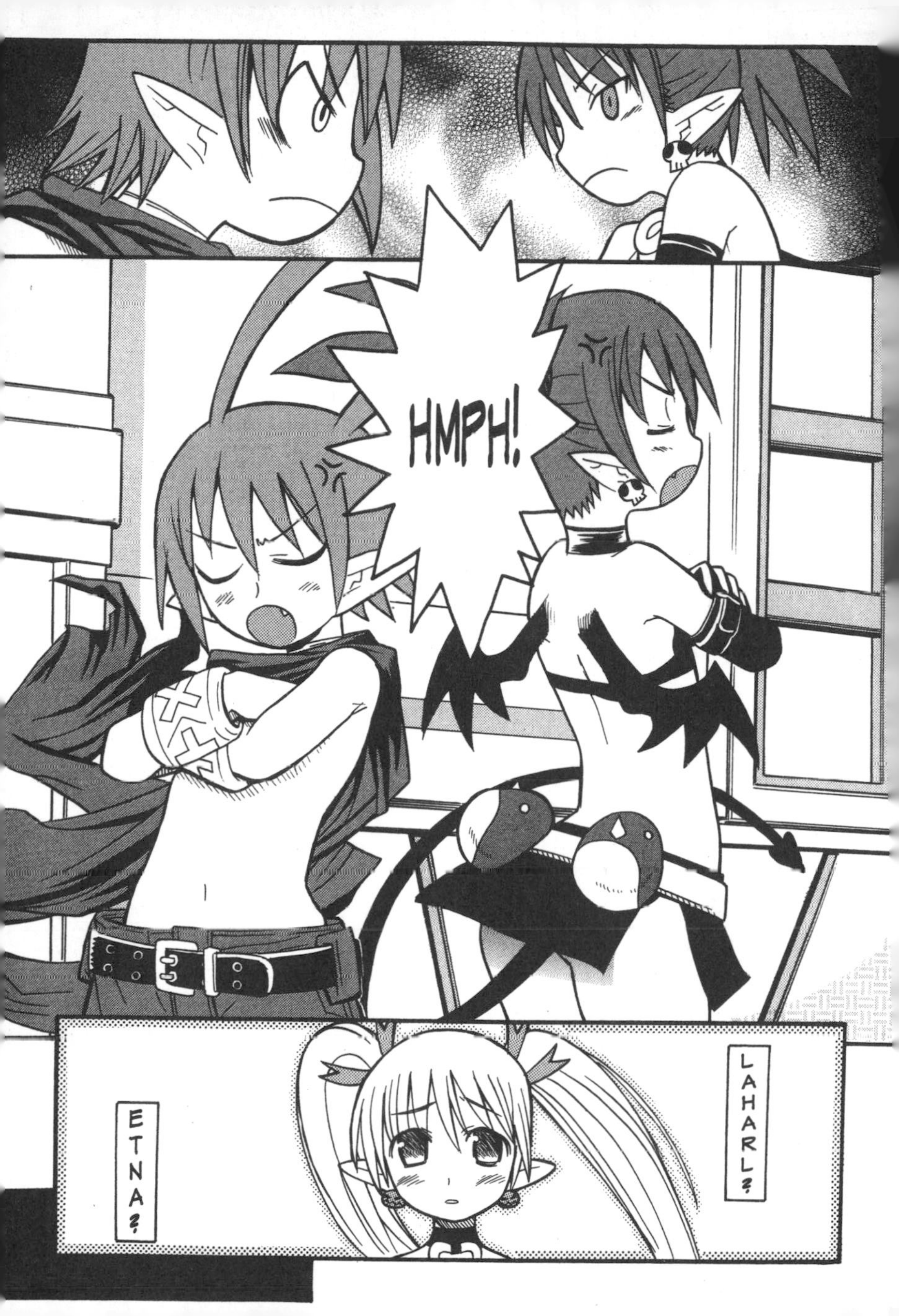
HMPH!
LAHARL?
ETNA?

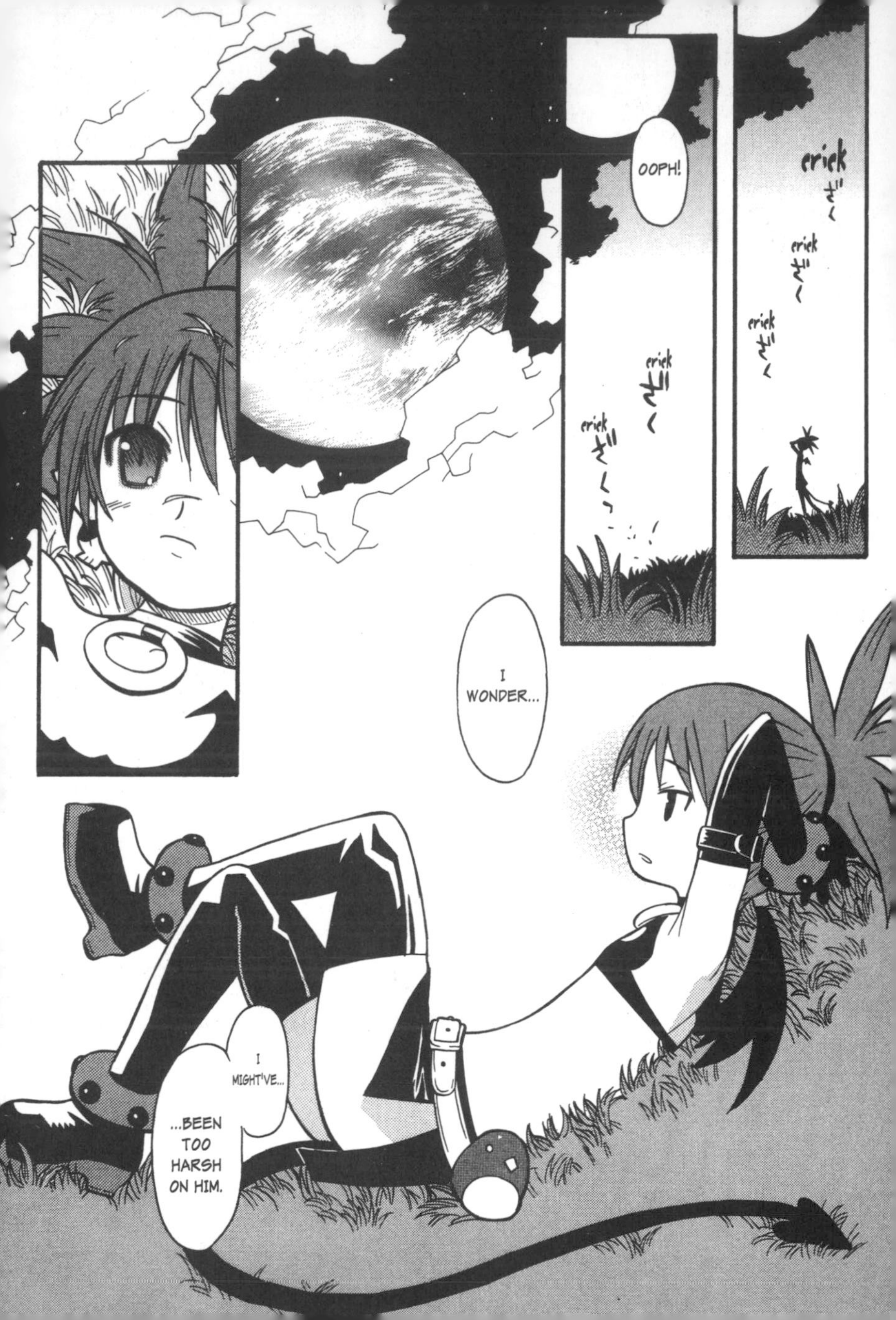
eriek
ざく
eriek
ざく
eriek
ざく
OOPH!
eriek
ざく
eriek
ざくっ
I WONDER...
I MIGHT'VE...
...BEEN TOO HARSH ON HIM.

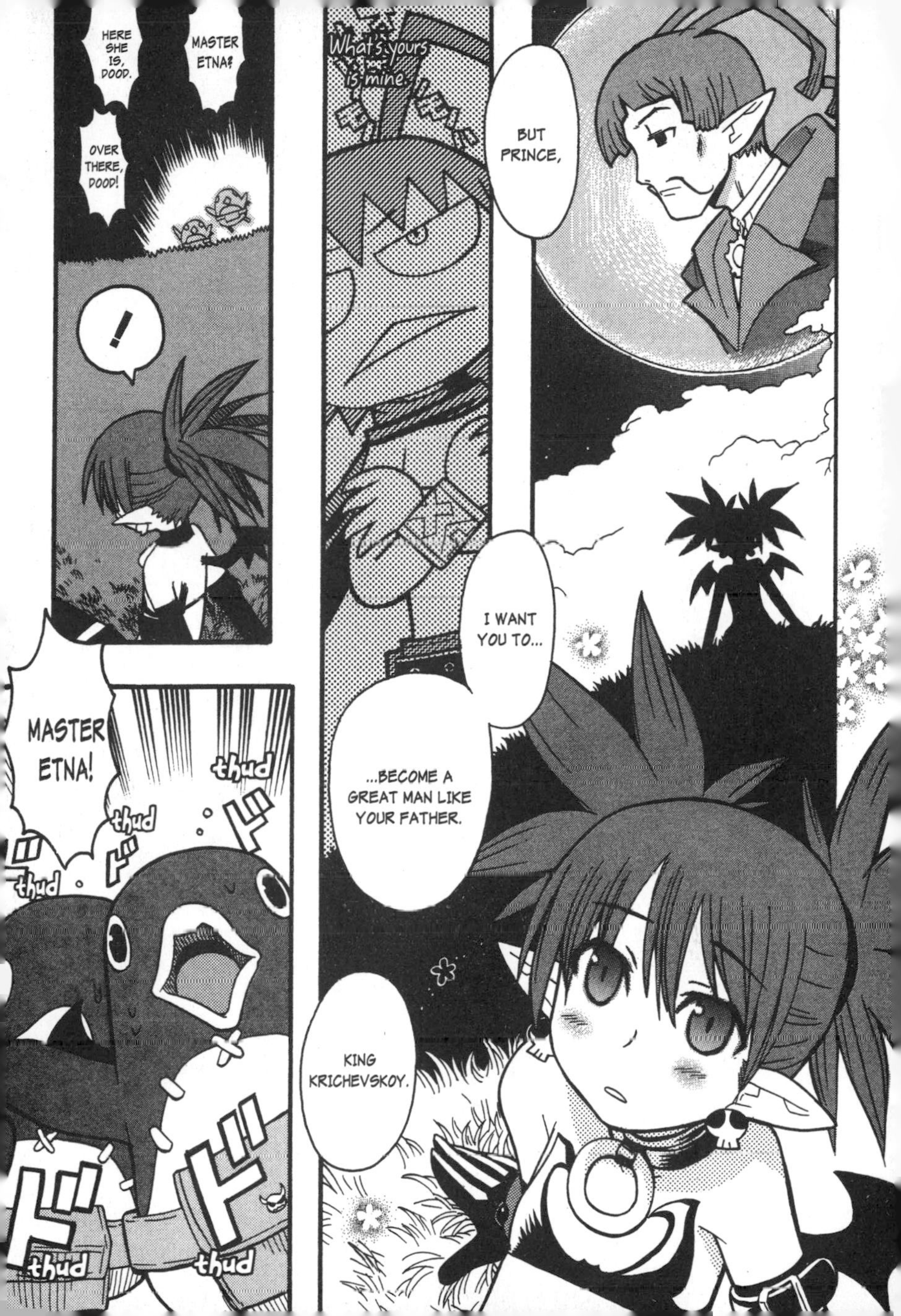
BUT PRINCE,
I WANT YOU TO...
...BECOME A GREAT MAN LIKE YOUR FATHER.
KING KRICHEVSKOY.
What's yours is mine.
MASTER ETNA?
HERE SHE IS, DOOD.
OVER THERE, DOOD!
!
MASTER ETNA!
thud
thud
thud
thud
thud

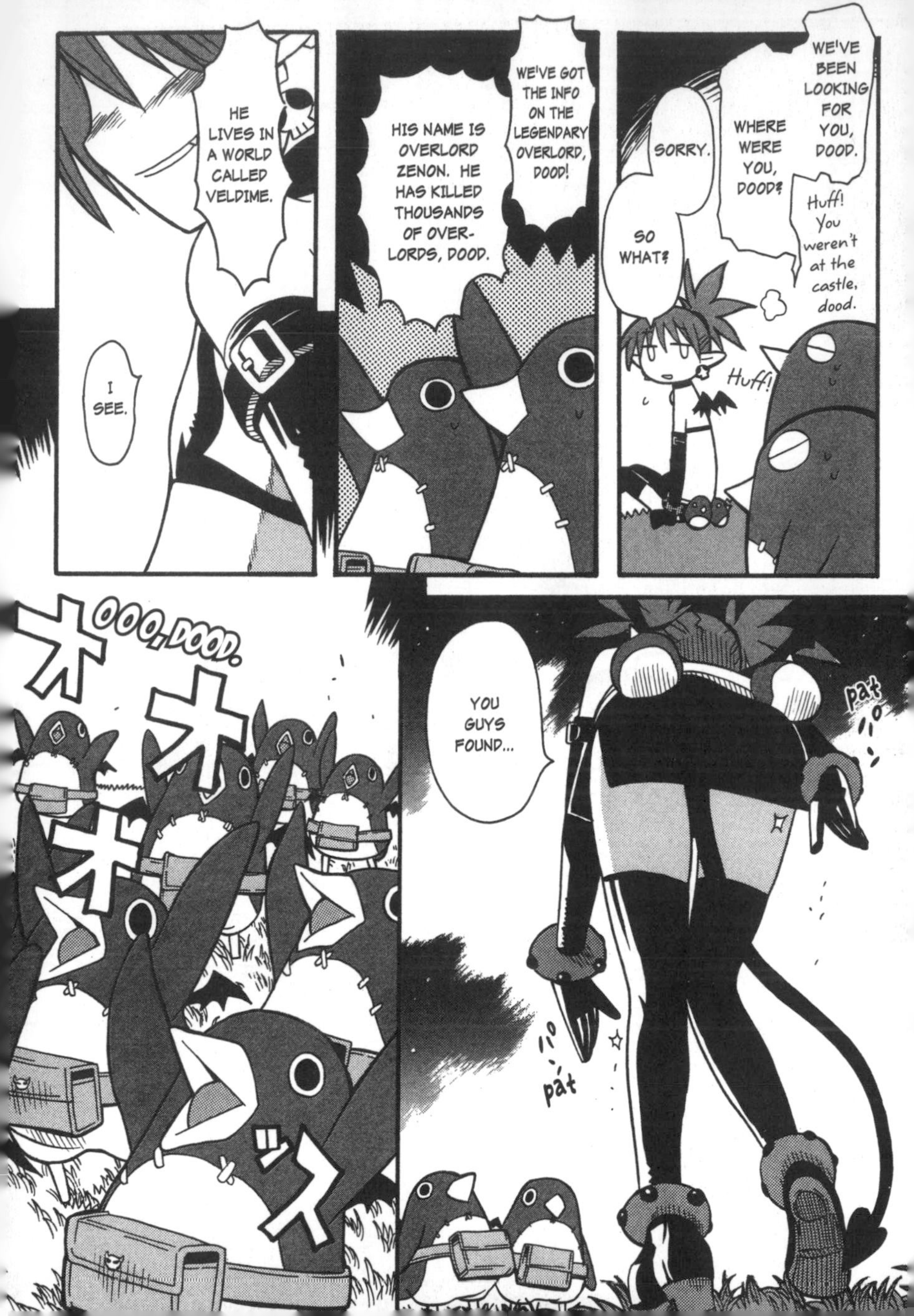
WE'VE BEEN LOOKING FOR YOU, DOOD.
Huff! You weren't at the castle, dood.
WHERE WERE YOU, DOOD?
SORRY.
SO WHAT?
Huff!
WE'VE GOT THE INFO ON THE LEGENDARY OVERLORD, DOOD!
HIS NAME IS OVERLORD ZENON. HE HAS KILLED THOUSANDS OF OVER-LORDS, DOOD.
HE LIVES IN A WORLD CALLED VELDIME.
I SEE.
YOU GUYS FOUND...
pat
pat
OOO, DOOD.

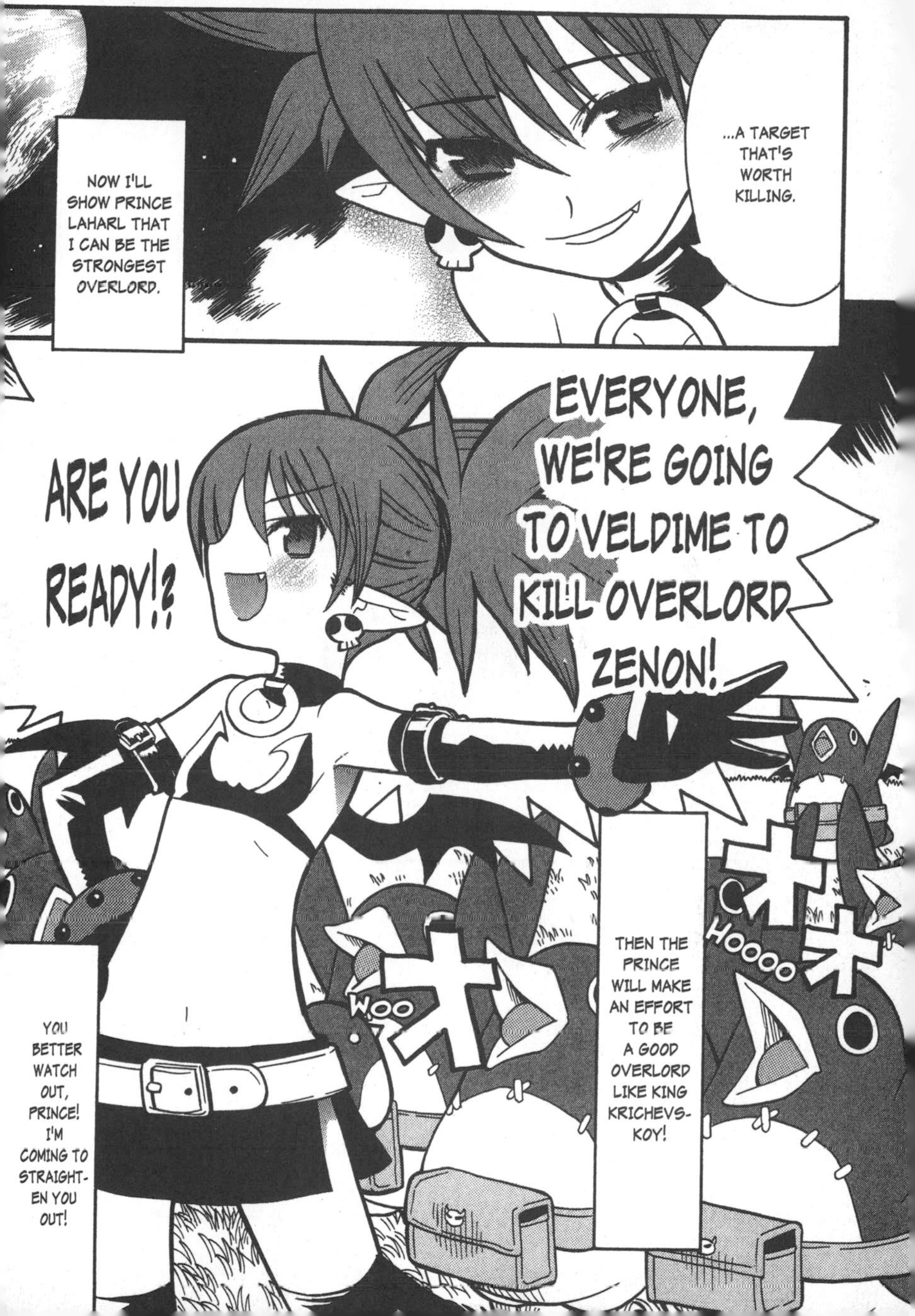
...A TARGET THAT'S WORTH KILLING.
NOW I'LL SHOW PRINCE LAHARL THAT I CAN BE THE STRONGEST OVERLORD.
EVERYONE, WE'RE GOING TO VELDIME TO KILL OVERLORD ZENON!
ARE YOU READY!?
HOOOOO
WOO
THEN THE PRINCE WILL MAKE AN EFFORT TO BE A GOOD OVERLORD LIKE KING KRICHEVS-KOY!
YOU BETTER WATCH OUT, PRINCE! I'M COMING TO STRAIGHT-EN YOU OUT!

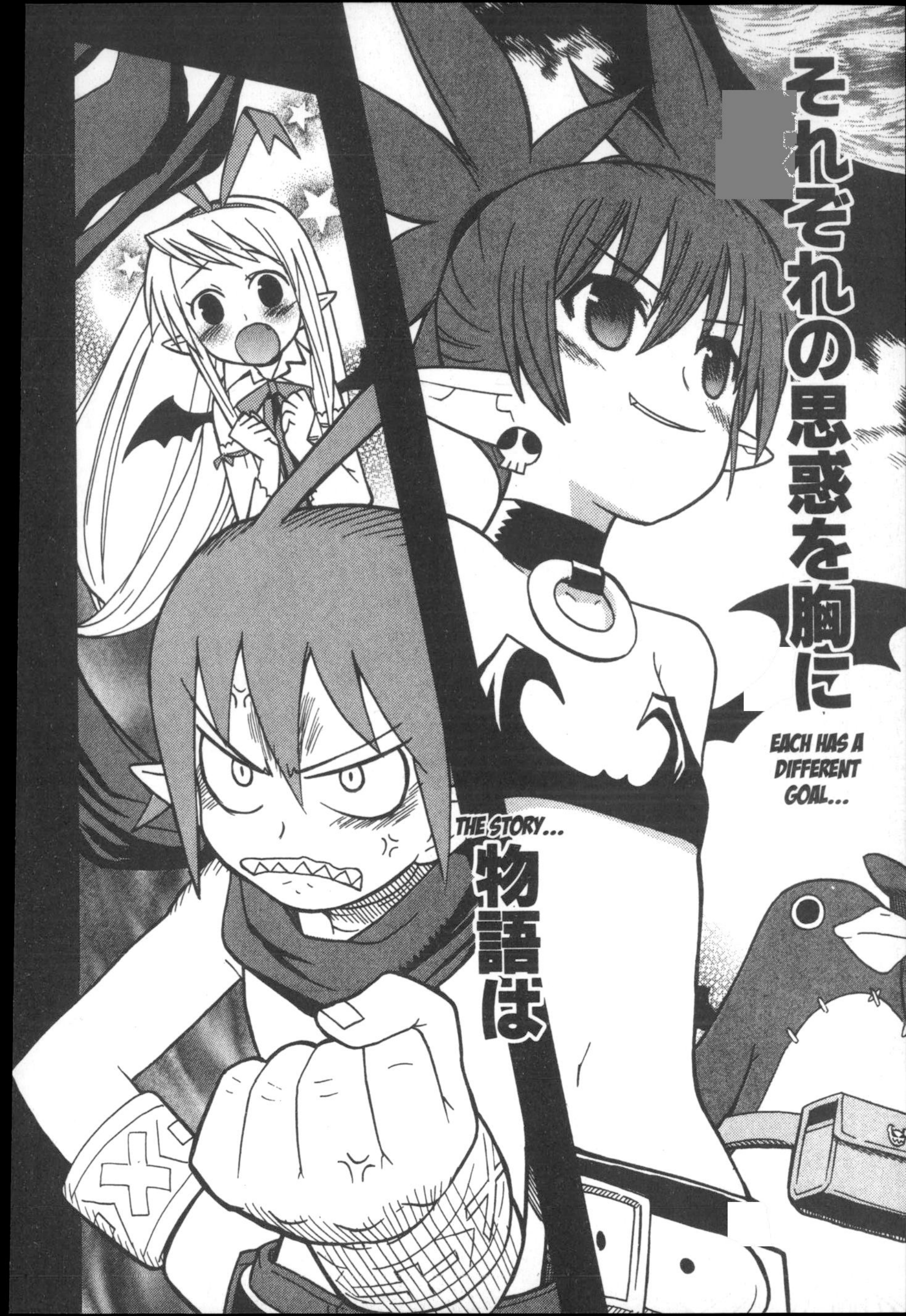
それぞれの思惑を胸に
EACH HAS A DIFFERENT GOAL...
物語は
THE STORY...

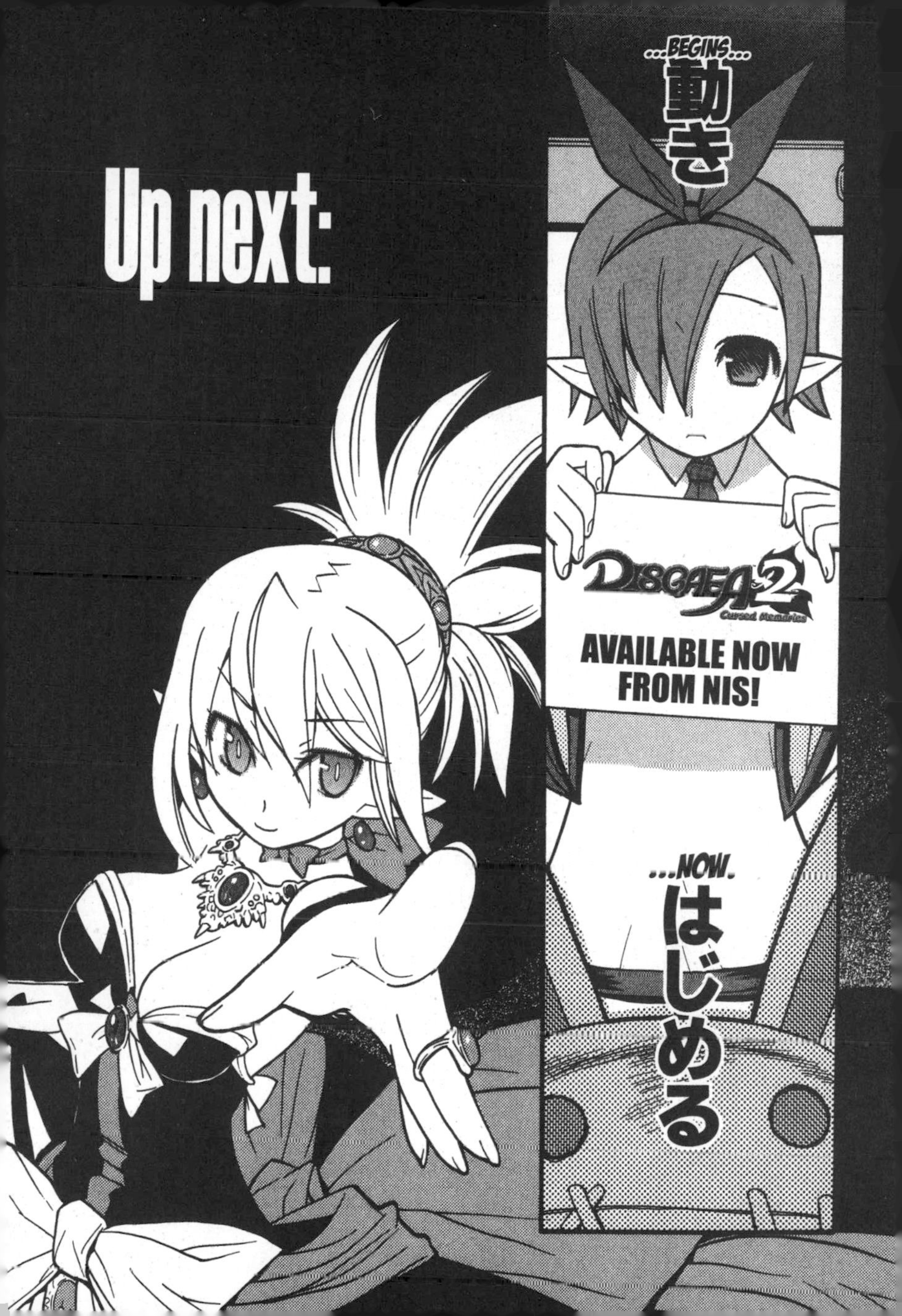

...BEGINS...
動き
DISGAEA 2 Cursed Memories
AVAILABLE NOW FROM NIS!
...NOW.
はじめる
Up next:

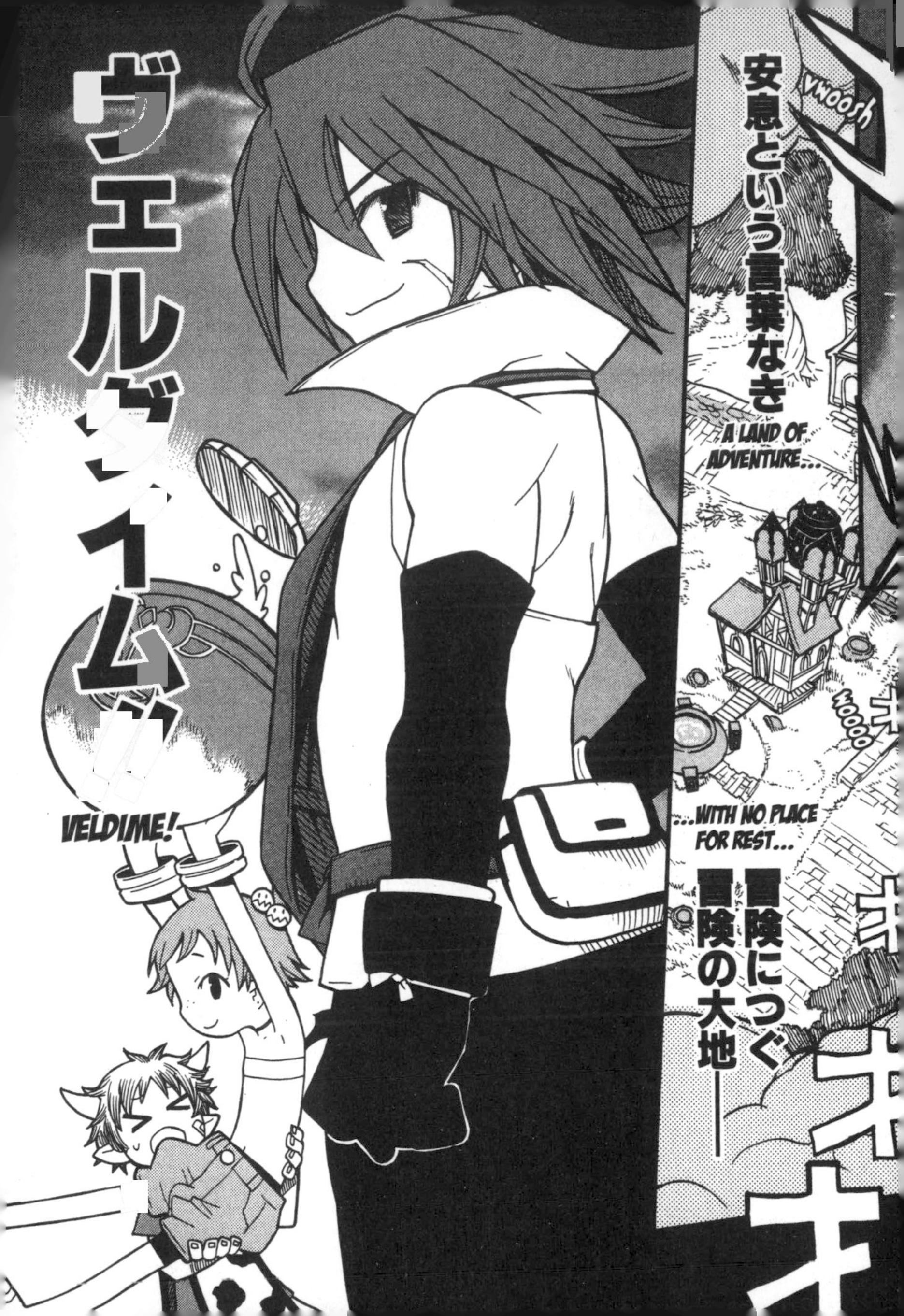
VWOOSH
安息という言葉なき
A LAND OF ADVENTURE...
WOOOO
...WITH NO PLACE FOR REST...
冒険につぐ冒険の大地——
VELDIME!

EPISODE PREVIEW

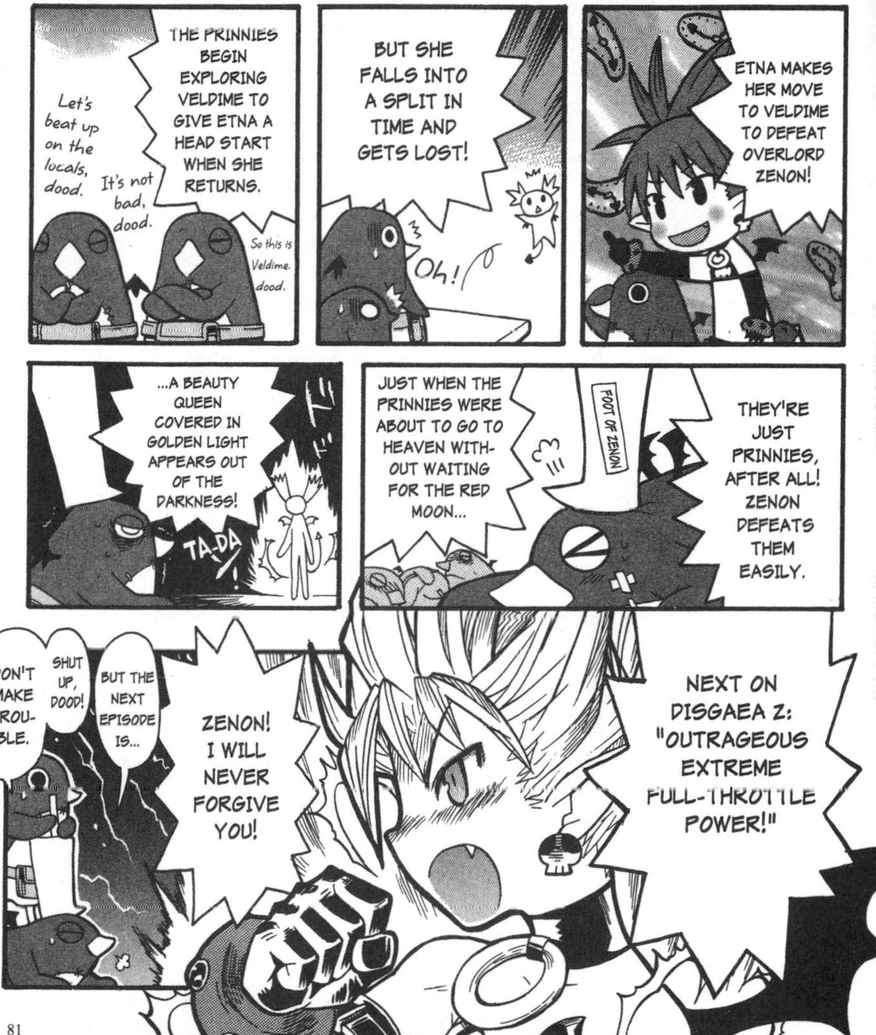
ETNA MAKES HER MOVE TO VELDIME TO DEFEAT OVERLORD ZENON!
BUT SHE FALLS INTO A SPLIT IN TIME AND GETS LOST!
Oh!
THE PRINNIES BEGIN EXPLORING VELDIME TO GIVE ETNA A HEAD START WHEN SHE RETURNS.
So this is Veldime. dood.
It's not bad, dood.
Let's beat up on the locals, dood.
JUST WHEN THE PRINNIES WERE ABOUT TO GO TO HEAVEN WITH-OUT WAITING FOR THE RED MOON...
FOOT OF ZENON
THEY'RE JUST PRINNIES, AFTER ALL! ZENON DEFEATS THEM EASILY.
...A BEAUTY QUEEN COVERED IN GOLDEN LIGHT APPEARS OUT OF THE DARKNESS!
TA-DA
NEXT ON DISGAEA Z: "OUTRAGEOUS EXTREME FULL-THROTTLE POWER!"
ZENON! I WILL NEVER FORGIVE YOU!
BUT THE NEXT EPISODE IS...
SHUT UP, DOOD!
DON'T MAKE TROUBLE.

Those who see him, laugh uncontrollably.
Those who have never met him still pray to the gods
for a man who is without pain or fear
and who will never give up
once he has made a promise.
The man kept his word.
His oath, in plain words, sounds cheap and easy.
In action, his oath is almost impossible to keep.

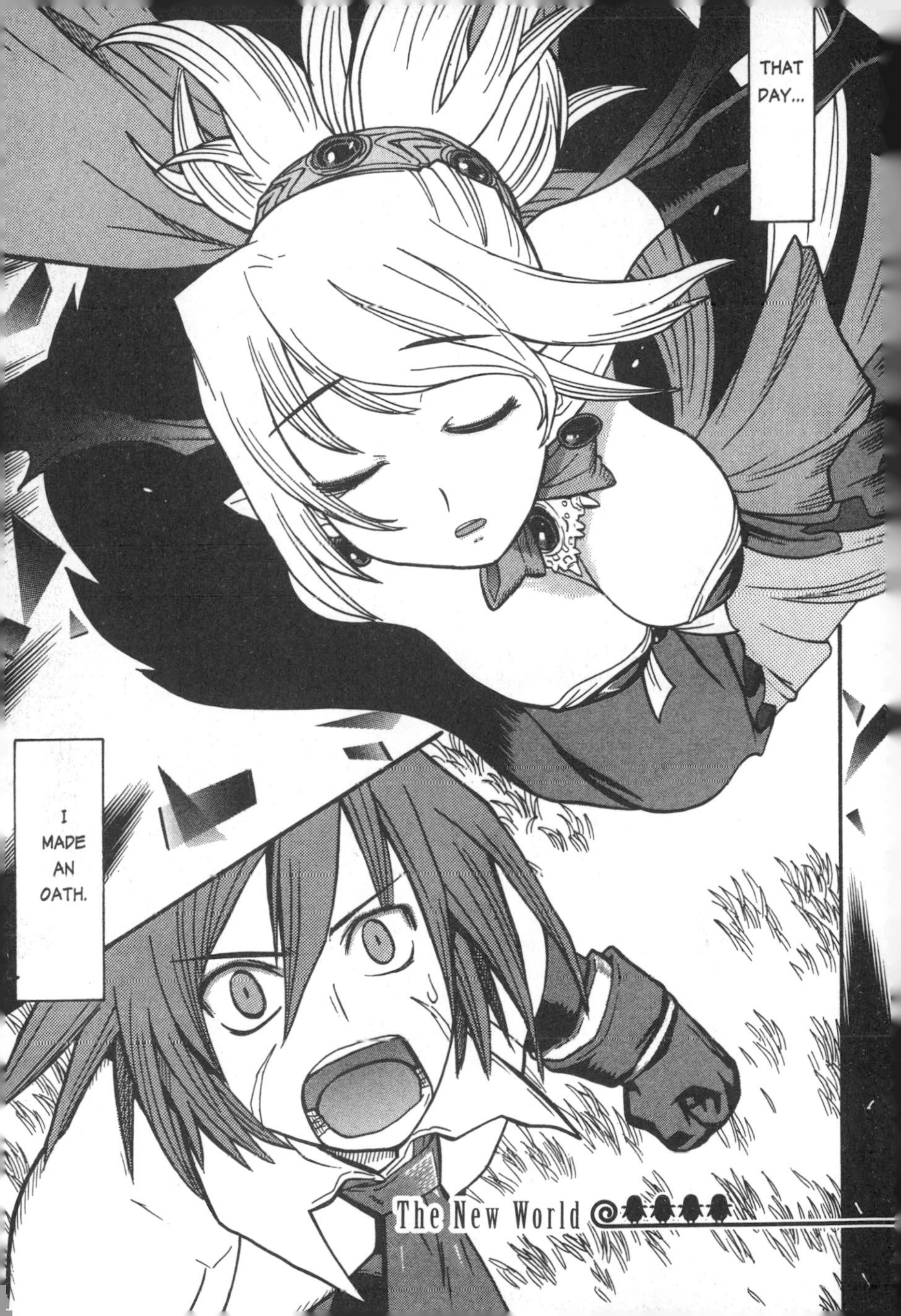
THAT DAY...
I MADE AN OATH.
The New World

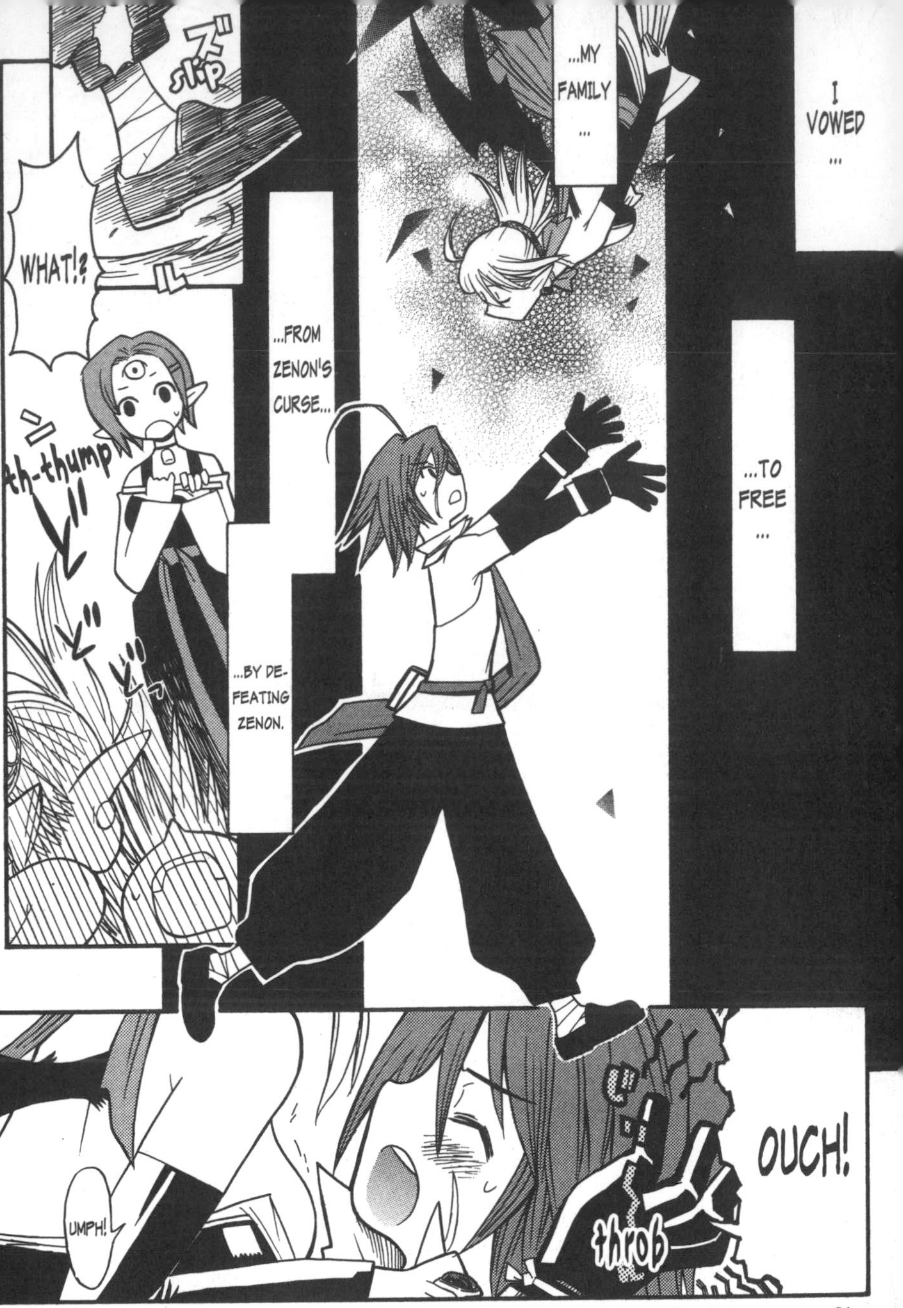
I VOWED ...
...TO FREE ...
...MY FAMILY ...
...FROM ZENON'S CURSE...
...BY DE-FEATING ZENON.
slip
WHAT!?
th-thump
OUCH!
throb
UMPH!

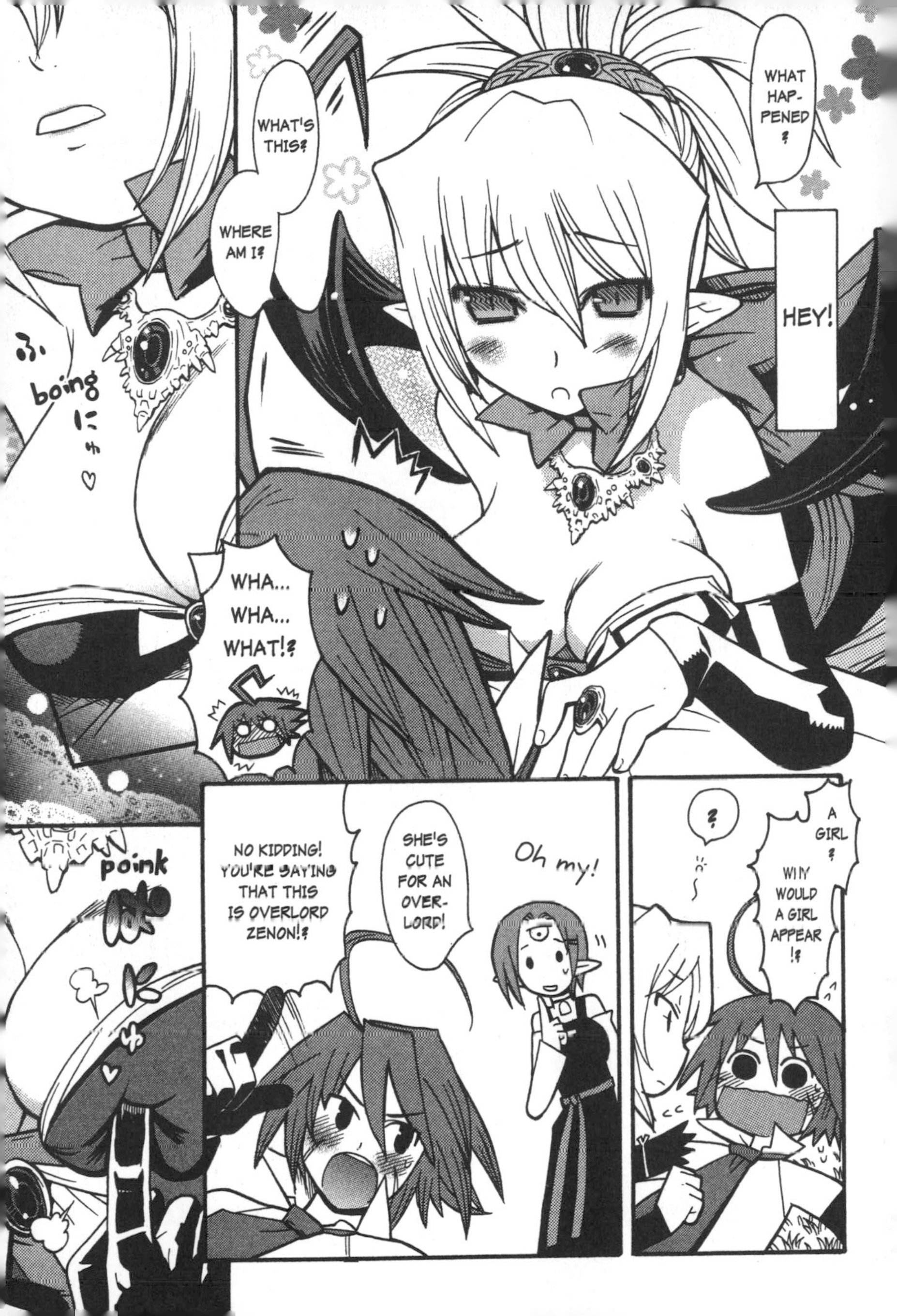
WHAT HAP-PENED?
HEY!
WHAT'S THIS?
WHERE AM I?
WHA... WHA... WHAT!?
ふ
boing
にゅ
♥
?
A GIRL?
WHY WOULD A GIRL APPEAR!?
Oh my!
SHE'S CUTE FOR AN OVER-LORD!
NO KIDDING! YOU'RE SAYING THAT THIS IS OVERLORD ZENON!?
poink

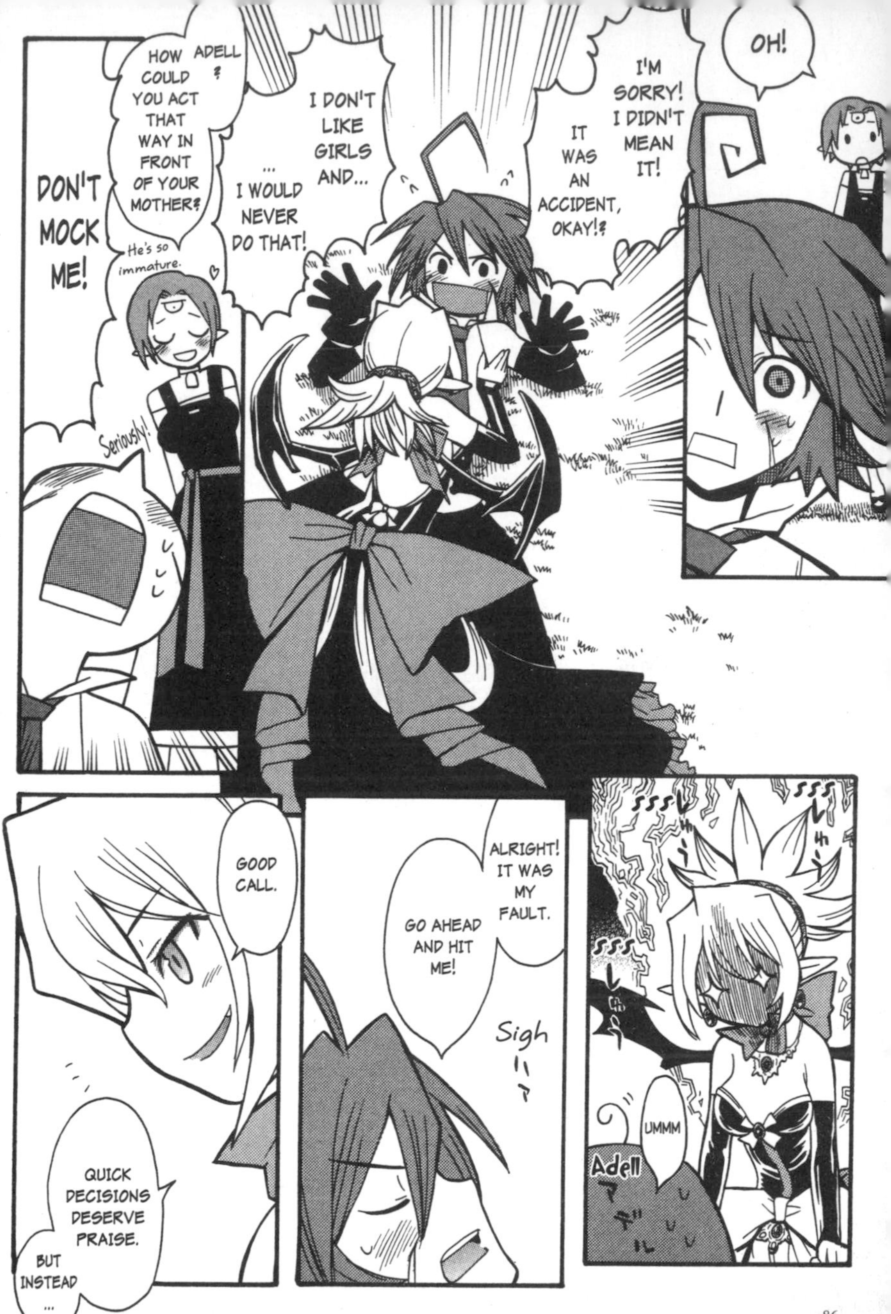
OH!
I'M SORRY! I DIDN'T MEAN IT!
IT WAS AN ACCIDENT, OKAY!?
I DON'T LIKE GIRLS AND...
... I WOULD NEVER DO THAT!
ADELL?
HOW COULD YOU ACT THAT WAY IN FRONT OF YOUR MOTHER?
He's so immature.
DON'T MOCK ME!
Seriously!
Adell
UMMM
ALRIGHT! IT WAS MY FAULT.
GO AHEAD AND HIT ME!
Sigh
GOOD CALL.
QUICK DECISIONS DESERVE PRAISE.
BUT INSTEAD ...

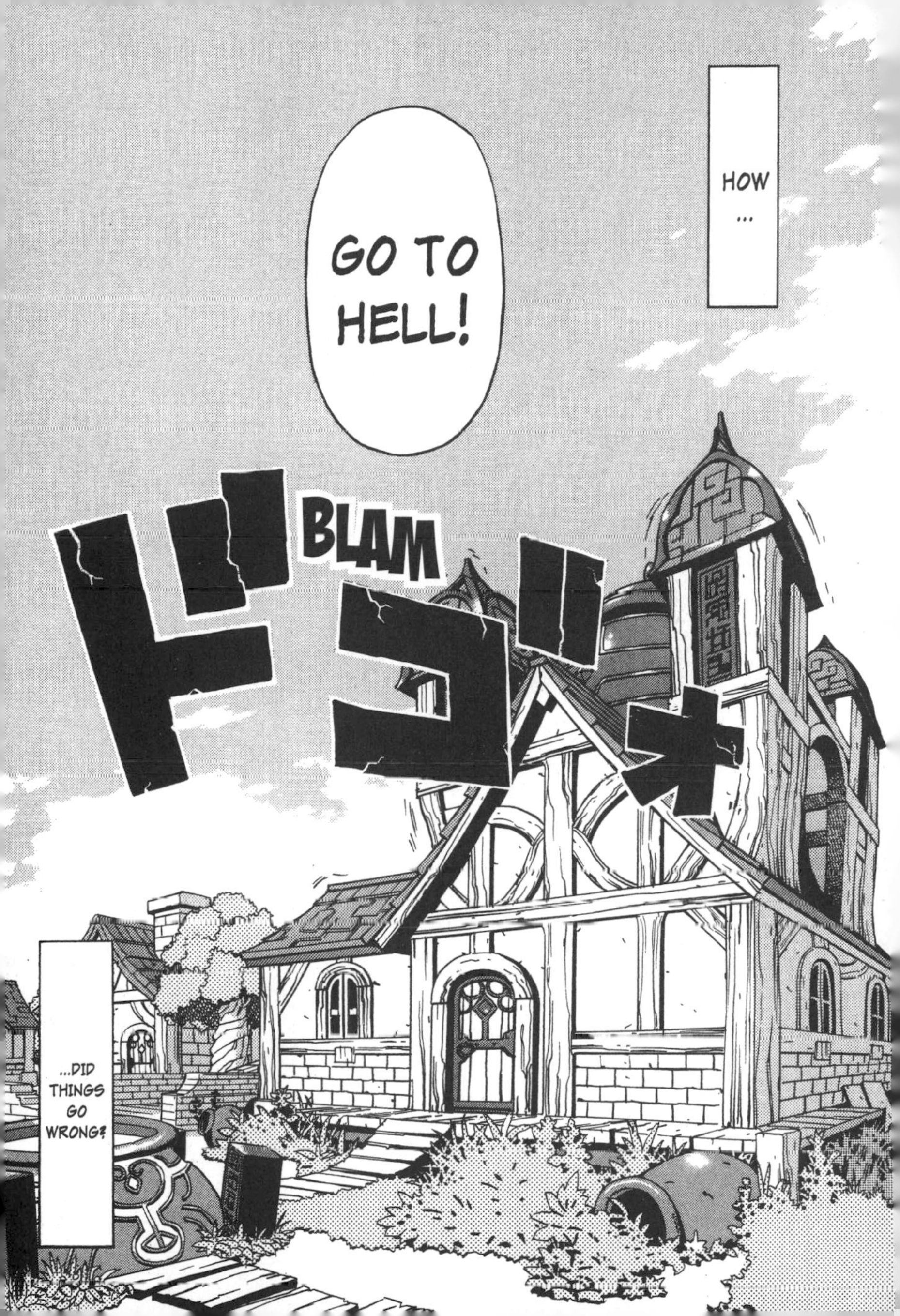
HOW ...
GO TO HELL!
BLAM
ドゴッ
...DID THINGS GO WRONG?

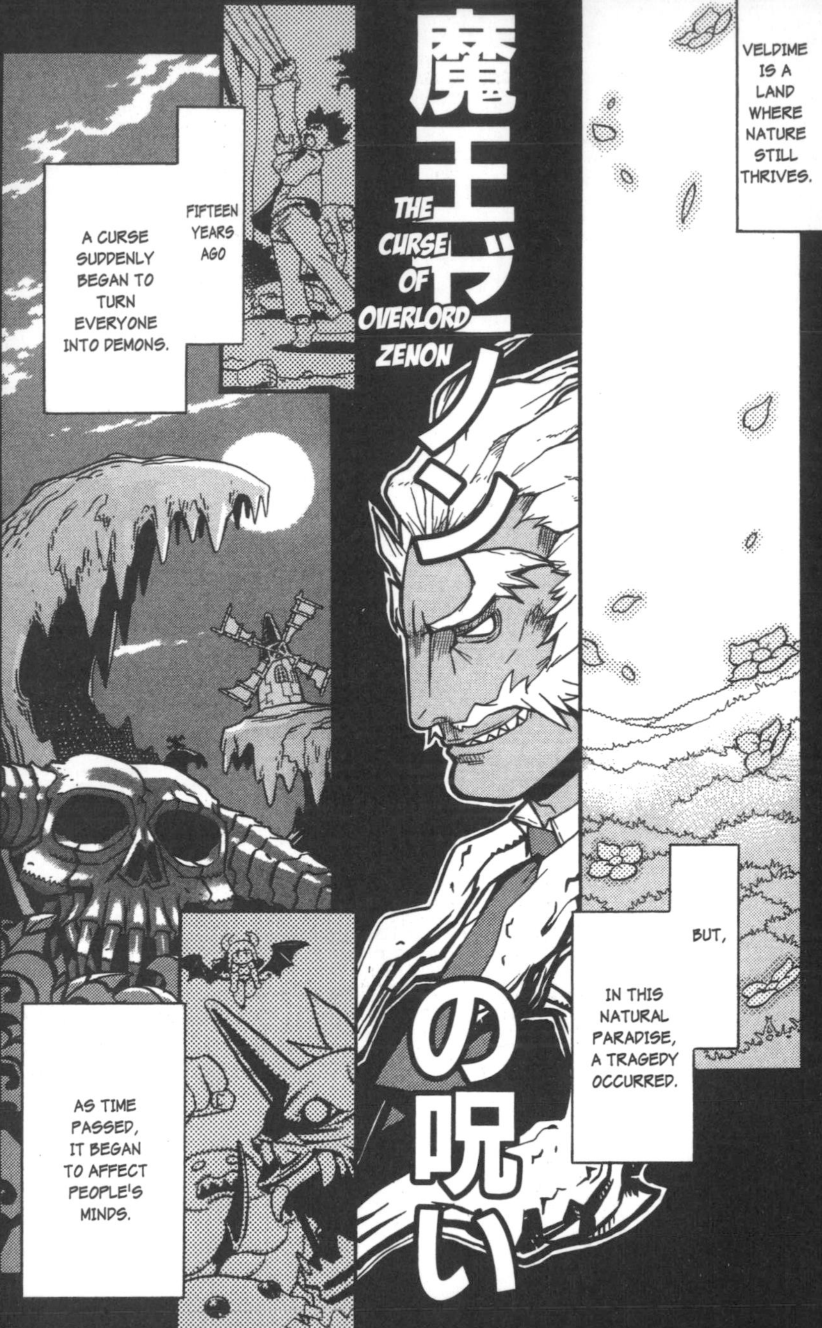
VELDIME IS A LAND WHERE NATURE STILL THRIVES.
BUT,
IN THIS NATURAL PARADISE, A TRAGEDY OCCURRED.
魔王ゼノンの呪い
THE CURSE OF OVERLORD ZENON
FIFTEEN YEARS AGO
A CURSE SUDDENLY BEGAN TO TURN EVERYONE INTO DEMONS.
AS TIME PASSED, IT BEGAN TO AFFECT PEOPLE'S MINDS.

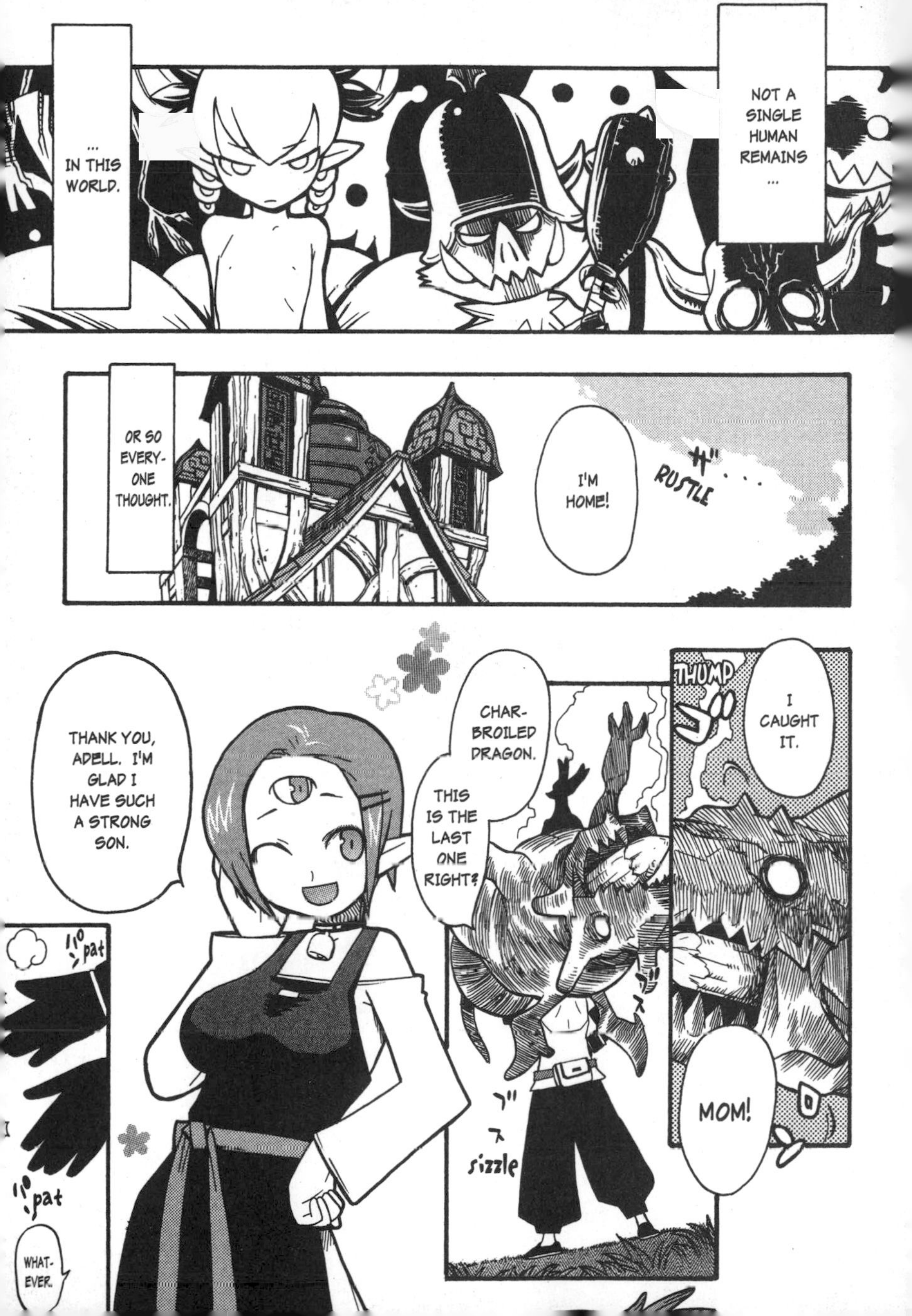
NOT A SINGLE HUMAN REMAINS ...
... IN THIS WORLD.
RUSTLE
I'M HOME!
OR SO EVERY-ONE THOUGHT.
THUMP
I CAUGHT IT.
MOM!
CHAR-BROILED DRAGON.
THIS IS THE LAST ONE RIGHT?
sizzle
THANK YOU, ADELL. I'M GLAD I HAVE SUCH A STRONG SON.
pat
pat
WHAT-EVER.

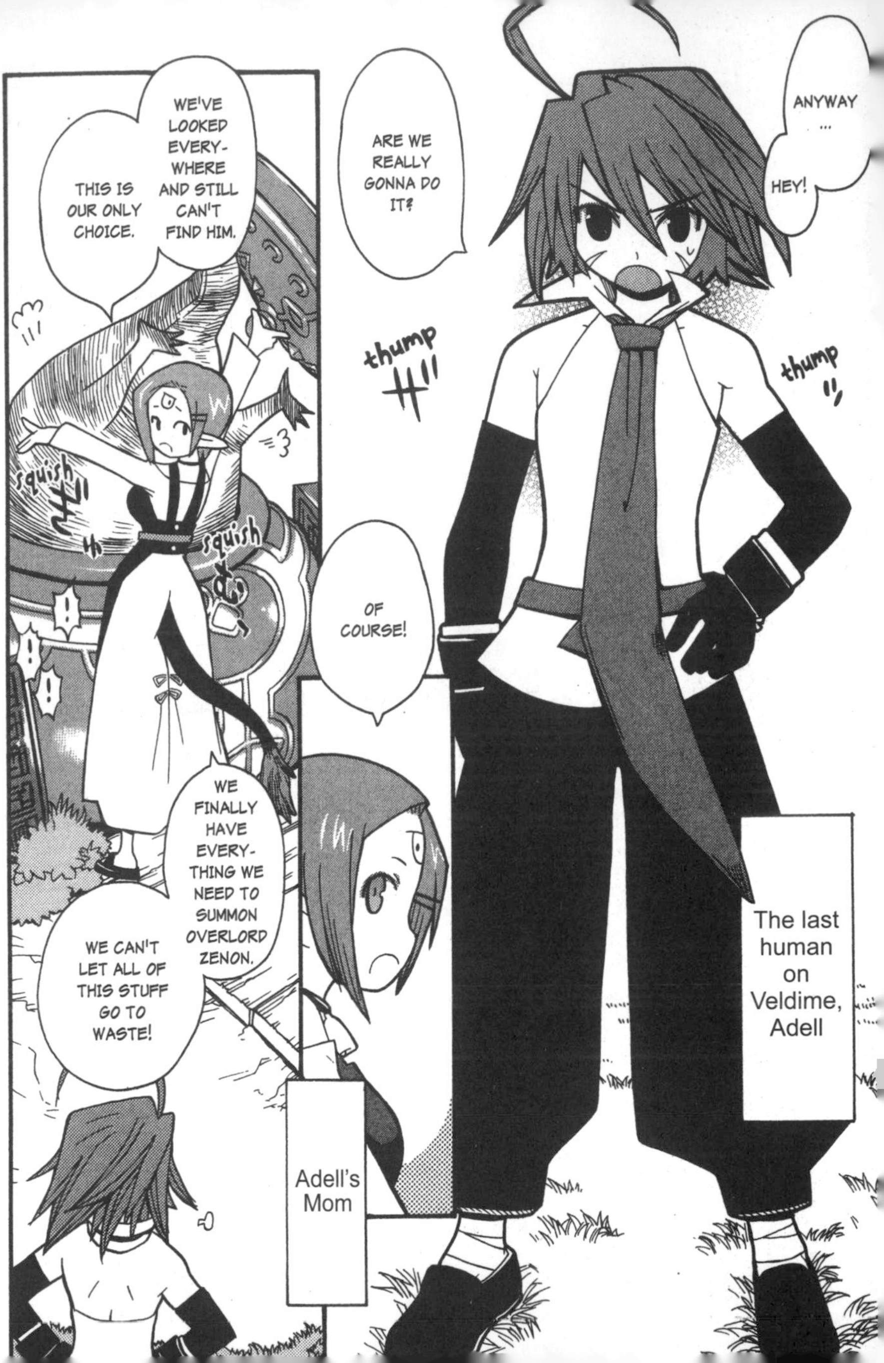
ANYWAY ... HEY!
ARE WE REALLY GONNA DO IT?
thump
thump
The last human on Veldime, Adell
WE'VE LOOKED EVERY-WHERE AND STILL CAN'T FIND HIM.
THIS IS OUR ONLY CHOICE.
squish
squish
OF COURSE!
Adell's Mom
WE FINALLY HAVE EVERY-THING WE NEED TO SUMMON OVERLORD ZENON.
WE CAN'T LET ALL OF THIS STUFF GO TO WASTE!

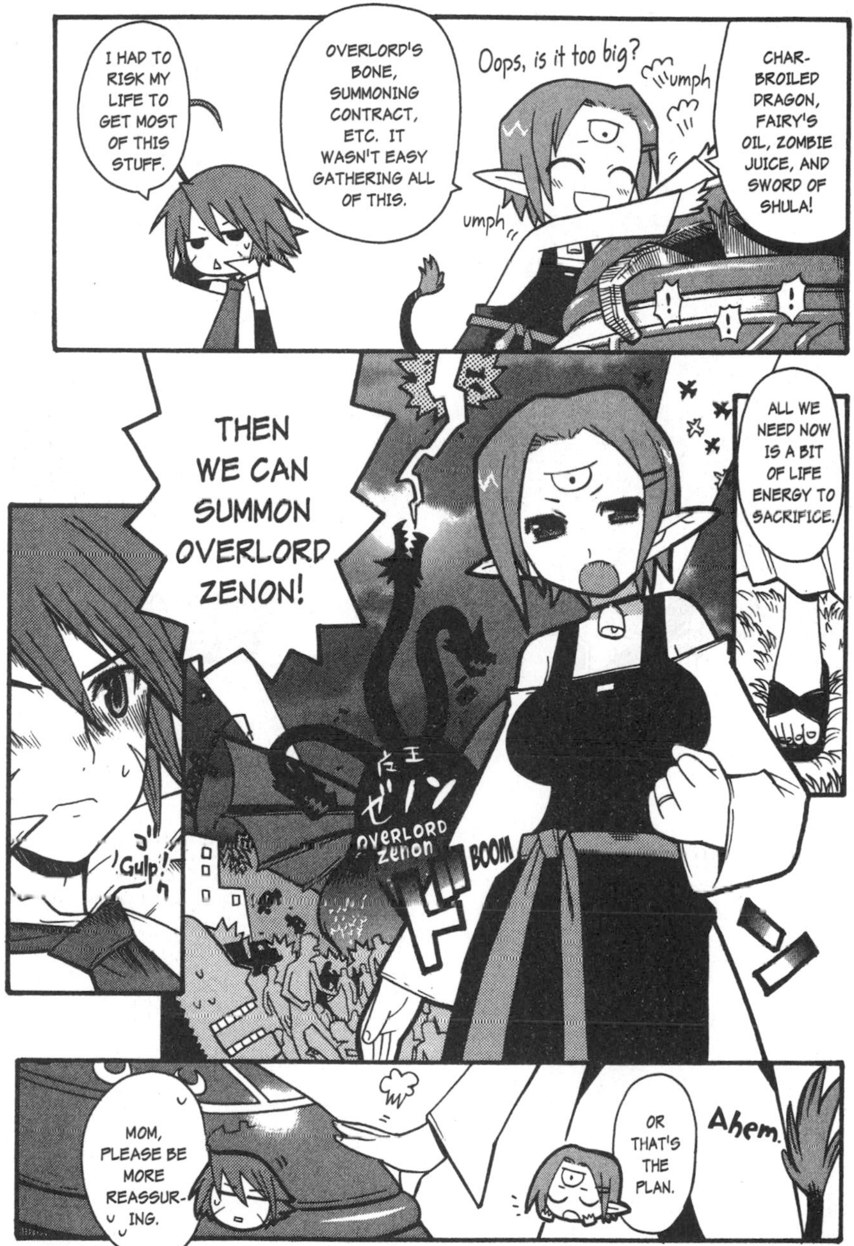
CHAR-BROILED DRAGON, FAIRY'S OIL, ZOMBIE JUICE, AND SWORD OF SHULA!
umph
Oops, is it too big?
umph
OVERLORD'S BONE, SUMMONING CONTRACT, ETC. IT WASN'T EASY GATHERING ALL OF THIS.
I HAD TO RISK MY LIFE TO GET MOST OF THIS STUFF.
ALL WE NEED NOW IS A BIT OF LIFE ENERGY TO SACRIFICE.
THEN WE CAN SUMMON OVERLORD ZENON!
OVERLORD Zenon
BOOM
Gulp!
Ahem.
OR THAT'S THE PLAN.
MOM, PLEASE BE MORE REASSURING.

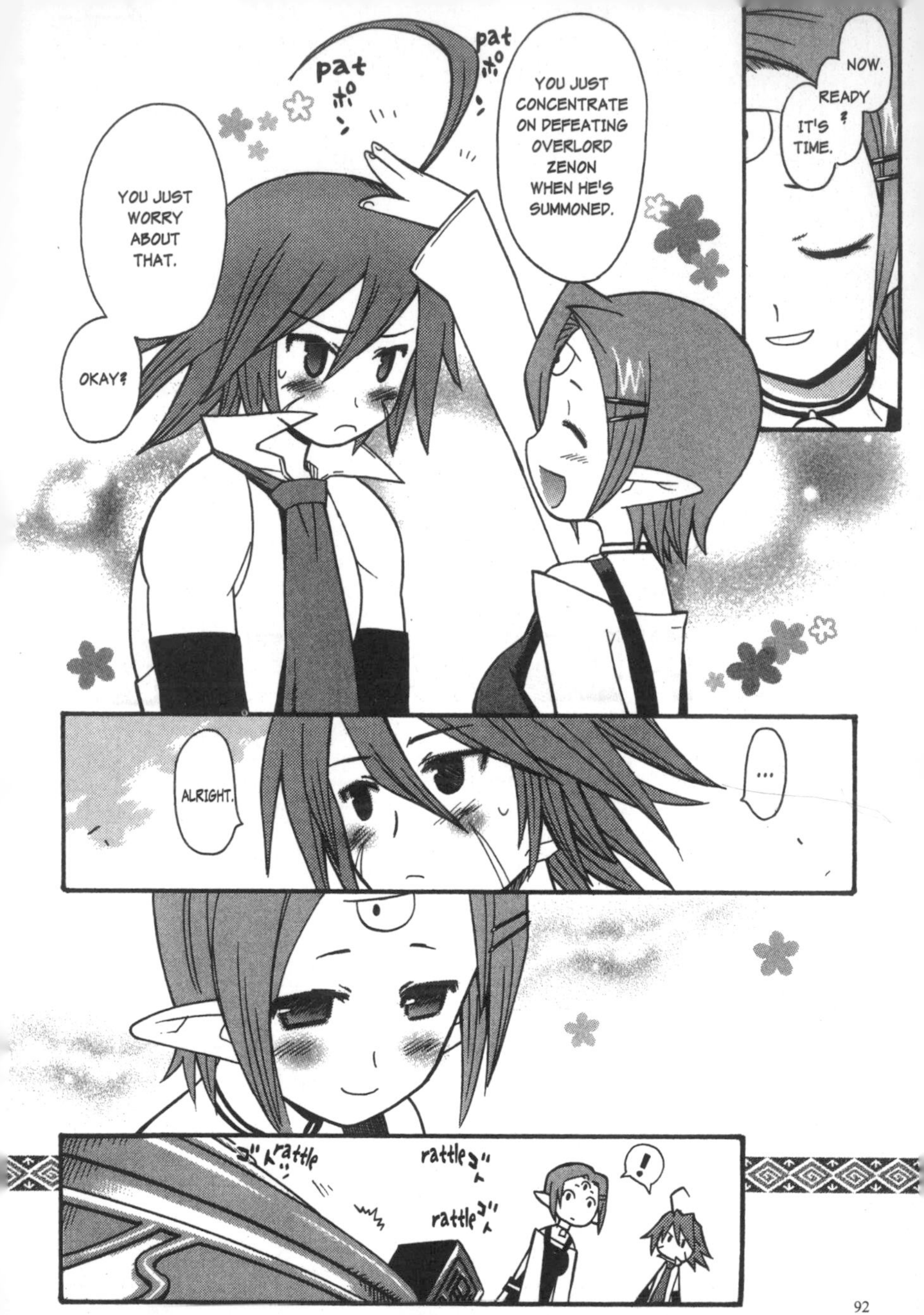
NOW.
READY?
IT'S TIME.
pat
pat
YOU JUST CONCENTRATE ON DEFEATING OVERLORD ZENON WHEN HE'S SUMMONED.
YOU JUST WORRY ABOUT THAT.
OKAY?
...
ALRIGHT.
!
rattle
rattle
rattle

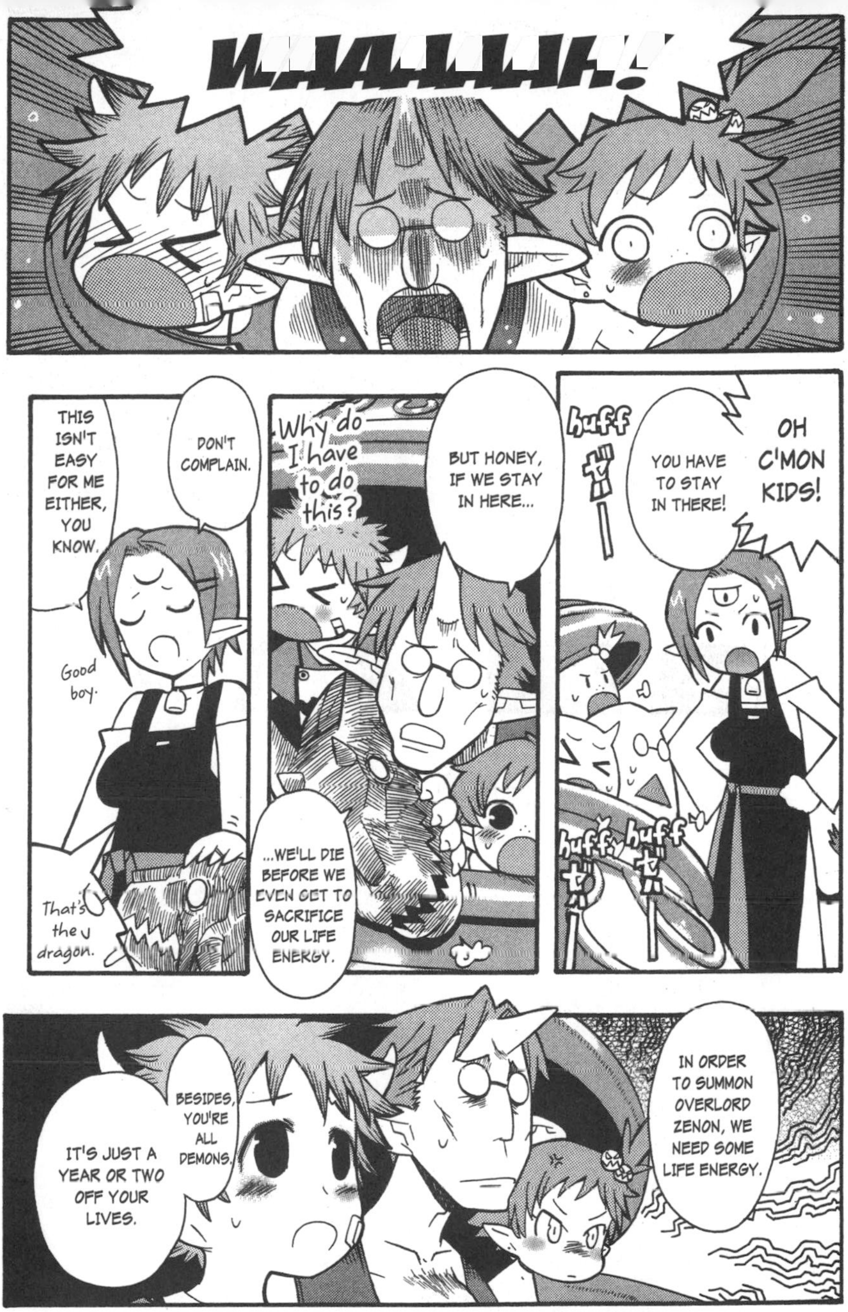
huff
OH C'MON KIDS!
YOU HAVE TO STAY IN THERE!
huffy huff
BUT HONEY, IF WE STAY IN HERE...
Why do I have to do this?
...WE'LL DIE BEFORE WE EVEN GET TO SACRIFICE OUR LIFE ENERGY.
DON'T COMPLAIN.
THIS ISN'T EASY FOR ME EITHER, YOU KNOW.
Good boy.
That's the dragon.
IN ORDER TO SUMMON OVERLORD ZENON, WE NEED SOME LIFE ENERGY.
BESIDES, YOU'RE ALL DEMONS.
IT'S JUST A YEAR OR TWO OFF YOUR LIVES.

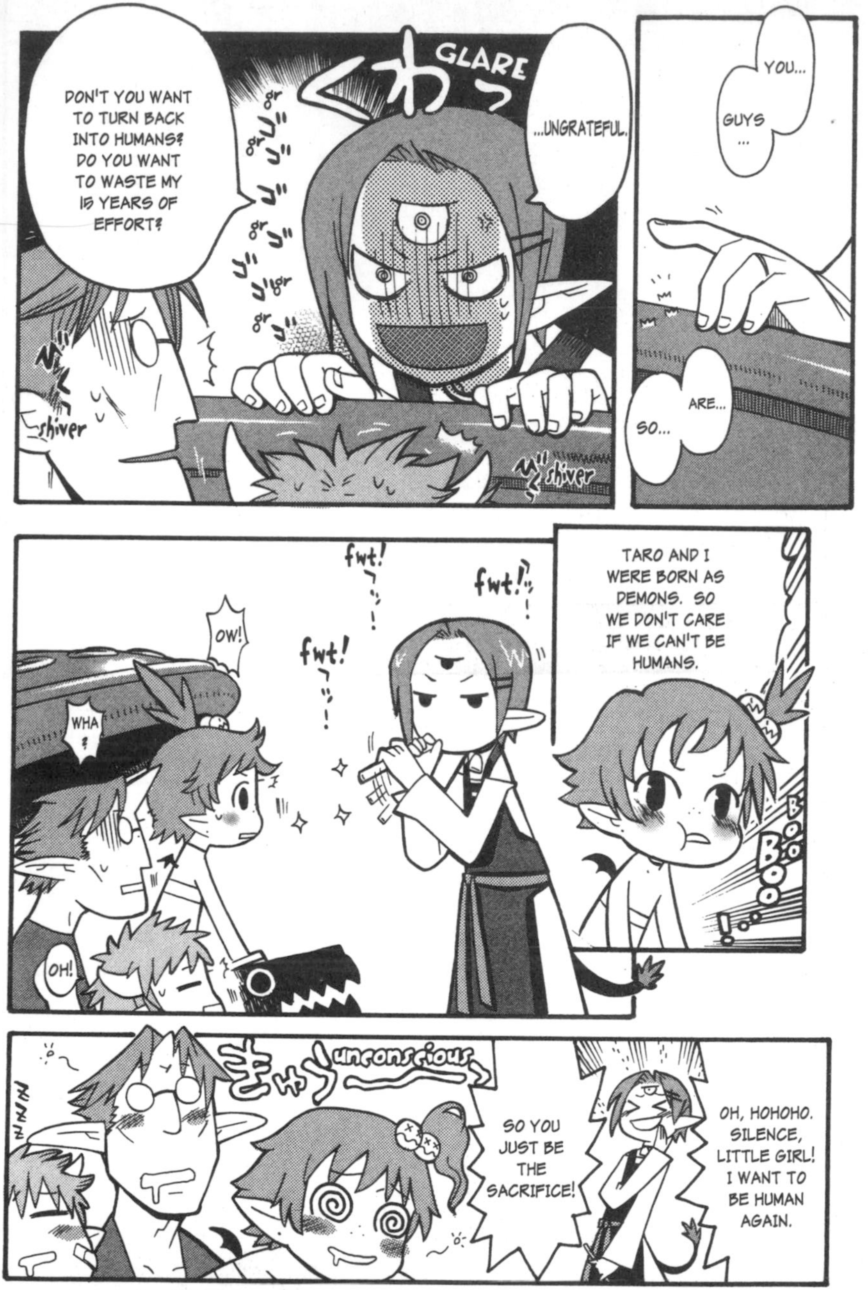
YOU... GUYS ...
ARE... SO...
GLARE
...UNGRATEFUL.
DON'T YOU WANT TO TURN BACK INTO HUMANS? DO YOU WANT TO WASTE MY 15 YEARS OF EFFORT?
shiver
shiver
TARO AND I WERE BORN AS DEMONS. SO WE DON'T CARE IF WE CAN'T BE HUMANS.
BOOBOO
fwt!
fwt!
fwt!
OW!
WHA?
OH!
OH, HOHOHO. SILENCE, LITTLE GIRL! I WANT TO BE HUMAN AGAIN.
SO YOU JUST BE THE SACRIFICE!
unconscious

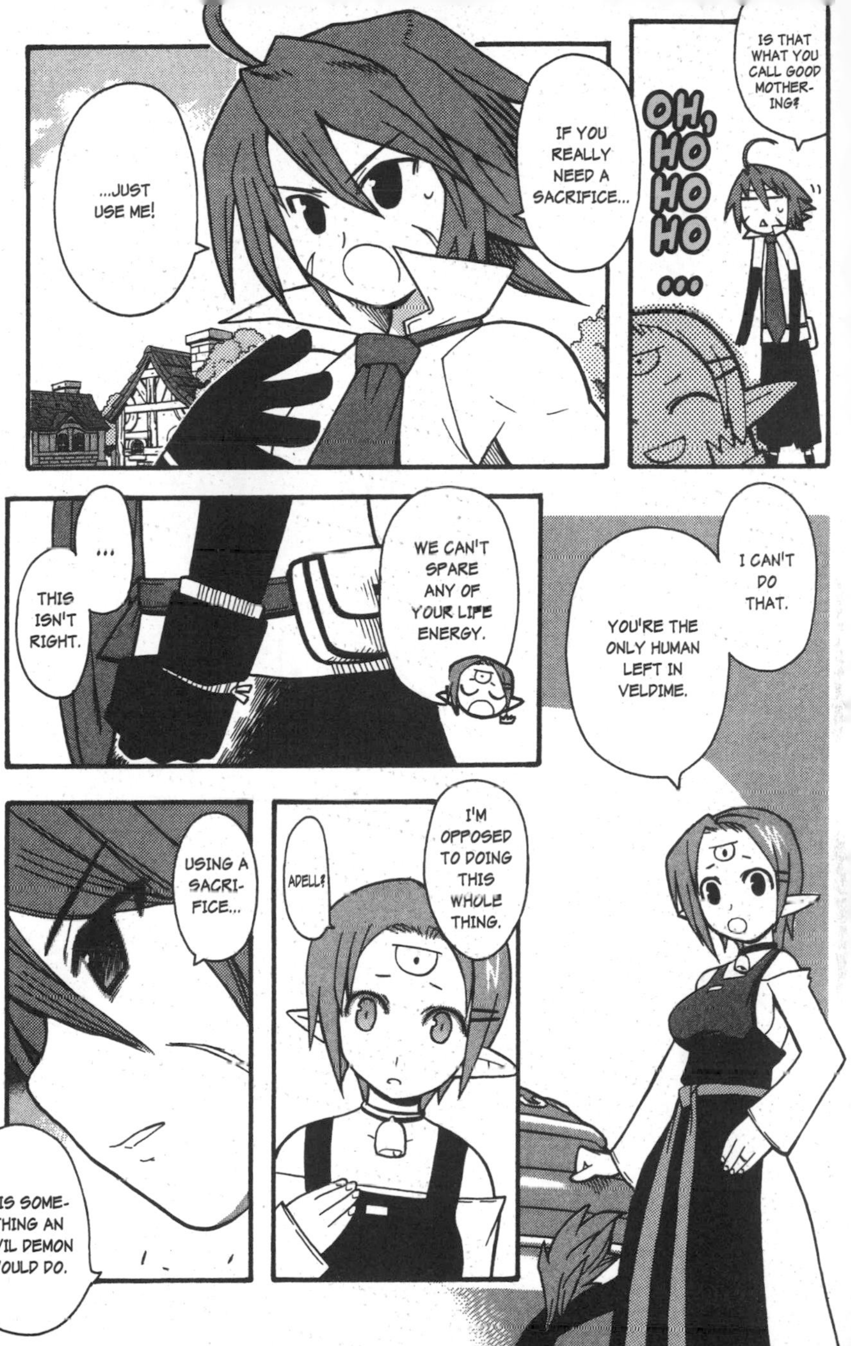
IS THAT WHAT YOU CALL GOOD MOTHERING?
OH, HO HO HO ...
IF YOU REALLY NEED A SACRIFICE...
...JUST USE ME!
I CAN'T DO THAT.
YOU'RE THE ONLY HUMAN LEFT IN VELDIME.
WE CAN'T SPARE ANY OF YOUR LIFE ENERGY.
...
THIS ISN'T RIGHT.
I'M OPPOSED TO DOING THIS WHOLE THING.
ADELL?
USING A SACRIFICE...
...IS SOMETHING AN EVIL DEMON WOULD DO.

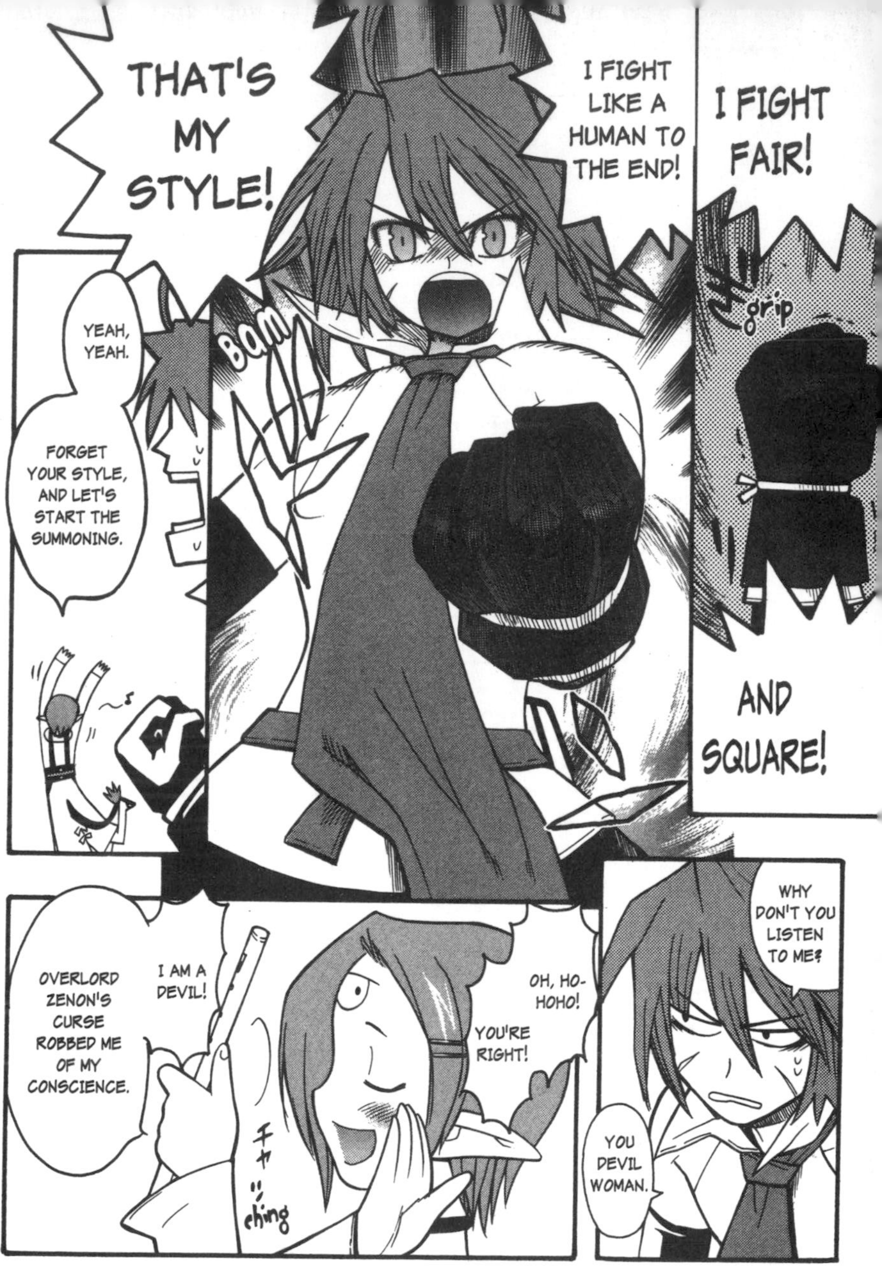
I FIGHT FAIR!
grip
AND SQUARE!
I FIGHT LIKE A HUMAN TO THE END!
THAT'S MY STYLE!
Bam
YEAH, YEAH.
FORGET YOUR STYLE, AND LET'S START THE SUMMONING.
WHY DON'T YOU LISTEN TO ME?
YOU DEVIL WOMAN.
OH, HO-HOHO!
YOU'RE RIGHT!
I AM A DEVIL!
OVERLORD ZENON'S CURSE ROBBED ME OF MY CONSCIENCE.
ching

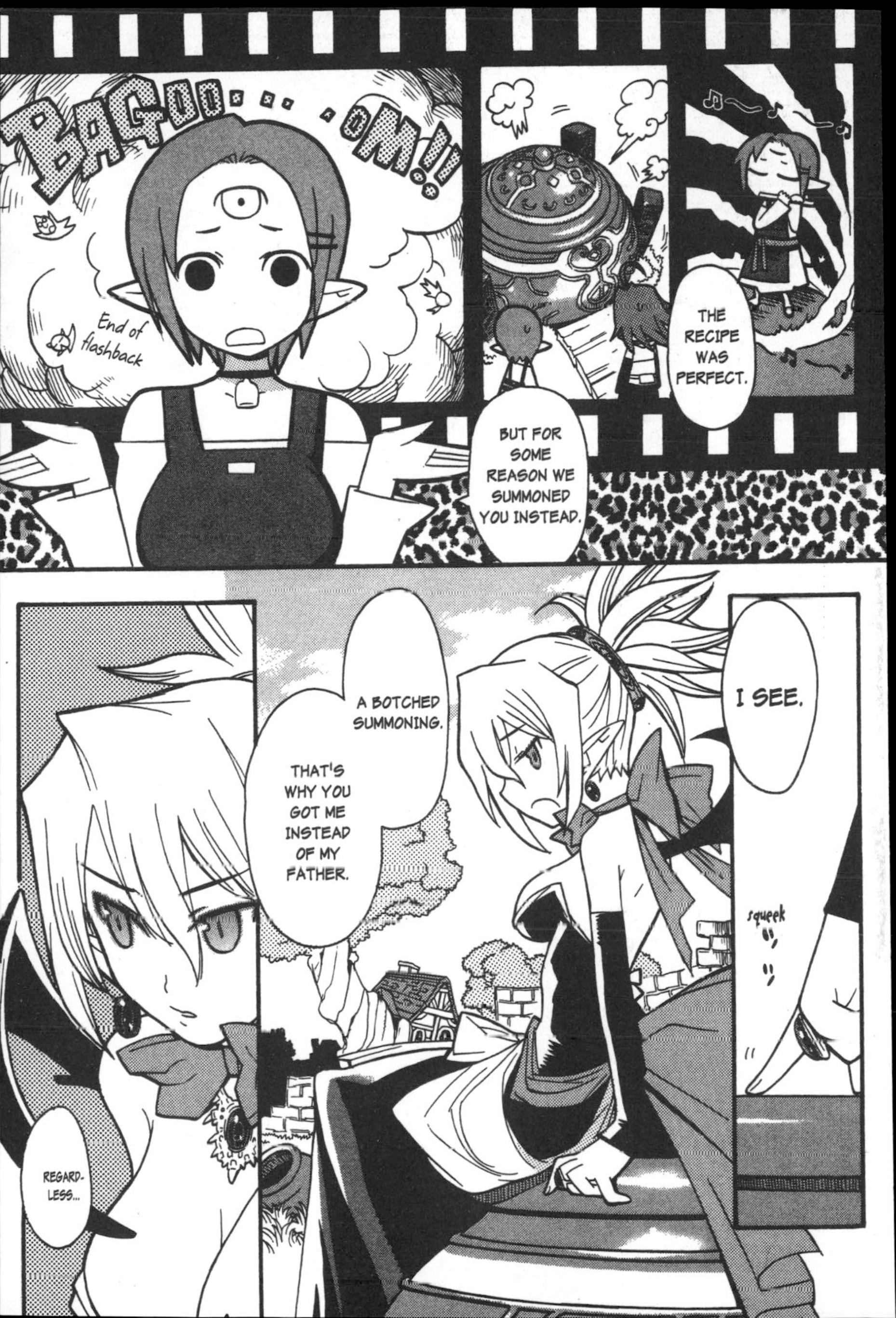
THE RECIPE WAS PERFECT.
BAGOO... ...OM!!
End of flashback
BUT FOR SOME REASON WE SUMMONED YOU INSTEAD.
I SEE.
squeek
A BOTCHED SUMMONING.
THAT'S WHY YOU GOT ME INSTEAD OF MY FATHER.
REGARD-LESS...

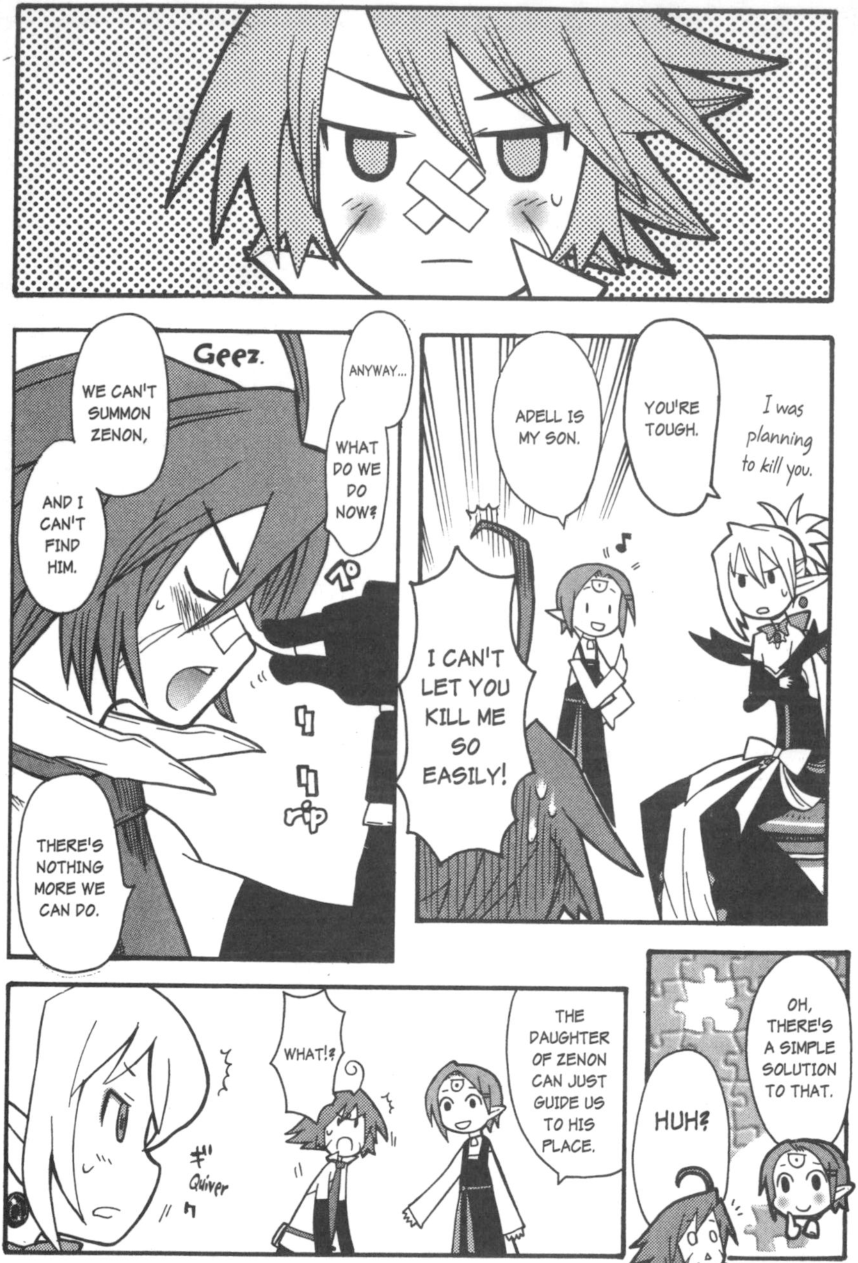
I was planning to kill you.
YOU'RE TOUGH.
ADELL IS MY SON.
I CAN'T LET YOU KILL ME SO EASILY!
ANYWAY...
WHAT DO WE DO NOW?
Geez.
WE CAN'T SUMMON ZENON,
AND I CAN'T FIND HIM.
rip
THERE'S NOTHING MORE WE CAN DO.
OH, THERE'S A SIMPLE SOLUTION TO THAT.
HUH?
THE DAUGHTER OF ZENON CAN JUST GUIDE US TO HIS PLACE.
WHAT!?
Quiver

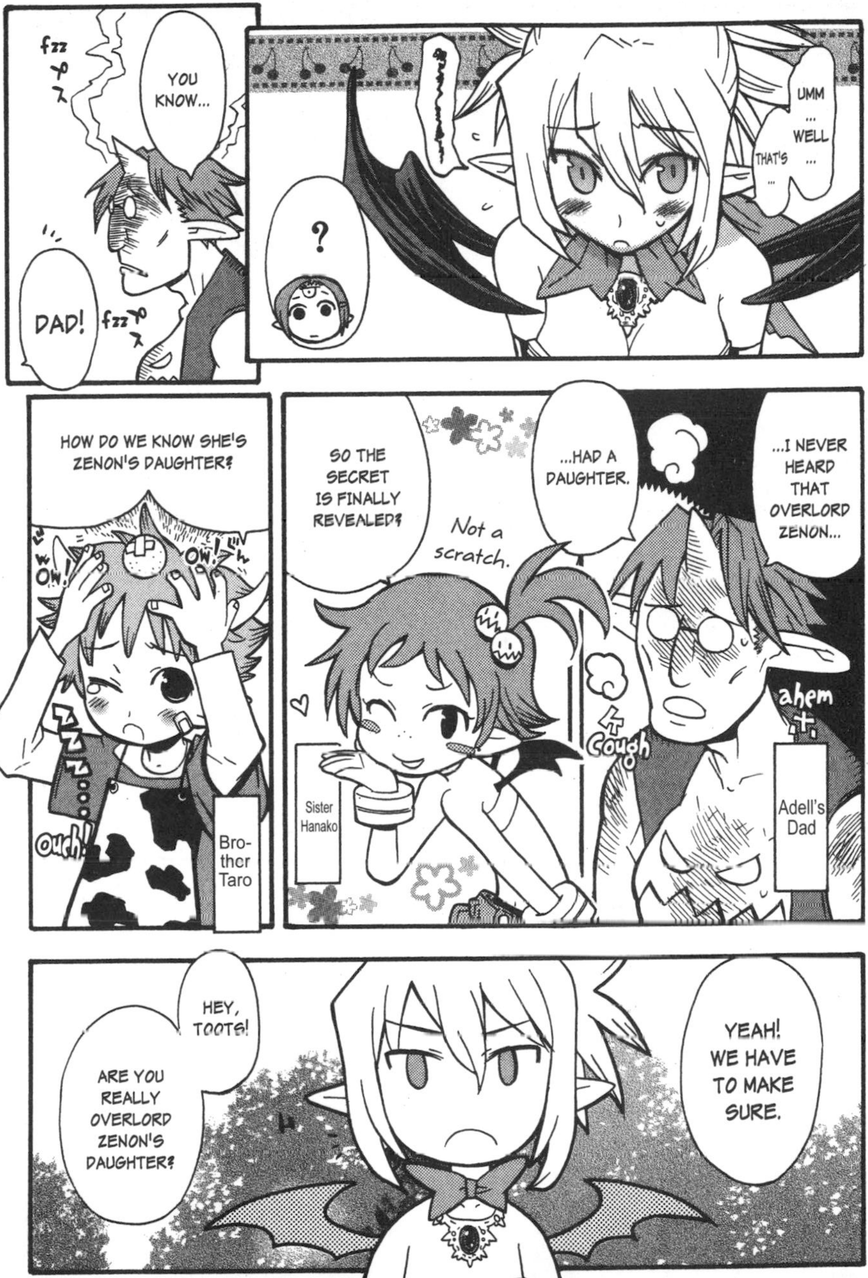

UMM ... WELL ... THAT'S ...
?
YOU KNOW...
fzz
DAD!
fzz
...I NEVER HEARD THAT OVERLORD ZENON...
...HAD A DAUGHTER.
ahem
cough
Adell's Dad
SO THE SECRET IS FINALLY REVEALED?
Not a scratch.
Sister Hanako
HOW DO WE KNOW SHE'S ZENON'S DAUGHTER?
OW!
OW!
ouch!
Bro-ther Taro
YEAH! WE HAVE TO MAKE SURE.
HEY, TOOTS!
ARE YOU REALLY OVERLORD ZENON'S DAUGHTER?

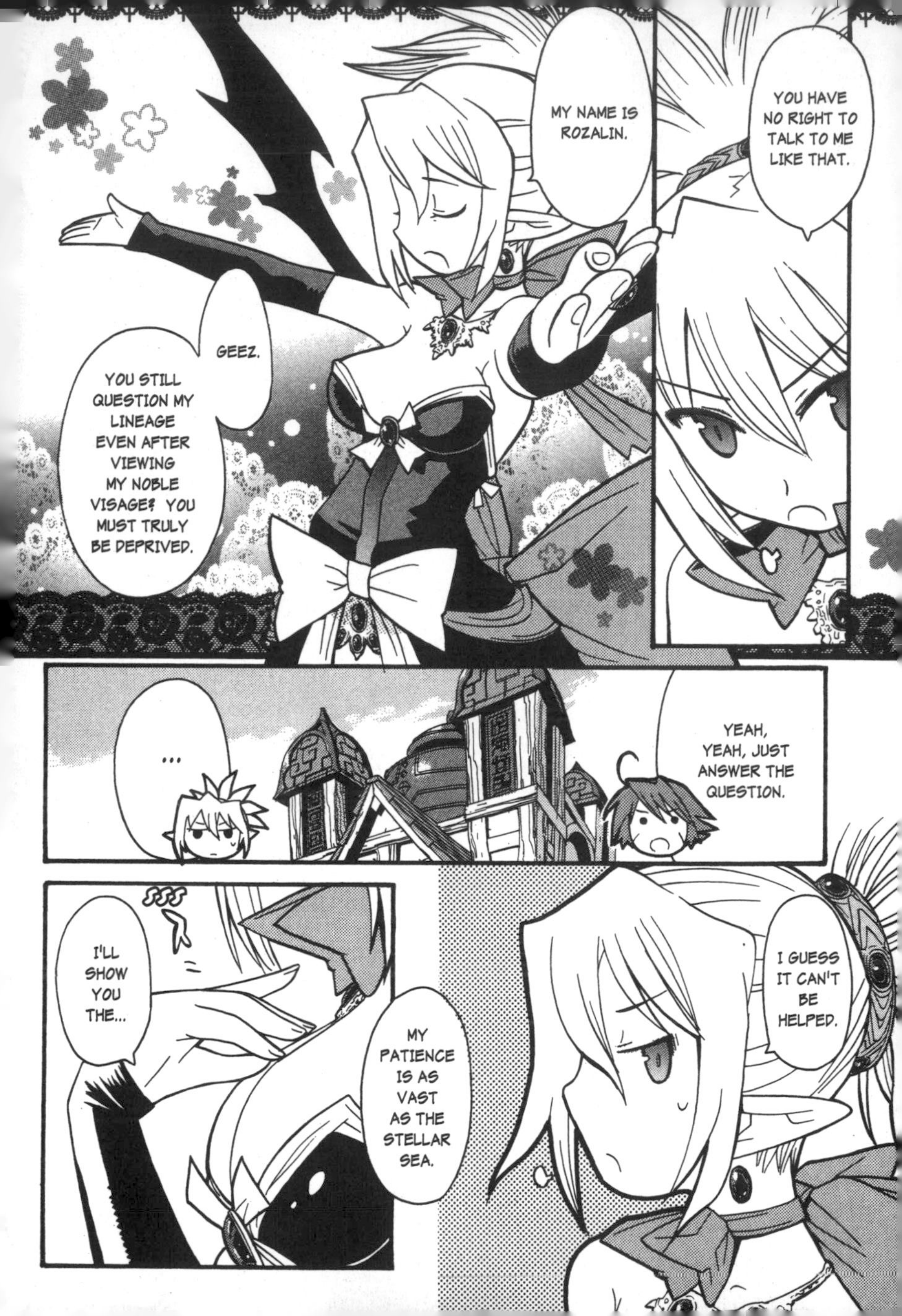
YOU HAVE NO RIGHT TO TALK TO ME LIKE THAT.
MY NAME IS ROZALIN.
GEEZ.
YOU STILL QUESTION MY LINEAGE EVEN AFTER VIEWING MY NOBLE VISAGE? YOU MUST TRULY BE DEPRIVED.
YEAH, YEAH, JUST ANSWER THE QUESTION.
...
I GUESS IT CAN'T BE HELPED.
MY PATIENCE IS AS VAST AS THE STELLAR SEA.
I'LL SHOW YOU THE...

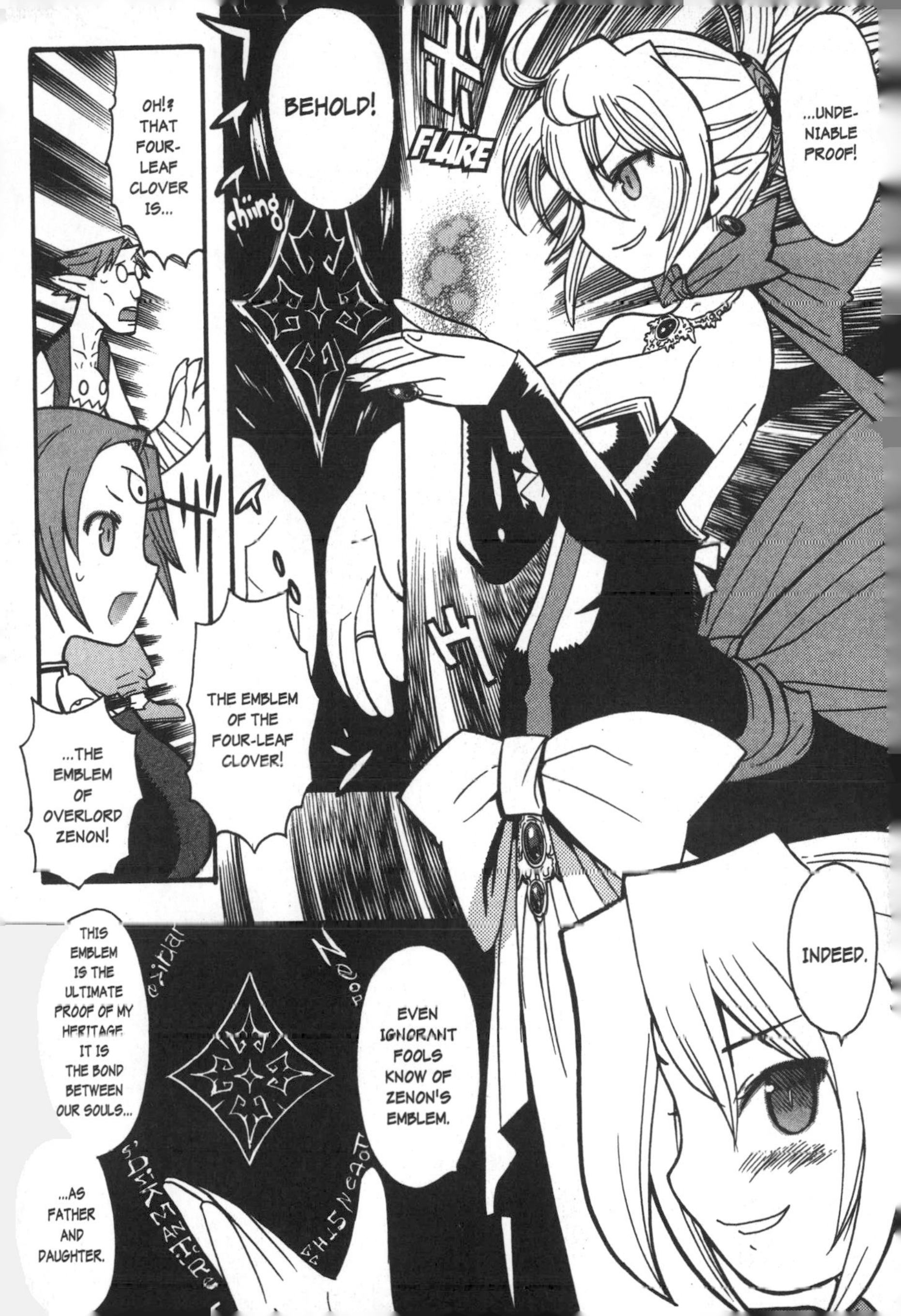
...UNDENIABLE PROOF!
BEHOLD!
FLARE
chiing
OH!? THAT FOUR-LEAF CLOVER IS...
THE EMBLEM OF THE FOUR-LEAF CLOVER!
...THE EMBLEM OF OVERLORD ZENON!
INDEED.
EVEN IGNORANT FOOLS KNOW OF ZENON'S EMBLEM.
THIS EMBLEM IS THE ULTIMATE PROOF OF MY HERITAGE. IT IS THE BOND BETWEEN OUR SOULS...
...AS FATHER AND DAUGHTER.

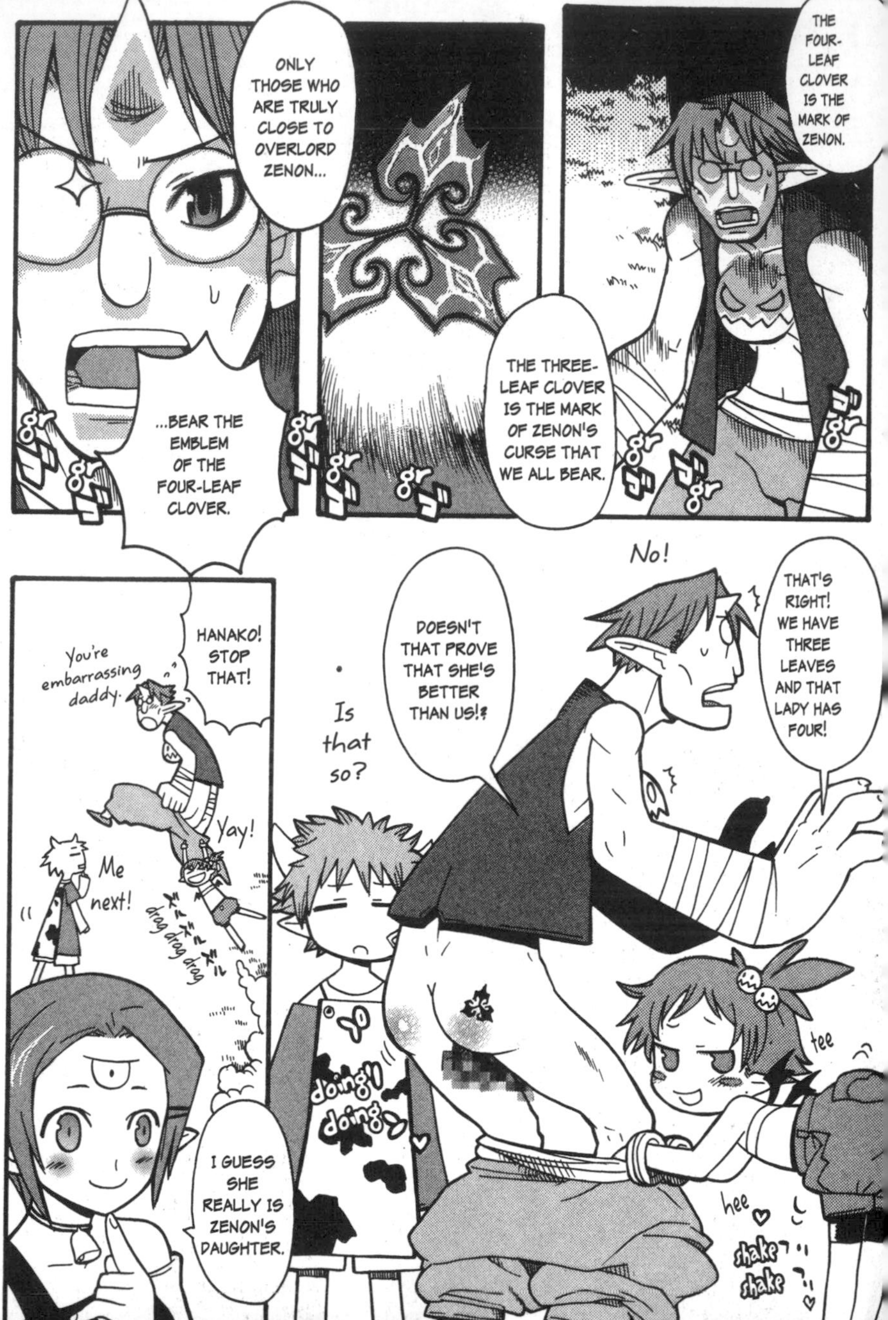
THE FOUR-LEAF CLOVER IS THE MARK OF ZENON.
THE THREE-LEAF CLOVER IS THE MARK OF ZENON'S CURSE THAT WE ALL BEAR.
gr gr
ONLY THOSE WHO ARE TRULY CLOSE TO OVERLORD ZENON...
gr gr
...BEAR THE EMBLEM OF THE FOUR-LEAF CLOVER.
gr gr
No!
THAT'S RIGHT! WE HAVE THREE LEAVES AND THAT LADY HAS FOUR!
DOESN'T THAT PROVE THAT SHE'S BETTER THAN US!?
Is that so?
tee
hee
shake shake
doing doing
I GUESS SHE REALLY IS ZENON'S DAUGHTER.
HANAKO! STOP THAT!
You're embarrassing daddy.
Yay!
Me next!
drag drag drag drag

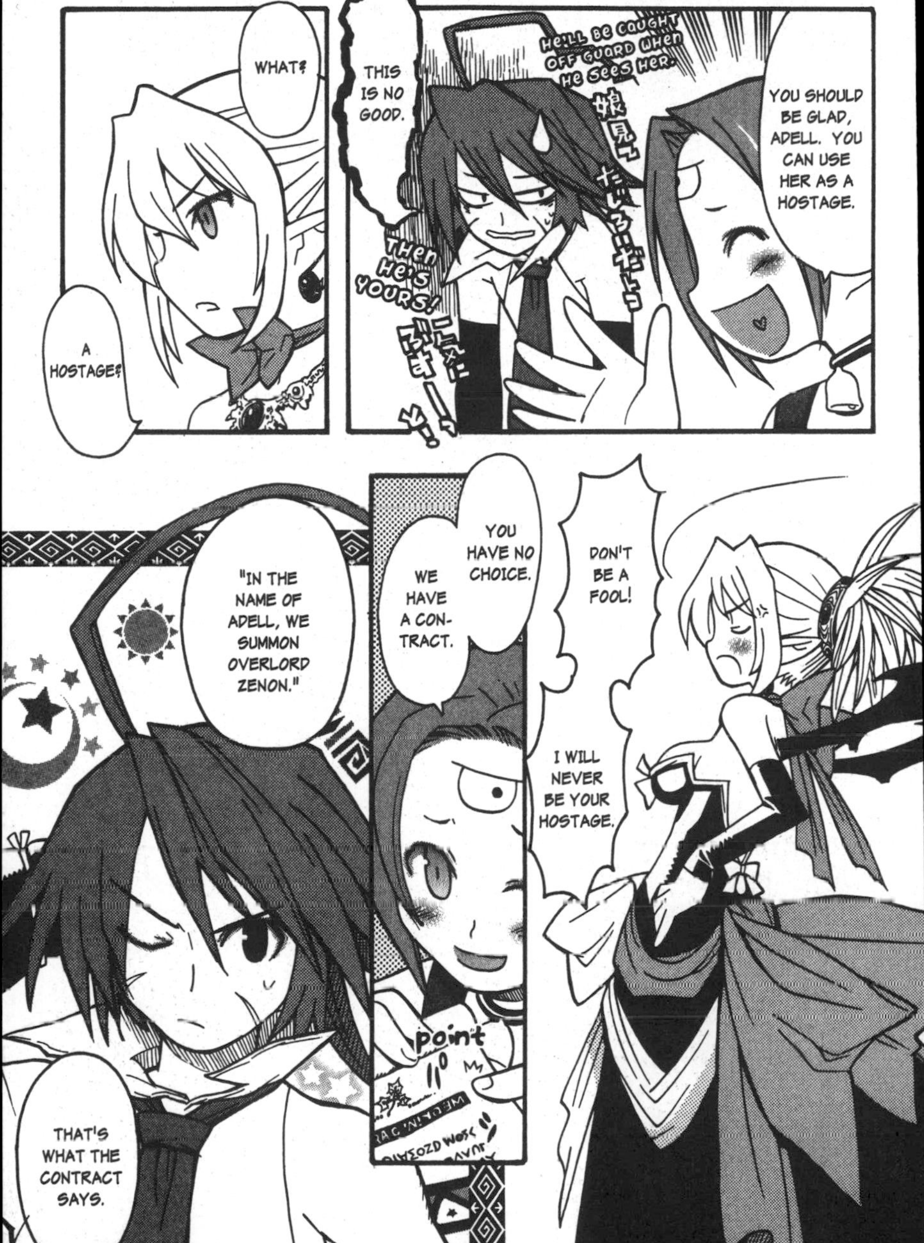

YOU SHOULD BE GLAD, ADELL. YOU CAN USE HER AS A HOSTAGE.
HE'LL BE CAUGHT OFF GUARD WHEN HE SEES HER.
THEN HE'S YOURS!
THIS IS NO GOOD.
WHAT?
A HOSTAGE?
DON'T BE A FOOL!
I WILL NEVER BE YOUR HOSTAGE.
YOU HAVE NO CHOICE.
WE HAVE A CONTRACT.
point
"IN THE NAME OF ADELL, WE SUMMON OVERLORD ZENON."
THAT'S WHAT THE CONTRACT SAYS.

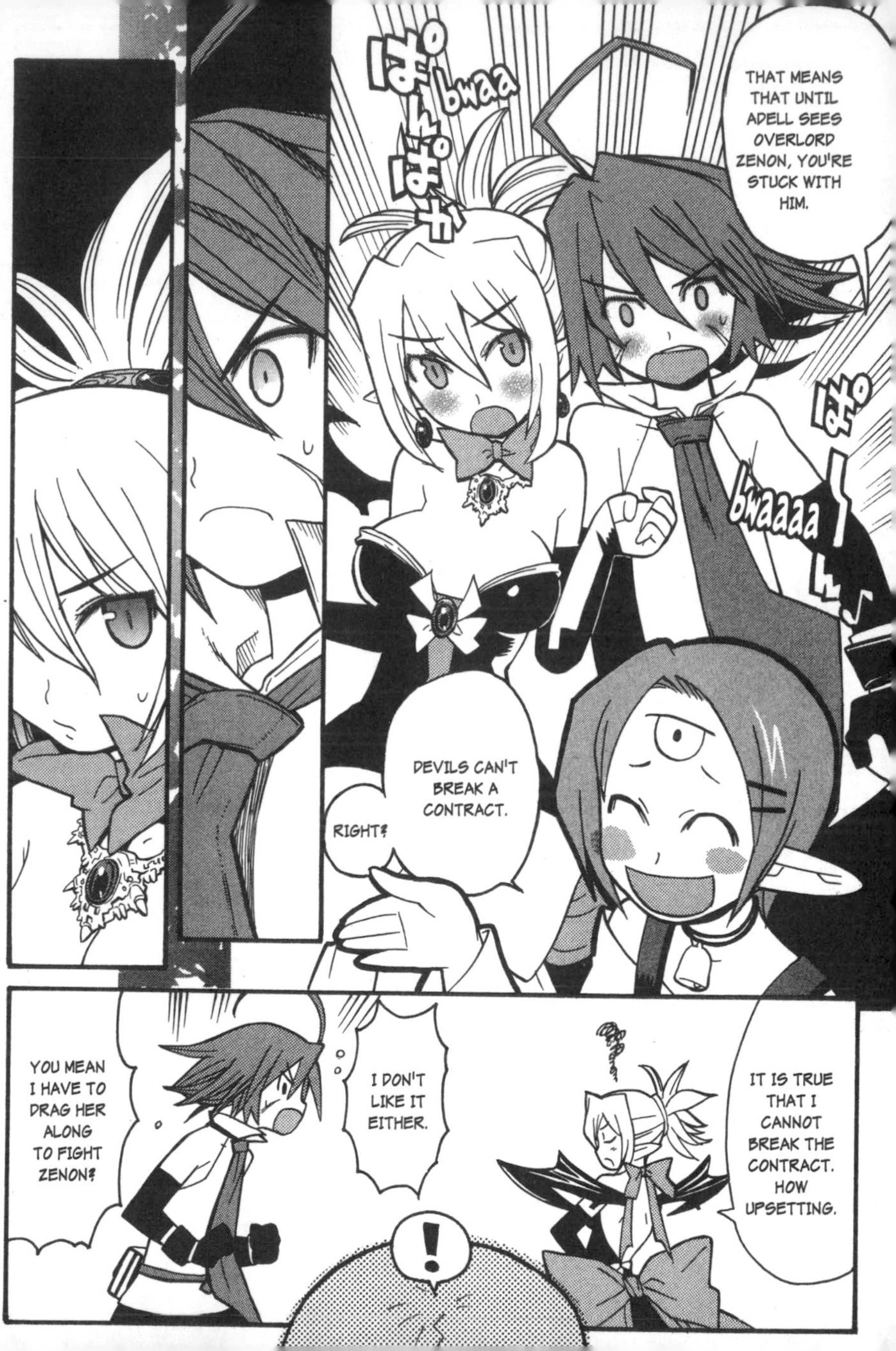
THAT MEANS THAT UNTIL ADELL SEES OVERLORD ZENON, YOU'RE STUCK WITH HIM.
bwaa
bwaaaa
DEVILS CAN'T BREAK A CONTRACT.
RIGHT?
IT IS TRUE THAT I CANNOT BREAK THE CONTRACT. HOW UPSETTING.
I DON'T LIKE IT EITHER.
YOU MEAN I HAVE TO DRAG HER ALONG TO FIGHT ZENON?
!

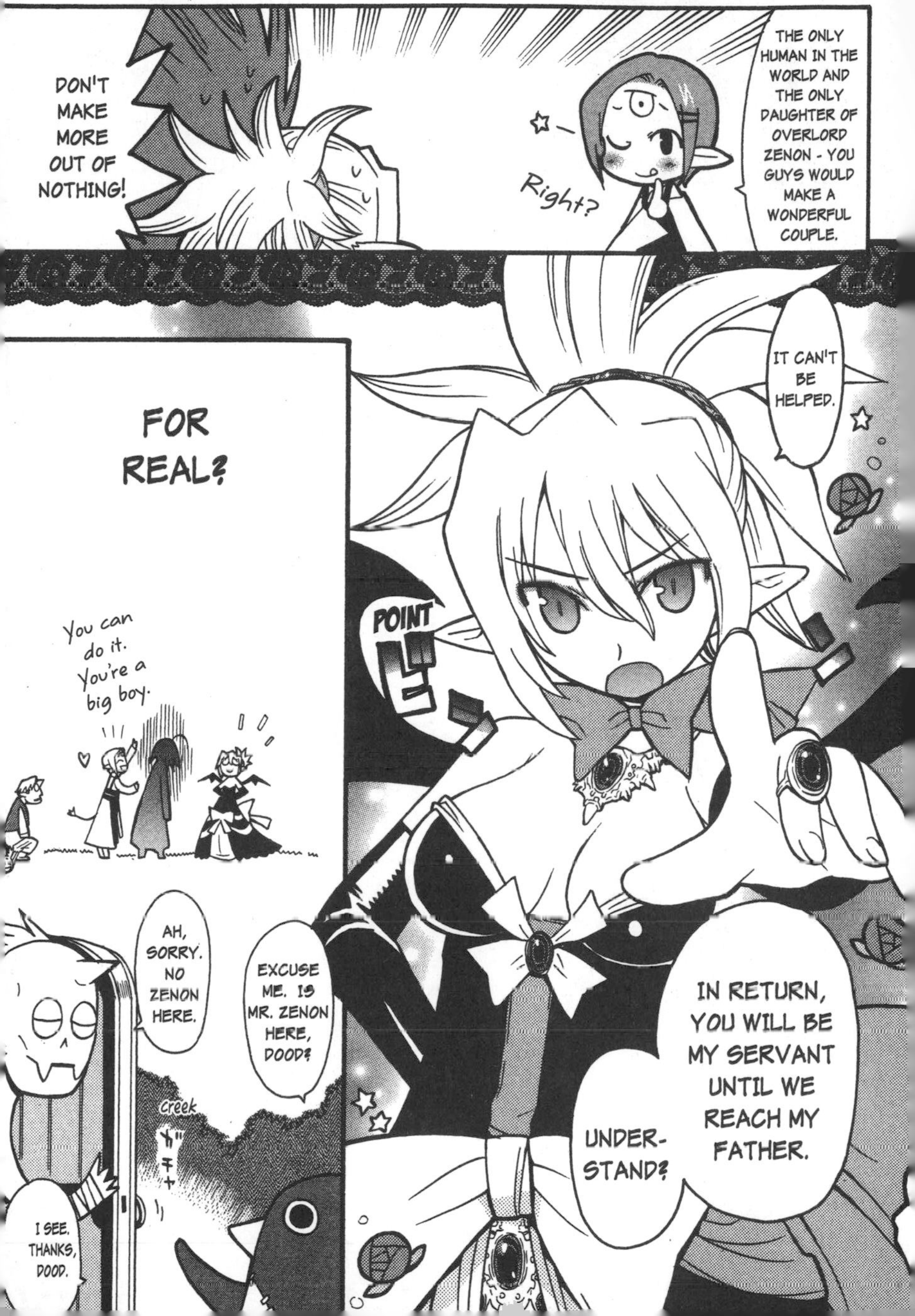
THE ONLY HUMAN IN THE WORLD AND THE ONLY DAUGHTER OF OVERLORD ZENON - YOU GUYS WOULD MAKE A WONDERFUL COUPLE.
Right?
DON'T MAKE MORE OUT OF NOTHING!
IT CAN'T BE HELPED.
POINT
IN RETURN, YOU WILL BE MY SERVANT UNTIL WE REACH MY FATHER.
UNDER-STAND?
FOR REAL?
You can do it. You're a big boy.
EXCUSE ME. IS MR. ZENON HERE, DOOD?
AH, SORRY. NO ZENON HERE.
creek
ガチャ
I SEE. THANKS, DOOD.

EPISODE PREVIEW

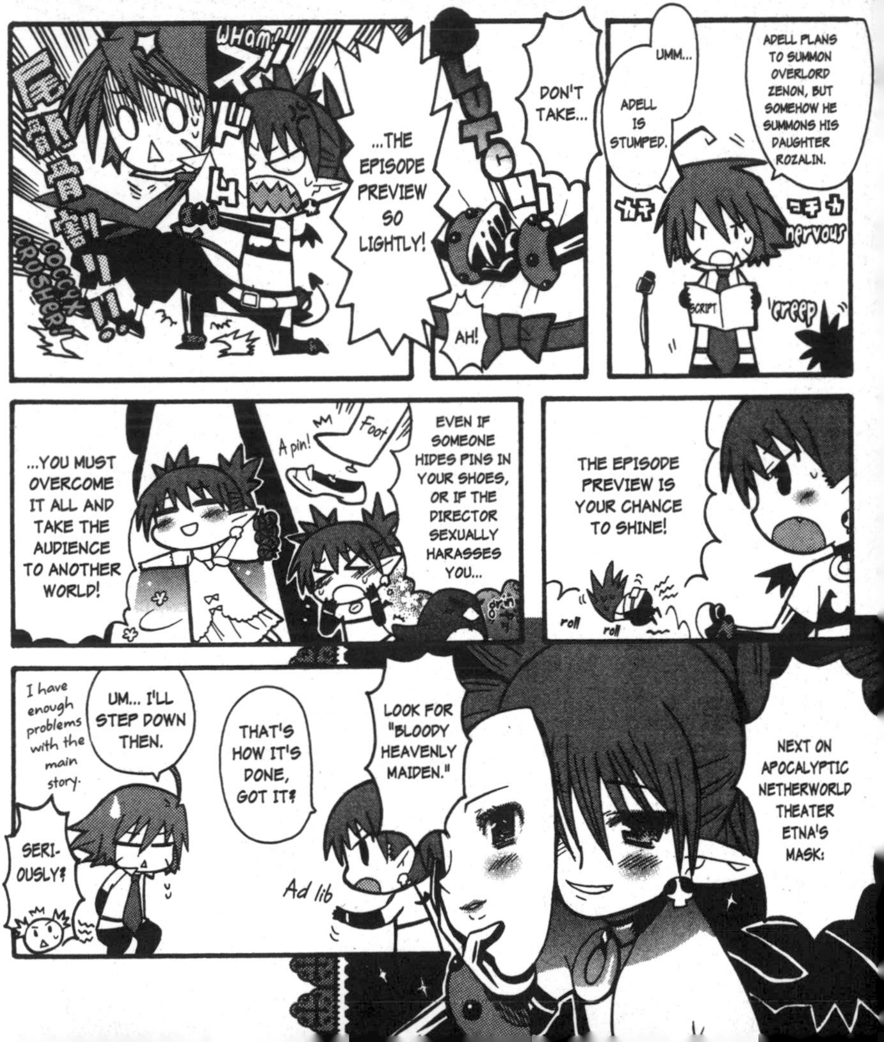
ADELL PLANS TO SUMMON OVERLORD ZENON, BUT SOMEHOW HE SUMMONS HIS DAUGHTER ROZALIN.
UMM... ADELL IS STUMPED.
nervous
SCRIPT
creep
DON'T TAKE...
AH!
...THE EPISODE PREVIEW SO LIGHTLY!
WHAM!
COCCYX CRUSHER!
THE EPISODE PREVIEW IS YOUR CHANCE TO SHINE!
roll
roll
EVEN IF SOMEONE HIDES PINS IN YOUR SHOES, OR IF THE DIRECTOR SEXUALLY HARASSES YOU...
Foot
A pin!
grin
...YOU MUST OVERCOME IT ALL AND TAKE THE AUDIENCE TO ANOTHER WORLD!
NEXT ON APOCALYPTIC NETHERWORLD THEATER ETNA'S MASK:
LOOK FOR "BLOODY HEAVENLY MAIDEN."
THAT'S HOW IT'S DONE, GOT IT?
Ad lib
UM... I'LL STEP DOWN THEN.
I have enough problems with the main story.
SERI-OUSLY?

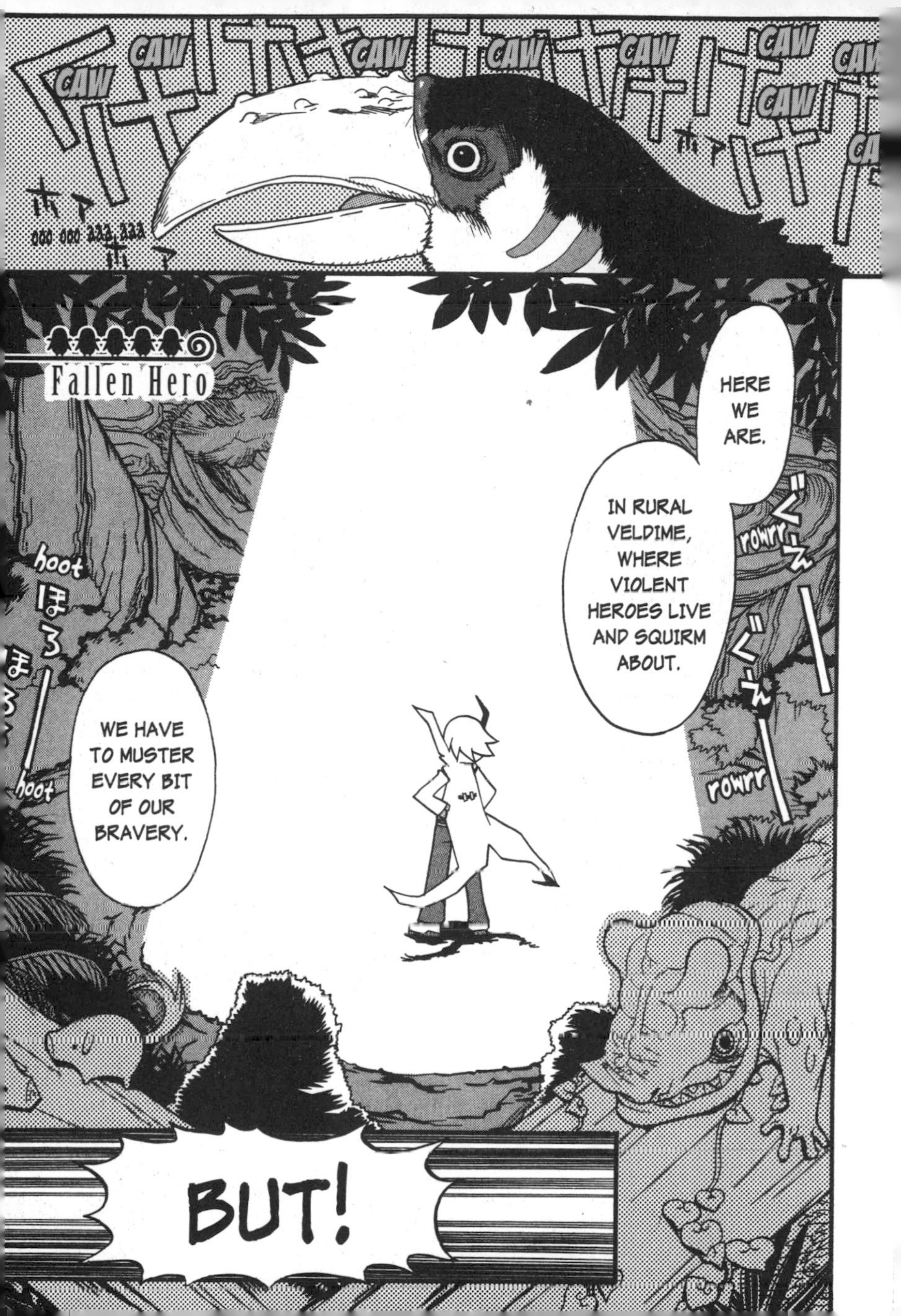
CAW
CAW
CAW
CAW
CAW
CAW
CAW
CAW
ooo ooo aaa aaa
Fallen Hero
HERE WE ARE.
IN RURAL VELDIME, WHERE VIOLENT HEROES LIVE AND SQUIRM ABOUT.
rowrr
rowrr
hoot
hoot
WE HAVE TO MUSTER EVERY BIT OF OUR BRAVERY.
BUT!

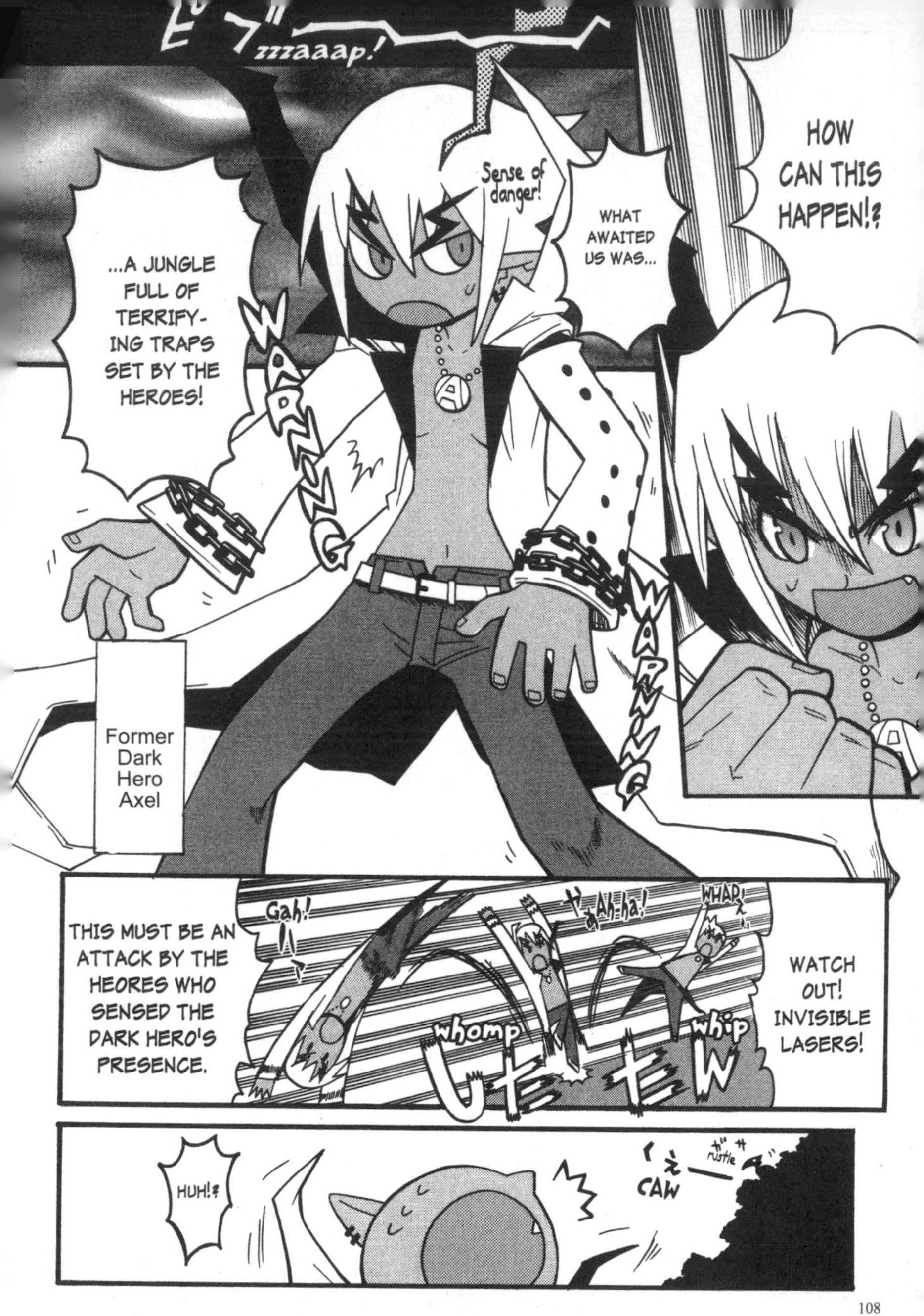
zzzaaap!
HOW CAN THIS HAPPEN!?
WHAT AWAITED US WAS...
Sense of danger!
...A JUNGLE FULL OF TERRIFY-ING TRAPS SET BY THE HEROES!
WARNING
WARNING
Former Dark Hero Axel
WATCH OUT! INVISIBLE LASERS!
WHAP!
Ah-ha!
Gah!
whip
whomp
THIS MUST BE AN ATTACK BY THE HEORES WHO SENSED THE DARK HERO'S PRESENCE.
rustle
CAW
HUH!?

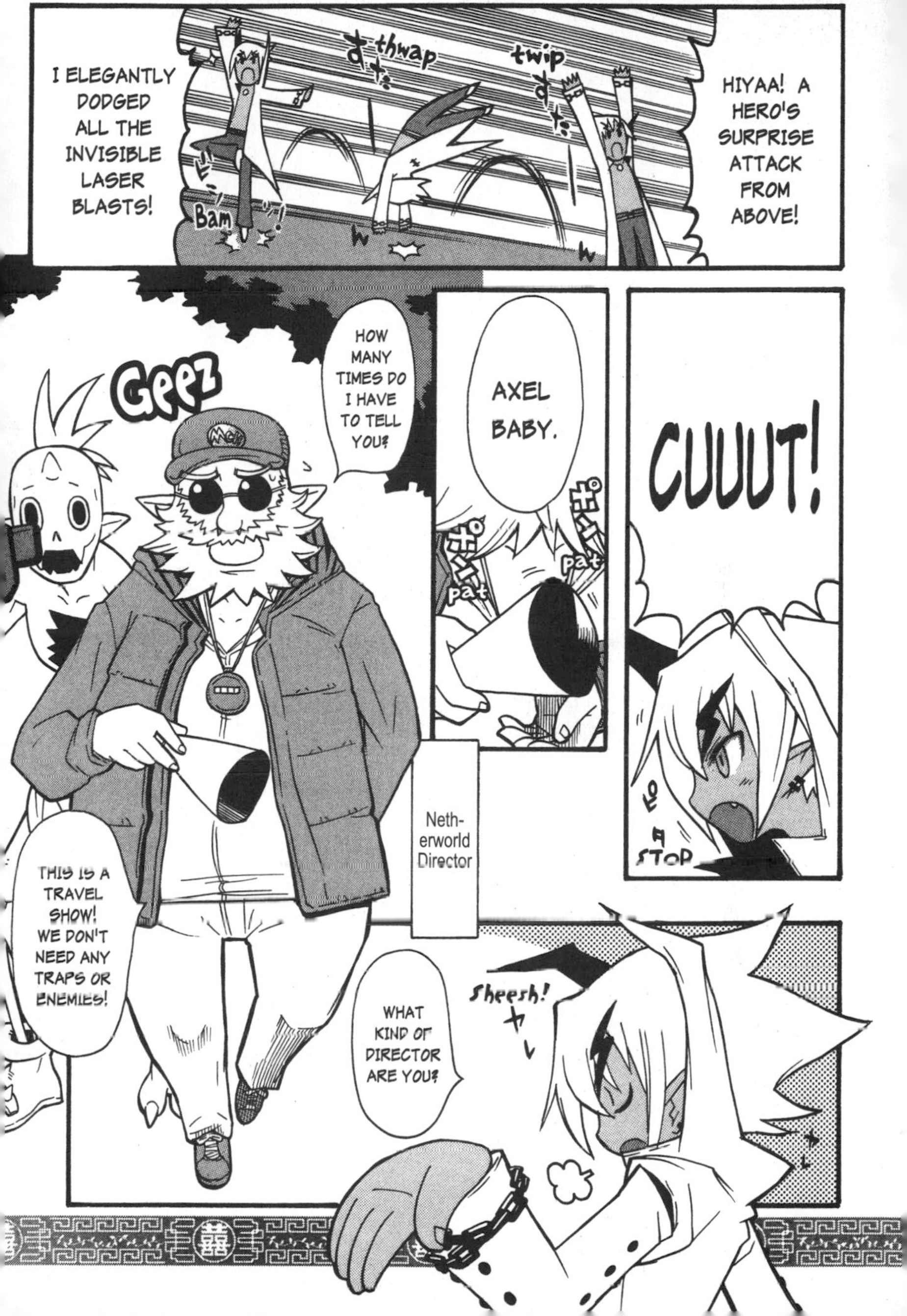
HIYAA! A HERO'S SURPRISE ATTACK FROM ABOVE!
twip
thwap
I ELEGANTLY DODGED ALL THE INVISIBLE LASER BLASTS!
Bam
CUUUT!
STOP
AXEL BABY.
pat
pat
Sheesh!
WHAT KIND OF DIRECTOR ARE YOU?
HOW MANY TIMES DO I HAVE TO TELL YOU?
Geez
Neth-erworld Director
THIS IS A TRAVEL SHOW! WE DON'T NEED ANY TRAPS OR ENEMIES!

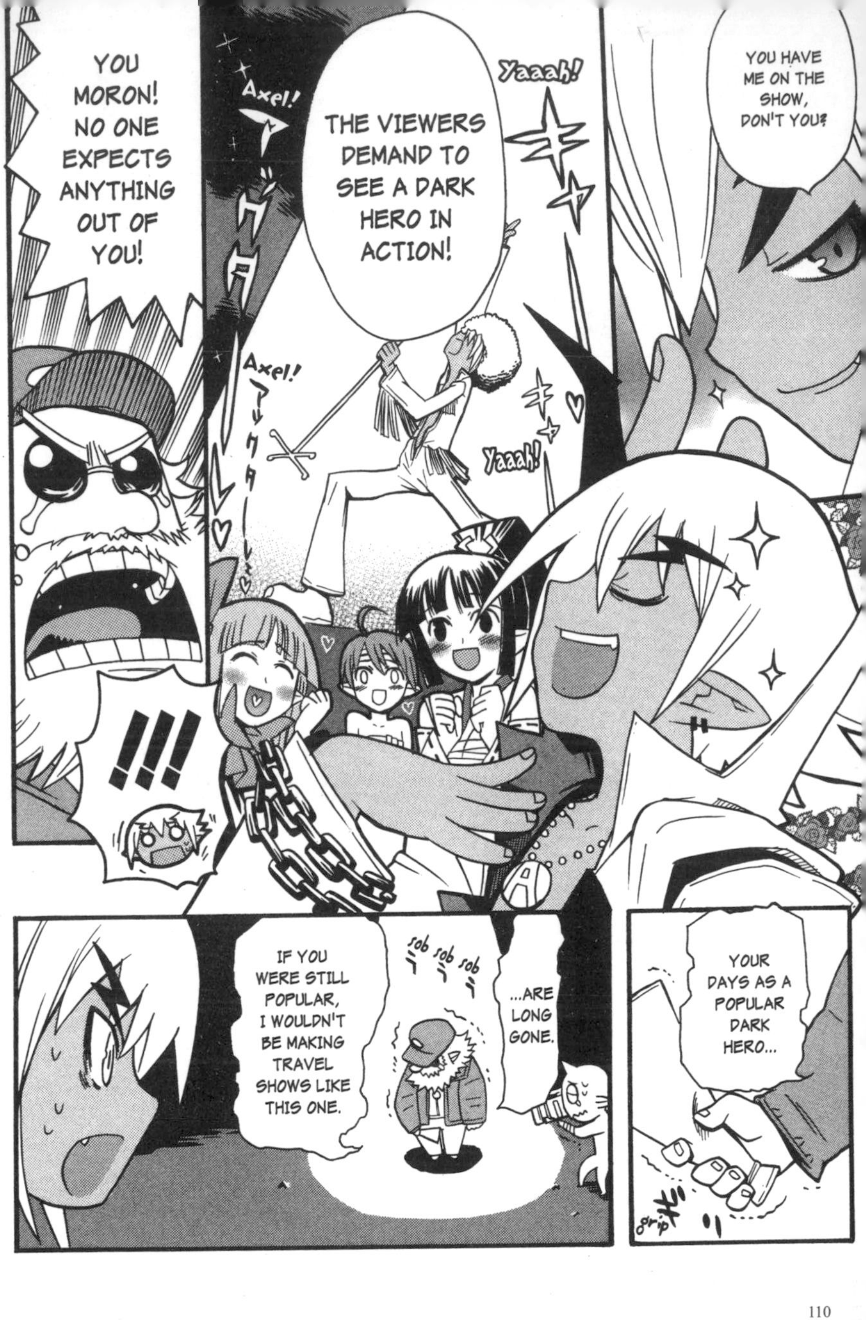
YOU HAVE ME ON THE SHOW, DON'T YOU?
Yaaah!
THE VIEWERS DEMAND TO SEE A DARK HERO IN ACTION!
Axel!
Yaaah!
Axel!
YOU MORON! NO ONE EXPECTS ANYTHING OUT OF YOU!
!!!
YOUR DAYS AS A POPULAR DARK HERO...
grip
...ARE LONG GONE.
sob sob sob
IF YOU WERE STILL POPULAR, I WOULDN'T BE MAKING TRAVEL SHOWS LIKE THIS ONE.

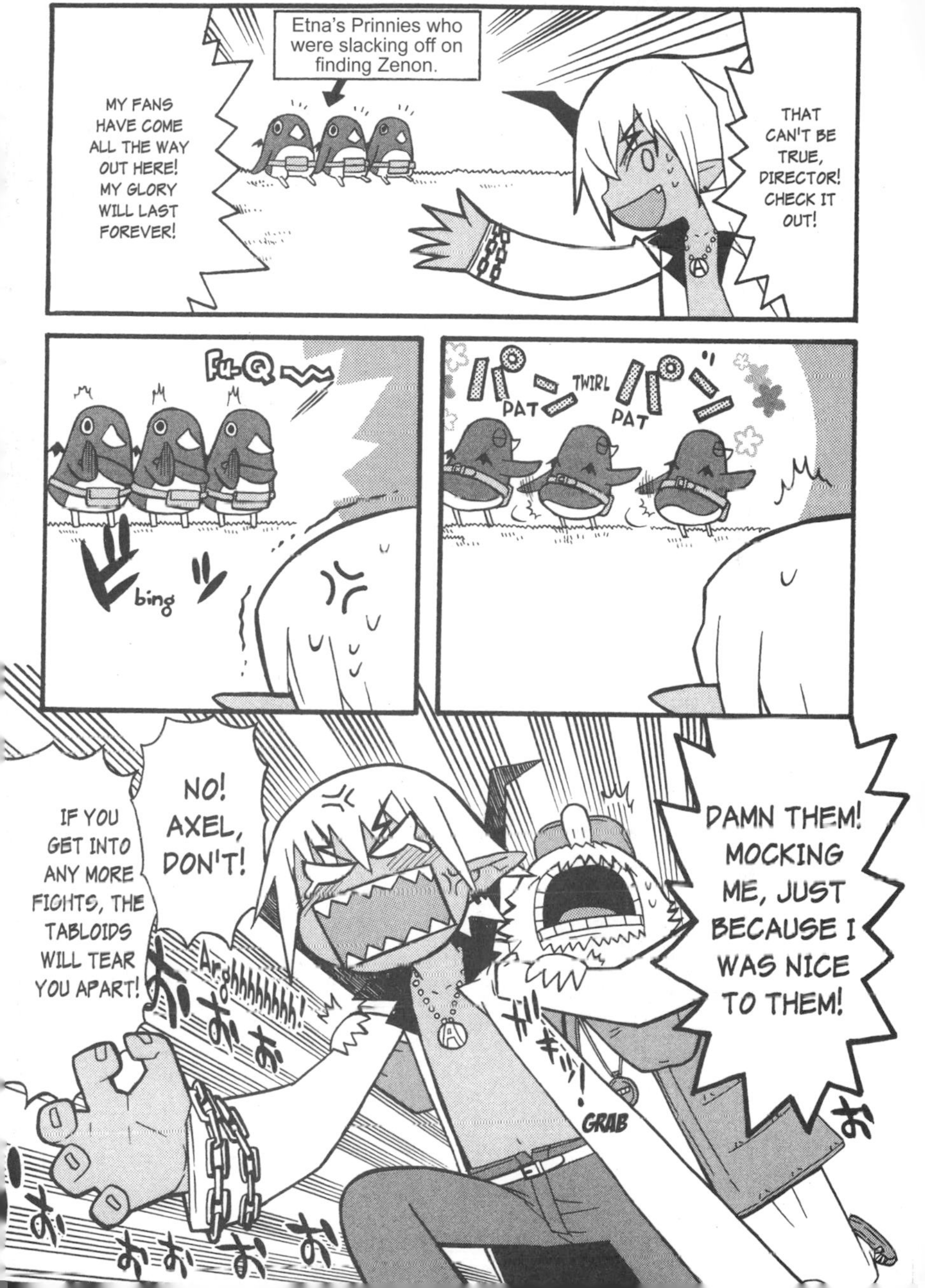
THAT CAN'T BE TRUE, DIRECTOR! CHECK IT OUT!
Etna's Prinnies who were slacking off on finding Zenon.
MY FANS HAVE COME ALL THE WAY OUT HERE! MY GLORY WILL LAST FOREVER!
PAT
TWIRL
PAT
Fu-Q~
bing
DAMN THEM! MOCKING ME, JUST BECAUSE I WAS NICE TO THEM!
GRAB
Arghhhhhhhhh!
NO! AXEL, DON'T!
IF YOU GET INTO ANY MORE FIGHTS, THE TABLOIDS WILL TEAR YOU APART!

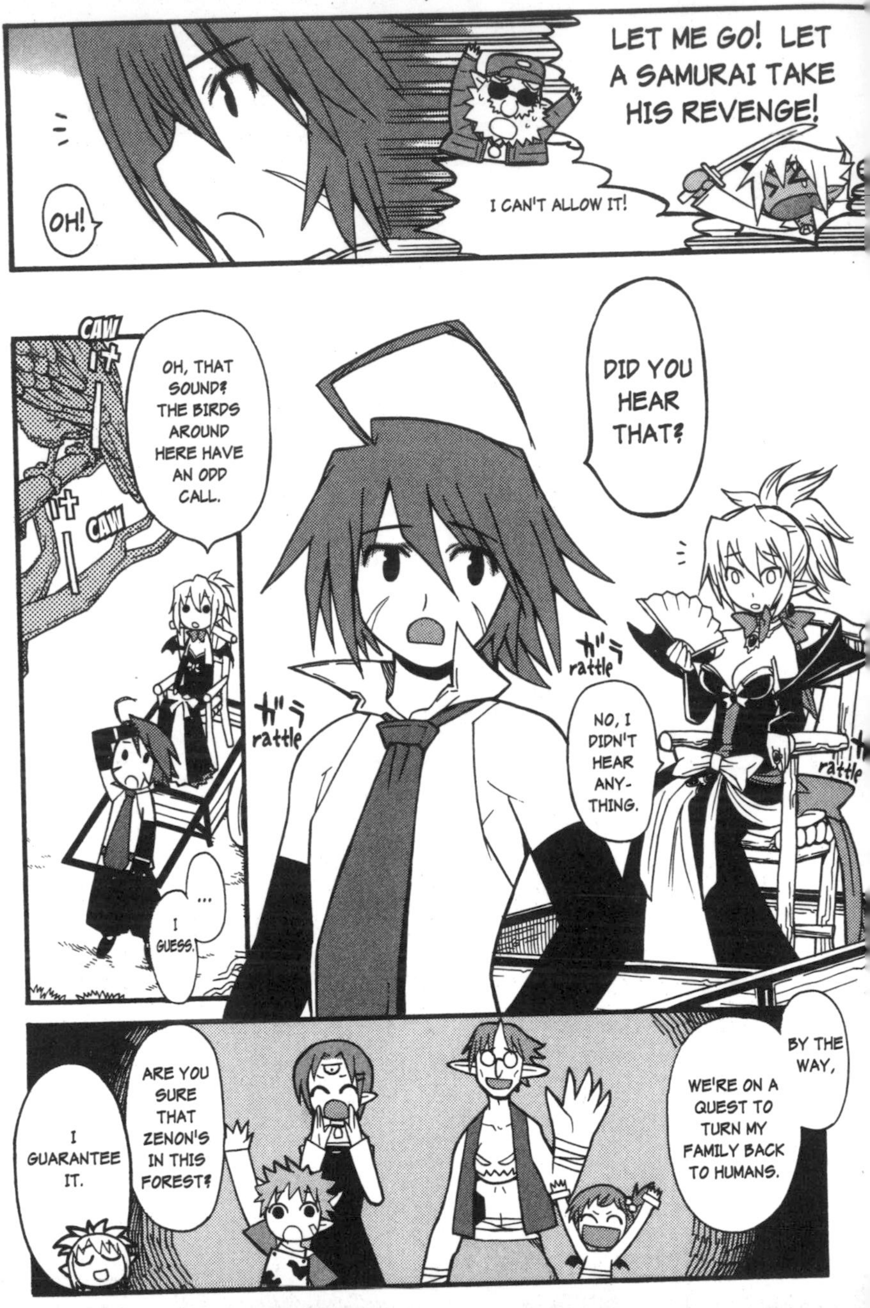
LET ME GO! LET A SAMURAI TAKE HIS REVENGE!
I CAN'T ALLOW IT!
OH!
DID YOU HEAR THAT?
rattle
NO, I DIDN'T HEAR ANYTHING.
rattle
rattle
CAW
OH, THAT SOUND? THE BIRDS AROUND HERE HAVE AN ODD CALL.
CAW
...
I GUESS.
BY THE WAY,
WE'RE ON A QUEST TO TURN MY FAMILY BACK TO HUMANS.
ARE YOU SURE THAT ZENON'S IN THIS FOREST?
I GUARANTEE IT.

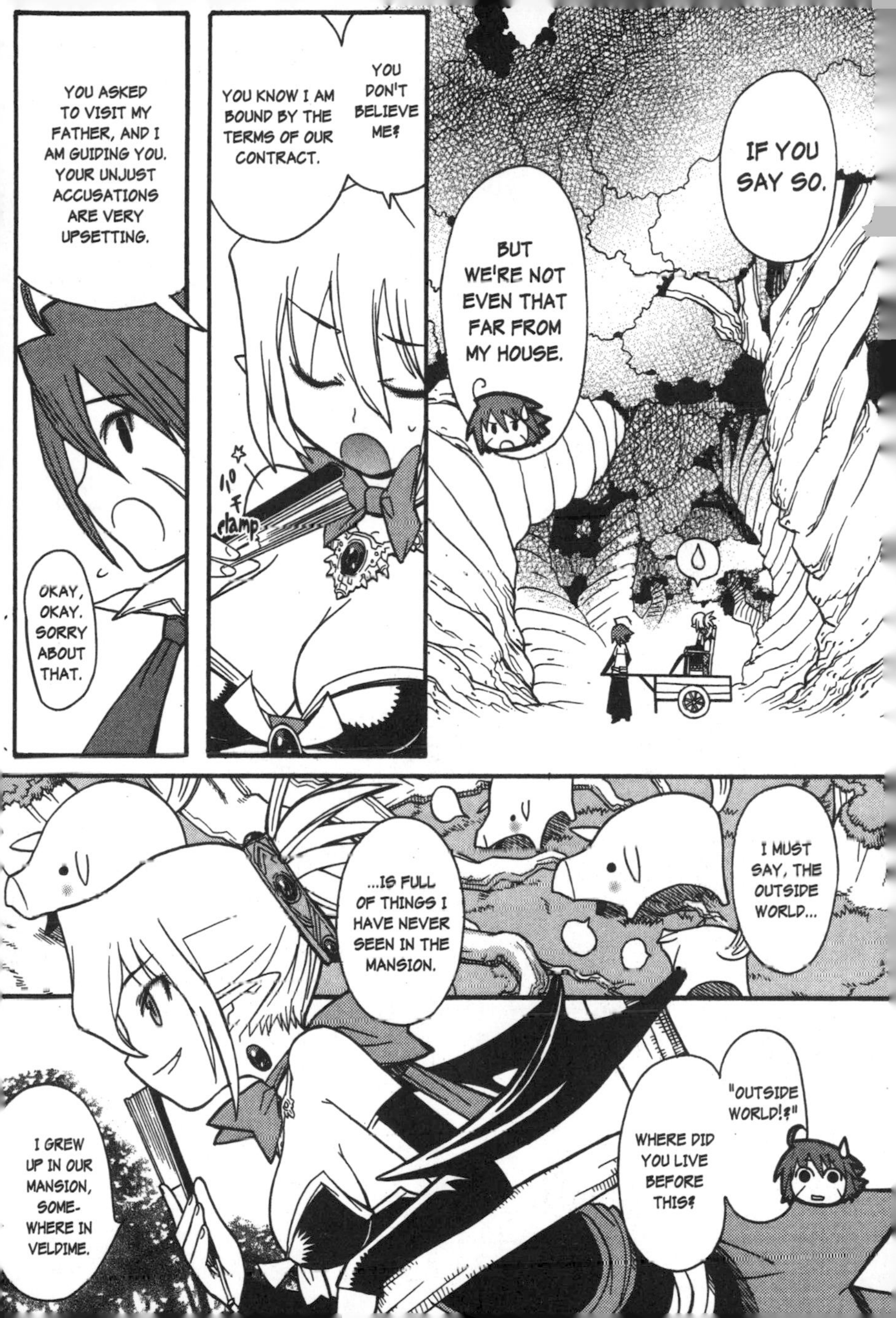
IF YOU SAY SO.
BUT WE'RE NOT EVEN THAT FAR FROM MY HOUSE.
YOU DON'T BELIEVE ME?
YOU KNOW I AM BOUND BY THE TERMS OF OUR CONTRACT.
clamp
YOU ASKED TO VISIT MY FATHER, AND I AM GUIDING YOU. YOUR UNJUST ACCUSATIONS ARE VERY UPSETTING.
OKAY, OKAY. SORRY ABOUT THAT.
I MUST SAY, THE OUTSIDE WORLD...
...IS FULL OF THINGS I HAVE NEVER SEEN IN THE MANSION.
"OUTSIDE WORLD!?"
WHERE DID YOU LIVE BEFORE THIS?
I GREW UP IN OUR MANSION, SOME-WHERE IN VELDIME.

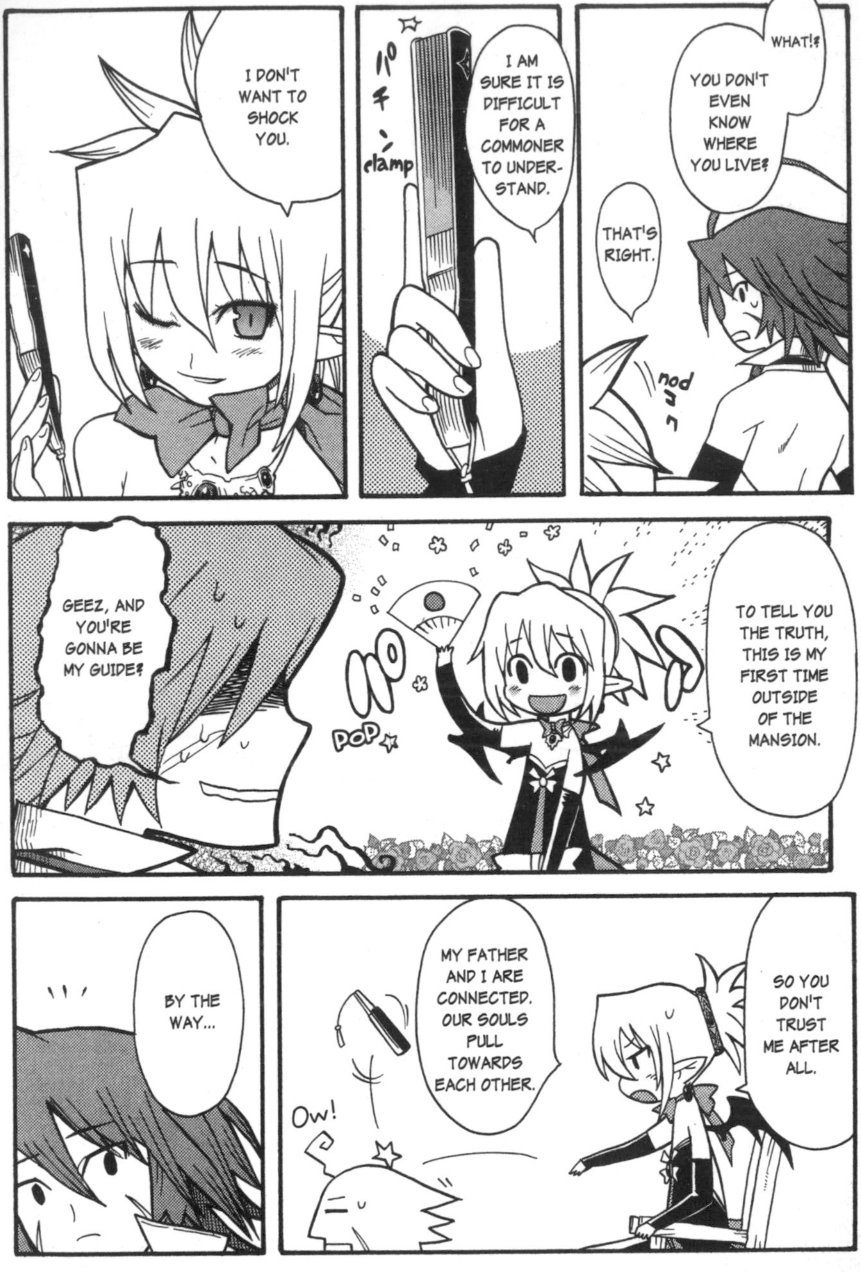
WHAT!?
YOU DON'T EVEN KNOW WHERE YOU LIVE?
THAT'S RIGHT.
nod nod
I AM SURE IT IS DIFFICULT FOR A COMMONER TO UNDERSTAND.
パチン
clamp
I DON'T WANT TO SHOCK YOU.
TO TELL YOU THE TRUTH, THIS IS MY FIRST TIME OUTSIDE OF THE MANSION.
POP
GEEZ, AND YOU'RE GONNA BE MY GUIDE?
SO YOU DON'T TRUST ME AFTER ALL.
MY FATHER AND I ARE CONNECTED. OUR SOULS PULL TOWARDS EACH OTHER.
Ow!
BY THE WAY...

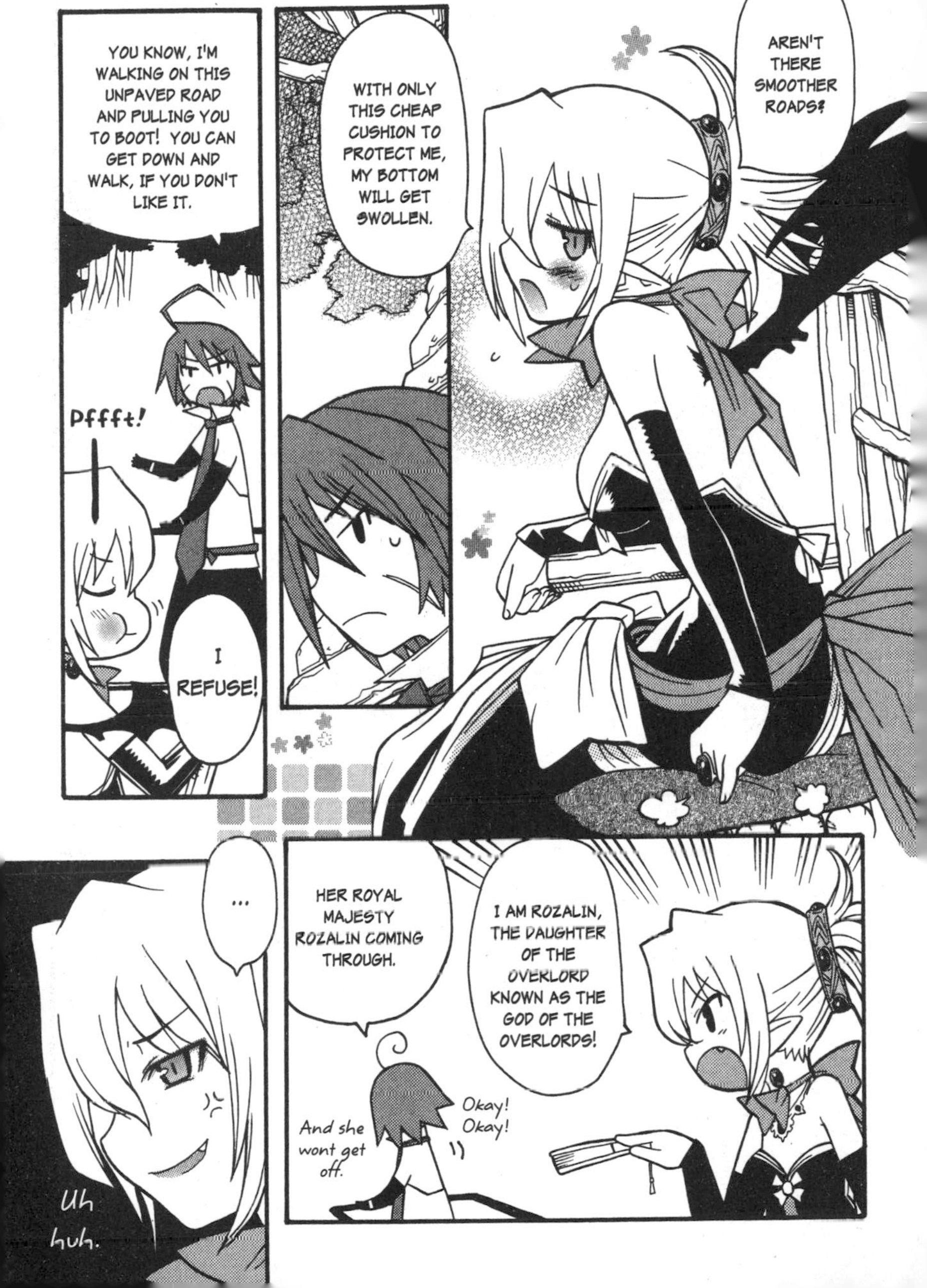
AREN'T THERE SMOOTHER ROADS?
WITH ONLY THIS CHEAP CUSHION TO PROTECT ME, MY BOTTOM WILL GET SWOLLEN.
YOU KNOW, I'M WALKING ON THIS UNPAVED ROAD AND PULLING YOU TO BOOT! YOU CAN GET DOWN AND WALK, IF YOU DON'T LIKE IT.
Pffft!
I REFUSE!
I AM ROZALIN, THE DAUGHTER OF THE OVERLORD KNOWN AS THE GOD OF THE OVERLORDS!
HER ROYAL MAJESTY ROZALIN COMING THROUGH.
Okay! Okay!
And she wont get off.
...
Uh huh.

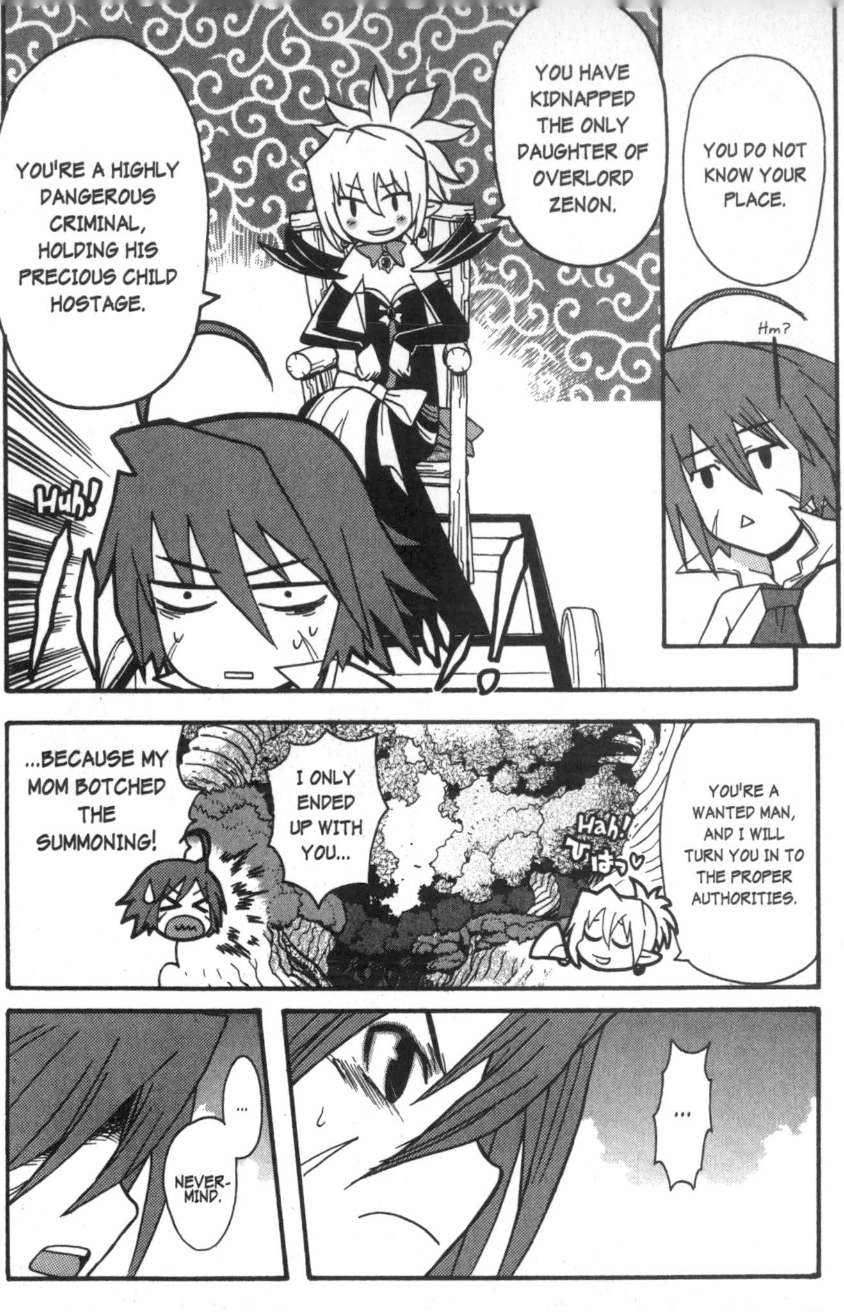
YOU DO NOT KNOW YOUR PLACE.
Hm?
YOU HAVE KIDNAPPED THE ONLY DAUGHTER OF OVERLORD ZENON.
YOU'RE A HIGHLY DANGEROUS CRIMINAL, HOLDING HIS PRECIOUS CHILD HOSTAGE.
Huh!
YOU'RE A WANTED MAN, AND I WILL TURN YOU IN TO THE PROPER AUTHORITIES.
Hah!
I ONLY ENDED UP WITH YOU...
...BECAUSE MY MOM BOTCHED THE SUMMONING!
...
...
NEVER-MIND.

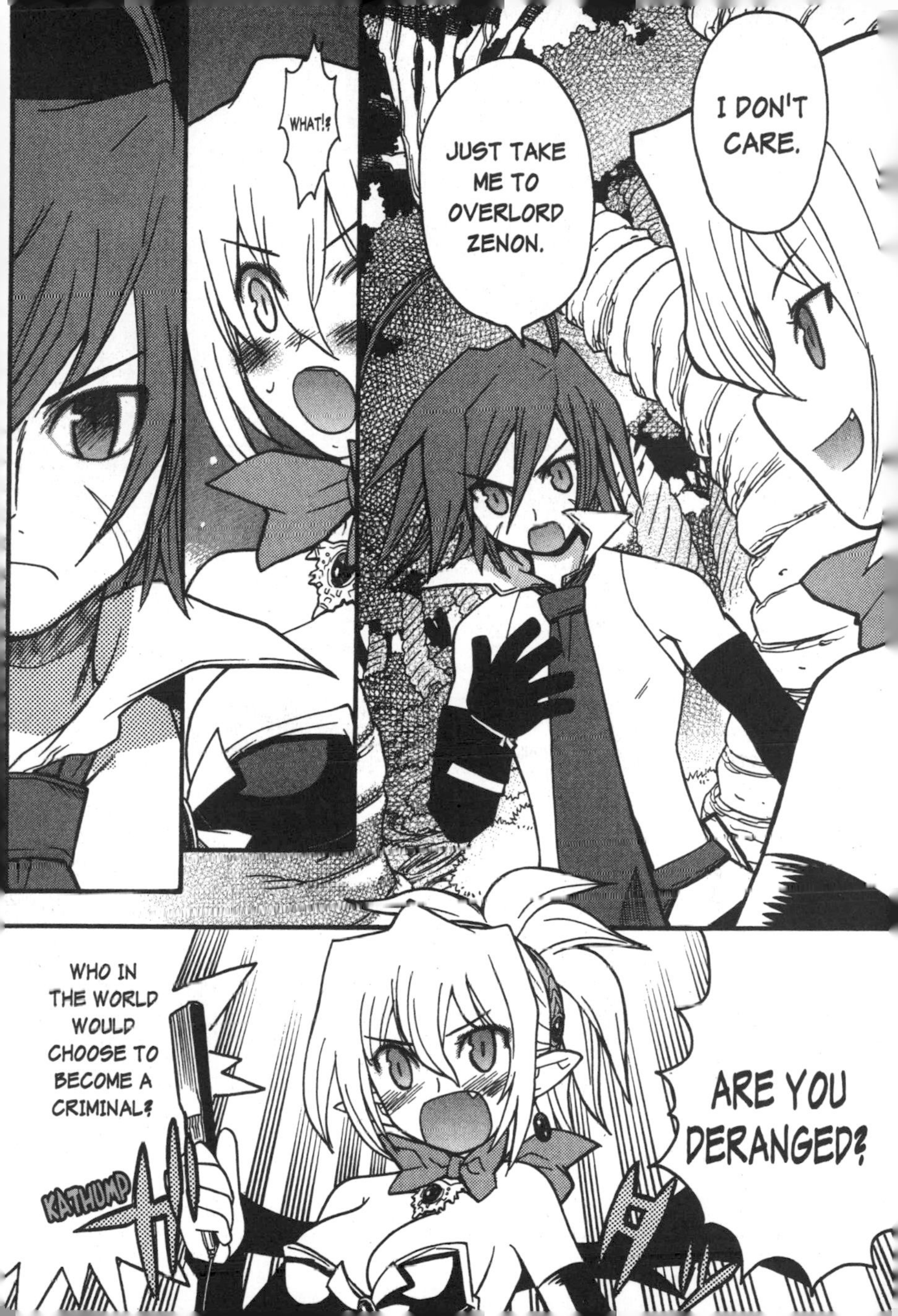
I DON'T CARE.
JUST TAKE ME TO OVERLORD ZENON.
WHAT!?
WHO IN THE WORLD WOULD CHOOSE TO BECOME A CRIMINAL?
ARE YOU DERANGED?
KATHUMP

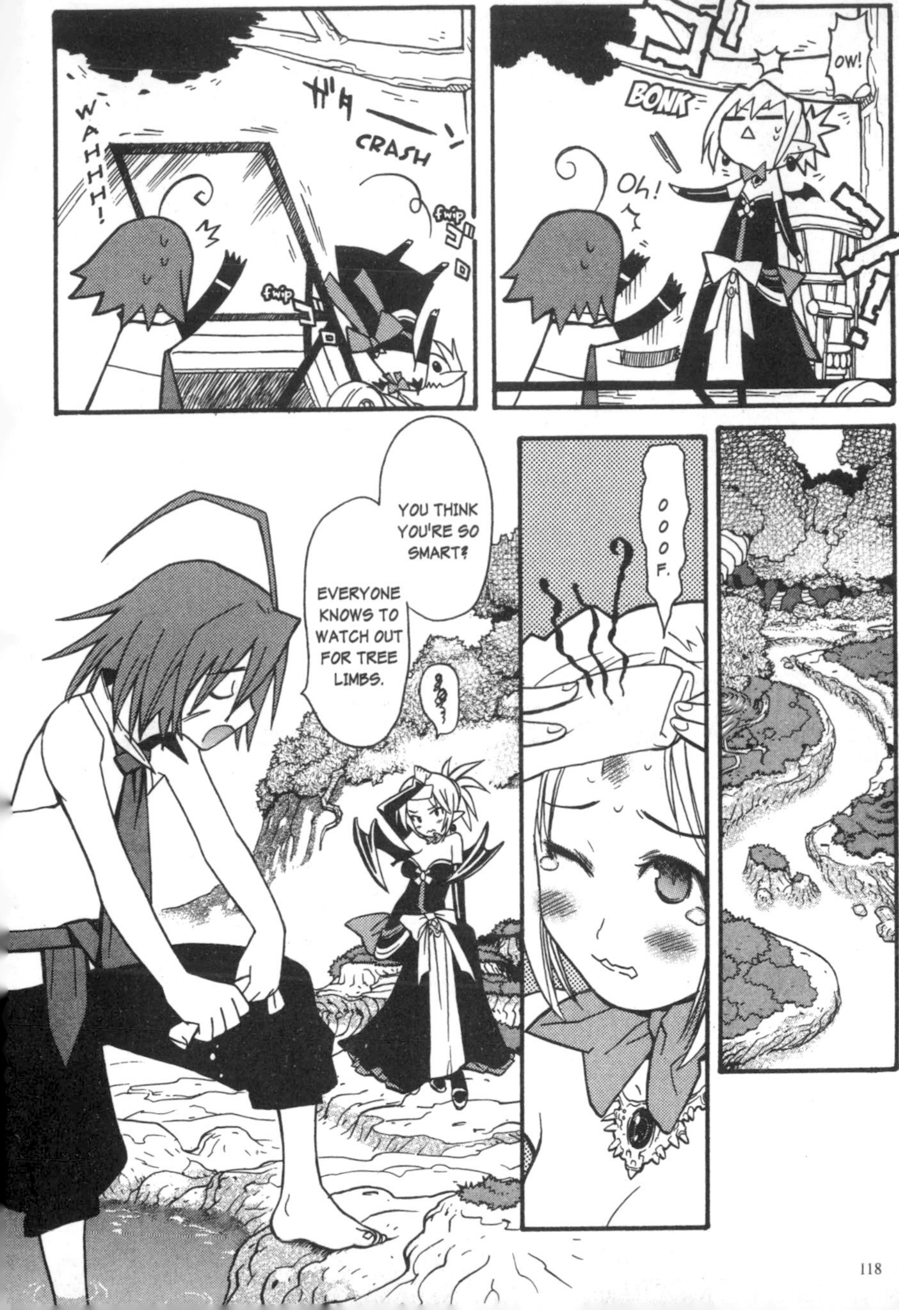
OW!
BONK
Oh!
WAHHHH!
CRASH
fwip
fwip
OOOF.
YOU THINK YOU'RE SO SMART?
EVERYONE KNOWS TO WATCH OUT FOR TREE LIMBS.

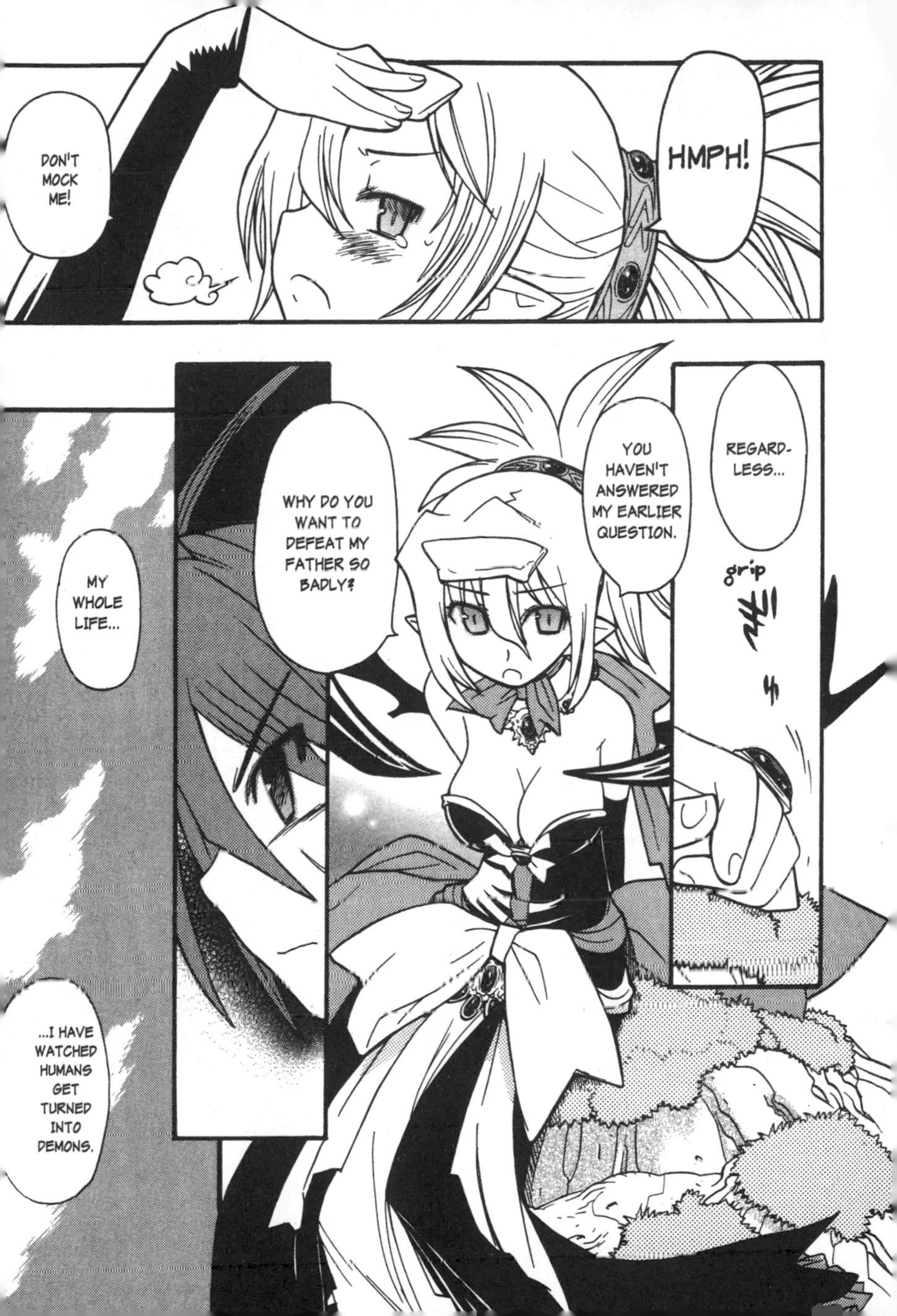
HMPH!
DON'T MOCK ME!
REGARD-LESS...
YOU HAVEN'T ANSWERED MY EARLIER QUESTION.
grip
WHY DO YOU WANT TO DEFEAT MY FATHER SO BADLY?
MY WHOLE LIFE...
...I HAVE WATCHED HUMANS GET TURNED INTO DEMONS.

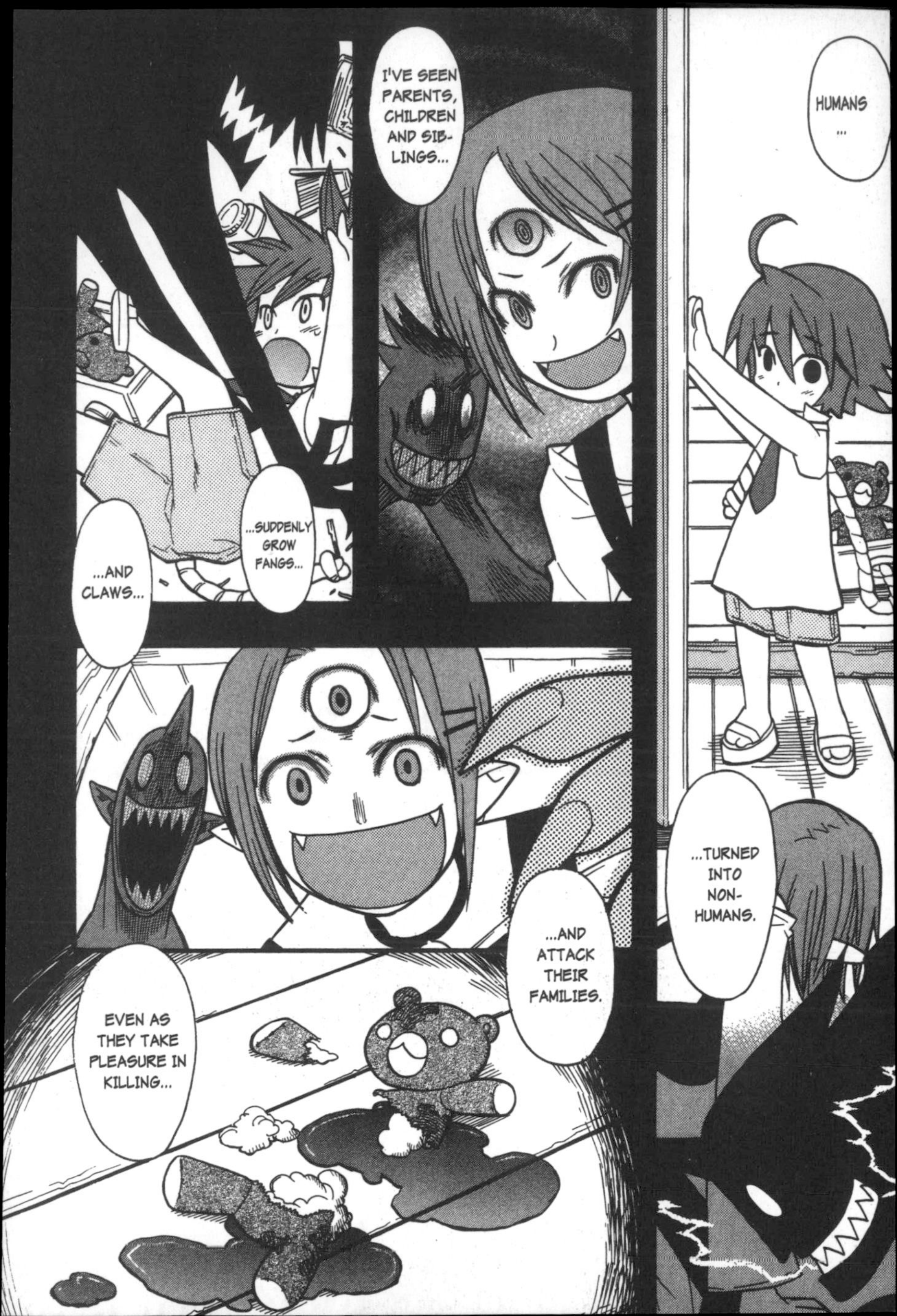
HUMANS ...
I'VE SEEN PARENTS, CHILDREN AND SIB-LINGS...
...TURNED INTO NON-HUMANS.
...SUDDENLY GROW FANGS...
...AND CLAWS...
...AND ATTACK THEIR FAMILIES.
EVEN AS THEY TAKE PLEASURE IN KILLING...

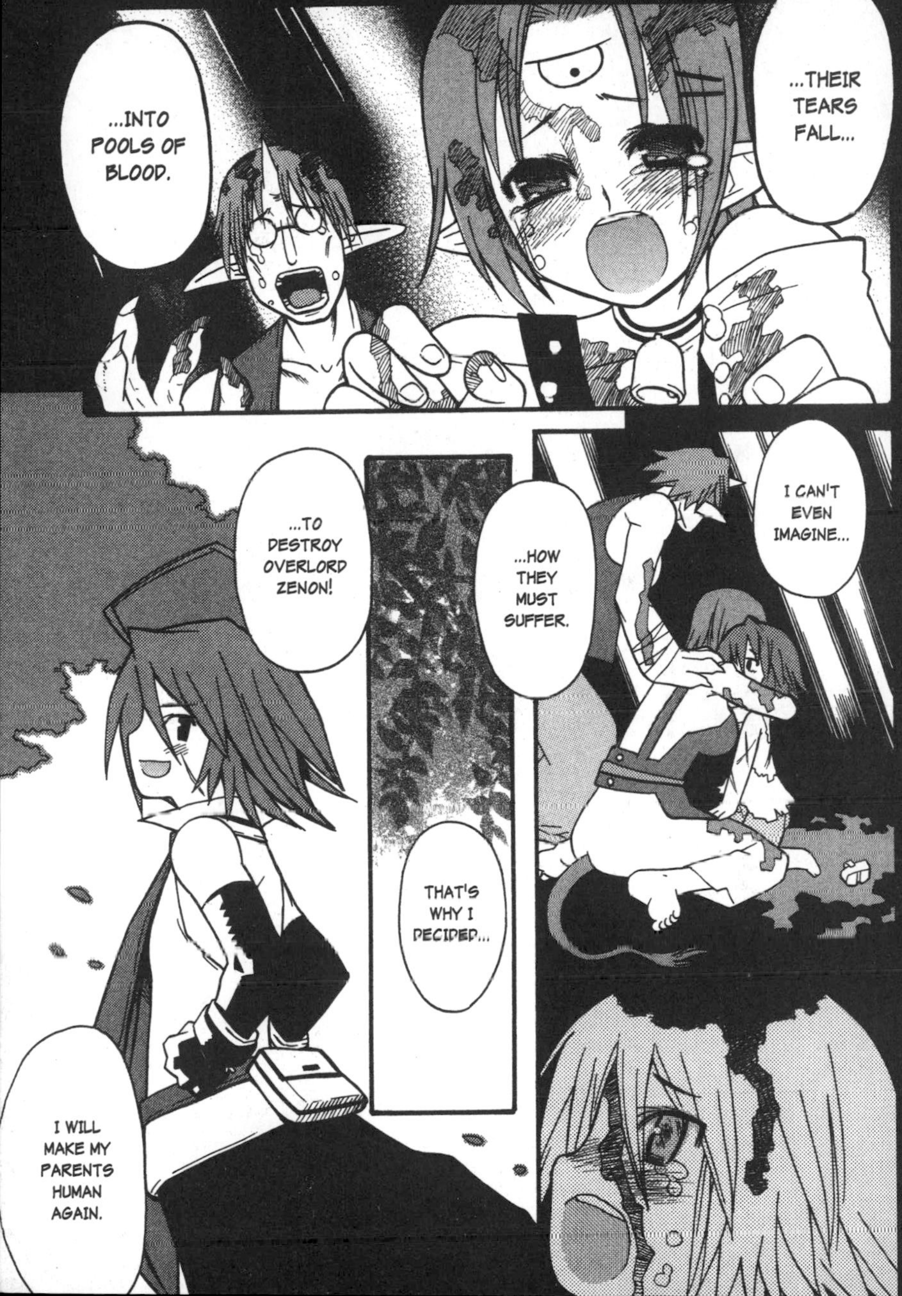
...THEIR TEARS FALL...
...INTO POOLS OF BLOOD.
I CAN'T EVEN IMAGINE...
...HOW THEY MUST SUFFER.
THAT'S WHY I DECIDED...
...TO DESTROY OVERLORD ZENON!
I WILL MAKE MY PARENTS HUMAN AGAIN.

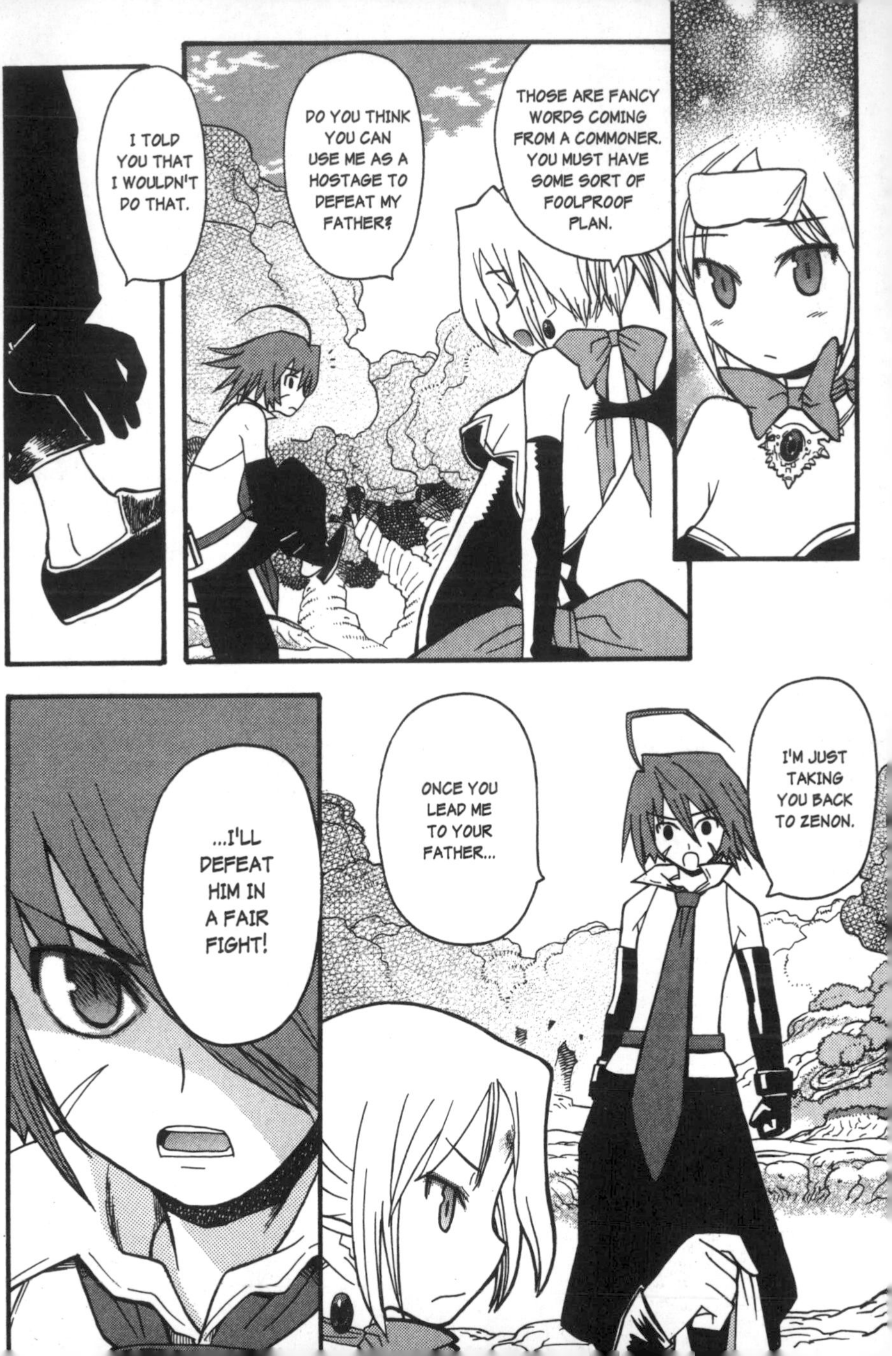
THOSE ARE FANCY WORDS COMING FROM A COMMONER. YOU MUST HAVE SOME SORT OF FOOLPROOF PLAN.
DO YOU THINK YOU CAN USE ME AS A HOSTAGE TO DEFEAT MY FATHER?
I TOLD YOU THAT I WOULDN'T DO THAT.
I'M JUST TAKING YOU BACK TO ZENON.
ONCE YOU LEAD ME TO YOUR FATHER...
...I'LL DEFEAT HIM IN A FAIR FIGHT!

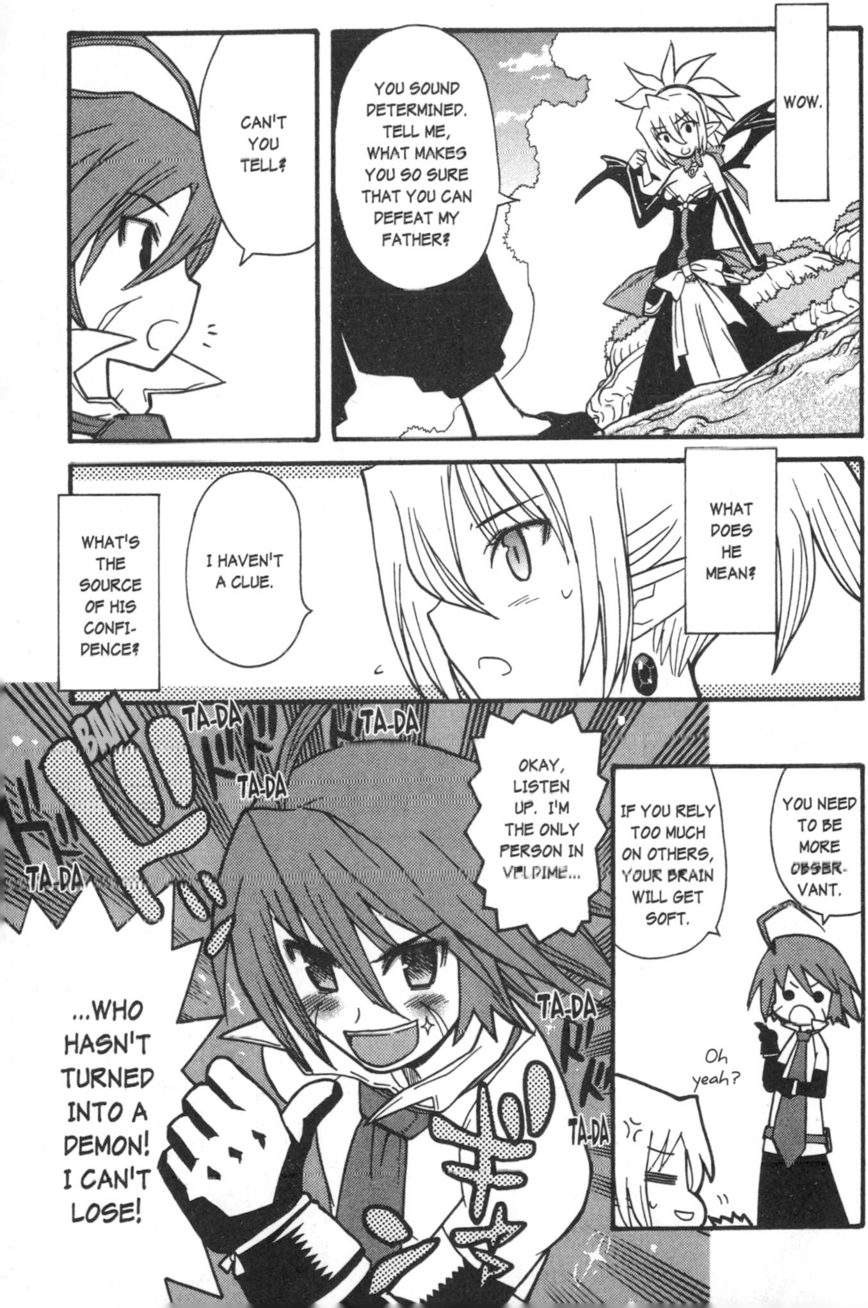

WOW.
YOU SOUND DETERMINED. TELL ME, WHAT MAKES YOU SO SURE THAT YOU CAN DEFEAT MY FATHER?
CAN'T YOU TELL?
WHAT DOES HE MEAN?
I HAVEN'T A CLUE.
WHAT'S THE SOURCE OF HIS CONFI-DENCE?
YOU NEED TO BE MORE OBSER-VANT.
IF YOU RELY TOO MUCH ON OTHERS, YOUR BRAIN WILL GET SOFT.
Oh yeah?
OKAY, LISTEN UP. I'M THE ONLY PERSON IN VELDIME...
TA-DA
BAM
TA-DA
TA-DA
TA-DA
TA-DA
TA-DA
...WHO HASN'T TURNED INTO A DEMON! I CAN'T LOSE!

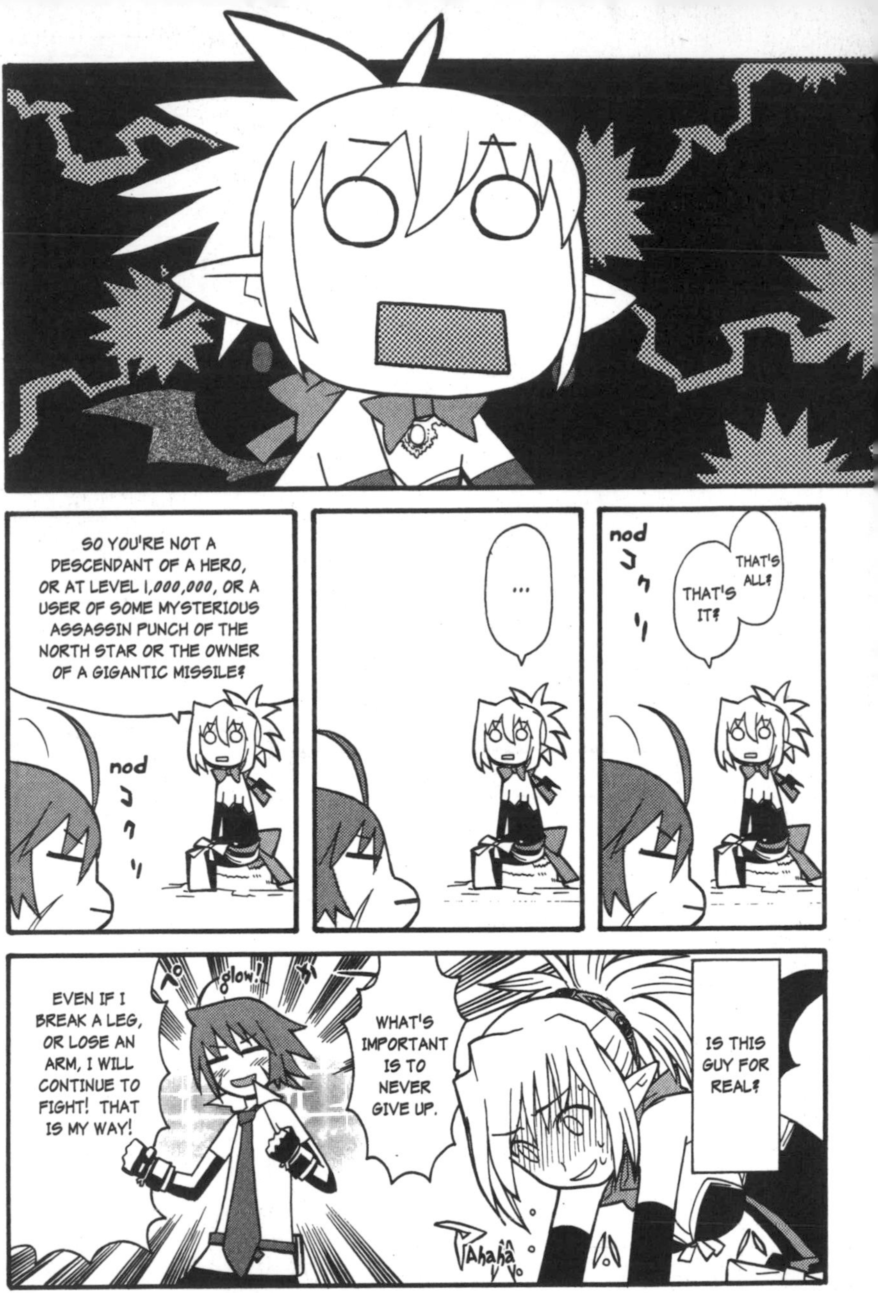
SO YOU'RE NOT A DESCENDANT OF A HERO, OR AT LEVEL 1,000,000, OR A USER OF SOME MYSTERIOUS ASSASSIN PUNCH OF THE NORTH STAR OR THE OWNER OF A GIGANTIC MISSILE?
nod
...
nod
THAT'S IT?
THAT'S ALL?
glow!
EVEN IF I BREAK A LEG, OR LOSE AN ARM, I WILL CONTINUE TO FIGHT! THAT IS MY WAY!
WHAT'S IMPORTANT IS TO NEVER GIVE UP.
Ahaha
IS THIS GUY FOR REAL?

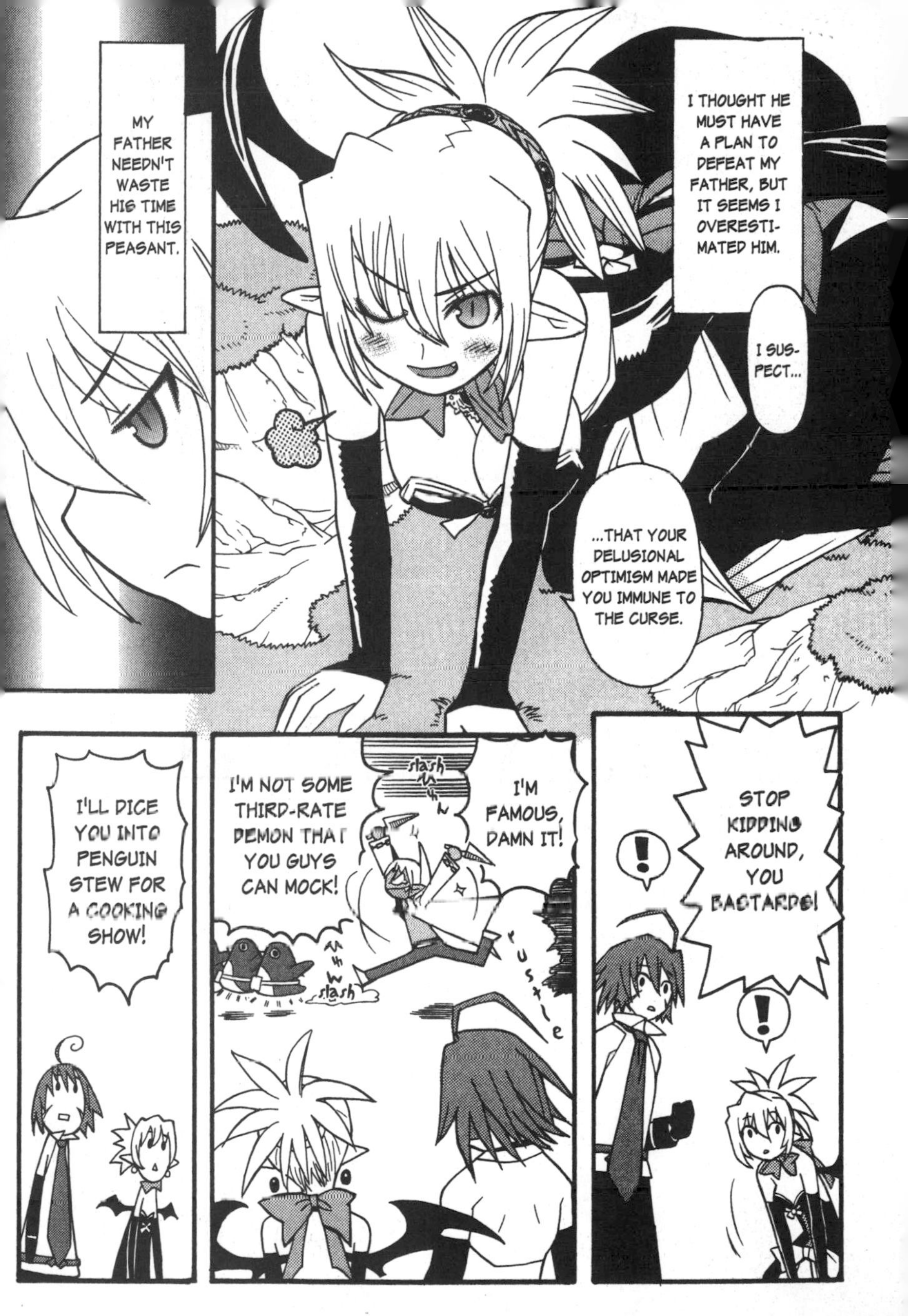
I THOUGHT HE MUST HAVE A PLAN TO DEFEAT MY FATHER, BUT IT SEEMS I OVERESTIMATED HIM.
I SUSPECT...
...THAT YOUR DELUSIONAL OPTIMISM MADE YOU IMMUNE TO THE CURSE.
MY FATHER NEEDN'T WASTE HIS TIME WITH THIS PEASANT.
STOP KIDDING AROUND, YOU BASTARDS!
!
!
I'M FAMOUS, DAMN IT!
I'M NOT SOME THIRD-RATE DEMON THAT YOU GUYS CAN MOCK!
slash
slash
rustle
I'LL DICE YOU INTO PENGUIN STEW FOR A COOKING SHOW!

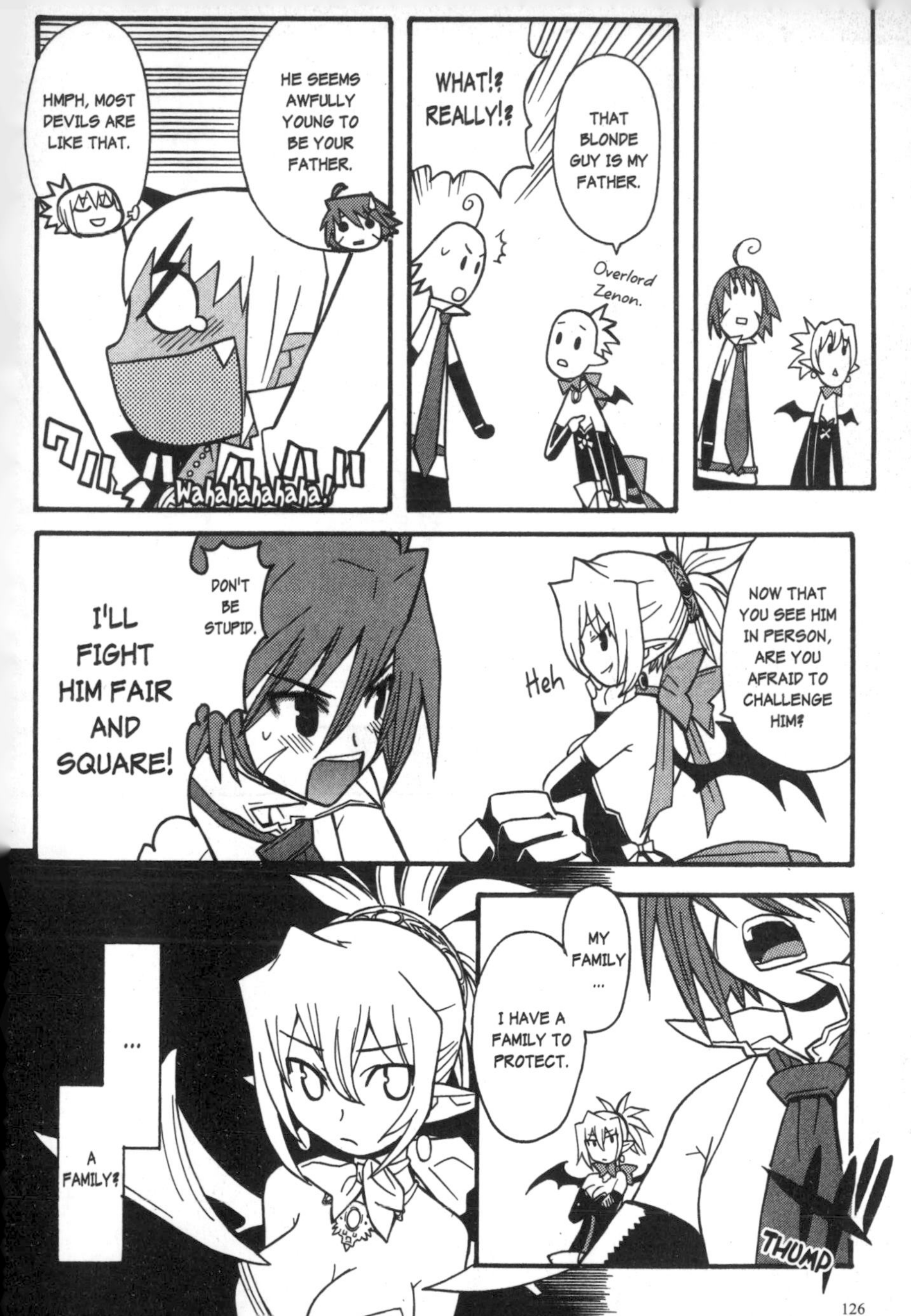
THAT BLONDE GUY IS MY FATHER.
Overlord Zenon.
WHAT!? REALLY!?
HE SEEMS AWFULLY YOUNG TO BE YOUR FATHER.
HMPH, MOST DEVILS ARE LIKE THAT.
Wahahahahaha!
NOW THAT YOU SEE HIM IN PERSON, ARE YOU AFRAID TO CHALLENGE HIM?
Heh
DON'T BE STUPID.
I'LL FIGHT HIM FAIR AND SQUARE!
MY FAMILY ...
I HAVE A FAMILY TO PROTECT.
THUMP
...
A FAMILY?

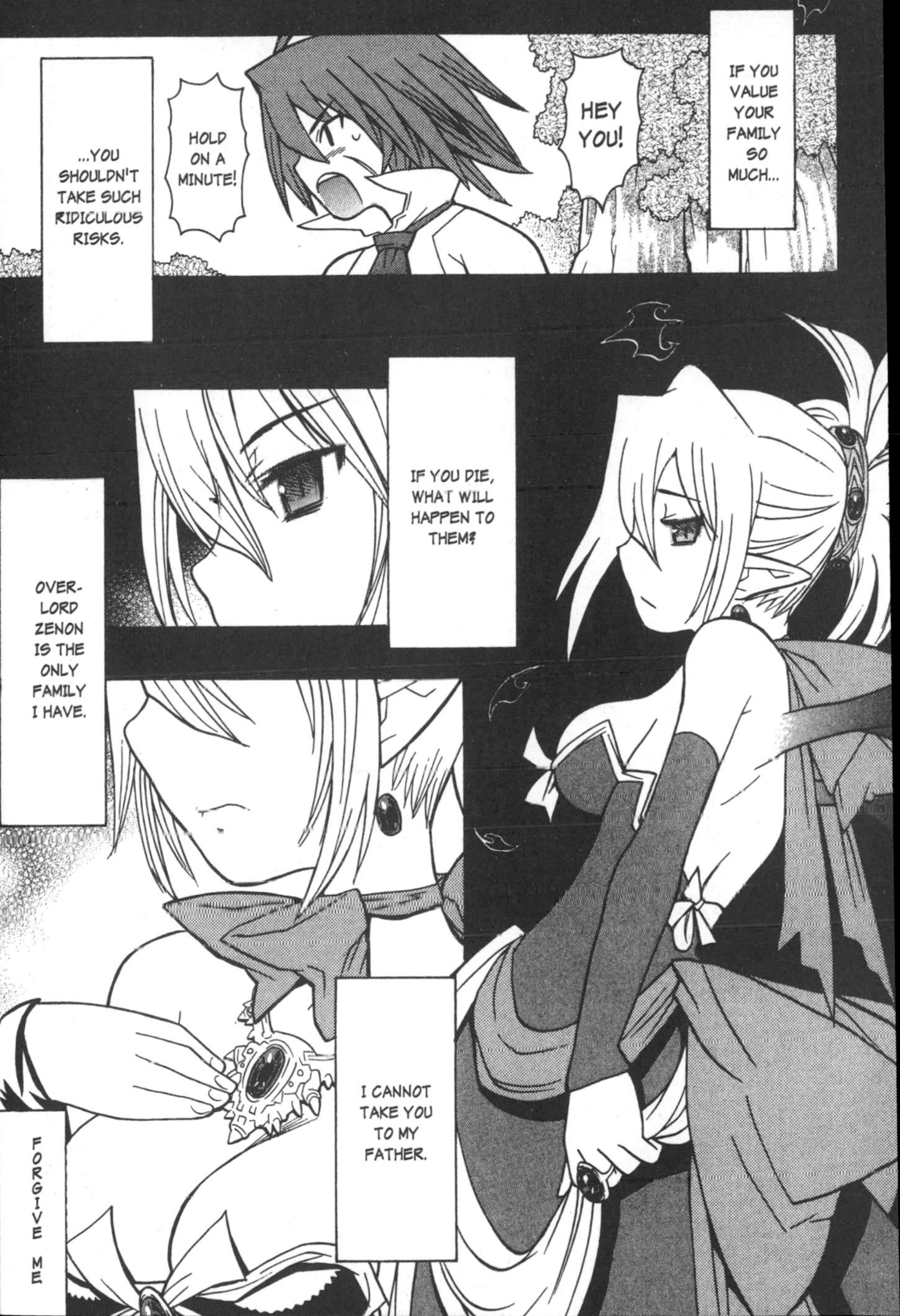
IF YOU VALUE YOUR FAMILY SO MUCH...
HEY YOU!
HOLD ON A MINUTE!
...YOU SHOULDN'T TAKE SUCH RIDICULOUS RISKS.
IF YOU DIE, WHAT WILL HAPPEN TO THEM?
I CANNOT TAKE YOU TO MY FATHER.
OVER-LORD ZENON IS THE ONLY FAMILY I HAVE.
FORGIVE ME

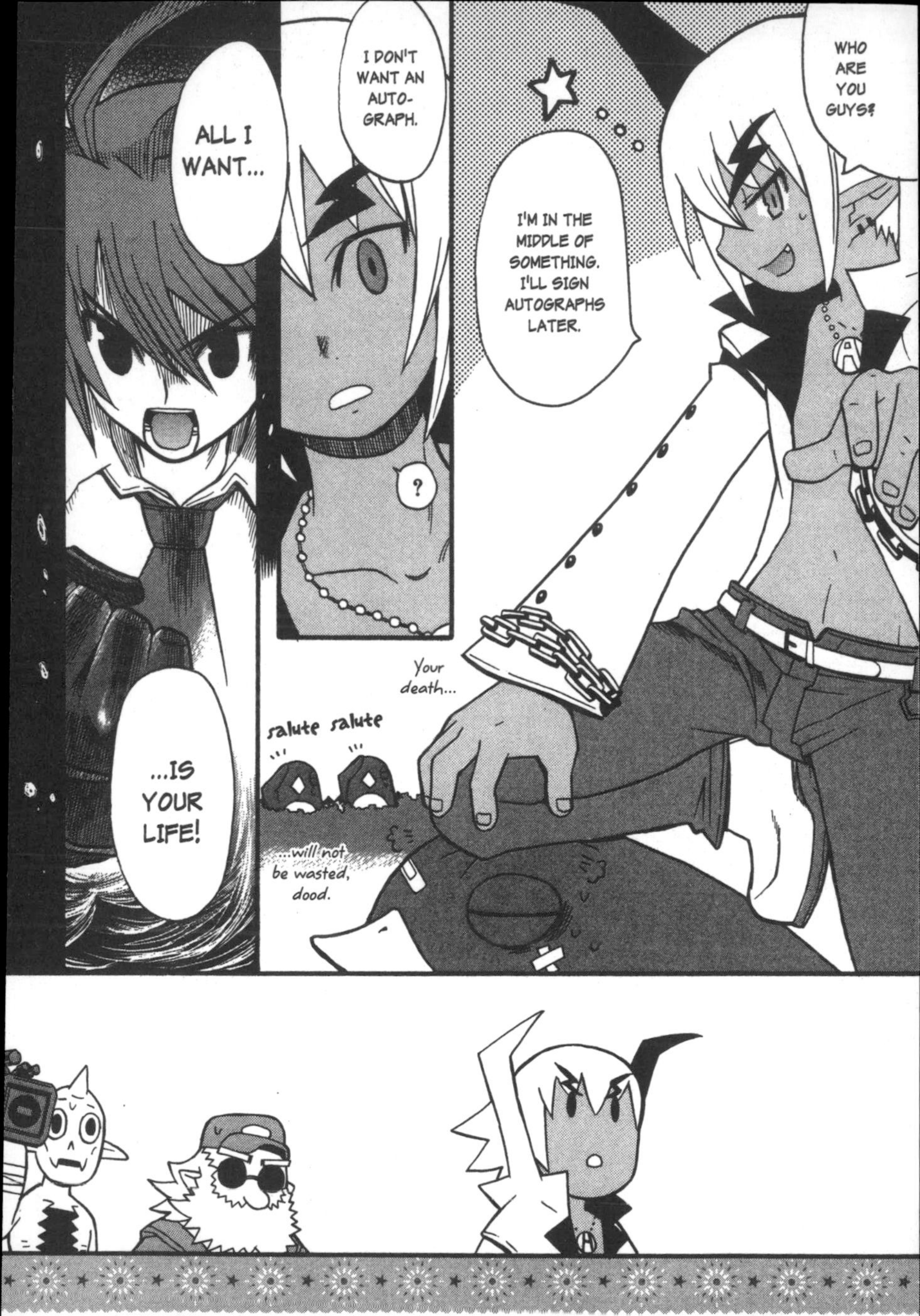
WHO ARE YOU GUYS?
I'M IN THE MIDDLE OF SOMETHING. I'LL SIGN AUTOGRAPHS LATER.
Your death...
salute salute
...will not be wasted, dood.
I DON'T WANT AN AUTOGRAPH.
?
ALL I WANT...
...IS YOUR LIFE!

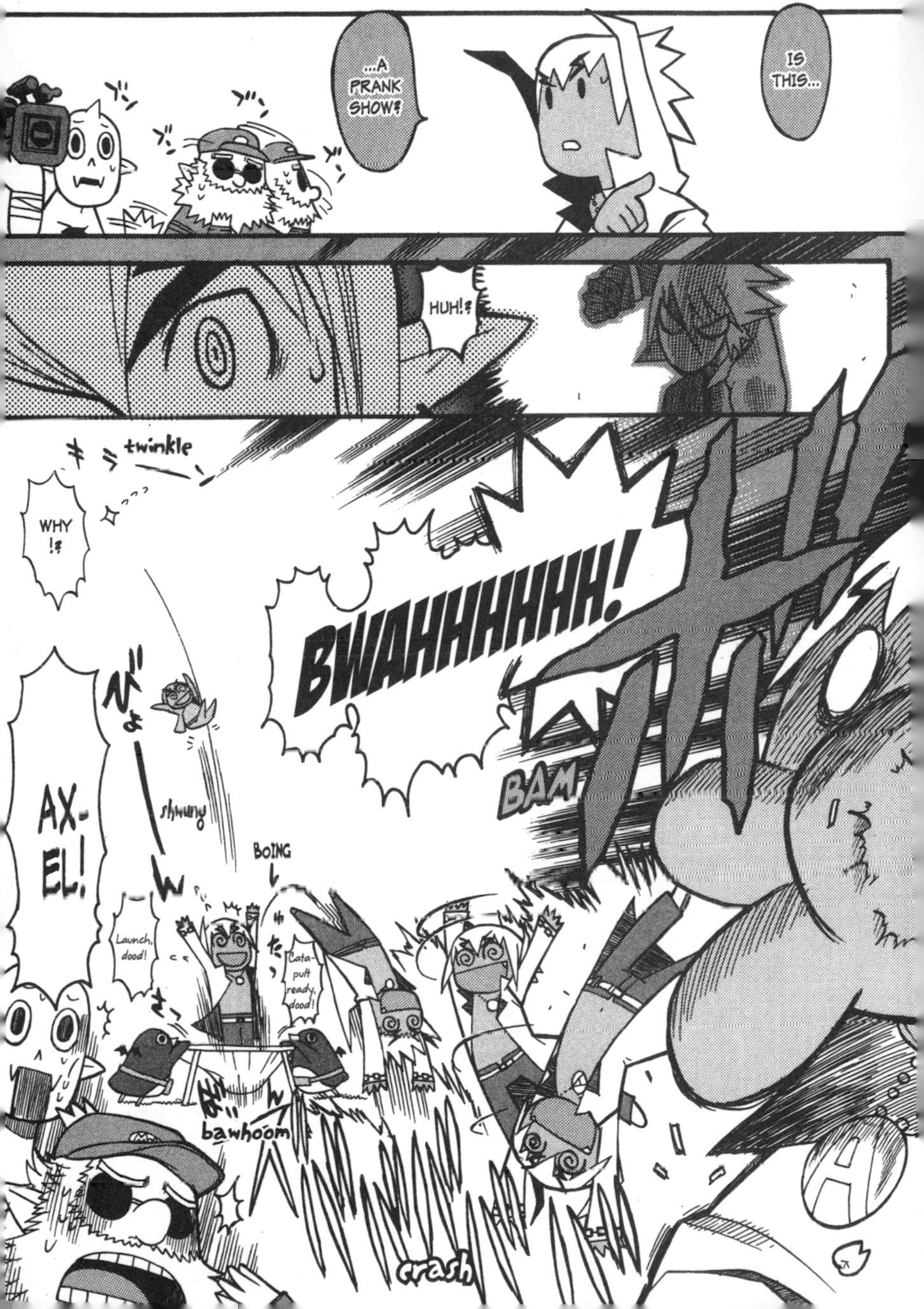
IS THIS...
...A PRANK SHOW!?
HUH!?
BWAHHHHHHH!
BAM
twinkle
WHY!?
AX-EL!
shwung
BOING
Cata-pult ready, dood!
Launch, dood!
bawhoom
crash

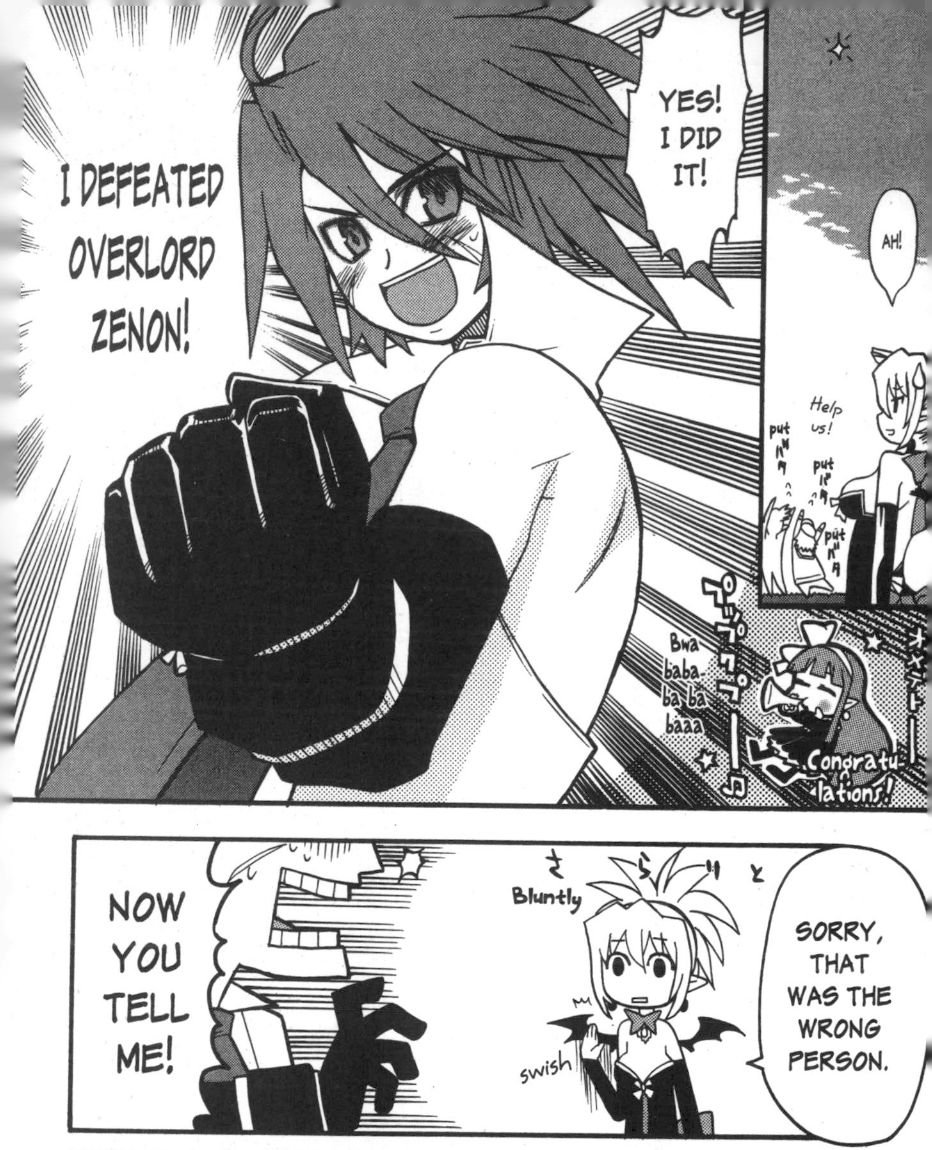
AH!
Help us!
put
put
put
YES! I DID IT!
I DEFEATED OVERLORD ZENON!
Bwa baba-ba ba baaa
Congratu-lations!
SORRY, THAT WAS THE WRONG PERSON.
Bluntly
swish
NOW YOU TELL ME!

ADELL THE CRIMINAL

1ST STRIKE

EPISODE PREVIEW

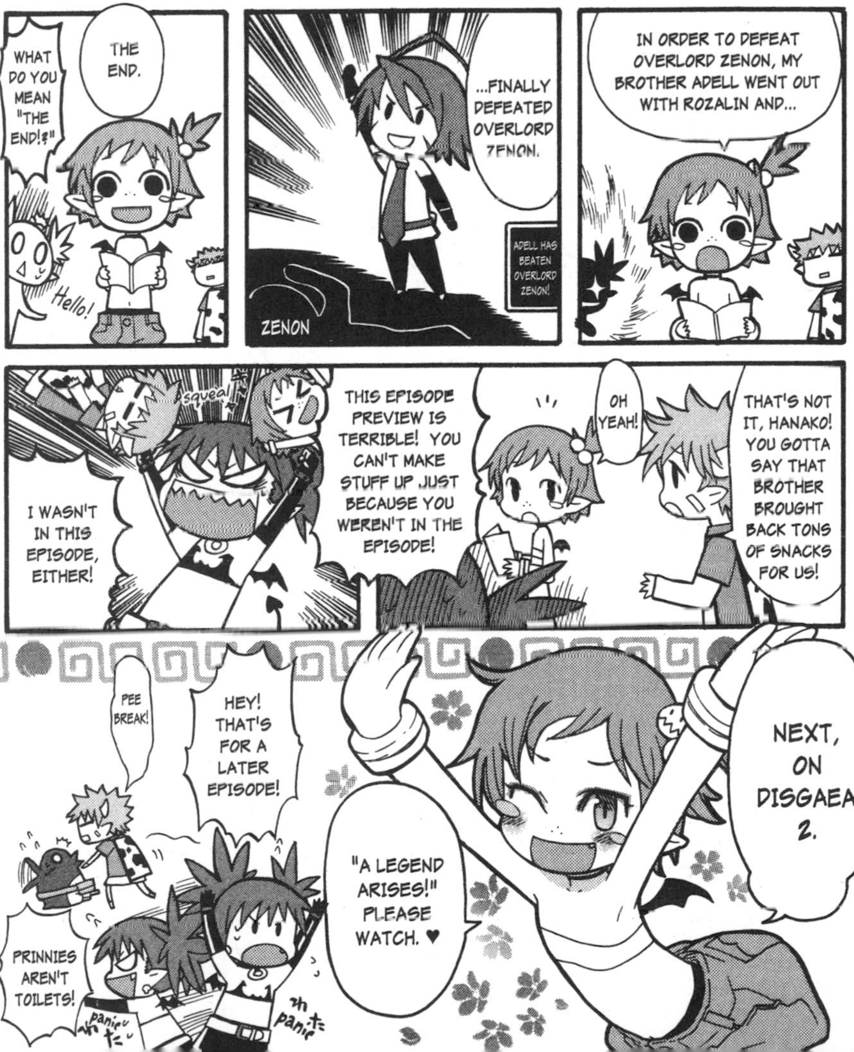

IN ORDER TO DEFEAT OVERLORD ZENON, MY BROTHER ADELL WENT OUT WITH ROZALIN AND...
...FINALLY DEFEATED OVERLORD ZENON.
ADELL HAS BEATEN OVERLORD ZENON!
ZENON
THE END.
WHAT DO YOU MEAN "THE END!?"
Hello!
THAT'S NOT IT, HANAKO! YOU GOTTA SAY THAT BROTHER BROUGHT BACK TONS OF SNACKS FOR US!
OH YEAH!
THIS EPISODE PREVIEW IS TERRIBLE! YOU CAN'T MAKE STUFF UP JUST BECAUSE YOU WEREN'T IN THE EPISODE!
squeal
I WASN'T IN THIS EPISODE, EITHER!
NEXT, ON DISGAEA 2.
"A LEGEND ARISES!" PLEASE WATCH. ♥
HEY! THAT'S FOR A LATER EPISODE!
PEE BREAK!
PRINNIES AREN'T TOILETS!
panic
panic

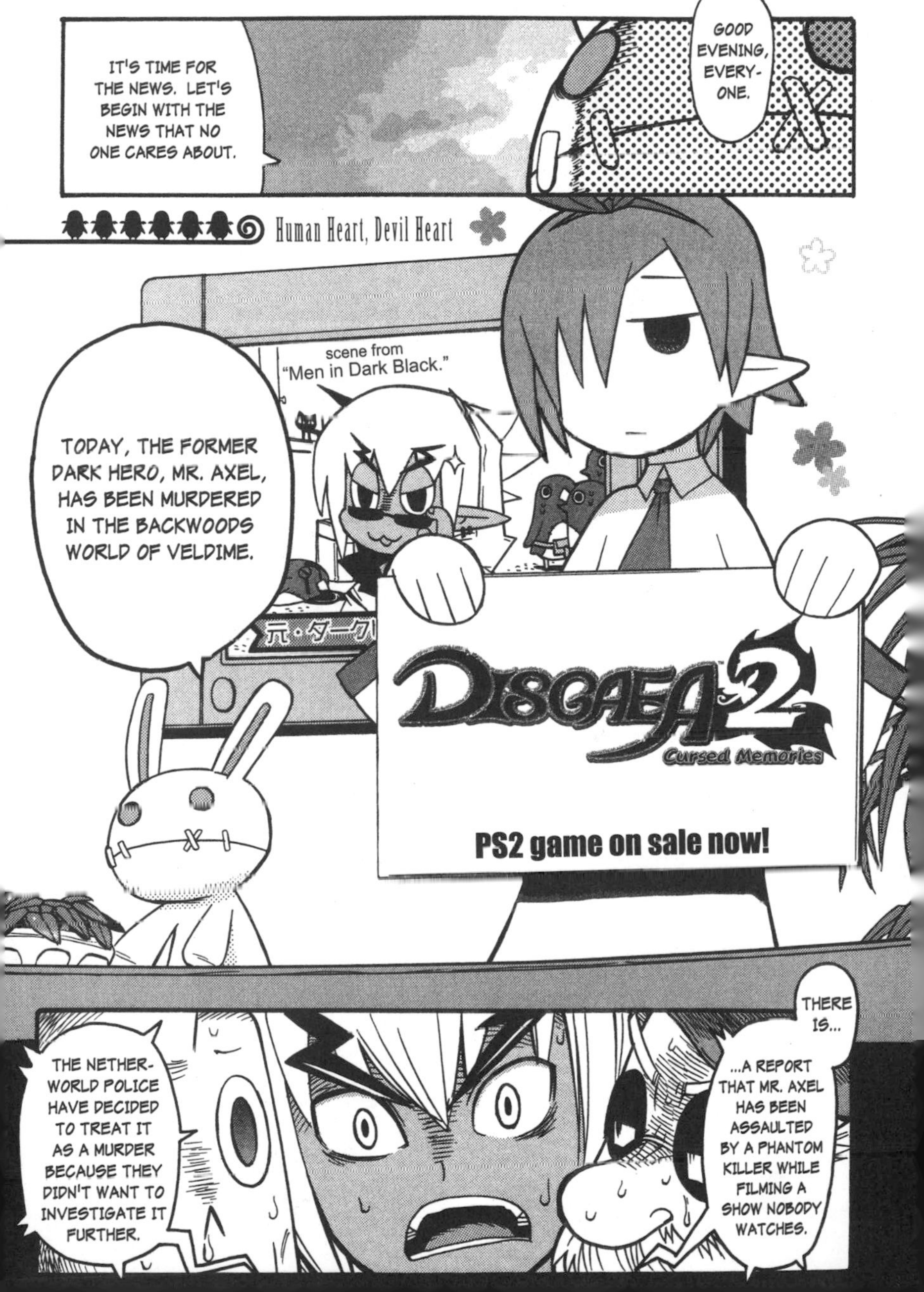
GOOD EVENING, EVERY-ONE.
IT'S TIME FOR THE NEWS. LET'S BEGIN WITH THE NEWS THAT NO ONE CARES ABOUT.
Human Heart, Devil Heart
scene from "Men in Dark Black."
TODAY, THE FORMER DARK HERO, MR. AXEL, HAS BEEN MURDERED IN THE BACKWOODS WORLD OF VELDIME.
元・ダーク
DISGAEA 2
Cursed Memories
PS2 game on sale now!
THERE IS...
...A REPORT THAT MR. AXEL HAS BEEN ASSAULTED BY A PHANTOM KILLER WHILE FILMING A SHOW NOBODY WATCHES.
THE NETHER-WORLD POLICE HAVE DECIDED TO TREAT IT AS A MURDER BECAUSE THEY DIDN'T WANT TO INVESTIGATE IT FURTHER.

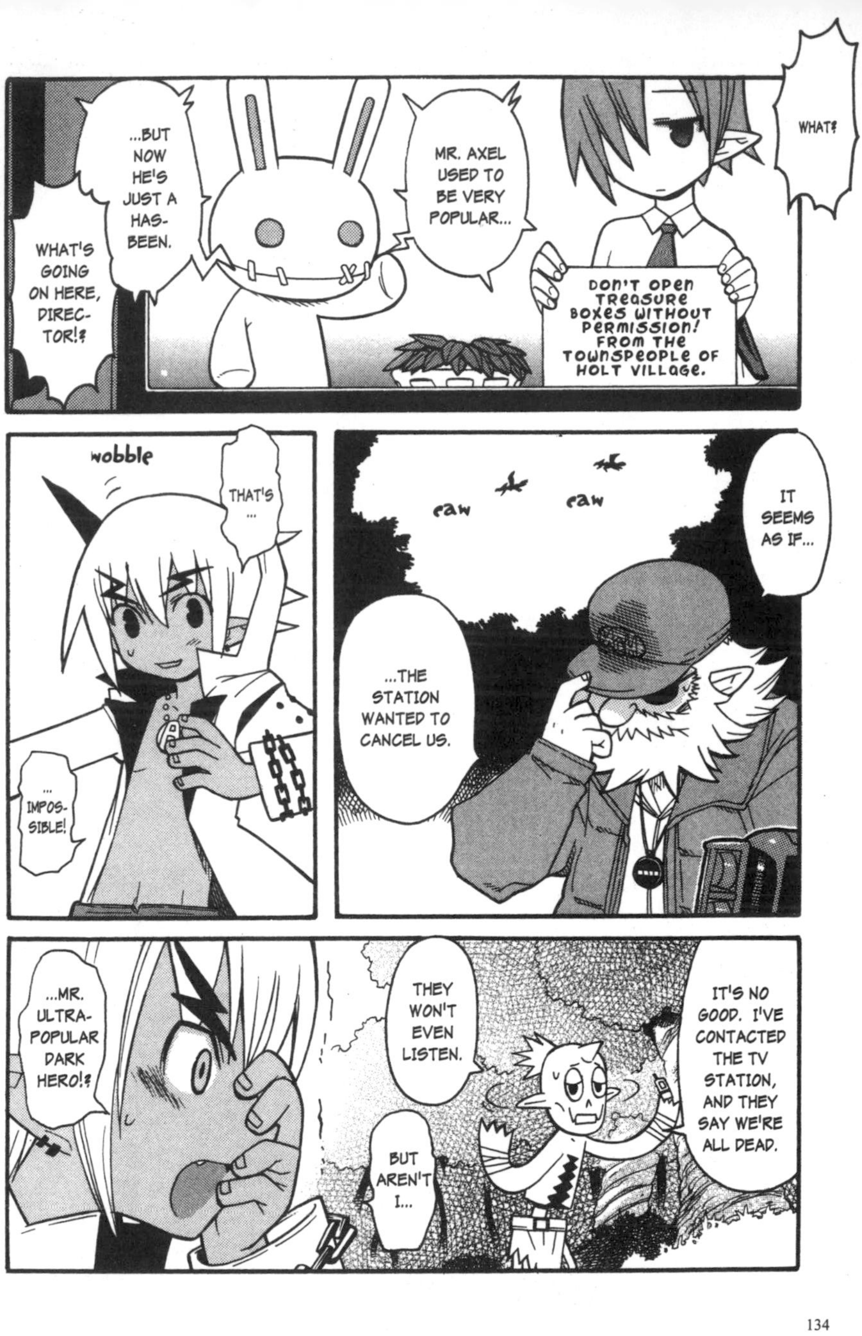
WHAT?
MR. AXEL USED TO BE VERY POPULAR...
...BUT NOW HE'S JUST A HAS-BEEN.
WHAT'S GOING ON HERE, DIRECTOR!?
DON'T OPEN TREASURE BOXES WITHOUT PERMISSION! FROM THE TOWNSPEOPLE OF HOLT VILLAGE.
caw
caw
IT SEEMS AS IF...
...THE STATION WANTED TO CANCEL US.
wobble
THAT'S ...
... IMPOSSIBLE!
IT'S NO GOOD. I'VE CONTACTED THE TV STATION, AND THEY SAY WE'RE ALL DEAD.
THEY WON'T EVEN LISTEN.
BUT AREN'T I...
...MR. ULTRA-POPULAR DARK HERO!?

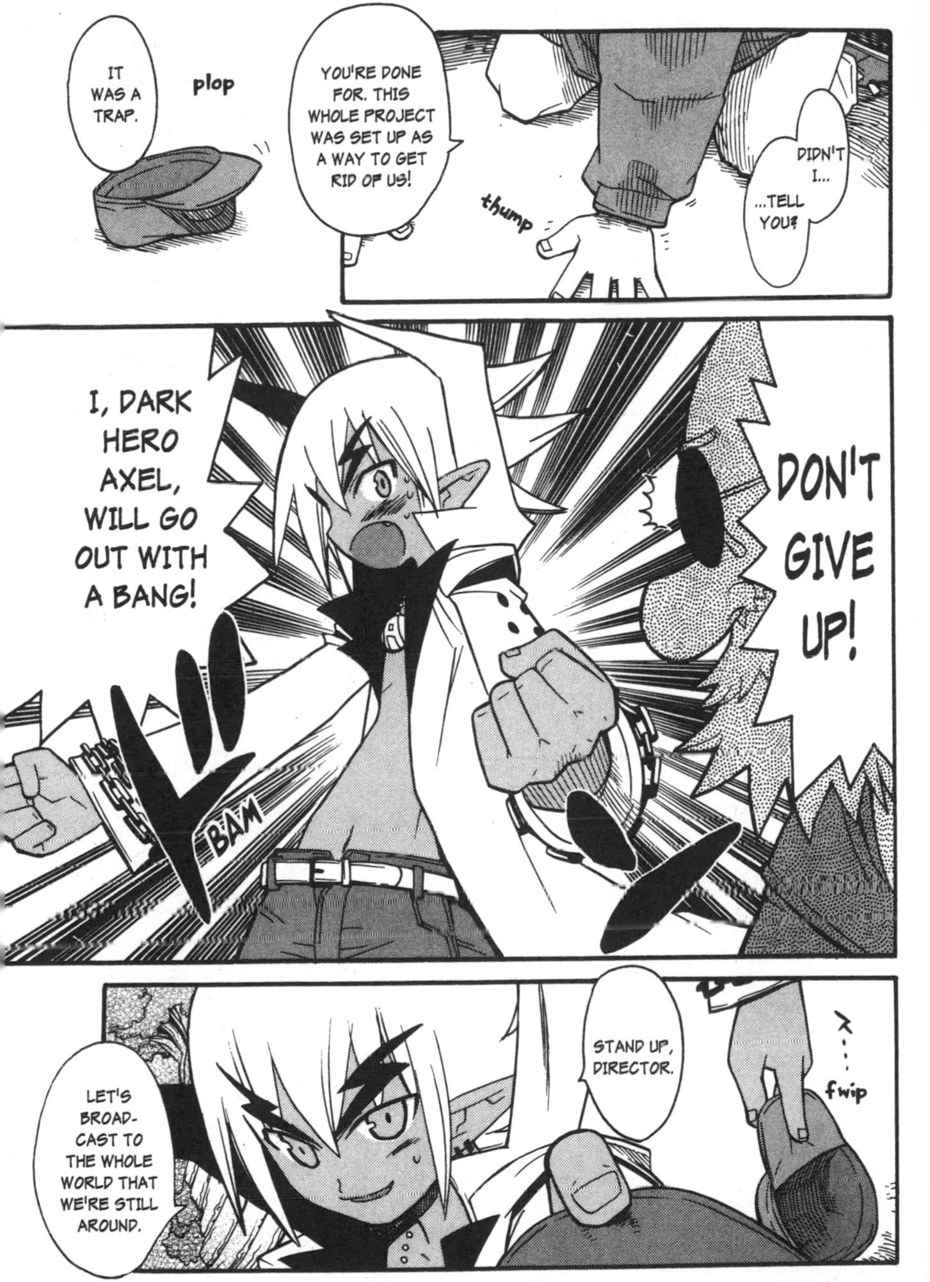
DIDN'T I...
...TELL YOU?
thump
YOU'RE DONE FOR. THIS WHOLE PROJECT WAS SET UP AS A WAY TO GET RID OF US!
plop
IT WAS A TRAP.
DON'T GIVE UP!
I, DARK HERO AXEL, WILL GO OUT WITH A BANG!
BAM
fwip
STAND UP, DIRECTOR.
LET'S BROAD-CAST TO THE WHOLE WORLD THAT WE'RE STILL AROUND.

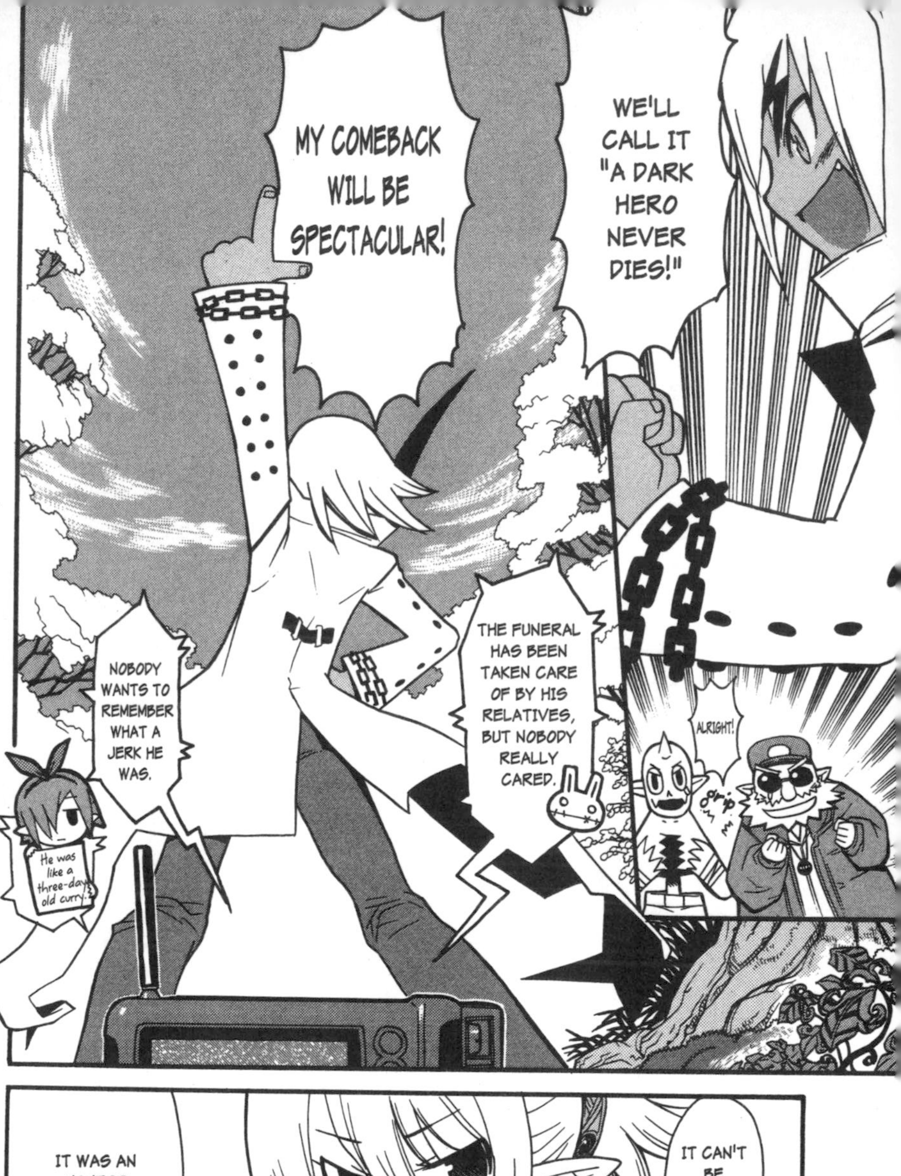
WE'LL CALL IT "A DARK HERO NEVER DIES!"
MY COMEBACK WILL BE SPECTACULAR!
ALRIGHT!
THE FUNERAL HAS BEEN TAKEN CARE OF BY HIS RELATIVES, BUT NOBODY REALLY CARED.
NOBODY WANTS TO REMEMBER WHAT A JERK HE WAS.
He was like a three-day old curry.
IT CAN'T BE HELPED NOW, CAN IT?
IT WAS AN HONEST MISTAKE.

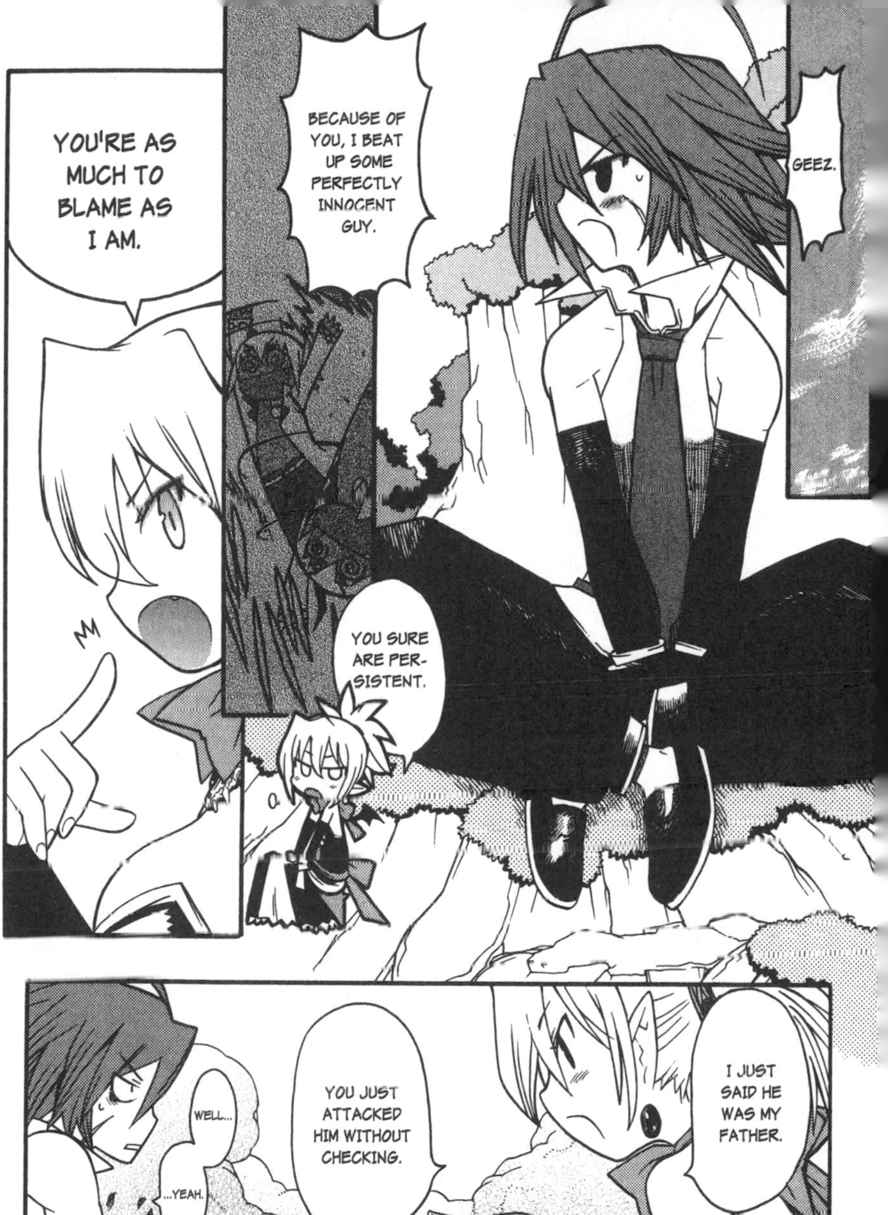
GEEZ.
BECAUSE OF YOU, I BEAT UP SOME PERFECTLY INNOCENT GUY.
YOU SURE ARE PER-SISTENT.
YOU'RE AS MUCH TO BLAME AS I AM.
M
I JUST SAID HE WAS MY FATHER.
YOU JUST ATTACKED HIM WITHOUT CHECKING.
WELL...
...YEAH.

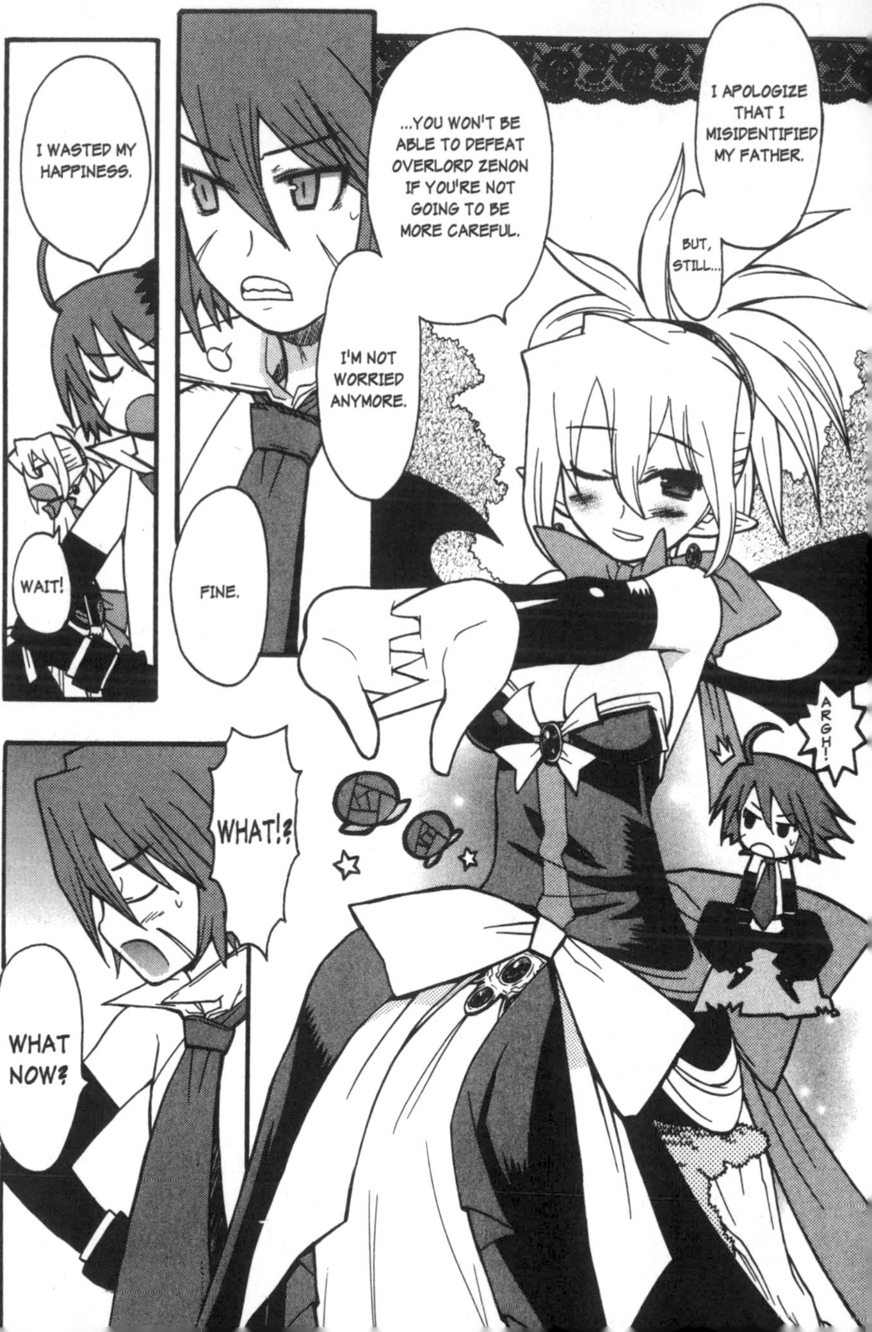
I APOLOGIZE THAT I MISIDENTIFIED MY FATHER.
BUT, STILL...
...YOU WON'T BE ABLE TO DEFEAT OVERLORD ZENON IF YOU'RE NOT GOING TO BE MORE CAREFUL.
I'M NOT WORRIED ANYMORE.
FINE.
I WASTED MY HAPPINESS.
WAIT!
ARGH!
WHAT!?
WHAT NOW?

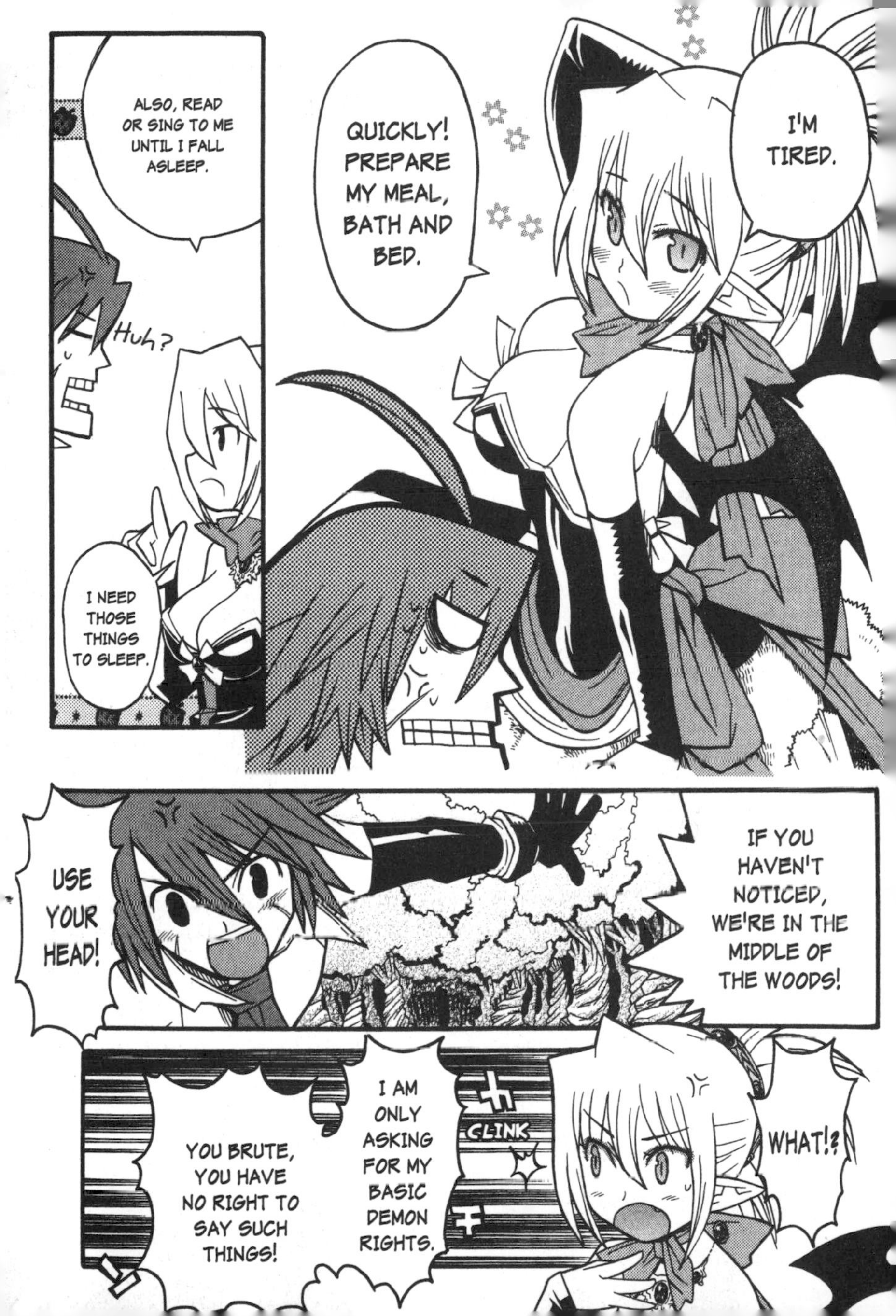
I'M TIRED.
QUICKLY! PREPARE MY MEAL, BATH AND BED.
ALSO, READ OR SING TO ME UNTIL I FALL ASLEEP.
Huh?
I NEED THOSE THINGS TO SLEEP.
IF YOU HAVEN'T NOTICED, WE'RE IN THE MIDDLE OF THE WOODS!
USE YOUR HEAD!
WHAT!?
CLINK
I AM ONLY ASKING FOR MY BASIC DEMON RIGHTS.
YOU BRUTE, YOU HAVE NO RIGHT TO SAY SUCH THINGS!

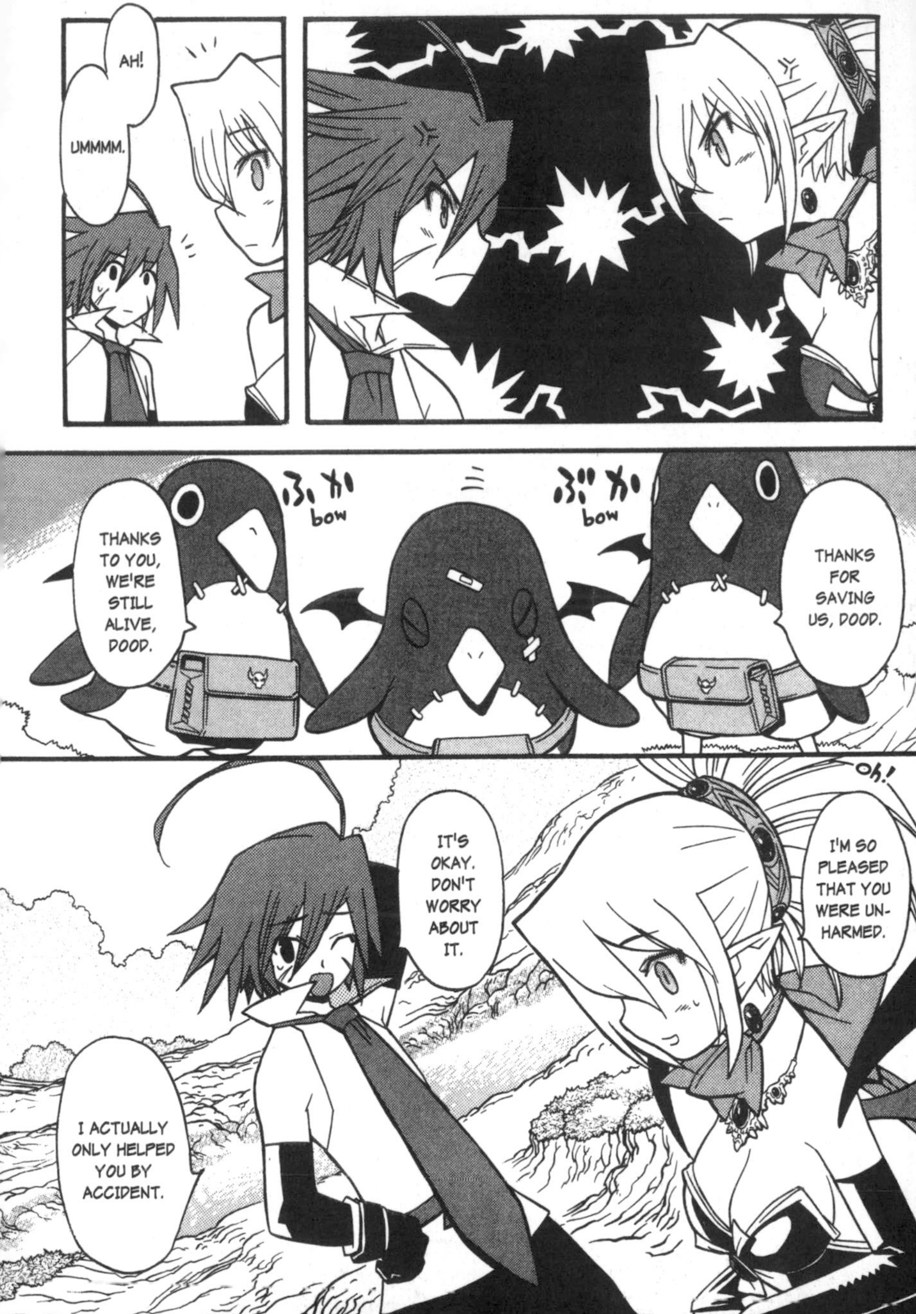
AH!
UMMMM.
THANKS FOR SAVING US, DOOD.
bow
bow
THANKS TO YOU, WE'RE STILL ALIVE, DOOD.
Oh!
I'M SO PLEASED THAT YOU WERE UN-HARMED.
IT'S OKAY. DON'T WORRY ABOUT IT.
I ACTUALLY ONLY HELPED YOU BY ACCIDENT.

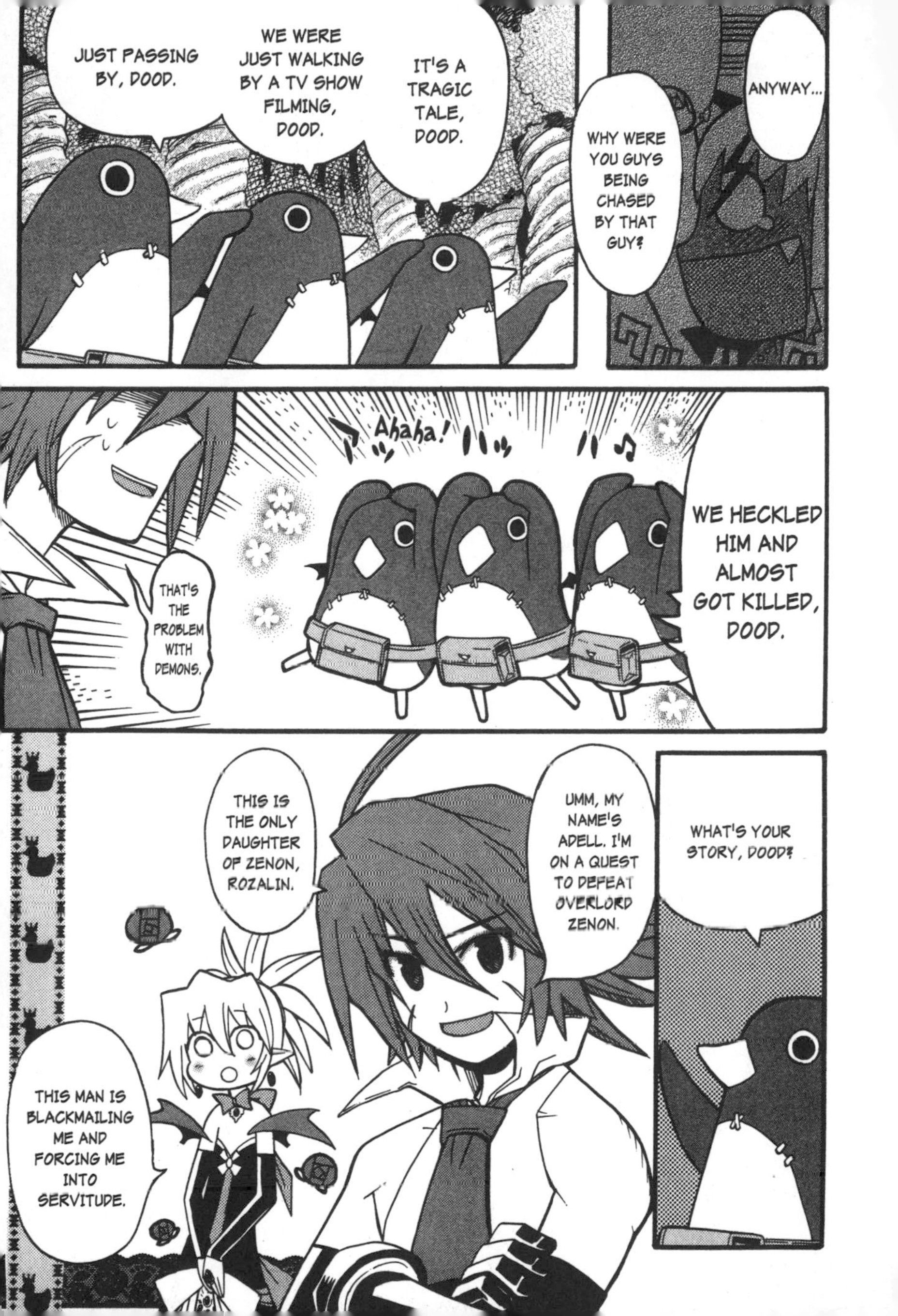
ANYWAY...
WHY WERE YOU GUYS BEING CHASED BY THAT GUY?
IT'S A TRAGIC TALE, DOOD.
WE WERE JUST WALKING BY A TV SHOW FILMING, DOOD.
JUST PASSING BY, DOOD.
WE HECKLED HIM AND ALMOST GOT KILLED, DOOD.
Ahaha!
THAT'S THE PROBLEM WITH DEMONS.
WHAT'S YOUR STORY, DOOD?
UMM, MY NAME'S ADELL. I'M ON A QUEST TO DEFEAT OVERLORD ZENON.
THIS IS THE ONLY DAUGHTER OF ZENON, ROZALIN.
THIS MAN IS BLACKMAILING ME AND FORCING ME INTO SERVITUDE.

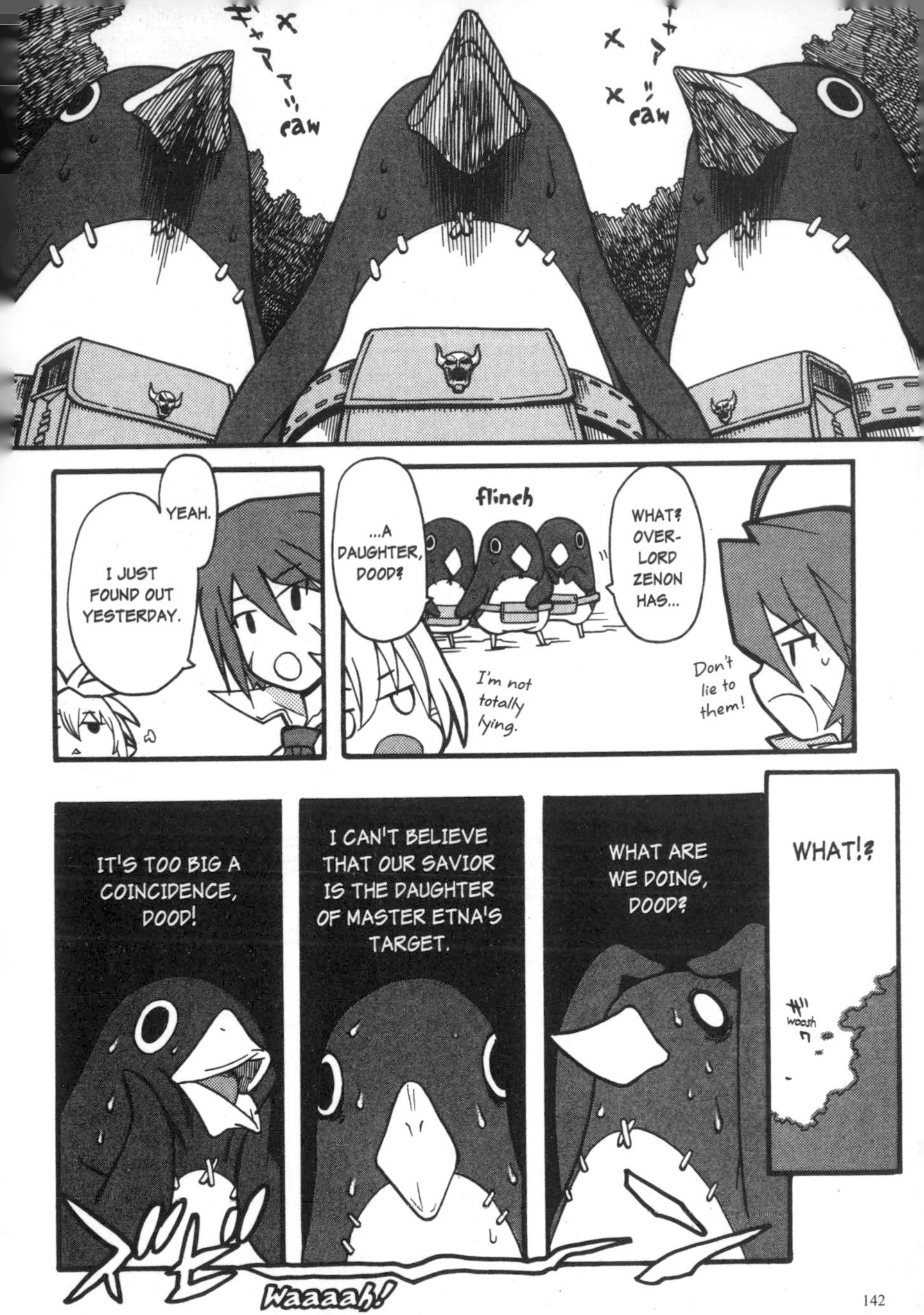
caw
caw
WHAT? OVER-LORD ZENON HAS...
Don't lie to them!
flinch
...A DAUGHTER, DOOD?
I'm not totally lying.
YEAH.
I JUST FOUND OUT YESTERDAY.
WHAT!?
woosh
WHAT ARE WE DOING, DOOD?
I CAN'T BELIEVE THAT OUR SAVIOR IS THE DAUGHTER OF MASTER ETNA'S TARGET.
IT'S TOO BIG A COINCIDENCE, DOOD!
Waaaah!

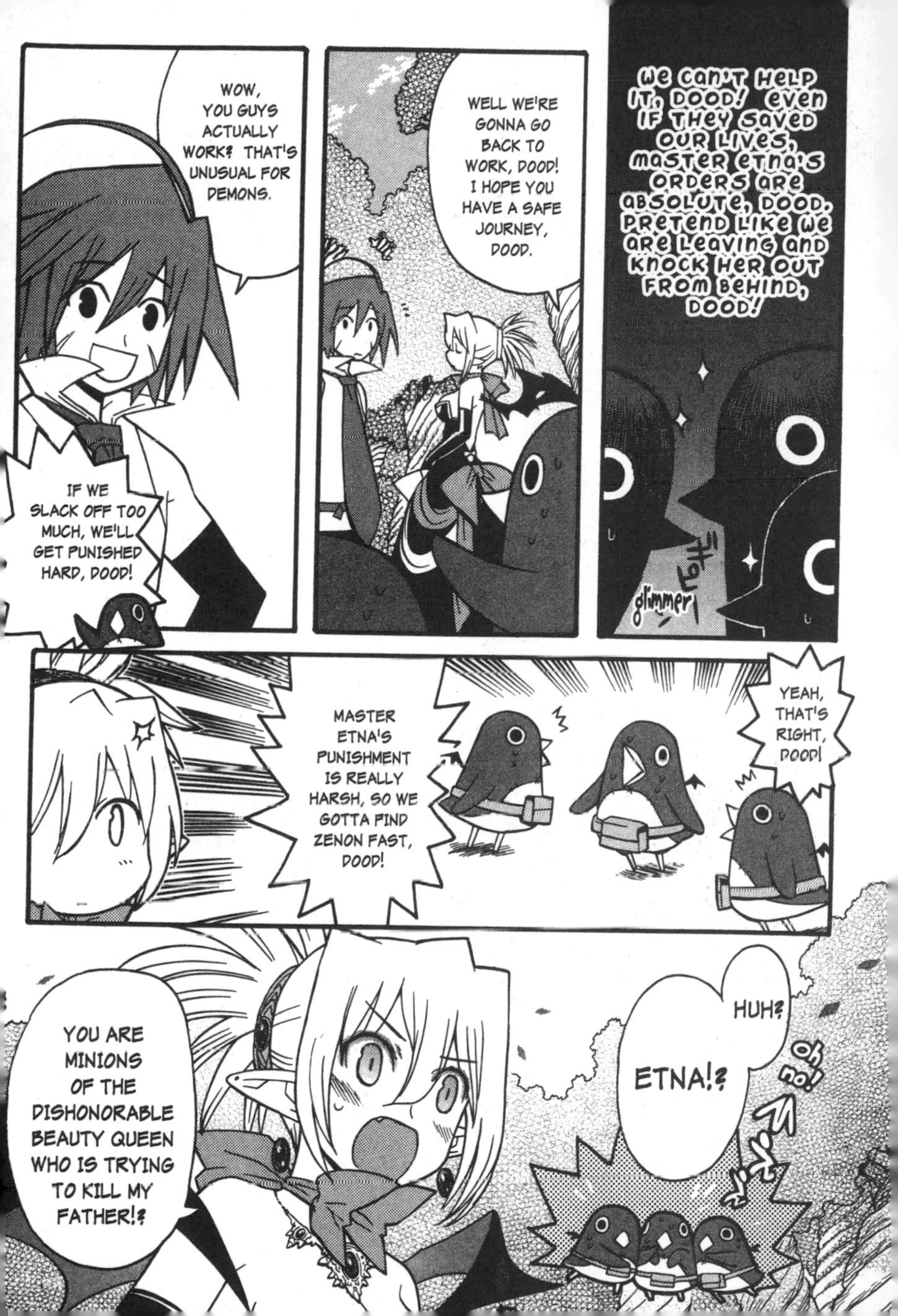
WE CAN'T HELP IT, DOOD! EVEN IF THEY SAVED OUR LIVES, MASTER ETNA'S ORDERS ARE ABSOLUTE, DOOD. PRETEND LIKE WE ARE LEAVING AND KNOCK HER OUT FROM BEHIND, DOOD!
glimmer
WELL WE'RE GONNA GO BACK TO WORK, DOOD! I HOPE YOU HAVE A SAFE JOURNEY, DOOD.
WOW, YOU GUYS ACTUALLY WORK? THAT'S UNUSUAL FOR DEMONS.
IF WE SLACK OFF TOO MUCH, WE'LL GET PUNISHED HARD, DOOD!
YEAH, THAT'S RIGHT, DOOD!
MASTER ETNA'S PUNISHMENT IS REALLY HARSH, SO WE GOTTA FIND ZENON FAST, DOOD!
HUH?
ETNA!?
oh no!
YOU ARE MINIONS OF THE DISHONORABLE BEAUTY QUEEN WHO IS TRYING TO KILL MY FATHER!?

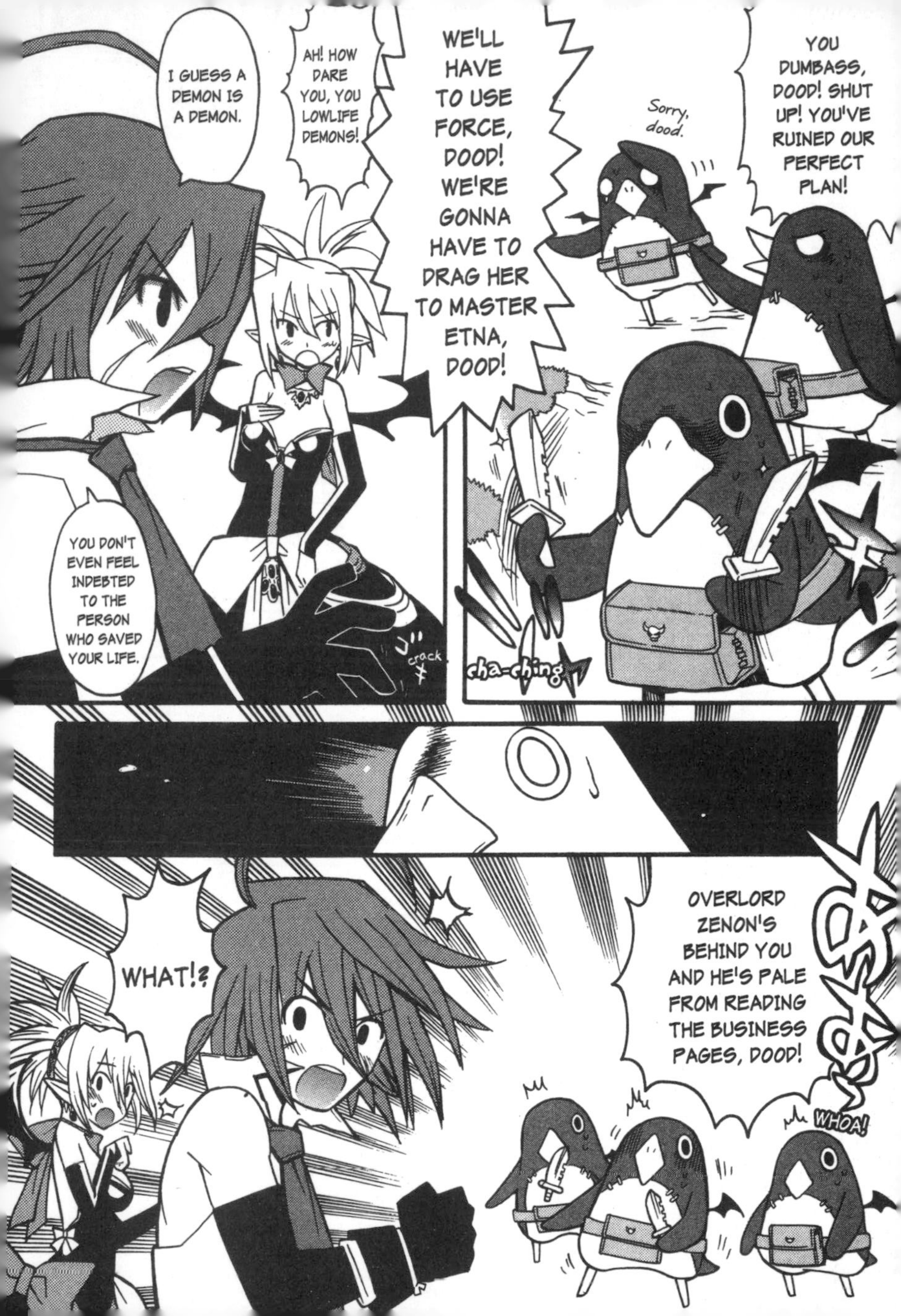
YOU DUMBASS, DOOD! SHUT UP! YOU'VE RUINED OUR PERFECT PLAN!
Sorry, dood.
WE'LL HAVE TO USE FORCE, DOOD! WE'RE GONNA HAVE TO DRAG HER TO MASTER ETNA, DOOD!
cha-ching
AH! HOW DARE YOU, YOU LOWLIFE DEMONS!
I GUESS A DEMON IS A DEMON.
YOU DON'T EVEN FEEL INDEBTED TO THE PERSON WHO SAVED YOUR LIFE.
crack
OVERLORD ZENON'S BEHIND YOU AND HE'S PALE FROM READING THE BUSINESS PAGES, DOOD!
WHOA!
WHAT!?

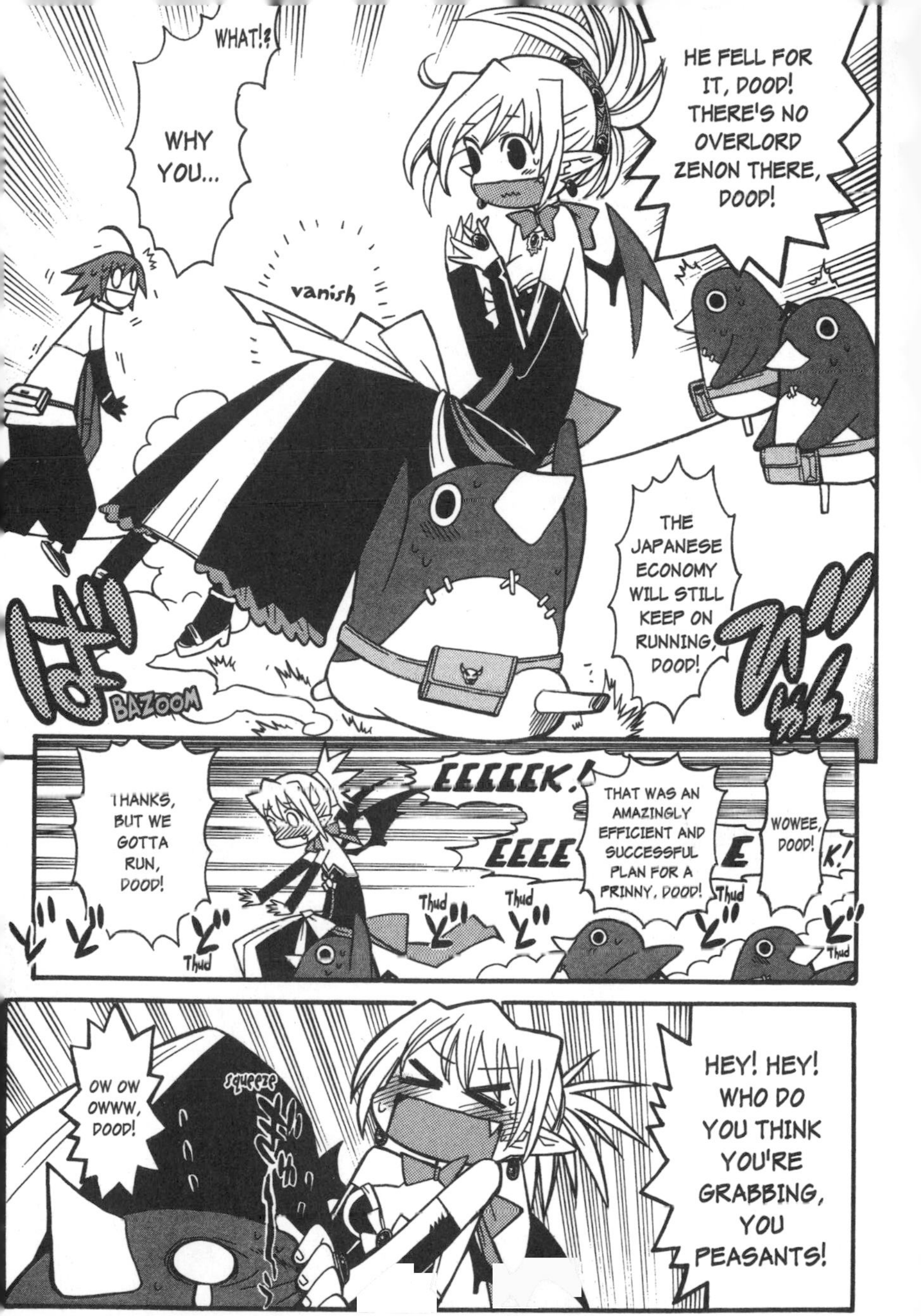
HE FELL FOR IT, DOOD! THERE'S NO OVERLORD ZENON THERE, DOOD!
WHAT!?
WHY YOU...
vanish
THE JAPANESE ECONOMY WILL STILL KEEP ON RUNNING, DOOD!
BAZOOM
WOWEE, DOOD!
THAT WAS AN AMAZINGLY EFFICIENT AND SUCCESSFUL PLAN FOR A PRINNY, DOOD!
EEEEEK!
EEEE E K!
THANKS, BUT WE GOTTA RUN, DOOD!
Thud
Thud
Thud
Thud
Thud
HEY! HEY! WHO DO YOU THINK YOU'RE GRABBING, YOU PEASANTS!
squeeze
OW OW OWWW, DOOD!

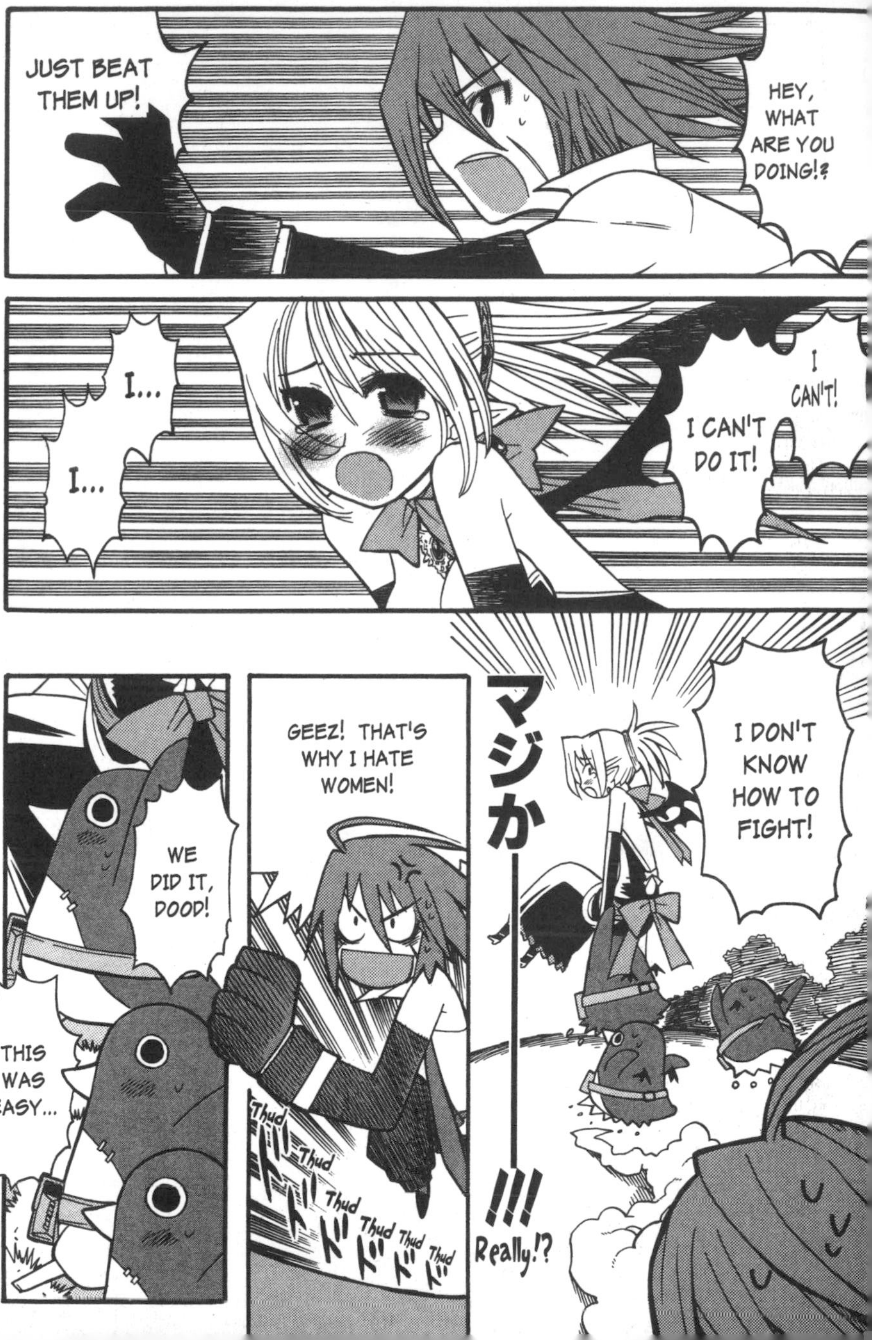
HEY, WHAT ARE YOU DOING!?
JUST BEAT THEM UP!
I CAN'T!
I CAN'T DO IT!
I...
I...
I DON'T KNOW HOW TO FIGHT!
マジか!!!
Really!?
GEEZ! THAT'S WHY I HATE WOMEN!
Thud Thud Thud Thud Thud Thud
WE DID IT, DOOD!
THIS WAS EASY...

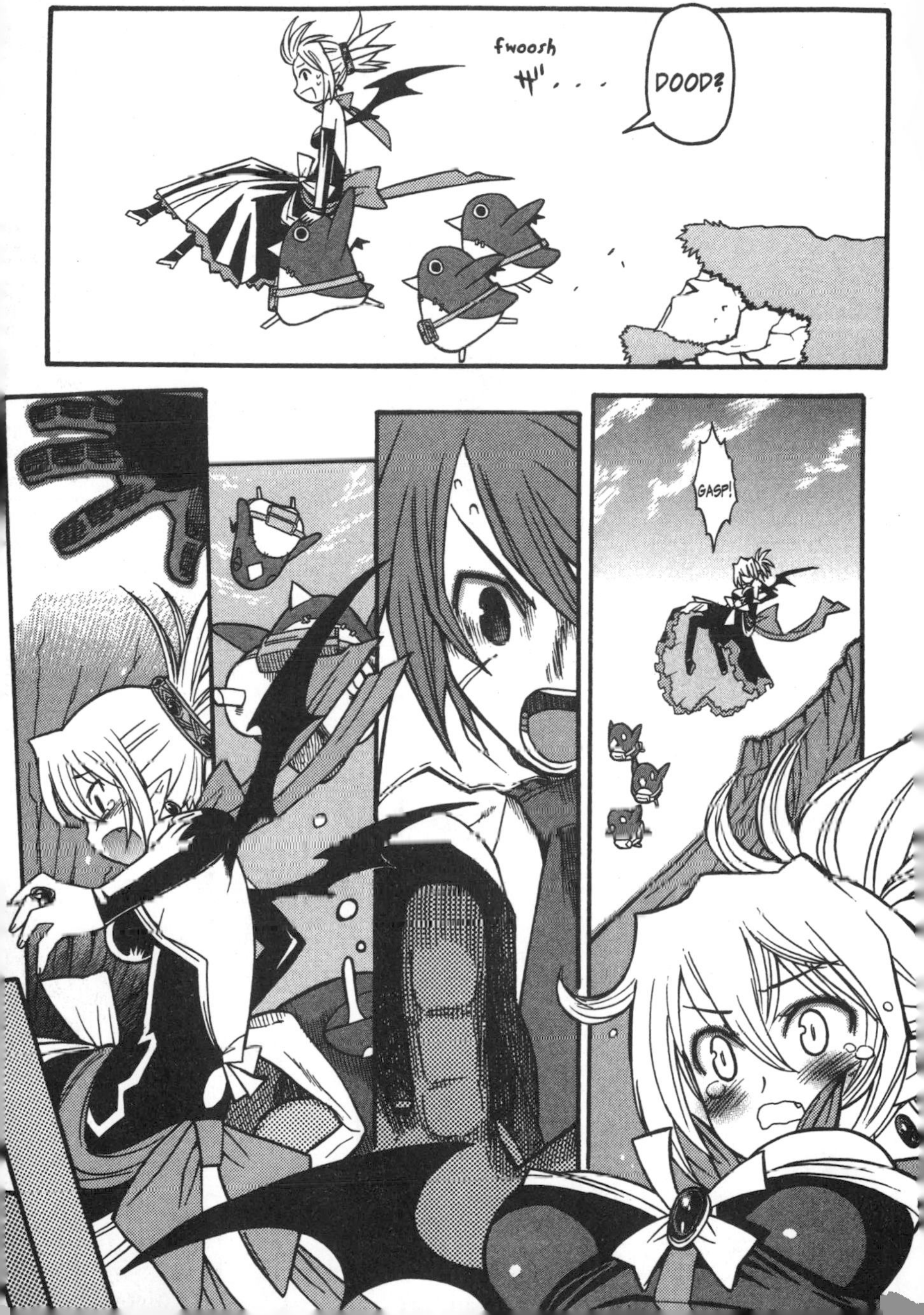
DOOD?
fwoosh
GASP!

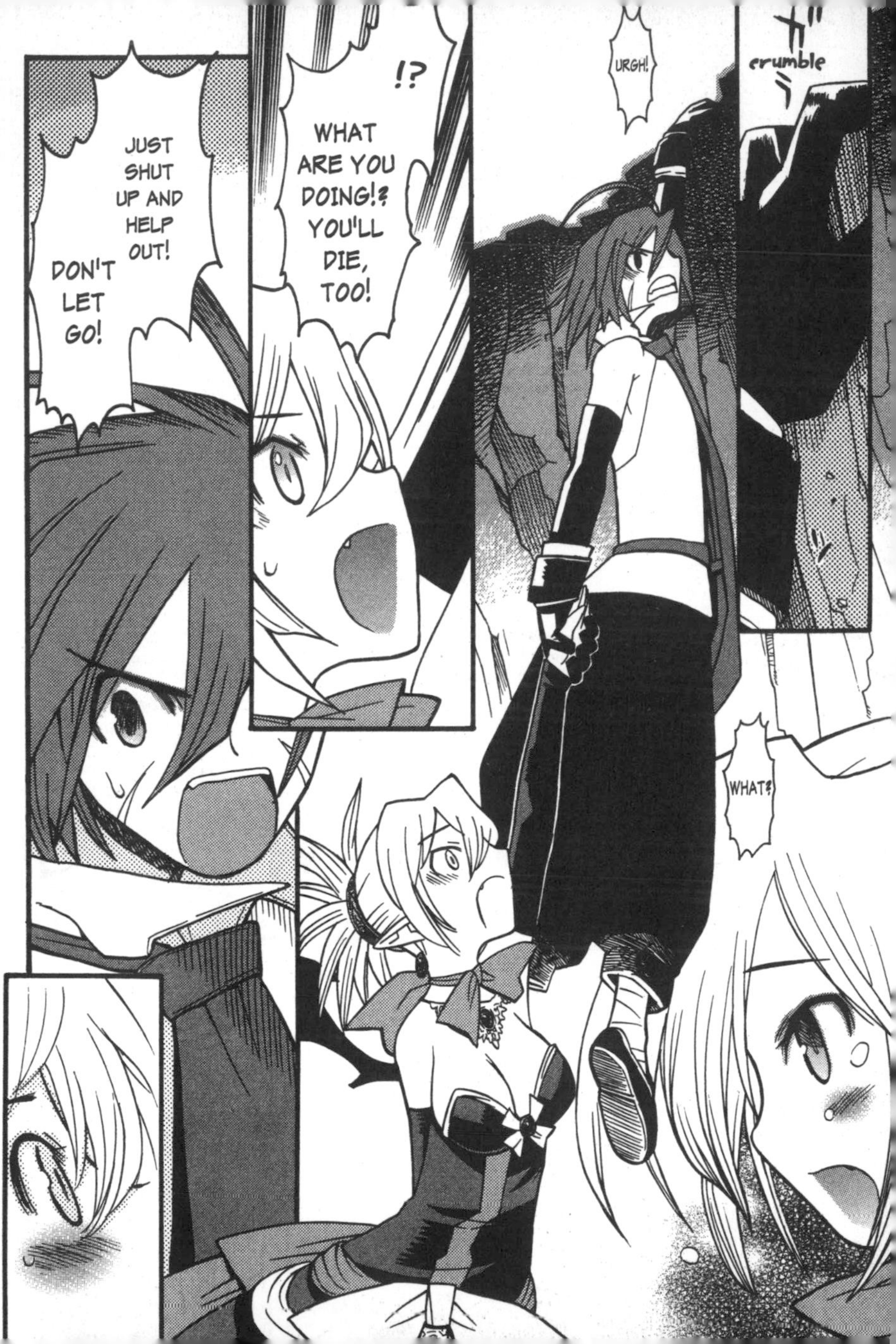
crumble
URGH!
!?
WHAT ARE YOU DOING!? YOU'LL DIE, TOO!
JUST SHUT UP AND HELP OUT!
DON'T LET GO!
WHAT!?

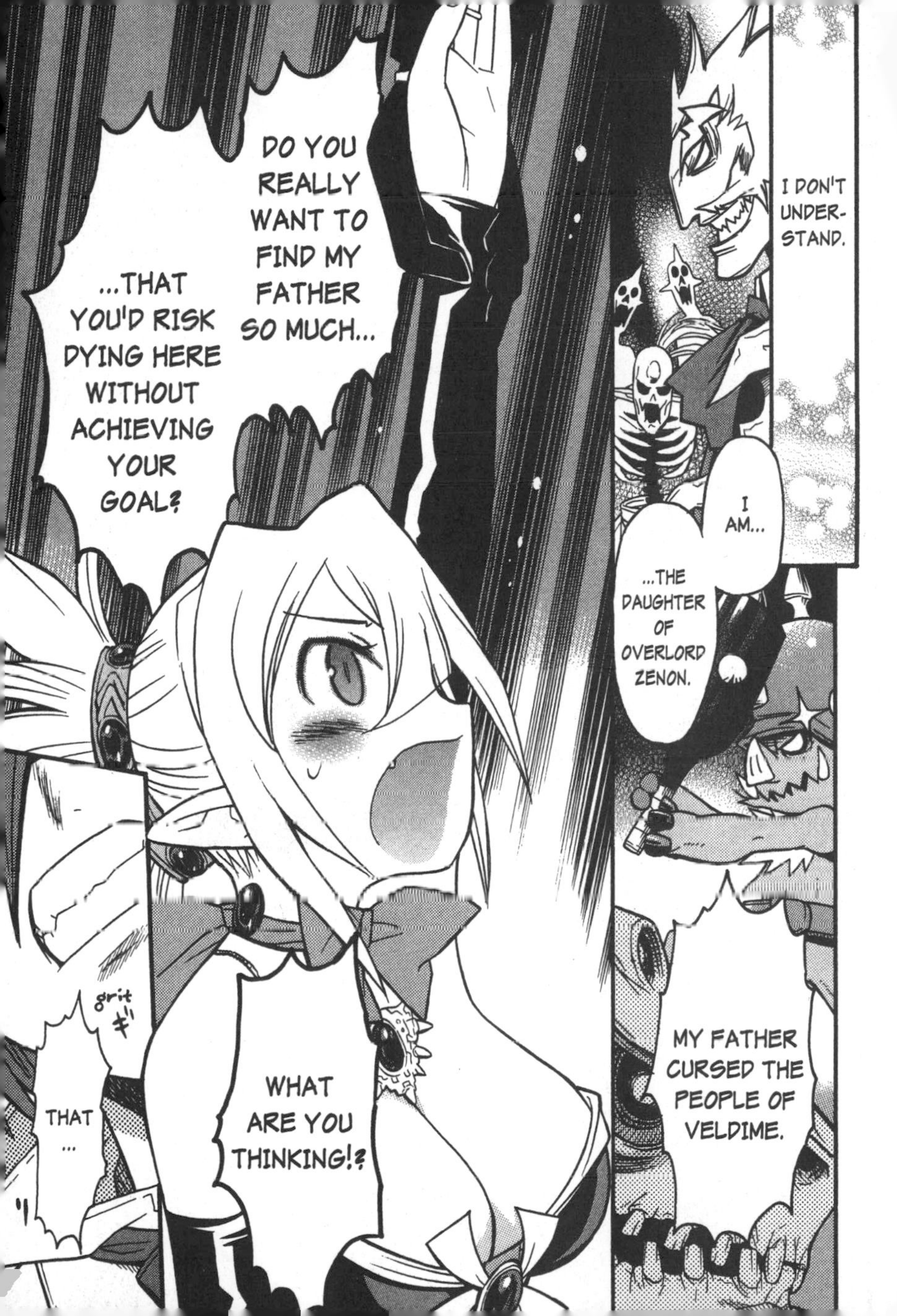
I DON'T UNDER-STAND.
I AM...
...THE DAUGHTER OF OVERLORD ZENON.
MY FATHER CURSED THE PEOPLE OF VELDIME.
DO YOU REALLY WANT TO FIND MY FATHER SO MUCH...
...THAT YOU'D RISK DYING HERE WITHOUT ACHIEVING YOUR GOAL?
WHAT ARE YOU THINKING!?
grit
THAT ...

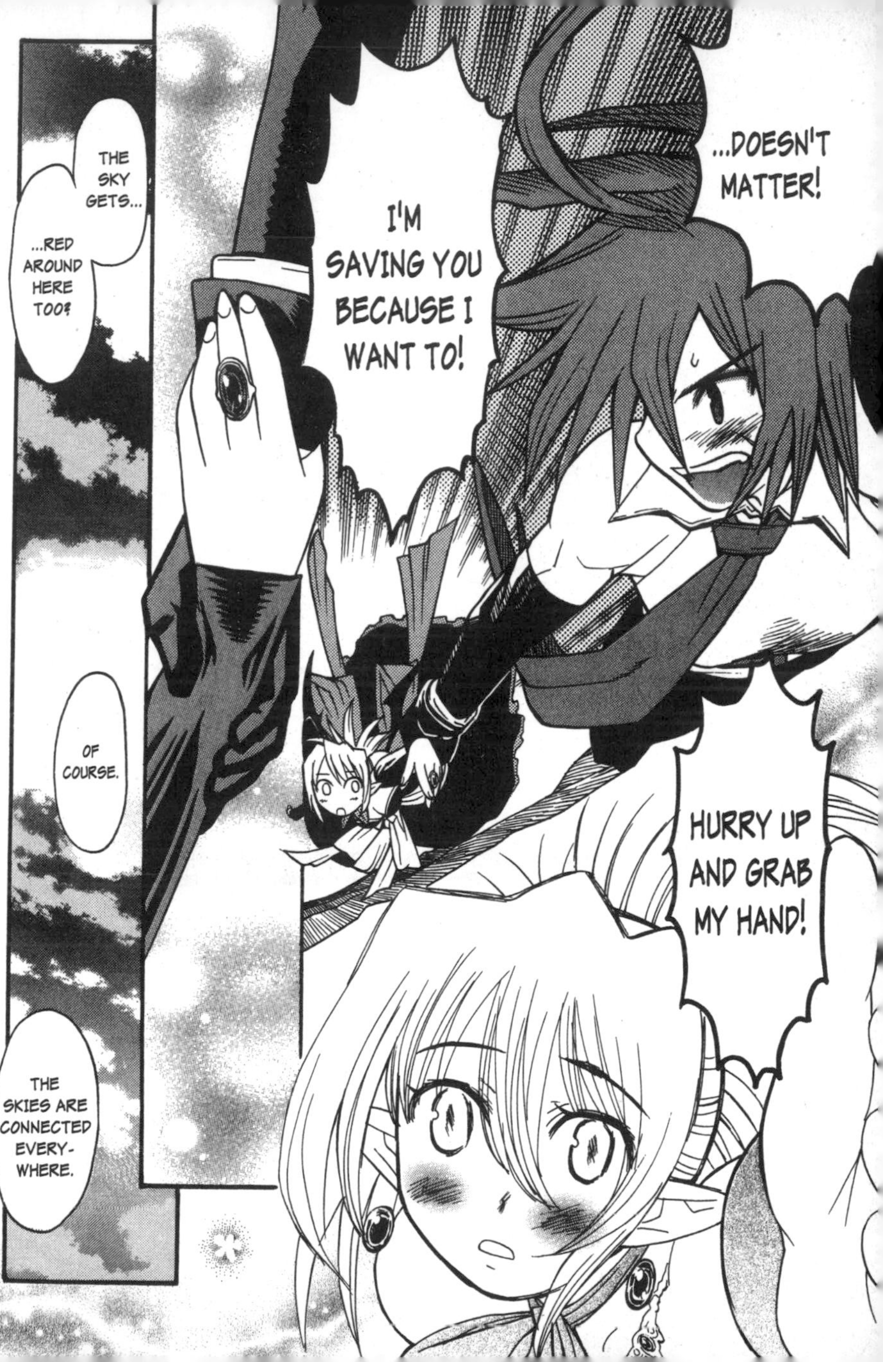
...DOESN'T MATTER!
I'M SAVING YOU BECAUSE I WANT TO!
HURRY UP AND GRAB MY HAND!
THE SKY GETS...
...RED AROUND HERE TOO?
OF COURSE.
THE SKIES ARE CONNECTED EVERY-WHERE.

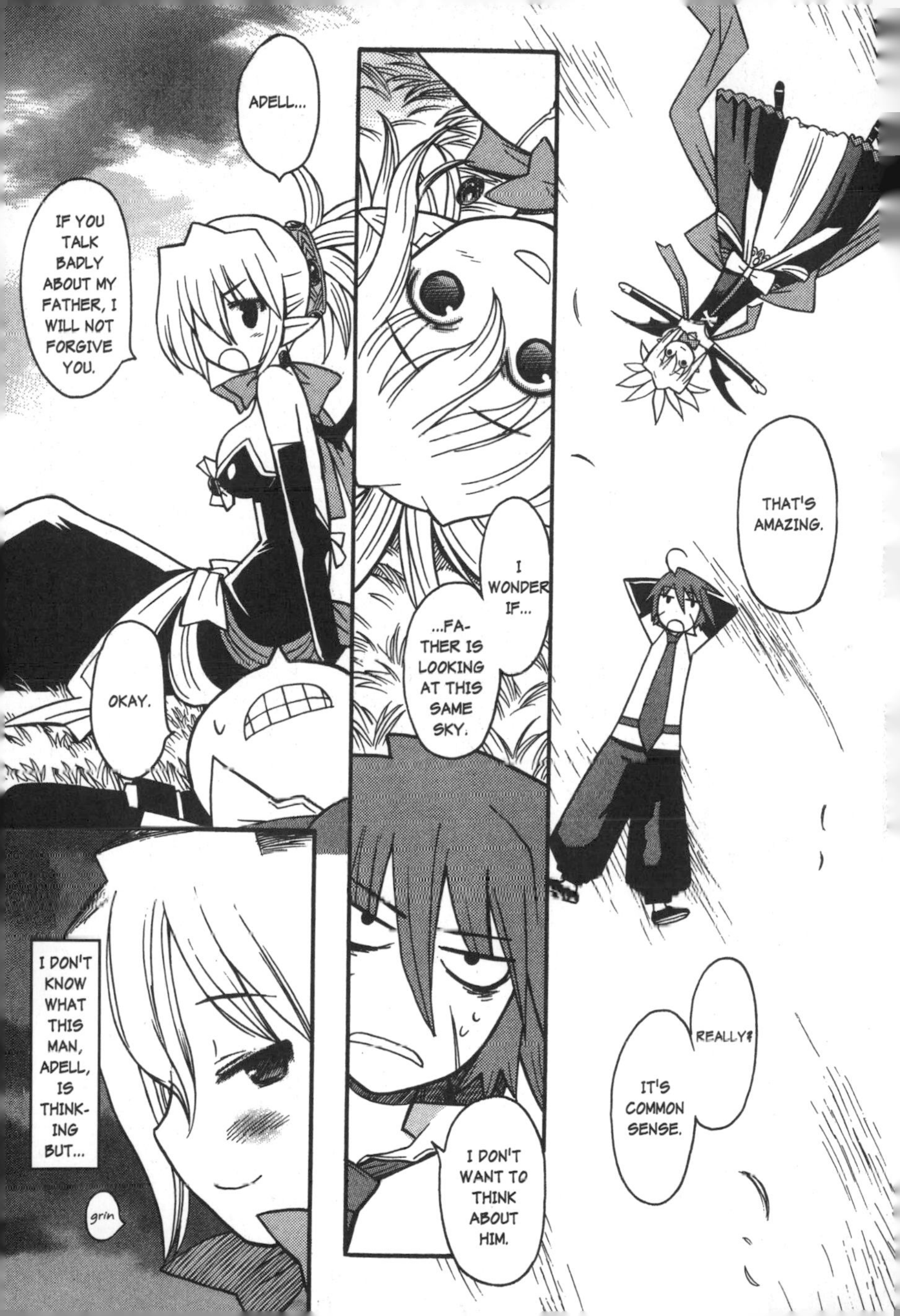
THAT'S AMAZING.
REALLY?
IT'S COMMON SENSE.
I WONDER IF...
...FA-THER IS LOOKING AT THIS SAME SKY.
I DON'T WANT TO THINK ABOUT HIM.
ADELL...
IF YOU TALK BADLY ABOUT MY FATHER, I WILL NOT FORGIVE YOU.
OKAY.
I DON'T KNOW WHAT THIS MAN, ADELL, IS THINKING BUT...
grin

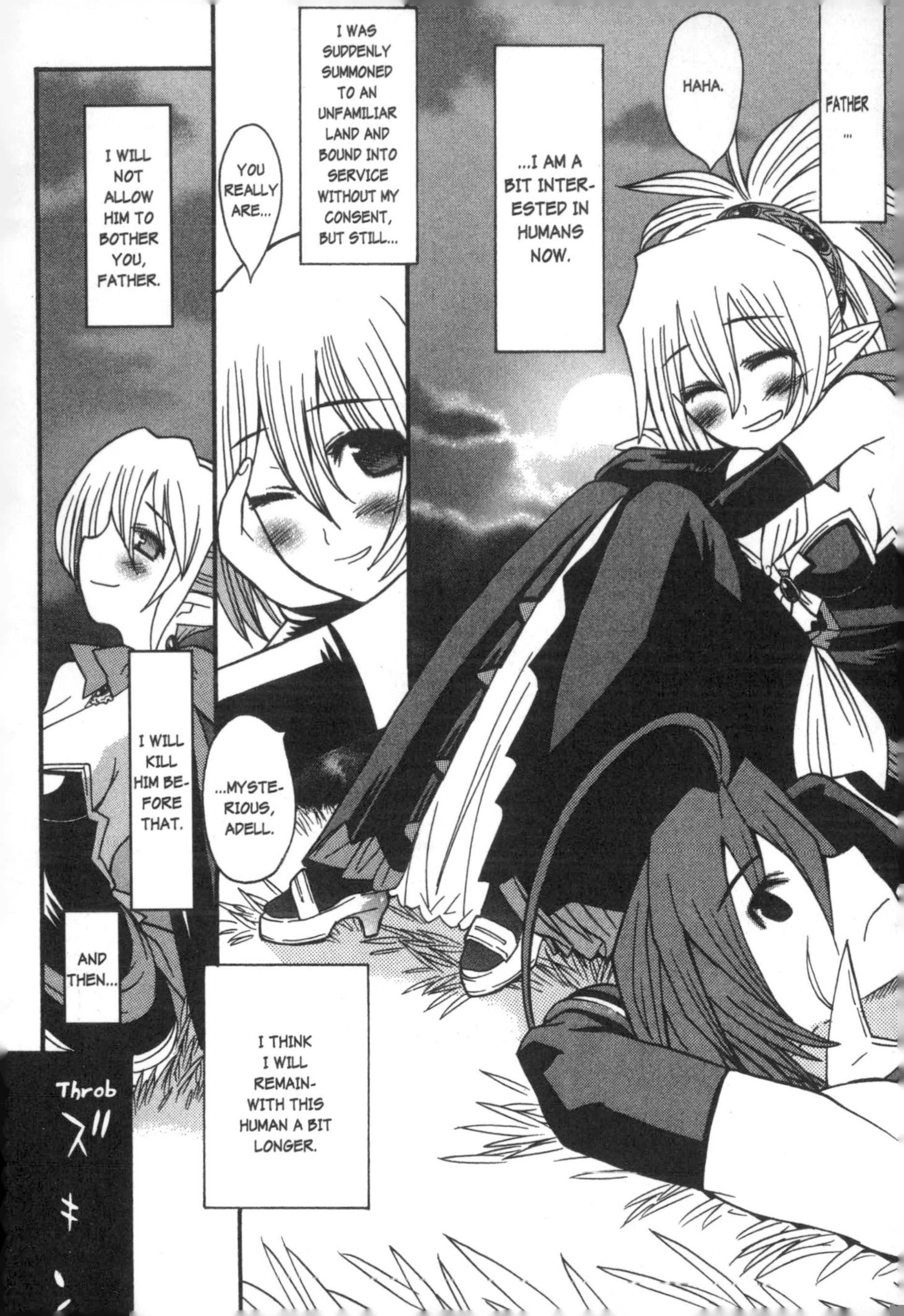
FATHER...
HAHA.
...I AM A BIT INTER-ESTED IN HUMANS NOW.
I WAS SUDDENLY SUMMONED TO AN UNFAMILIAR LAND AND BOUND INTO SERVICE WITHOUT MY CONSENT, BUT STILL...
YOU REALLY ARE...
...MYSTE-RIOUS, ADELL.
I THINK I WILL REMAIN-WITH THIS HUMAN A BIT LONGER.
I WILL NOT ALLOW HIM TO BOTHER YOU, FATHER.
I WILL KILL HIM BE-FORE THAT.
AND THEN...
Throb

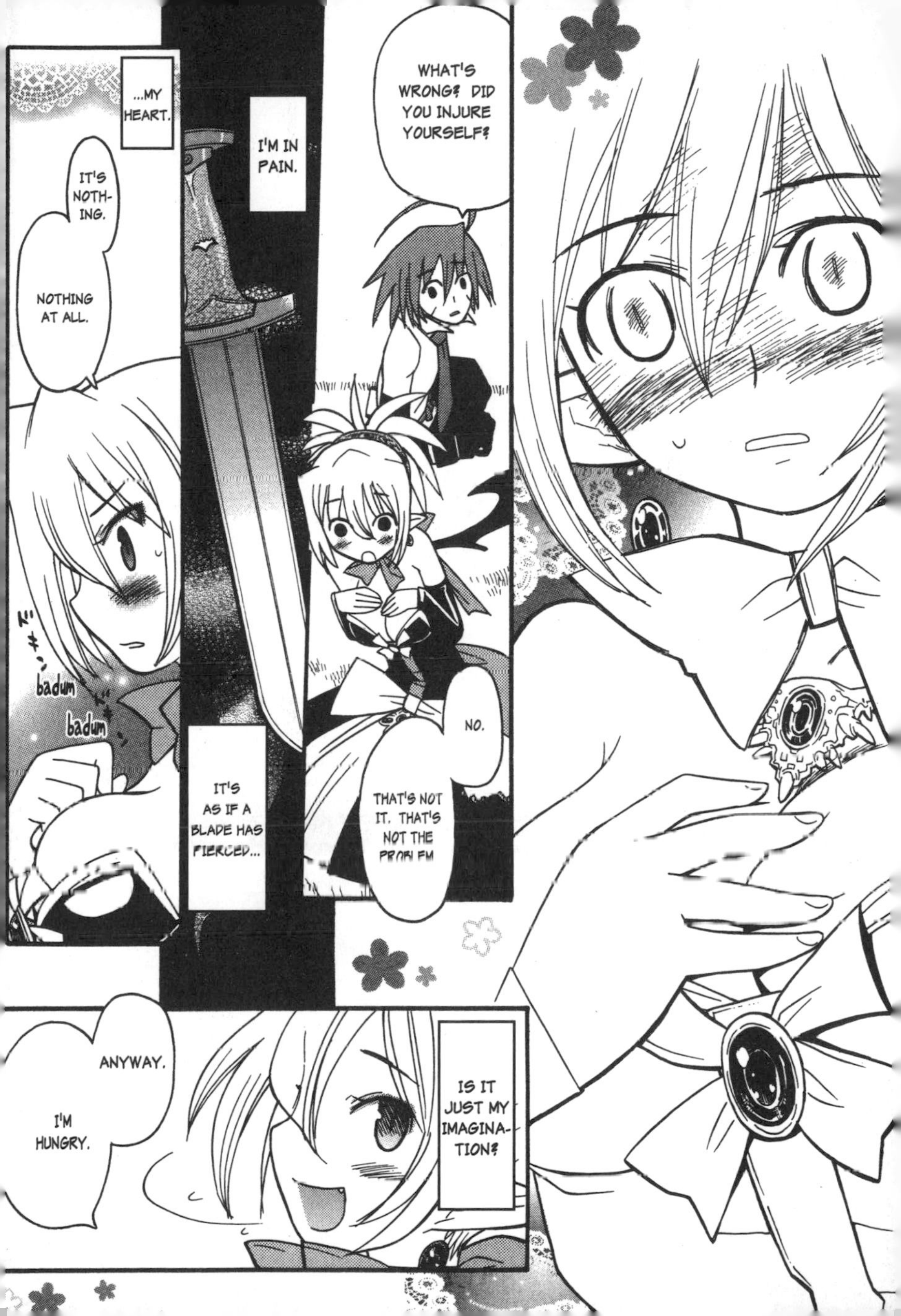
WHAT'S WRONG? DID YOU INJURE YOURSELF?
NO.
THAT'S NOT IT. THAT'S NOT THE PROBLEM
I'M IN PAIN.
IT'S AS IF A BLADE HAS PIERCED...
...MY HEART.
IT'S NOTHING.
NOTHING AT ALL.
badum
badum
IS IT JUST MY IMAGINATION?
ANYWAY.
I'M HUNGRY.

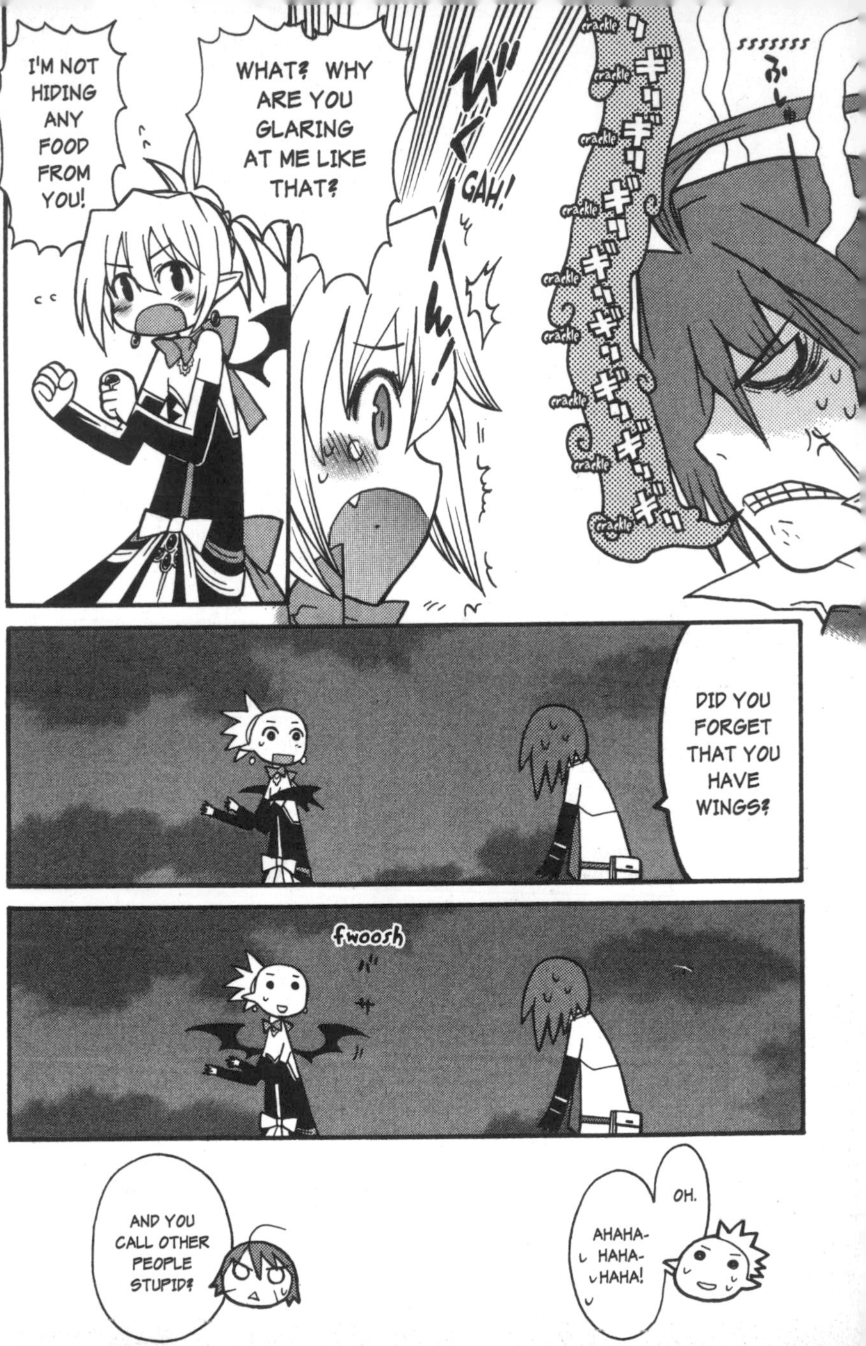
sssssss
crackle
crackle
crackle
crackle
crackle
crackle
crackle
crackle
crackle
WHAT? WHY ARE YOU GLARING AT ME LIKE THAT?
GAH!
I'M NOT HIDING ANY FOOD FROM YOU!
DID YOU FORGET THAT YOU HAVE WINGS?
fwoosh
OH.
AHAHA-HAHA-HAHA!
AND YOU CALL OTHER PEOPLE STUPID?

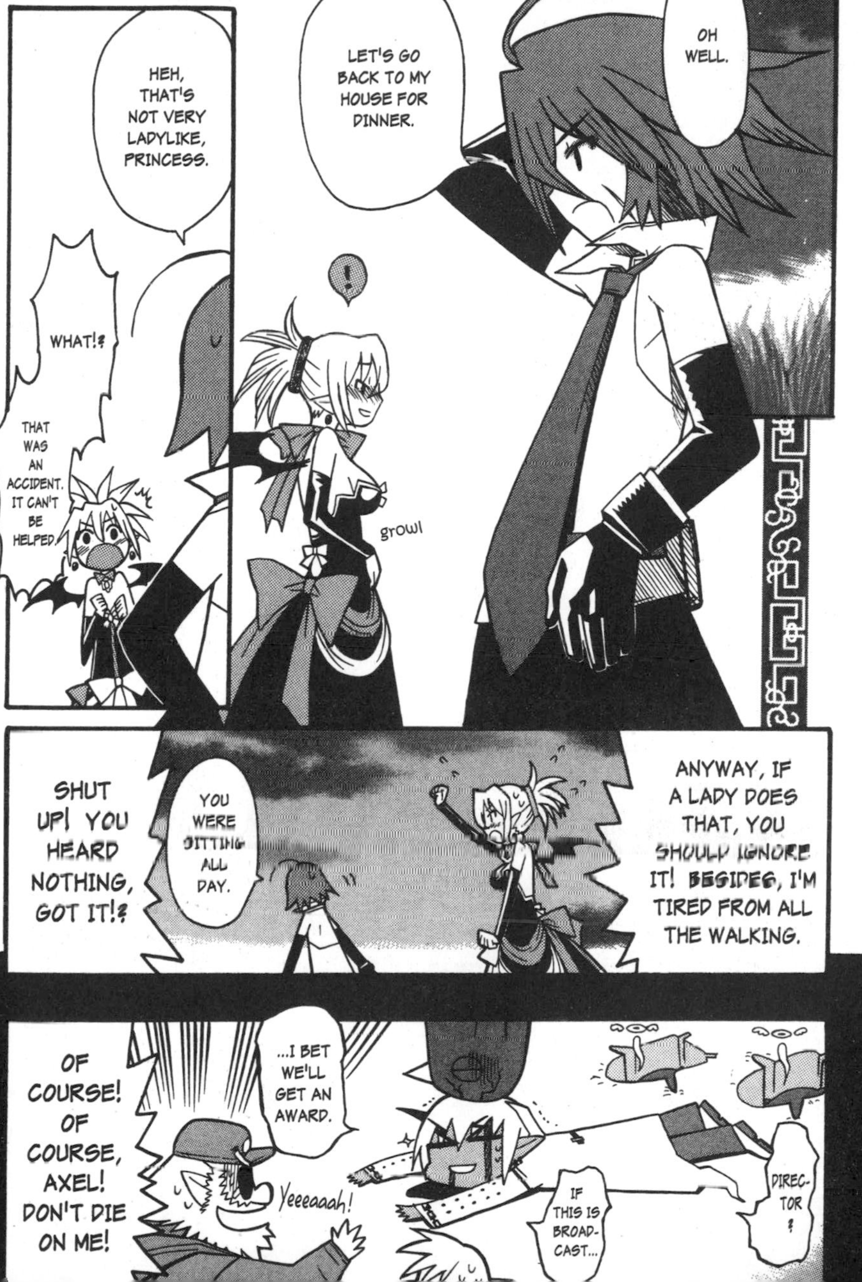
OH WELL.
LET'S GO BACK TO MY HOUSE FOR DINNER.
!
growl
HEH, THAT'S NOT VERY LADYLIKE, PRINCESS.
WHAT!?
THAT WAS AN ACCIDENT. IT CAN'T BE HELPED.
ANYWAY, IF A LADY DOES THAT, YOU SHOULD IGNORE IT! BESIDES, I'M TIRED FROM ALL THE WALKING.
YOU WERE SITTING ALL DAY.
SHUT UP! YOU HEARD NOTHING, GOT IT!?
DIRECTOR?
IF THIS IS BROADCAST...
...I BET WE'LL GET AN AWARD.
Yeeeaaah!
OF COURSE! OF COURSE, AXEL! DON'T DIE ON ME!

EPISODE PREVIEW

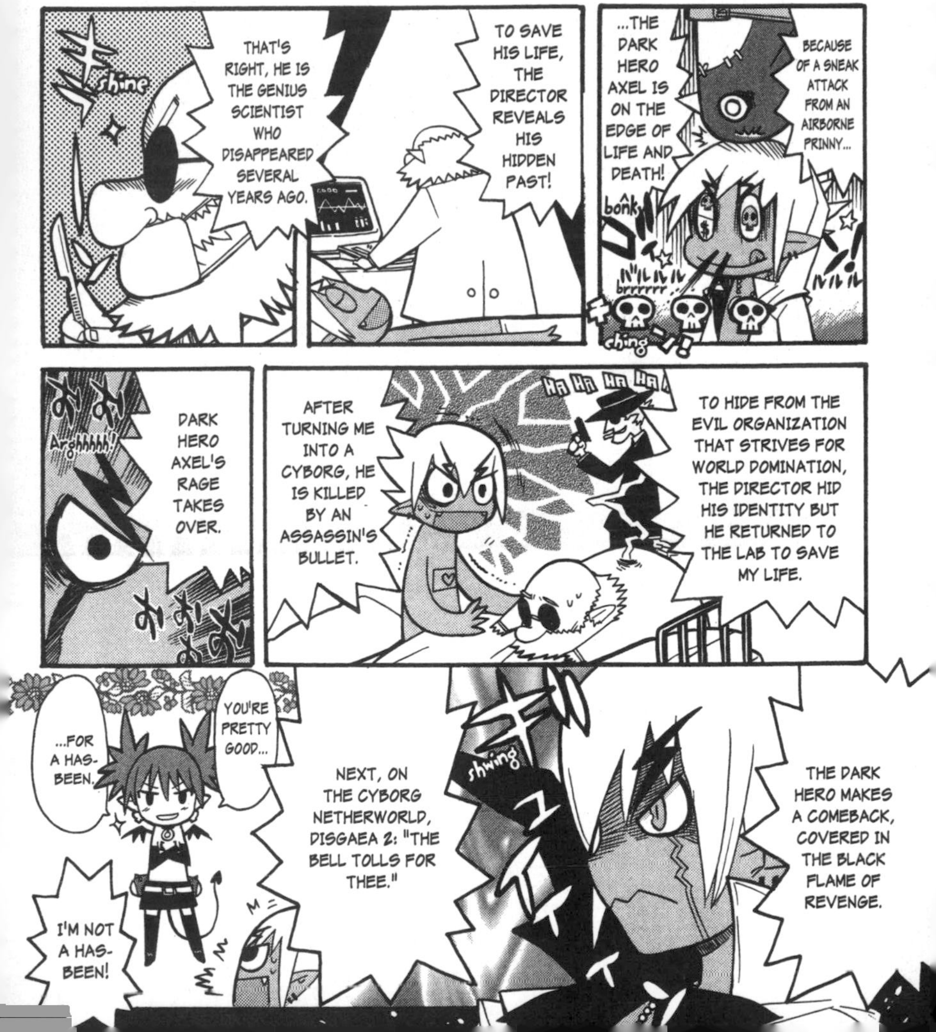
BECAUSE OF A SNEAK ATTACK FROM AN AIRBORNE PRINNY...
...THE DARK HERO AXEL IS ON THE EDGE OF LIFE AND DEATH!
bonk
brrrrrr
ching
TO SAVE HIS LIFE, THE DIRECTOR REVEALS HIS HIDDEN PAST!
THAT'S RIGHT, HE IS THE GENIUS SCIENTIST WHO DISAPPEARED SEVERAL YEARS AGO.
shine
TO HIDE FROM THE EVIL ORGANIZATION THAT STRIVES FOR WORLD DOMINATION, THE DIRECTOR HID HIS IDENTITY BUT HE RETURNED TO THE LAB TO SAVE MY LIFE.
HA HA HA HA
AFTER TURNING ME INTO A CYBORG, HE IS KILLED BY AN ASSASSIN'S BULLET.
DARK HERO AXEL'S RAGE TAKES OVER.
Arghhhhh!
THE DARK HERO MAKES A COMEBACK, COVERED IN THE BLACK FLAME OF REVENGE.
shwing
NEXT, ON THE CYBORG NETHERWORLD, DISGAEA 2: "THE BELL TOLLS FOR THEE."
YOU'RE PRETTY GOOD...
...FOR A HAS-BEEN.
I'M NOT A HAS-BEEN!

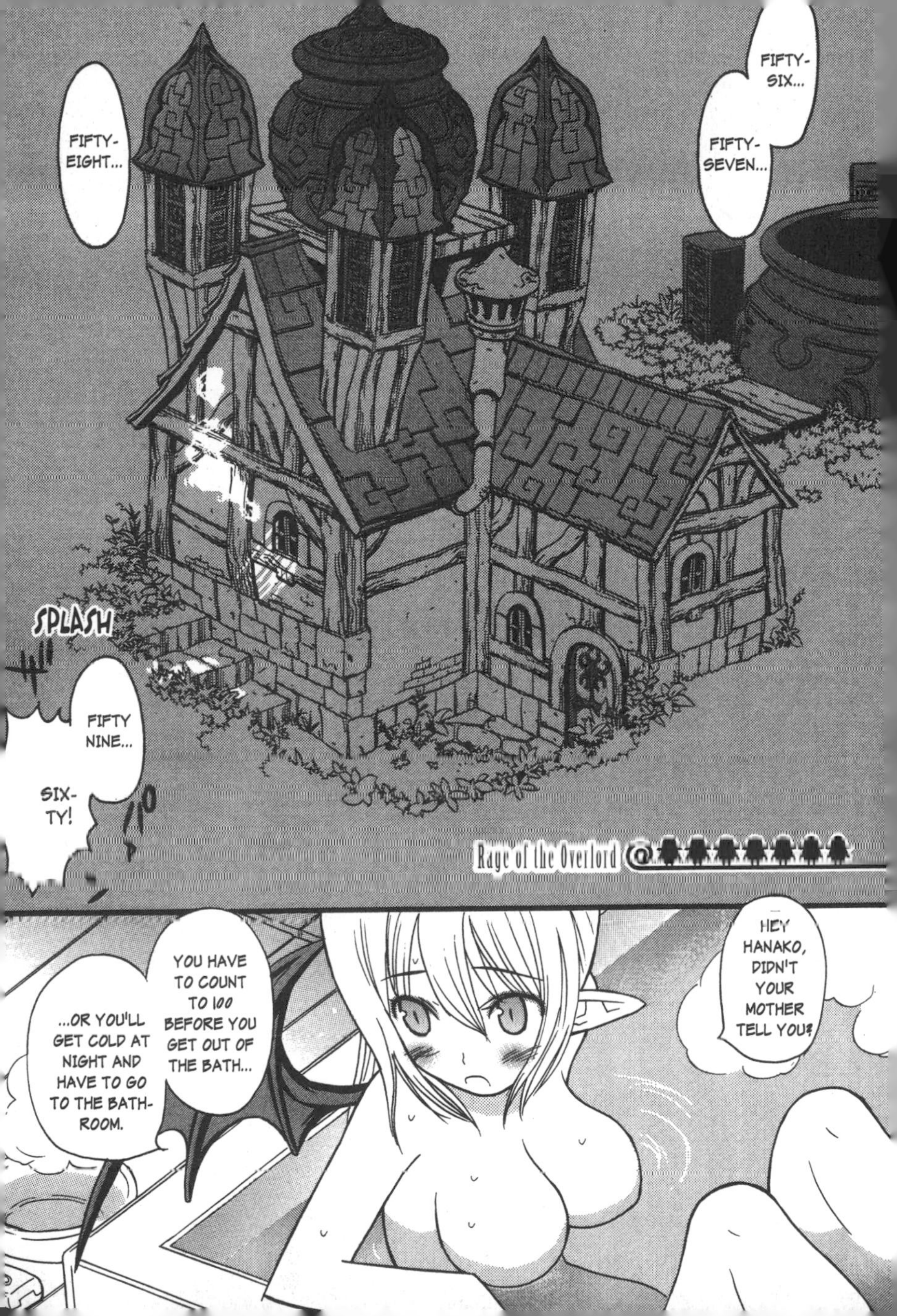
FIFTY-SIX...
FIFTY-SEVEN...
FIFTY-EIGHT...
SPLASH
FIFTY NINE...
SIX-TY!
Rage of the Overlord
HEY HANAKO, DIDN'T YOUR MOTHER TELL YOU?
YOU HAVE TO COUNT TO 100 BEFORE YOU GET OUT OF THE BATH...
...OR YOU'LL GET COLD AT NIGHT AND HAVE TO GO TO THE BATH-ROOM.

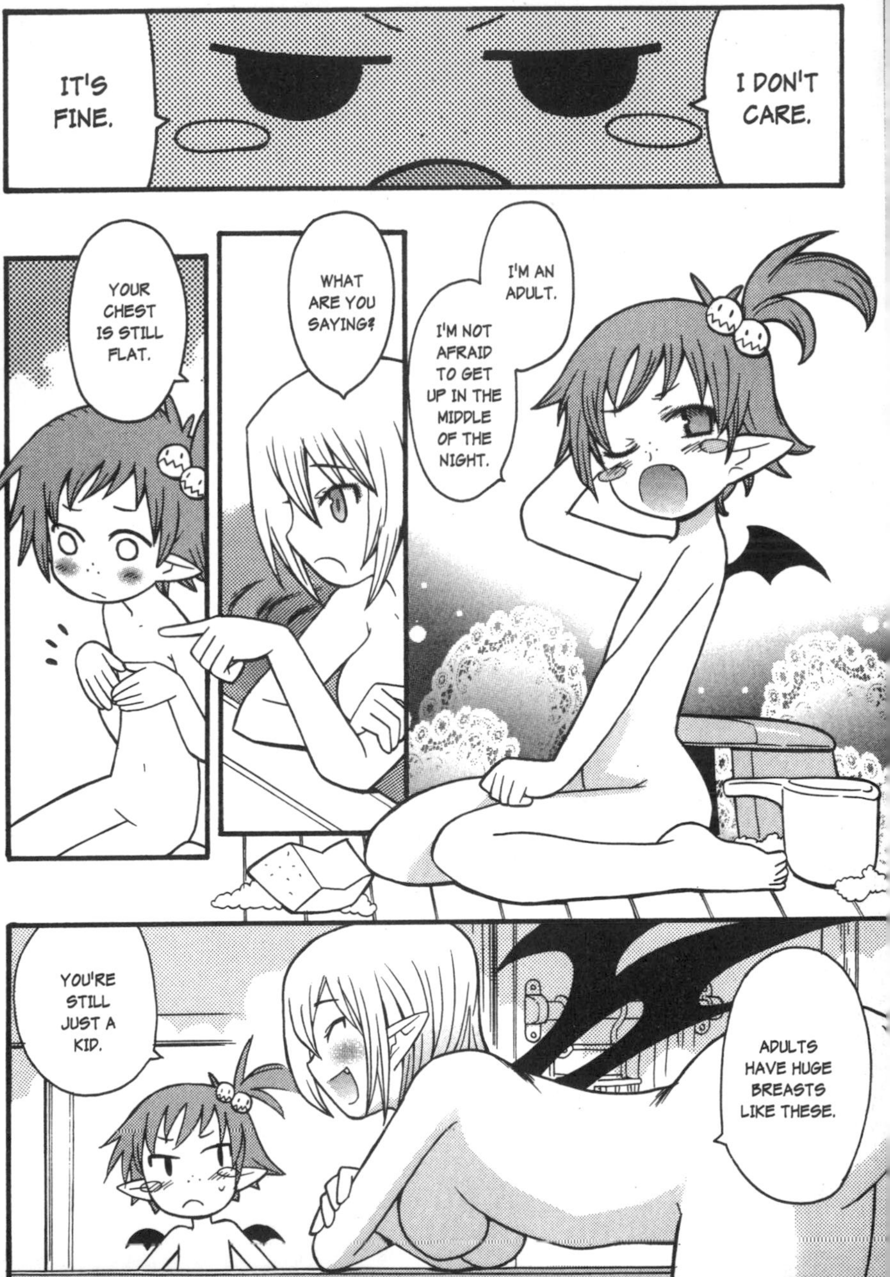
I DON'T CARE.
IT'S FINE.
I'M AN ADULT.
I'M NOT AFRAID TO GET UP IN THE MIDDLE OF THE NIGHT.
WHAT ARE YOU SAYING?
YOUR CHEST IS STILL FLAT.
ADULTS HAVE HUGE BREASTS LIKE THESE.
YOU'RE STILL JUST A KID.

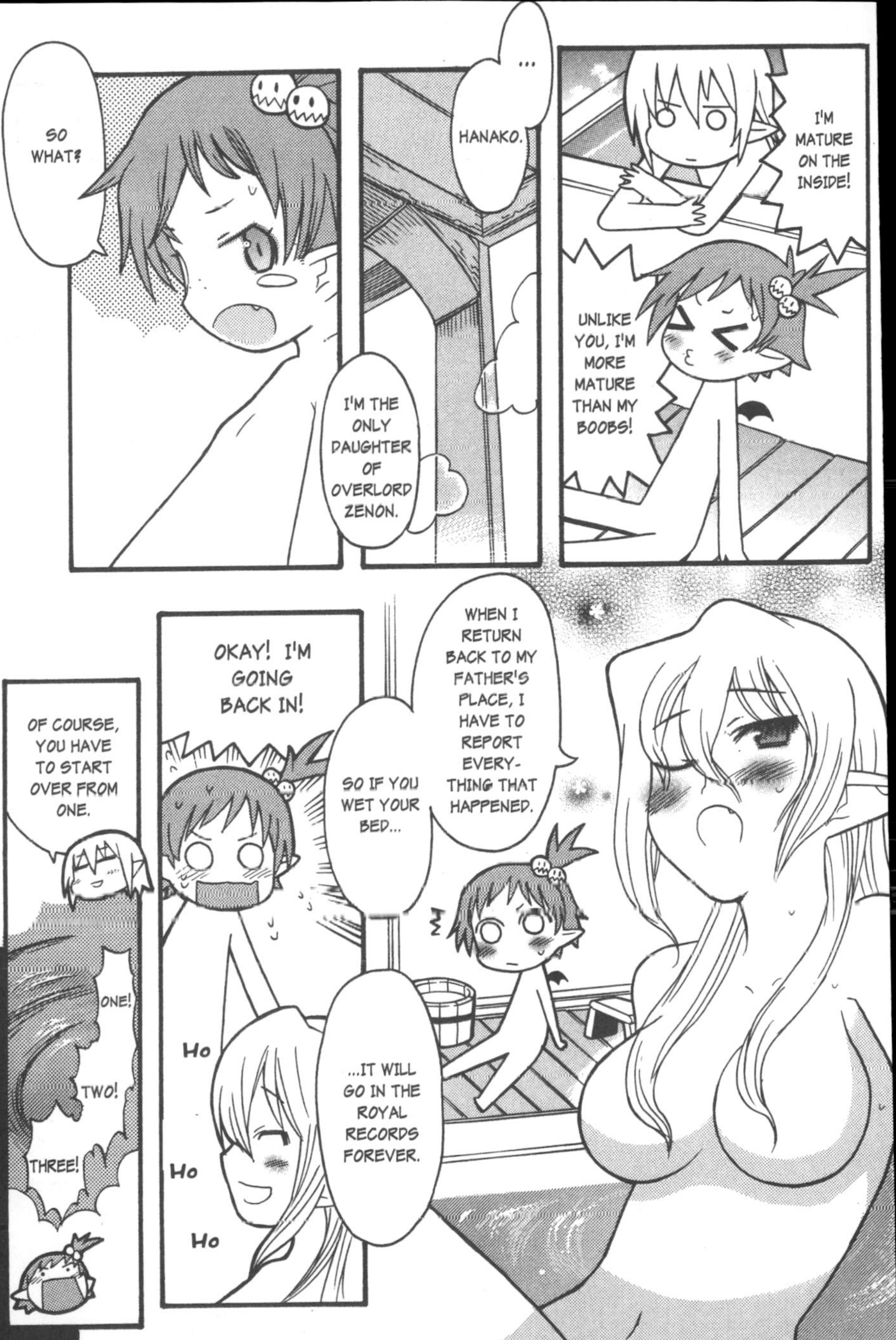
I'M MATURE ON THE INSIDE!
UNLIKE YOU, I'M MORE MATURE THAN MY BOOBS!
...
HANAKO.
I'M THE ONLY DAUGHTER OF OVERLORD ZENON.
SO WHAT?
WHEN I RETURN BACK TO MY FATHER'S PLACE, I HAVE TO REPORT EVERY-THING THAT HAPPENED.
SO IF YOU WET YOUR BED...
...IT WILL GO IN THE ROYAL RECORDS FOREVER.
OKAY! I'M GOING BACK IN!
Ho
Ho
Ho
OF COURSE, YOU HAVE TO START OVER FROM ONE.
ONE!
TWO!
THREE!

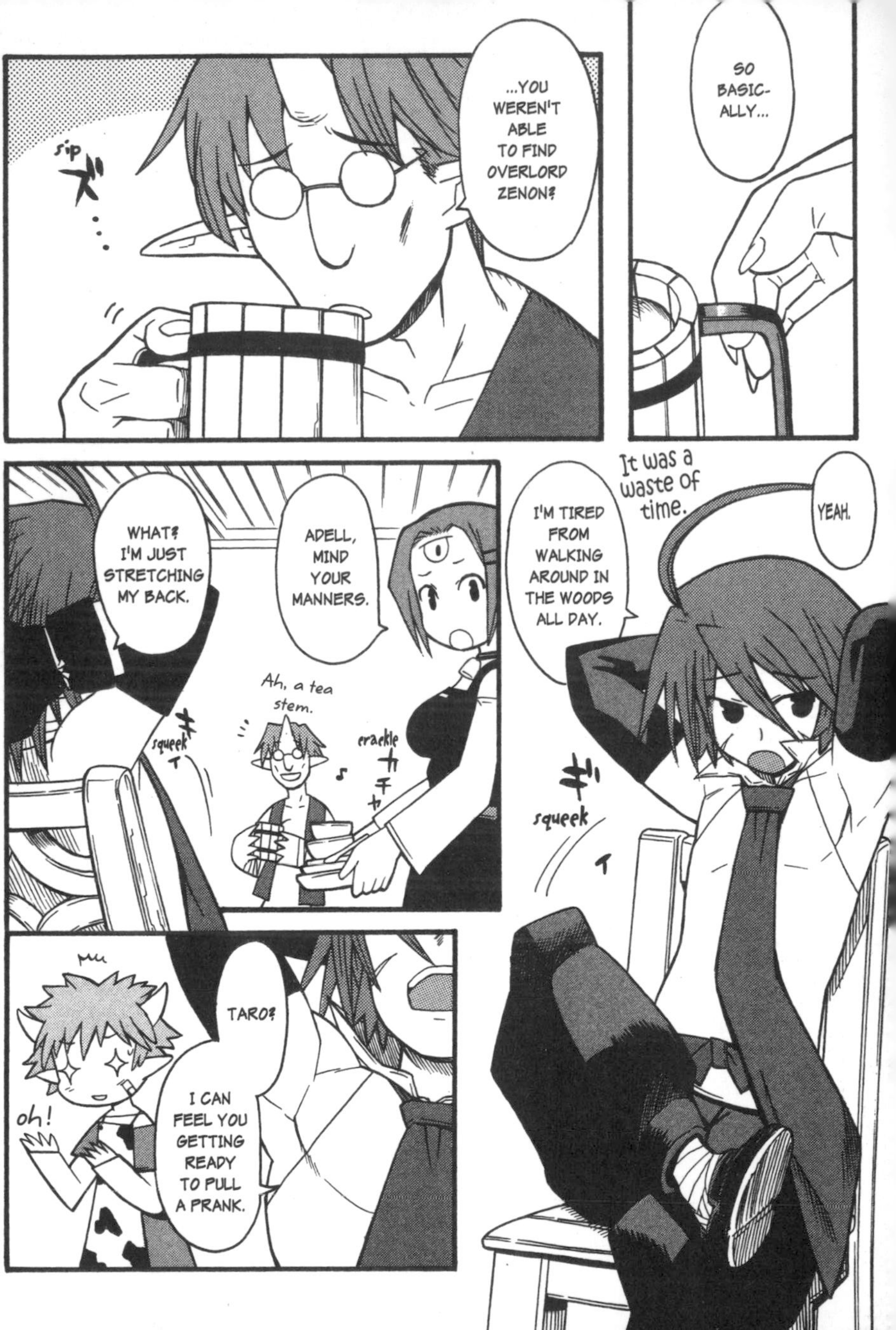
SO BASIC-ALLY...
...YOU WEREN'T ABLE TO FIND OVERLORD ZENON?
sip
YEAH.
It was a waste of time.
I'M TIRED FROM WALKING AROUND IN THE WOODS ALL DAY.
squeek
ADELL, MIND YOUR MANNERS.
WHAT? I'M JUST STRETCHING MY BACK.
Ah, a tea stem.
crackle
squeek
TARO?
I CAN FEEL YOU GETTING READY TO PULL A PRANK.
oh!

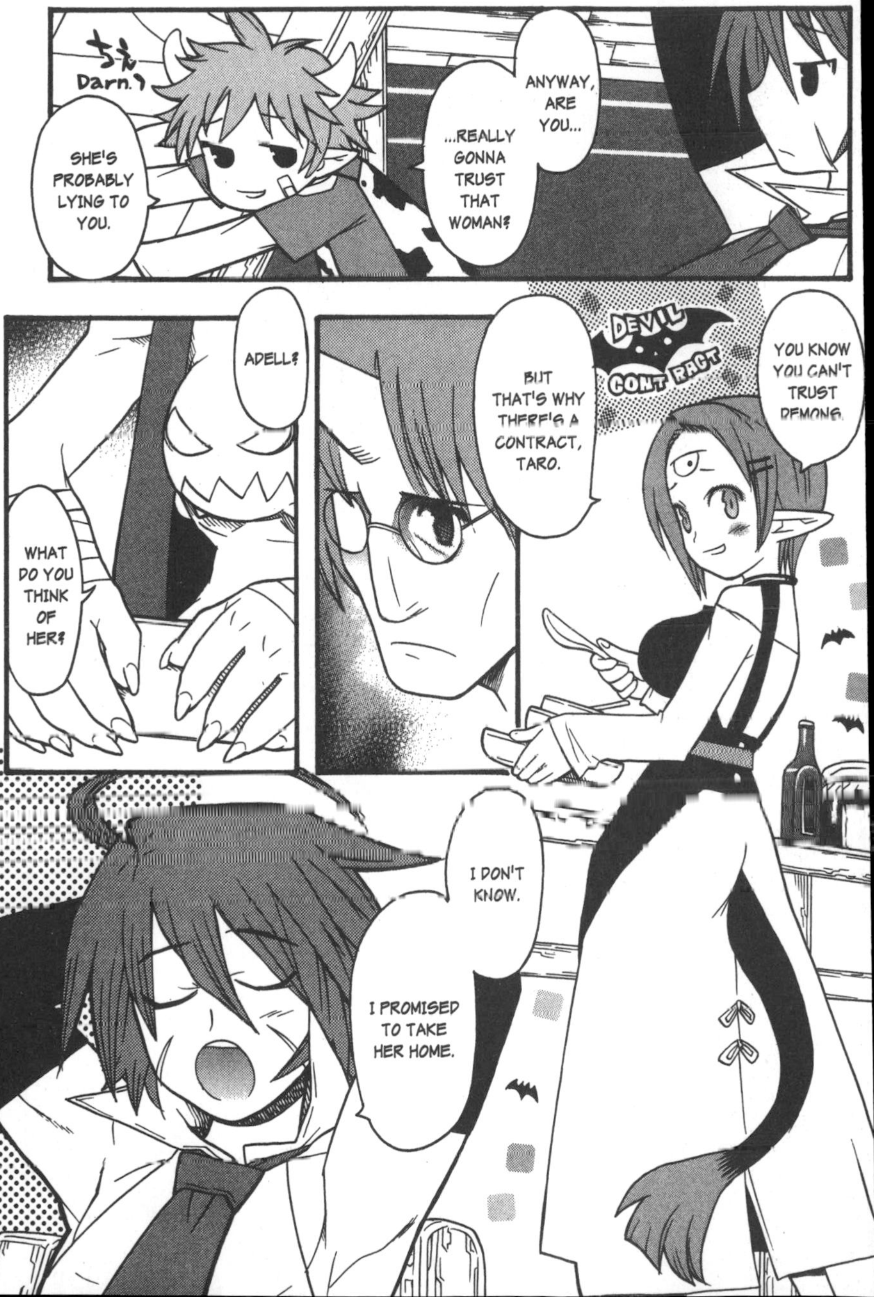
ANYWAY, ARE YOU...
...REALLY GONNA TRUST THAT WOMAN?
ちぇ
Darn.
SHE'S PROBABLY LYING TO YOU.
YOU KNOW YOU CAN'T TRUST DEMONS.
DEVIL CONTRACT
BUT THAT'S WHY THERE'S A CONTRACT, TARO.
ADELL?
WHAT DO YOU THINK OF HER?
I DON'T KNOW.
I PROMISED TO TAKE HER HOME.

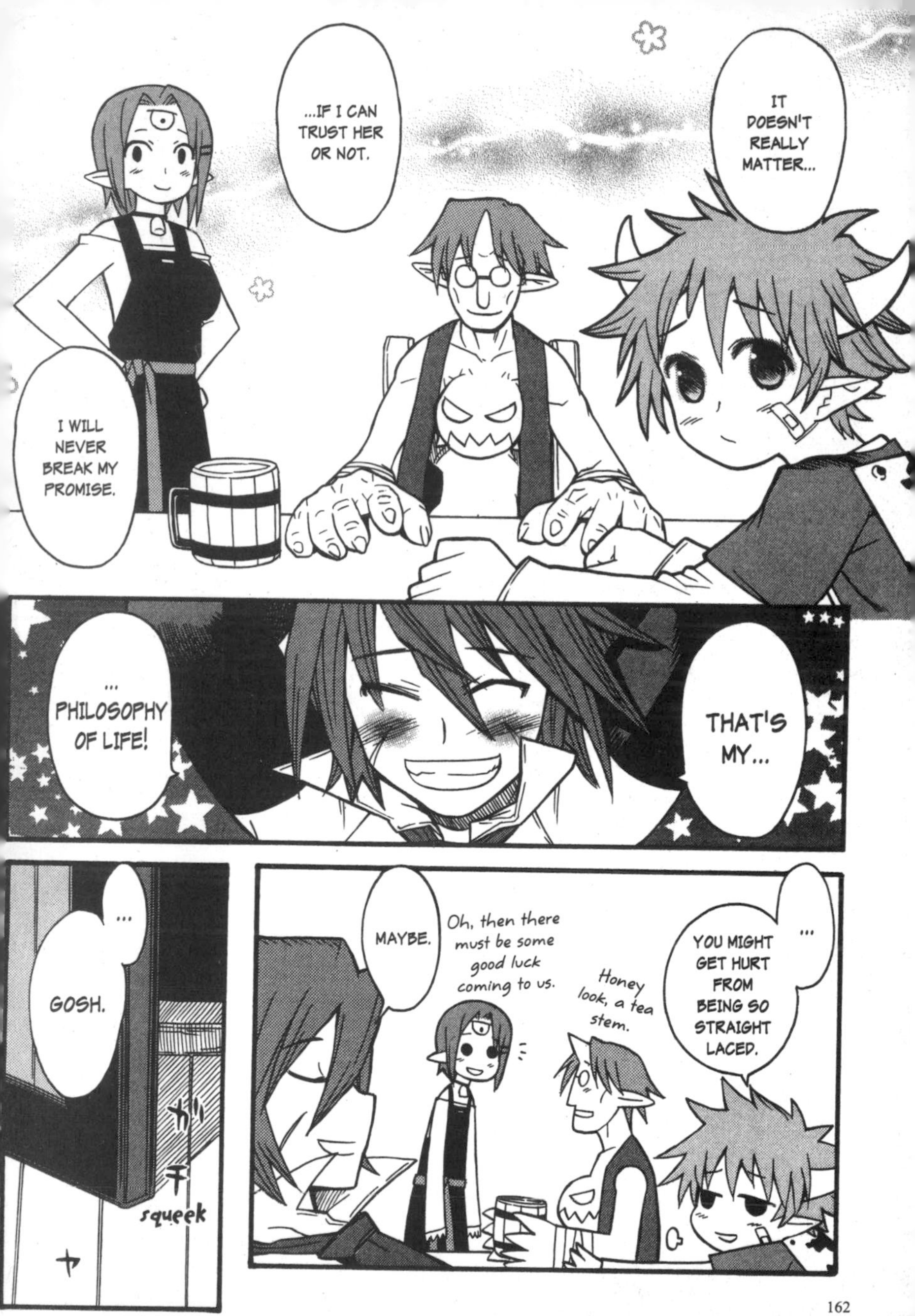
IT DOESN'T REALLY MATTER...
...IF I CAN TRUST HER OR NOT.
I WILL NEVER BREAK MY PROMISE.
THAT'S MY...
... PHILOSOPHY OF LIFE!
...
YOU MIGHT GET HURT FROM BEING SO STRAIGHT LACED.
Honey look, a tea stem.
Oh, then there must be some good luck coming to us.
MAYBE.
...
GOSH.
squeek

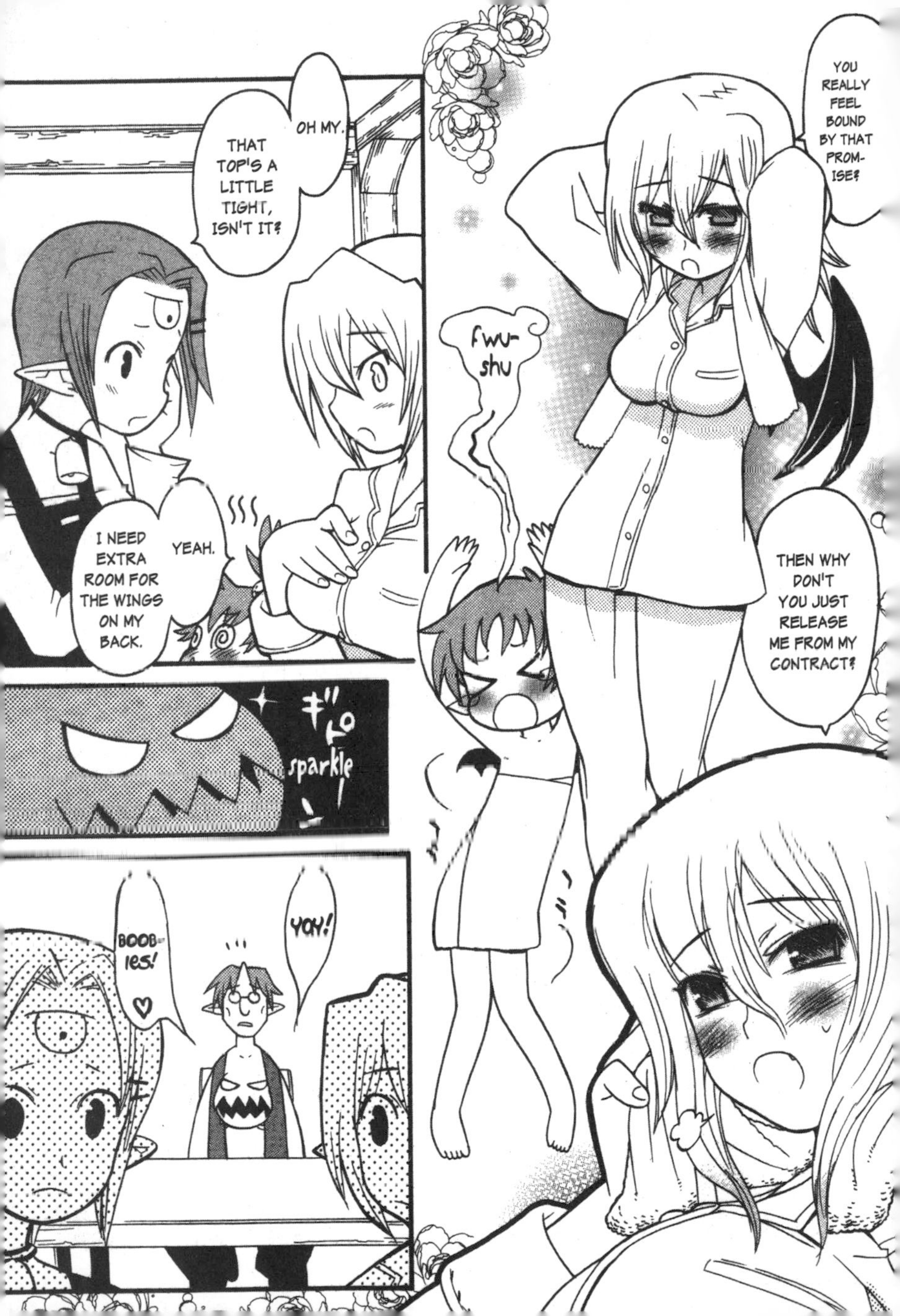
YOU REALLY FEEL BOUND BY THAT PROMISE?
fwu-shu
THEN WHY DON'T YOU JUST RELEASE ME FROM MY CONTRACT?
OH MY.
THAT TOP'S A LITTLE TIGHT, ISN'T IT?
YEAH.
I NEED EXTRA ROOM FOR THE WINGS ON MY BACK.
sparkle
YAY!
BOOB-IES! ♥

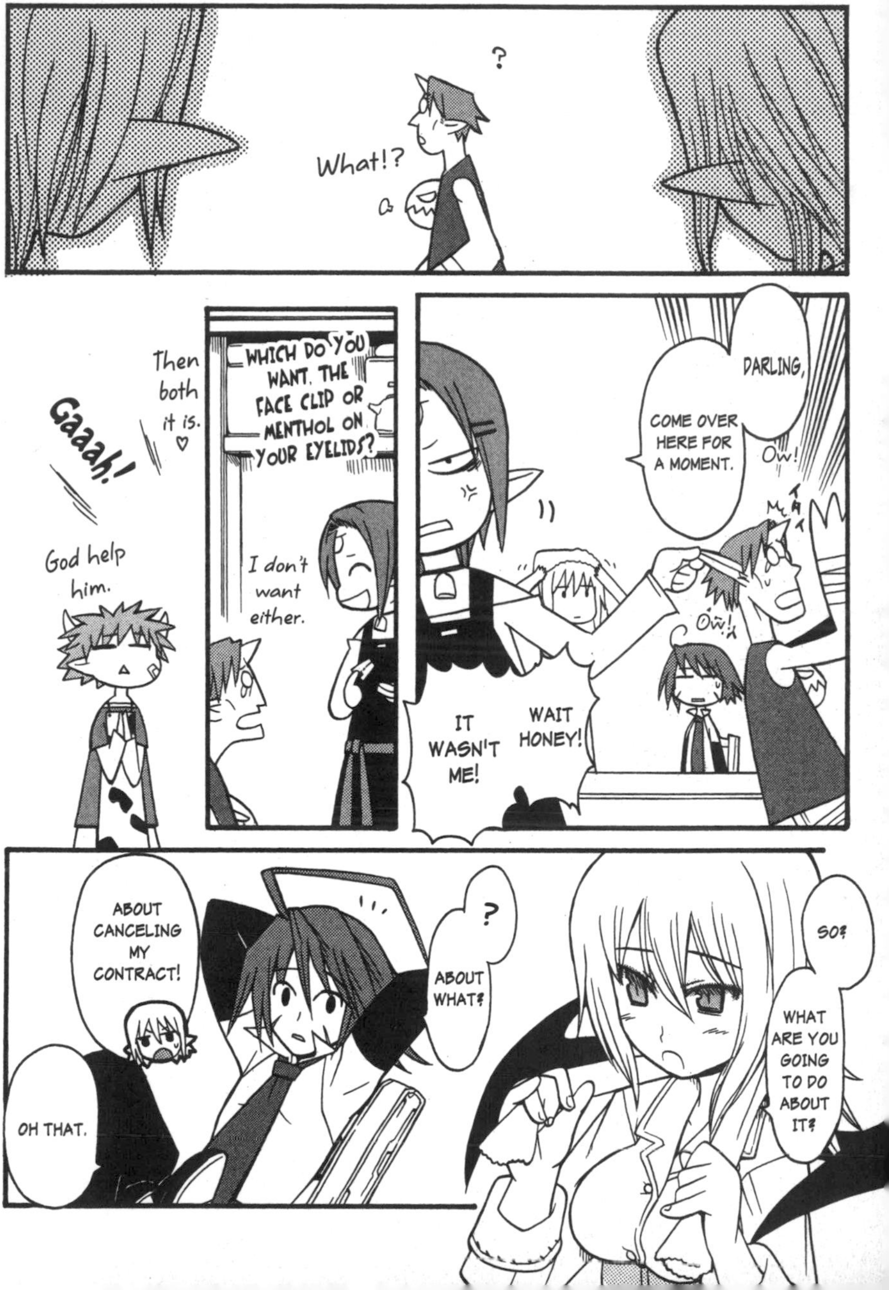
?
What!?
DARLING,
COME OVER HERE FOR A MOMENT.
Ow!
Ow!
WAIT HONEY!
IT WASN'T ME!
WHICH DO YOU WANT, THE FACE CLIP OR MENTHOL ON YOUR EYELIDS?
I don't want either.
Then both it is. ♡
Gaaah!
God help him.
SO?
WHAT ARE YOU GOING TO DO ABOUT IT?
?
ABOUT WHAT?
ABOUT CANCELING MY CONTRACT!
OH THAT.

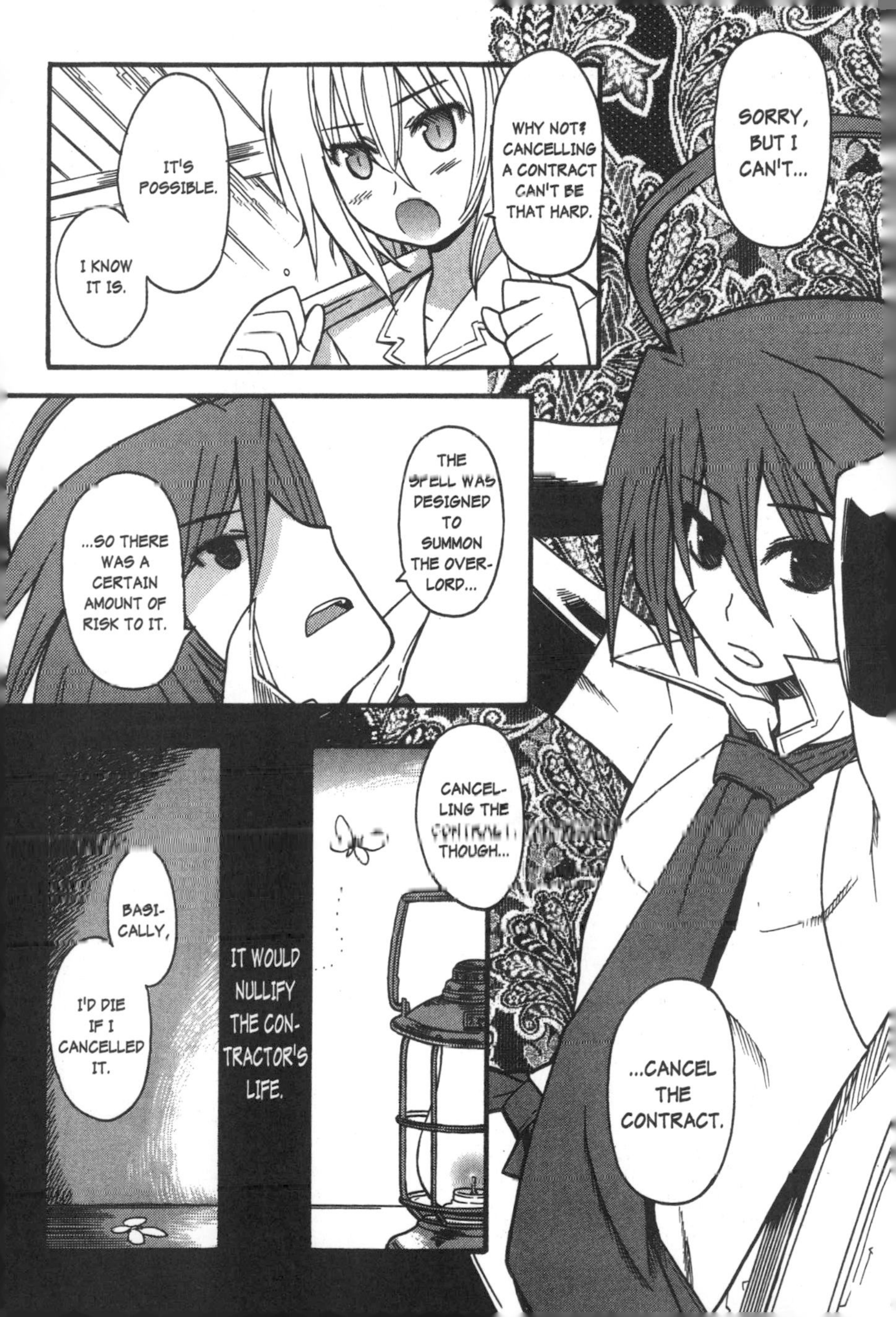
SORRY, BUT I CAN'T...
...CANCEL THE CONTRACT.
WHY NOT? CANCELLING A CONTRACT CAN'T BE THAT HARD.
IT'S POSSIBLE.
I KNOW IT IS.
THE SPELL WAS DESIGNED TO SUMMON THE OVERLORD...
...SO THERE WAS A CERTAIN AMOUNT OF RISK TO IT.
CANCELLING THE
THOUGH...
IT WOULD NULLIFY THE CONTRACTOR'S LIFE.
BASICALLY,
I'D DIE IF I CANCELLED IT.

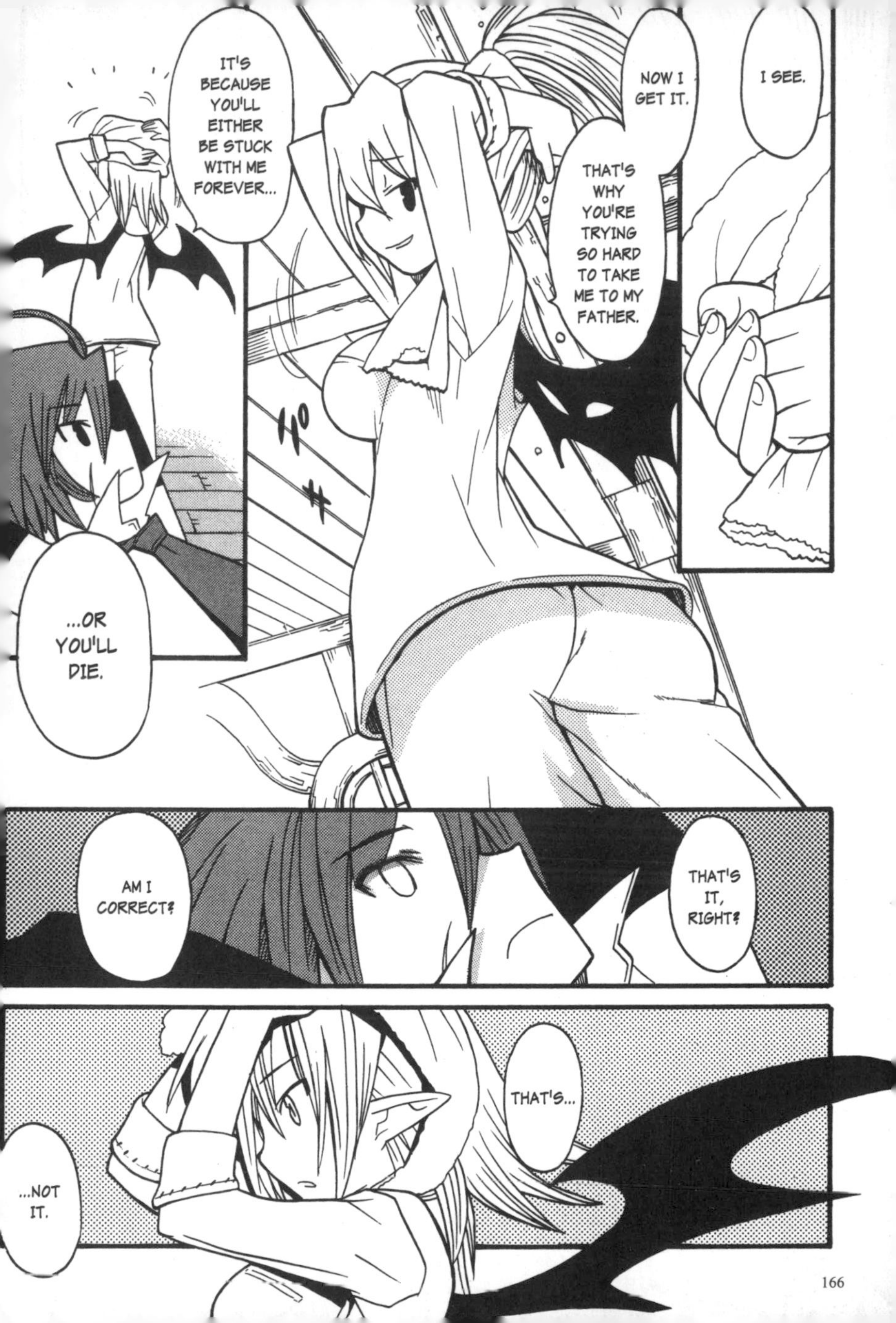
I SEE.
NOW I GET IT.
THAT'S WHY YOU'RE TRYING SO HARD TO TAKE ME TO MY FATHER.
IT'S BECAUSE YOU'LL EITHER BE STUCK WITH ME FOREVER...
...OR YOU'LL DIE.
THAT'S IT, RIGHT?
AM I CORRECT?
THAT'S...
...NOT IT.

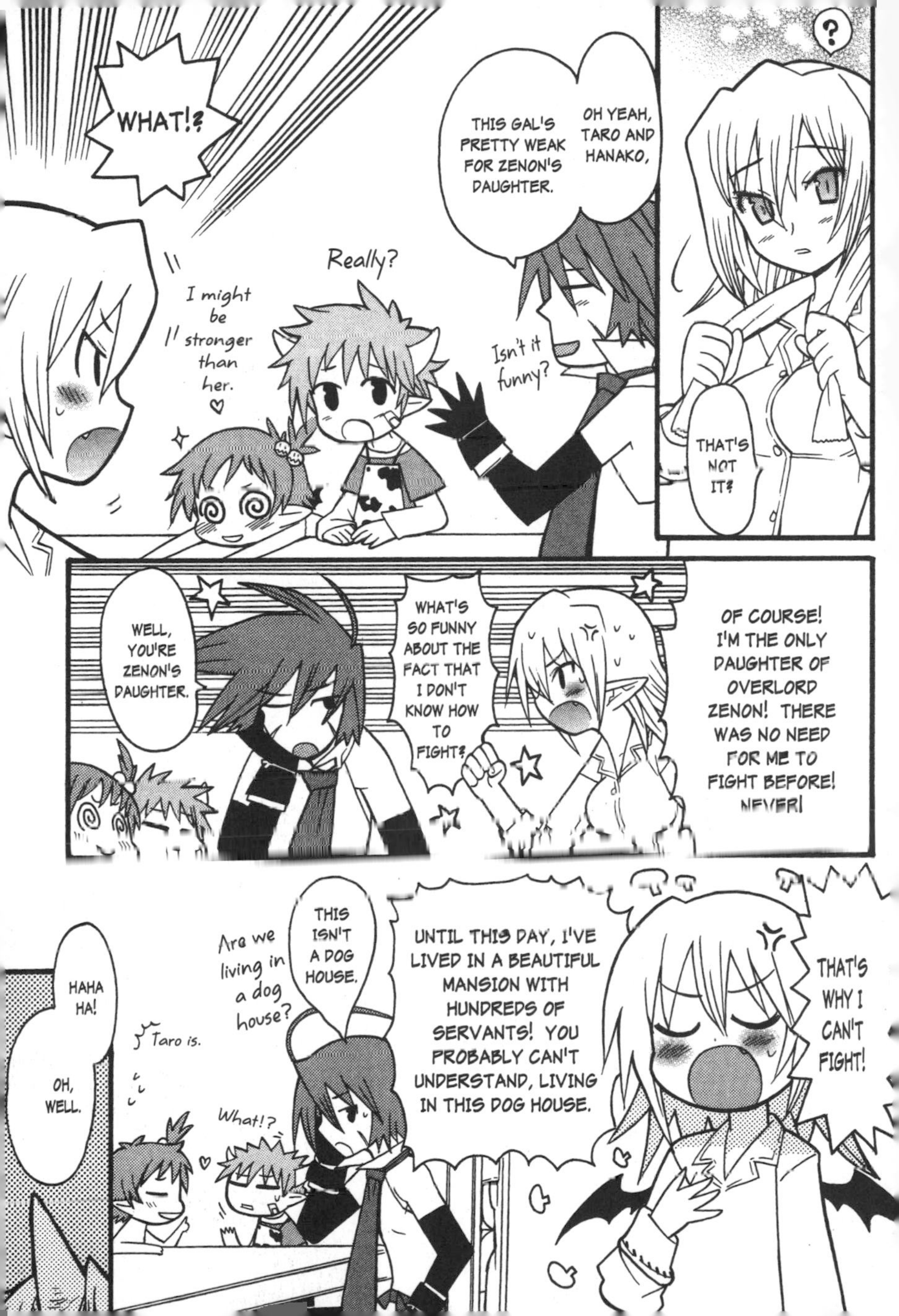
?
THAT'S NOT IT?
OH YEAH, TARO AND HANAKO,
THIS GAL'S PRETTY WEAK FOR ZENON'S DAUGHTER.
Isn't it funny?
Really?
I might be stronger than her. ♡
WHAT!?
OF COURSE! I'M THE ONLY DAUGHTER OF OVERLORD ZENON! THERE WAS NO NEED FOR ME TO FIGHT BEFORE! NEVER!
WHAT'S SO FUNNY ABOUT THE FACT THAT I DON'T KNOW HOW TO FIGHT?
WELL, YOU'RE ZENON'S DAUGHTER.
THAT'S WHY I CAN'T FIGHT!
UNTIL THIS DAY, I'VE LIVED IN A BEAUTIFUL MANSION WITH HUNDREDS OF SERVANTS! YOU PROBABLY CAN'T UNDERSTAND, LIVING IN THIS DOG HOUSE.
THIS ISN'T A DOG HOUSE.
Are we living in a dog house?
What!?
Taro is.
HAHA HA!
OH, WELL.

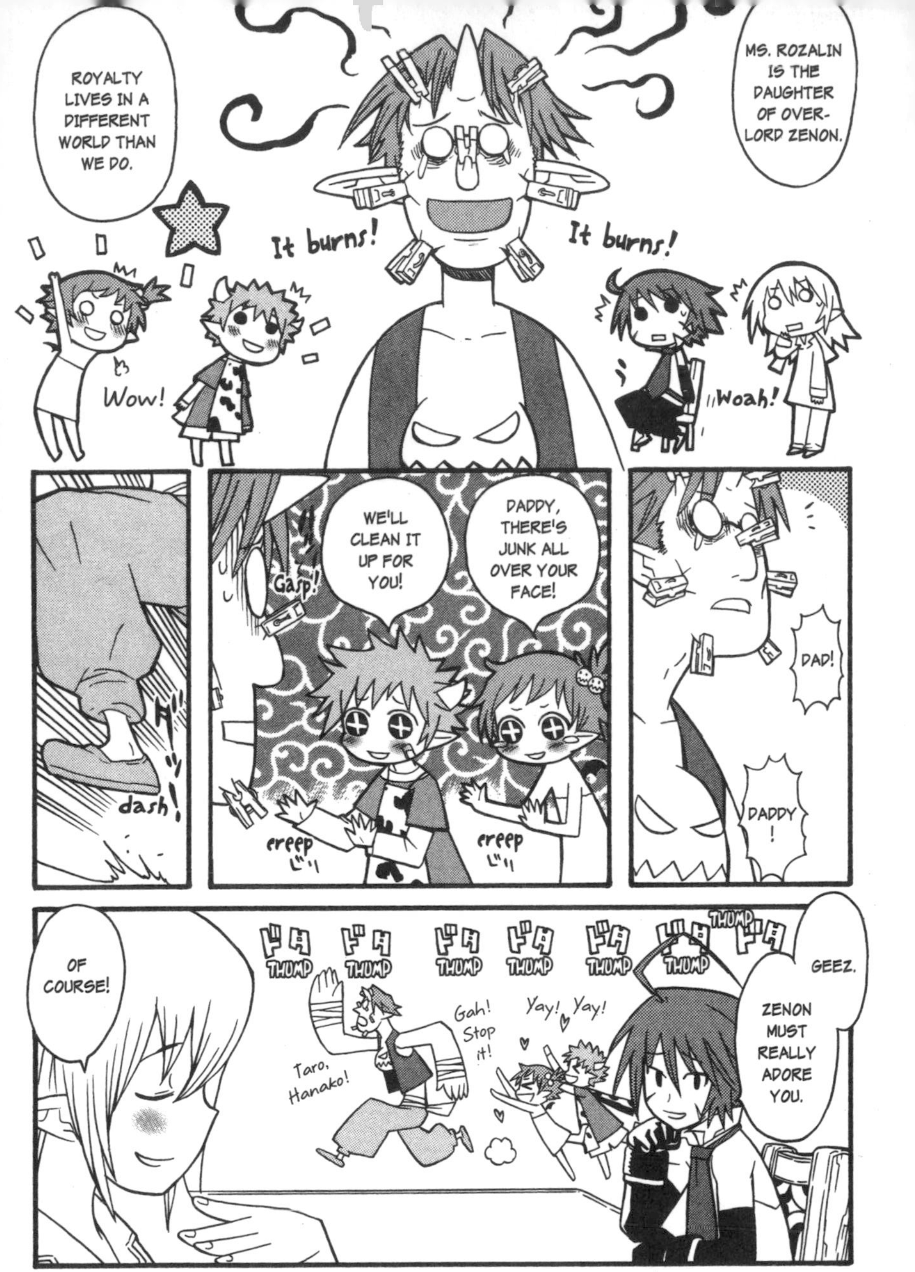
MS. ROZALIN IS THE DAUGHTER OF OVER-LORD ZENON.
It burns!
It burns!
ROYALTY LIVES IN A DIFFERENT WORLD THAN WE DO.
Woah!
Wow!
DAD!
DADDY!
DADDY, THERE'S JUNK ALL OVER YOUR FACE!
WE'LL CLEAN IT UP FOR YOU!
Gasp!
creep
creep
dash!
GEEZ.
ZENON MUST REALLY ADORE YOU.
THUMP THUMP THUMP THUMP THUMP THUMP THUMP
Yay! Yay!
Gah! Stop it!
Taro, Hanako!
OF COURSE!

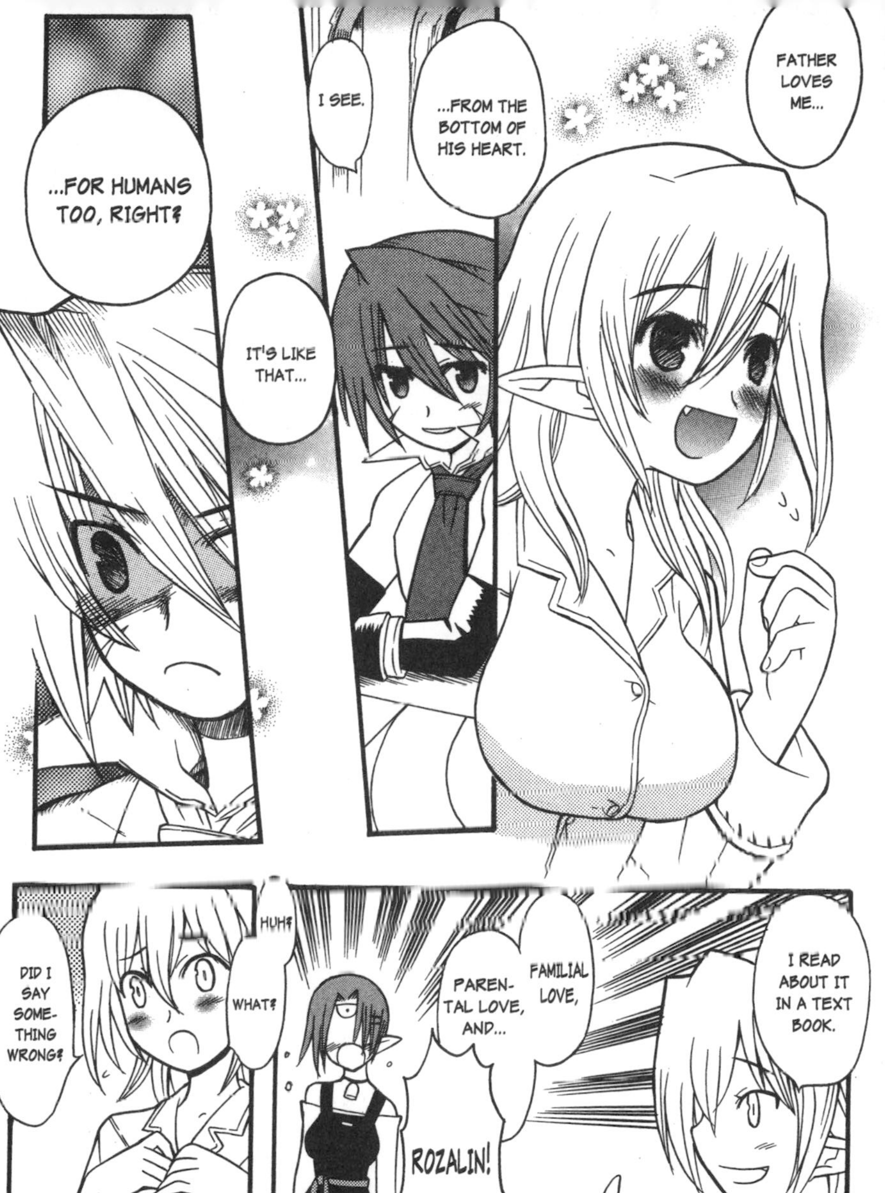
FATHER LOVES ME...
...FROM THE BOTTOM OF HIS HEART.
I SEE.
IT'S LIKE THAT...
...FOR HUMANS TOO, RIGHT?
I READ ABOUT IT IN A TEXT BOOK.
FAMILIAL LOVE,
PAREN-TAL LOVE, AND...
ROZALIN!
HUH?
WHAT?
DID I SAY SOME-THING WRONG?

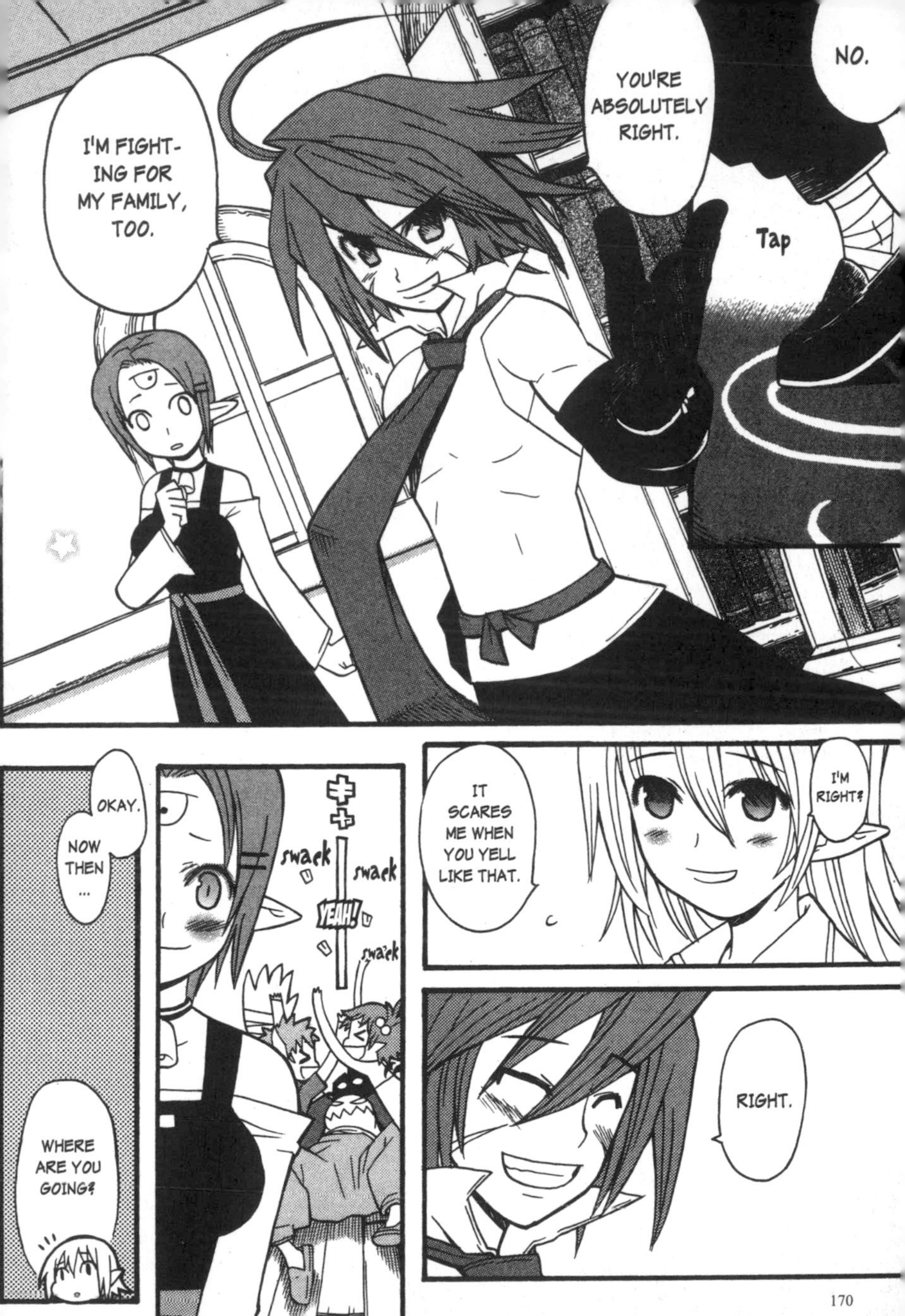

NO.
YOU'RE ABSOLUTELY RIGHT.
Tap
I'M FIGHT-ING FOR MY FAMILY, TOO.
I'M RIGHT?
IT SCARES ME WHEN YOU YELL LIKE THAT.
RIGHT.
swack
swack
YEAH!
swack
OKAY.
NOW THEN ...
WHERE ARE YOU GOING?

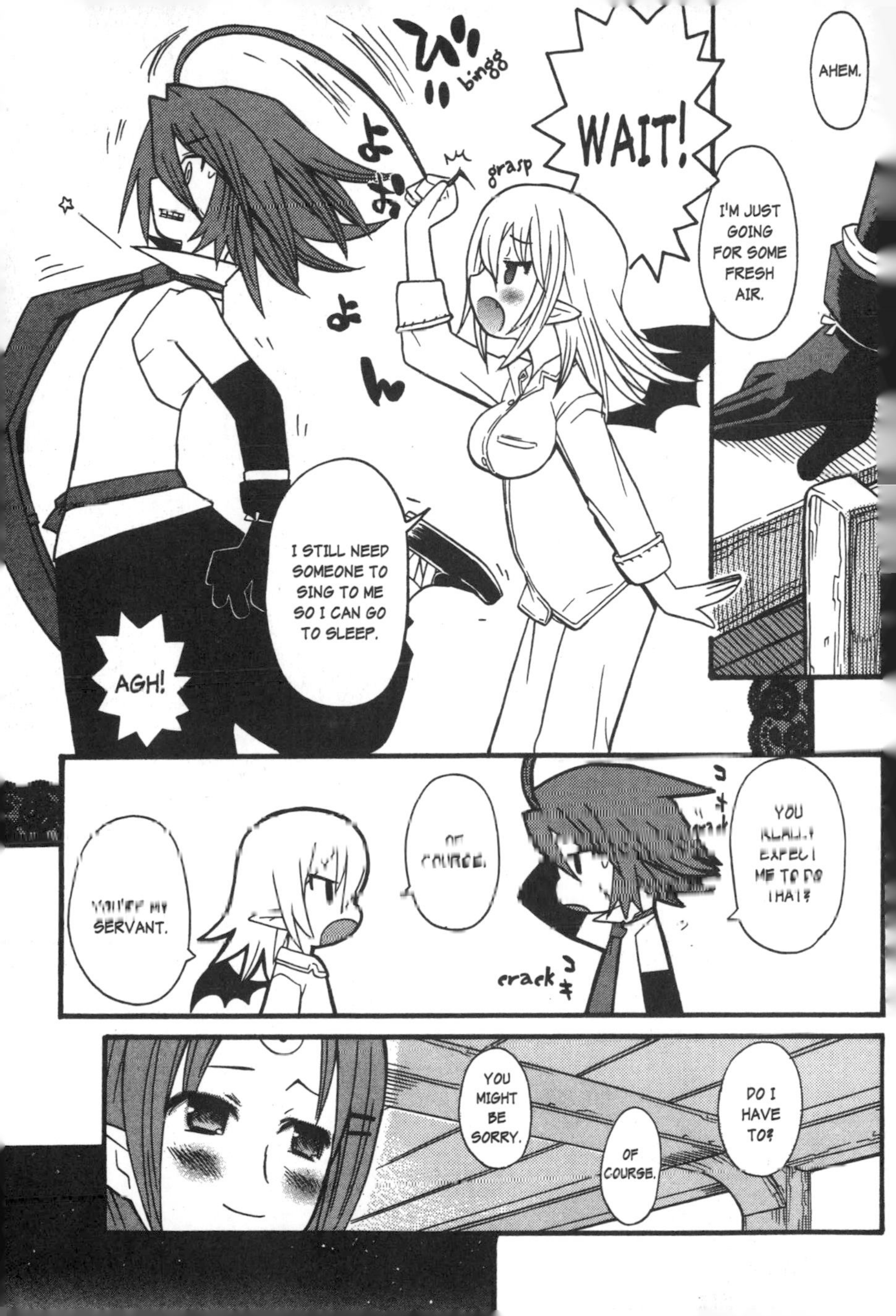
AHEM.
I'M JUST GOING FOR SOME FRESH AIR.
WAIT!
grasp
I STILL NEED SOMEONE TO SING TO ME SO I CAN GO TO SLEEP.
AGH!
YOU REALLY EXPECT ME TO DO THAT?
crack
OF COURSE.
YOU'RE MY SERVANT.
DO I HAVE TO?
OF COURSE.
YOU MIGHT BE SORRY.

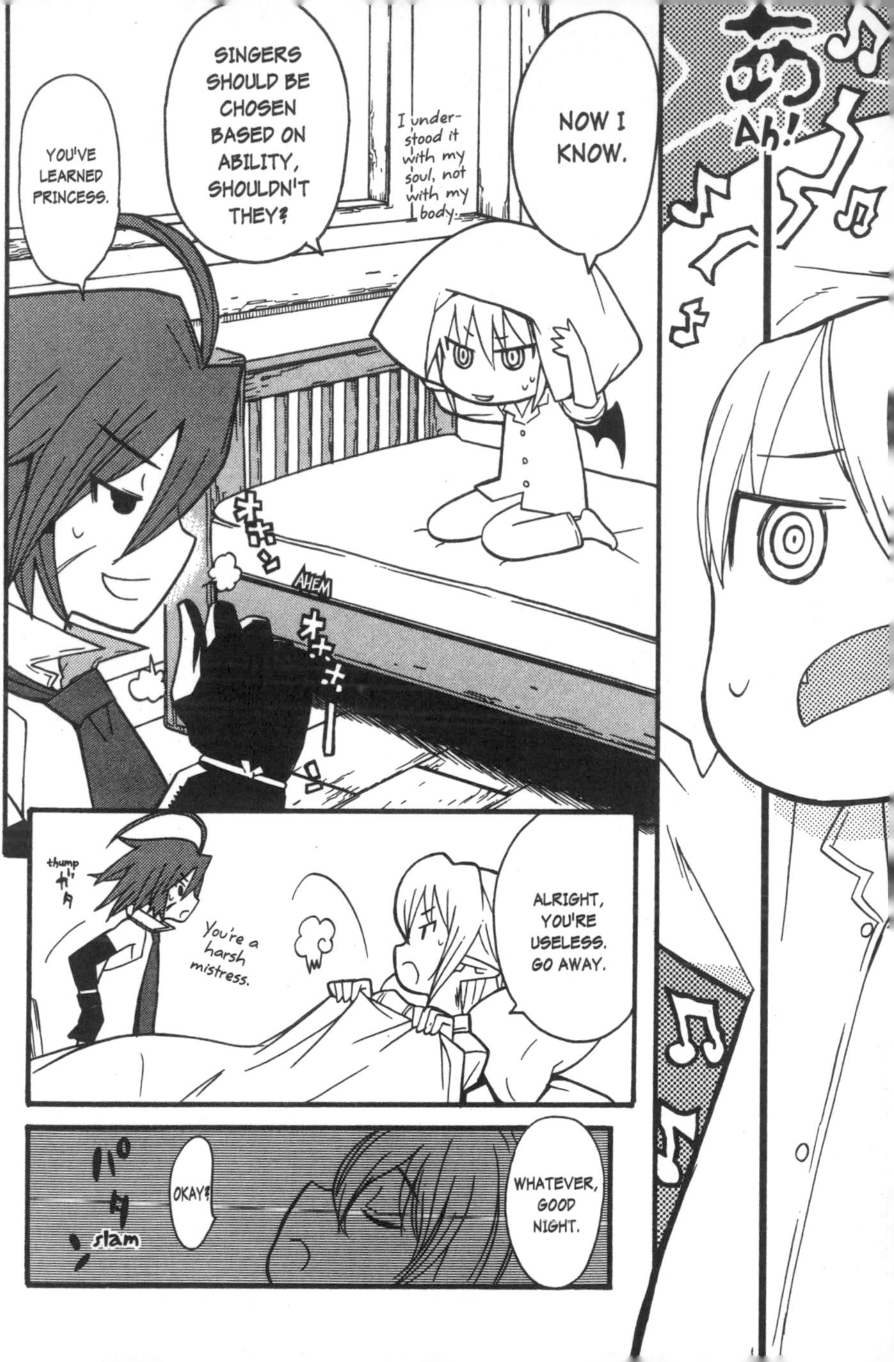

Ah!
NOW I KNOW.
I understood it with my soul, not with my body.
SINGERS SHOULD BE CHOSEN BASED ON ABILITY, SHOULDN'T THEY?
YOU'VE LEARNED PRINCESS.
AHEM
ALRIGHT, YOU'RE USELESS. GO AWAY.
You're a harsh mistress.
thump
WHATEVER, GOOD NIGHT.
OKAY?
slam

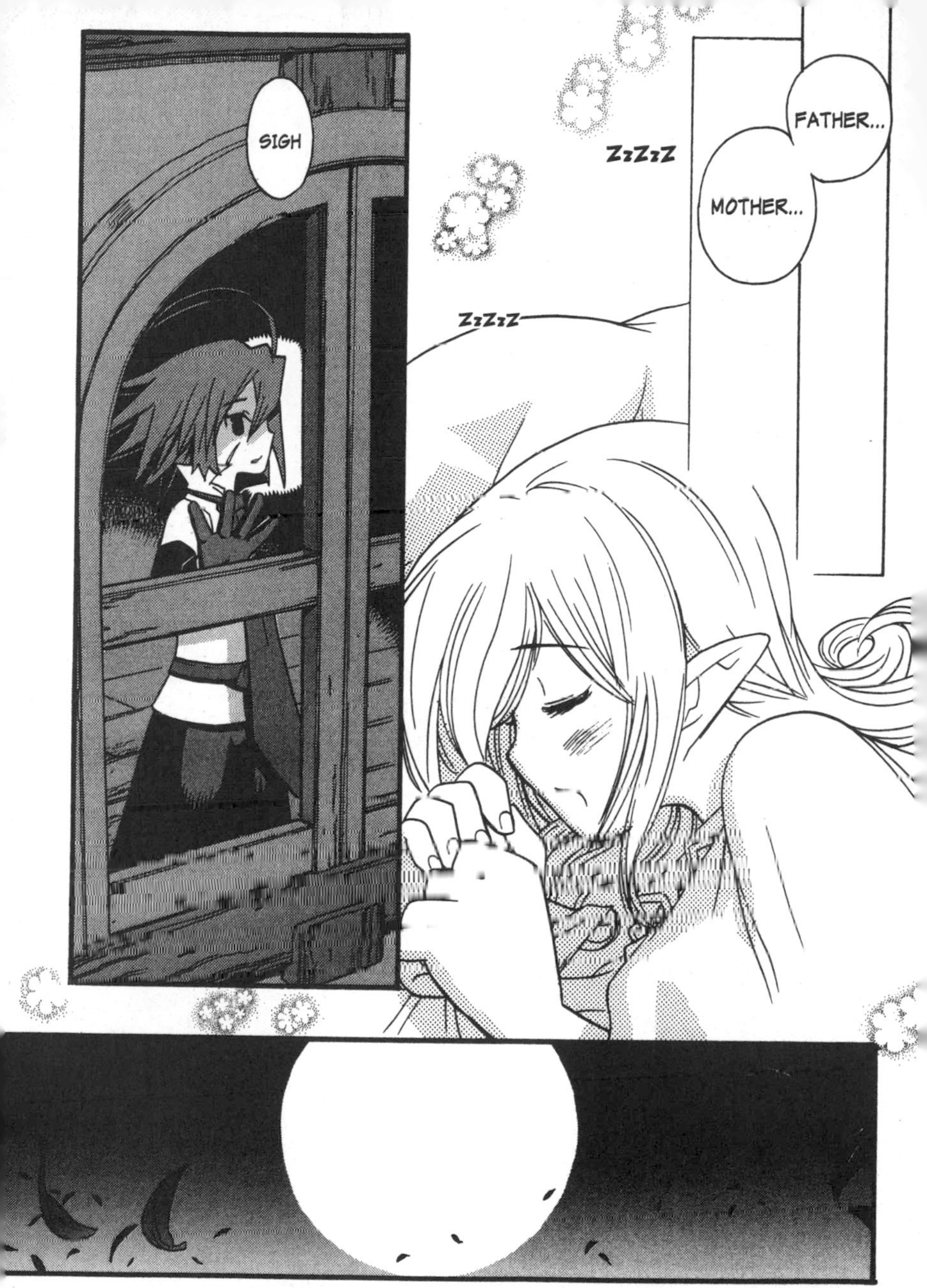
FATHER...
MOTHER...
ZzZzZ
ZzZzZ
SIGH

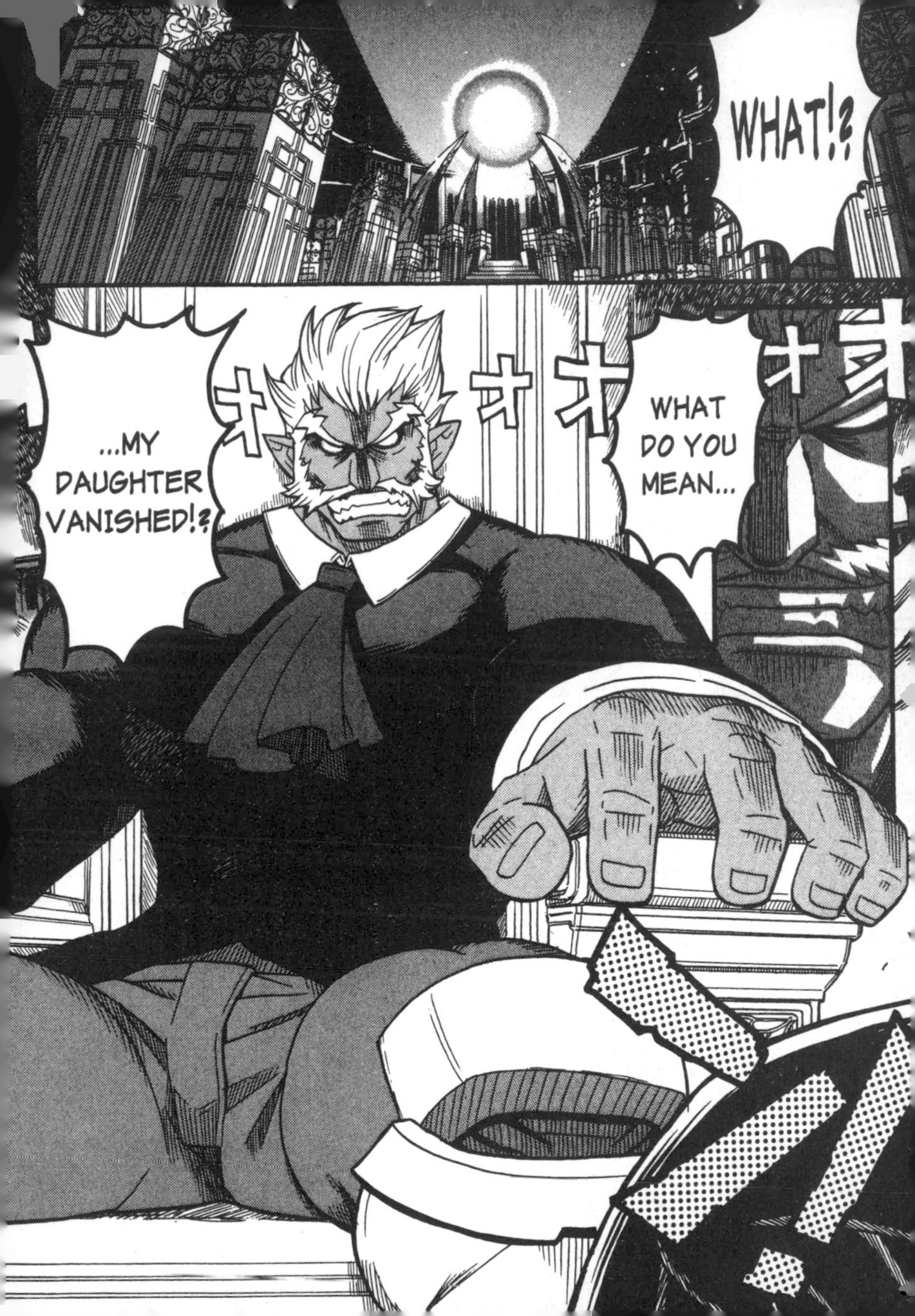
WHAT!?
WHAT DO YOU MEAN...
...MY DAUGHTER VANISHED!?

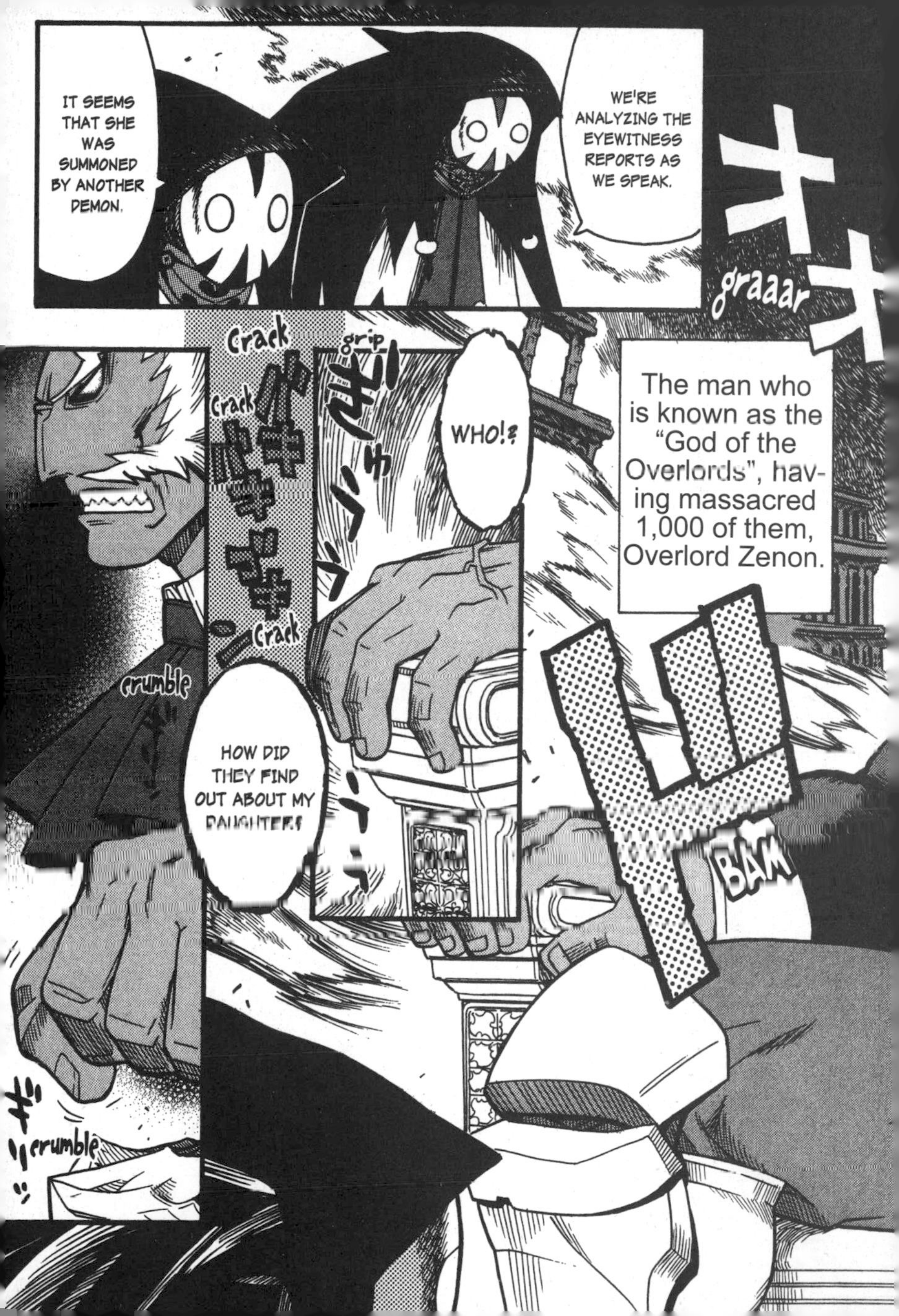
WE'RE ANALYZING THE EYEWITNESS REPORTS AS WE SPEAK.
IT SEEMS THAT SHE WAS SUMMONED BY ANOTHER DEMON.
graaar
The man who is known as the "God of the Overlords", having massacred 1,000 of them, Overlord Zenon.
BAM
WHO!?
grip
Crack
Crack
Crack
HOW DID THEY FIND OUT ABOUT MY DAUGHTER
crumble
crumble

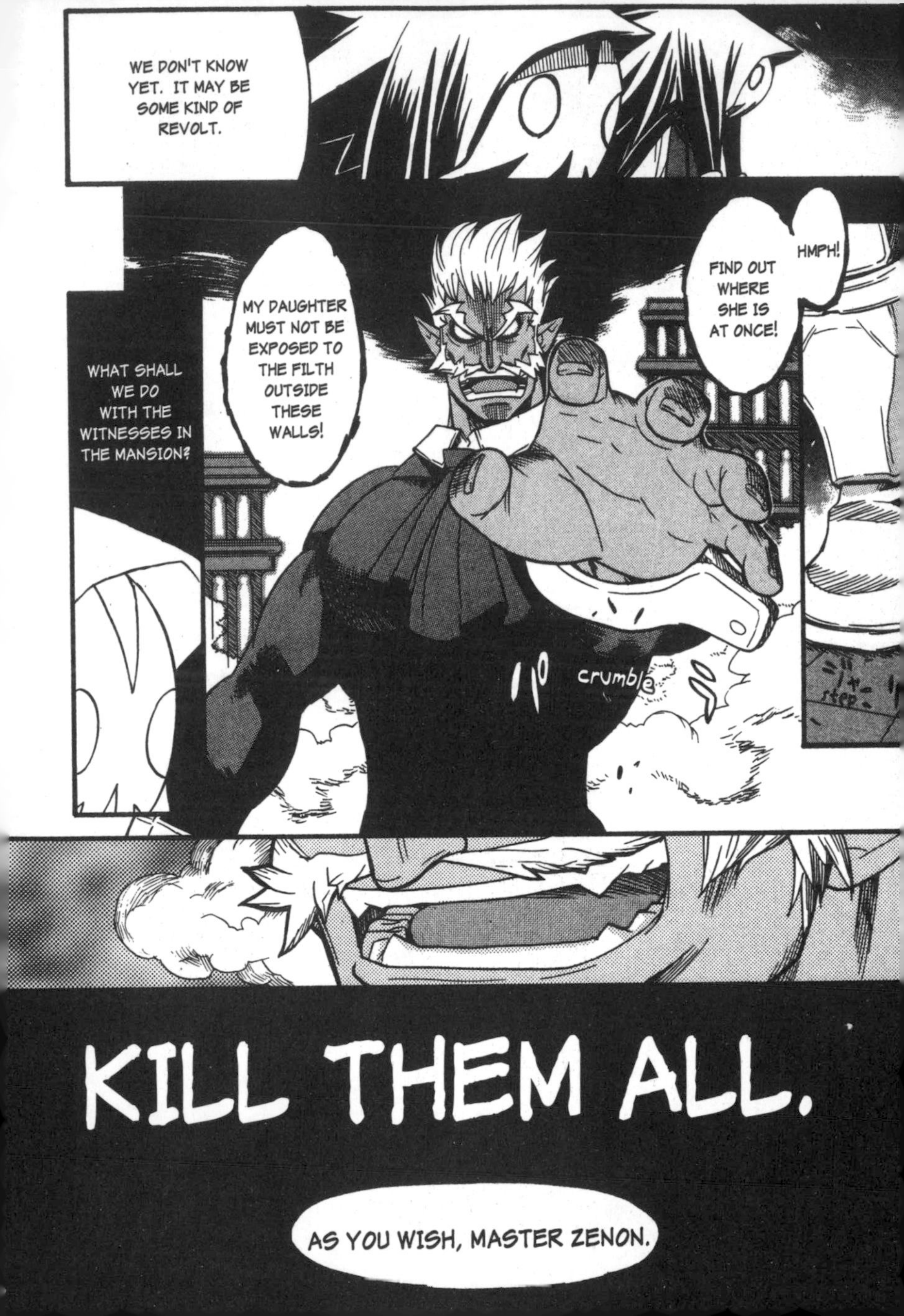
WE DON'T KNOW YET. IT MAY BE SOME KIND OF REVOLT.
HMPH!
FIND OUT WHERE SHE IS AT ONCE!
MY DAUGHTER MUST NOT BE EXPOSED TO THE FILTH OUTSIDE THESE WALLS!
WHAT SHALL WE DO WITH THE WITNESSES IN THE MANSION?
step
crumble
KILL THEM ALL.
AS YOU WISH, MASTER ZENON.

EPISODE PREVIEW

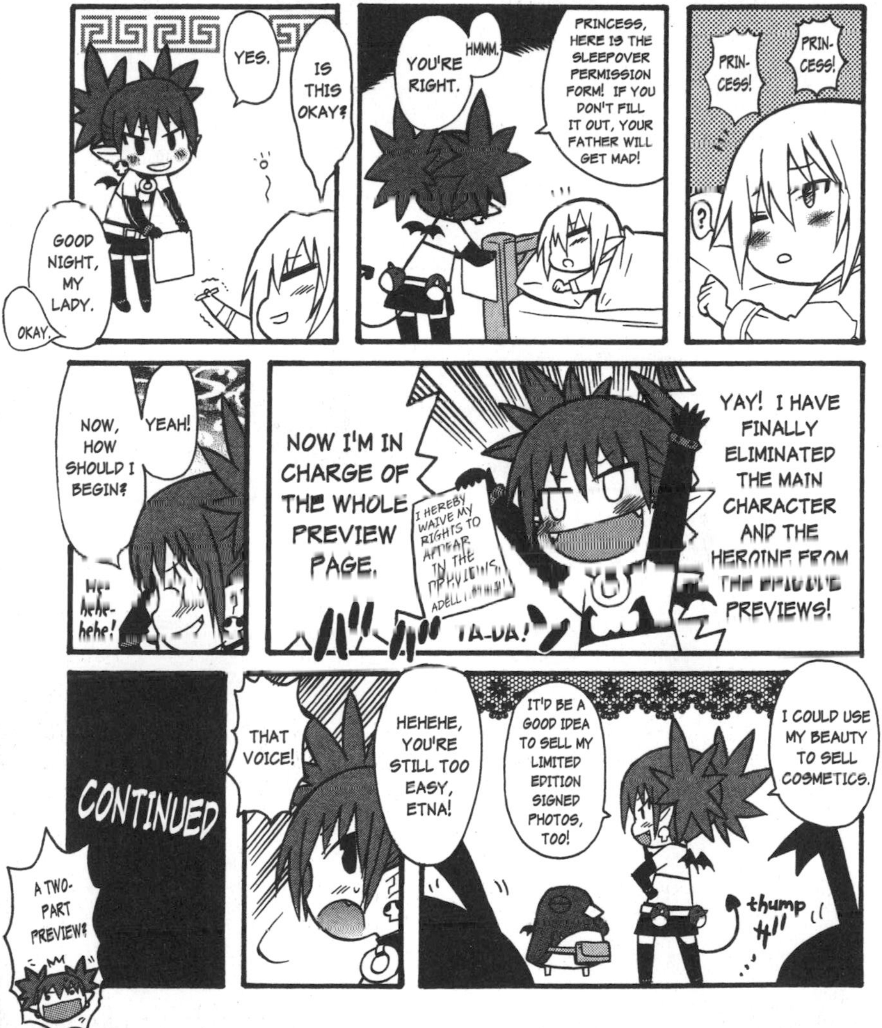
PRIN-CESS!
PRIN-CESS!
?
PRINCESS, HERE IS THE SLEEPOVER PERMISSION FORM! IF YOU DON'T FILL IT OUT, YOUR FATHER WILL GET MAD!
HMMM.
YOU'RE RIGHT.
IS THIS OKAY?
YES.
GOOD NIGHT, MY LADY.
OKAY.
YAY! I HAVE FINALLY ELIMINATED THE MAIN CHARACTER AND THE
PREVIEWS!
NOW I'M IN CHARGE OF THE WHOLE PREVIEW PAGE.
I HEREBY WAIVE MY RIGHTS TO
YEAH!
NOW, HOW SHOULD I BEGIN?
hehe-hehe!
I COULD USE MY BEAUTY TO SELL COSMETICS.
IT'D BE A GOOD IDEA TO SELL MY LIMITED EDITION SIGNED PHOTOS, TOO!
thump
HEHEHE, YOU'RE STILL TOO EASY, ETNA!
THAT VOICE!
CONTINUED
A TWO-PART PREVIEW?

IT'S COMING...

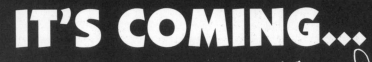

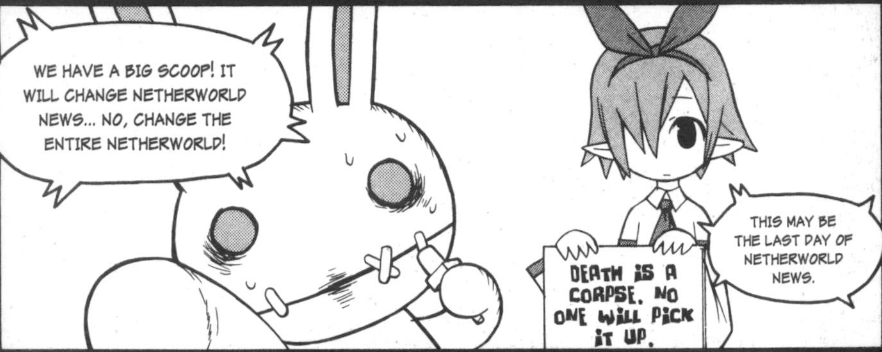
WE HAVE A BIG SCOOP! IT WILL CHANGE NETHERWORLD NEWS... NO, CHANGE THE ENTIRE NETHERWORLD!
DEATH IS A CORPSE. NO ONE WILL PICK IT UP.
THIS MAY BE THE LAST DAY OF NETHERWORLD NEWS.

After three years of silence... it has been resurrected in our world.

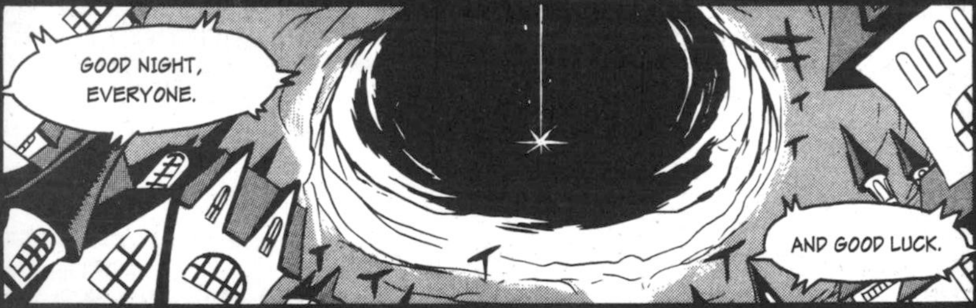
GOOD NIGHT, EVERYONE.
AND GOOD LUCK.

The sleep-depriving RPG sequel...

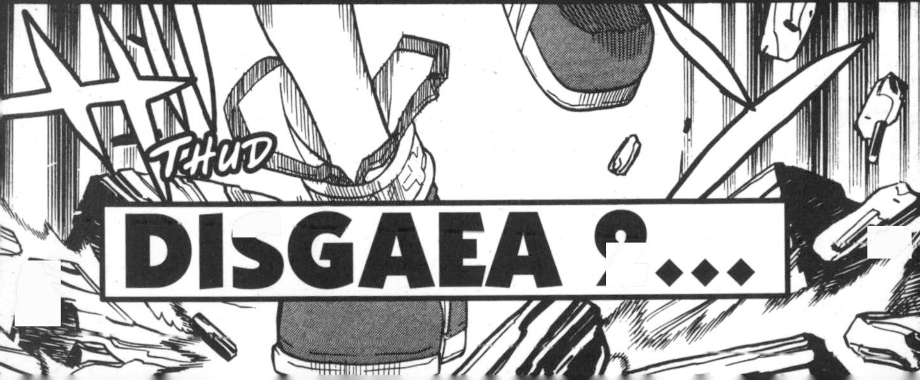
THUD
DISGAEA 2...

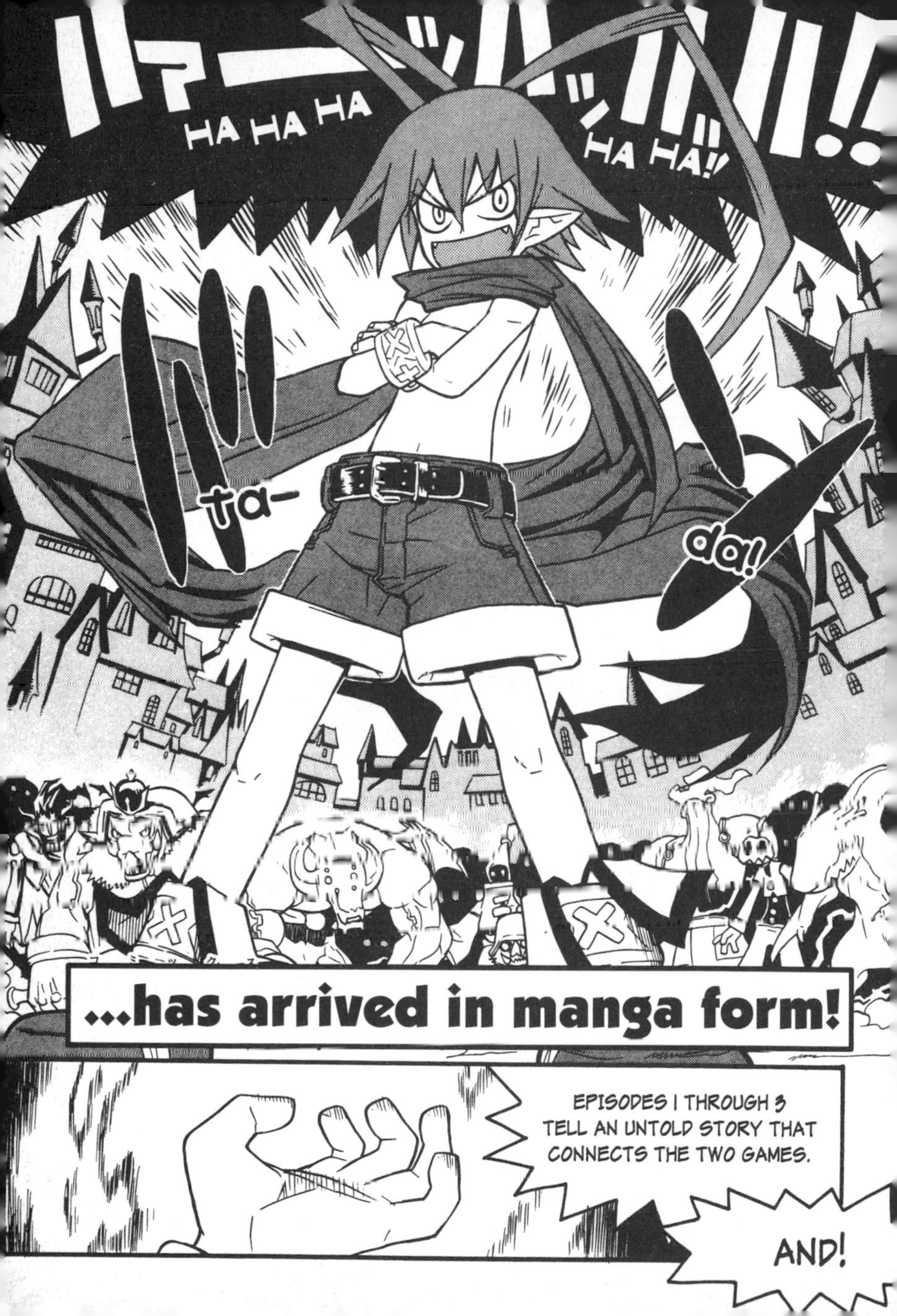
HA HA HA
HA HA!!
ta-
da!
...has arrived in manga form!
EPISODES 1 THROUGH 3 TELL AN UNTOLD STORY THAT CONNECTS THE TWO GAMES.
AND!

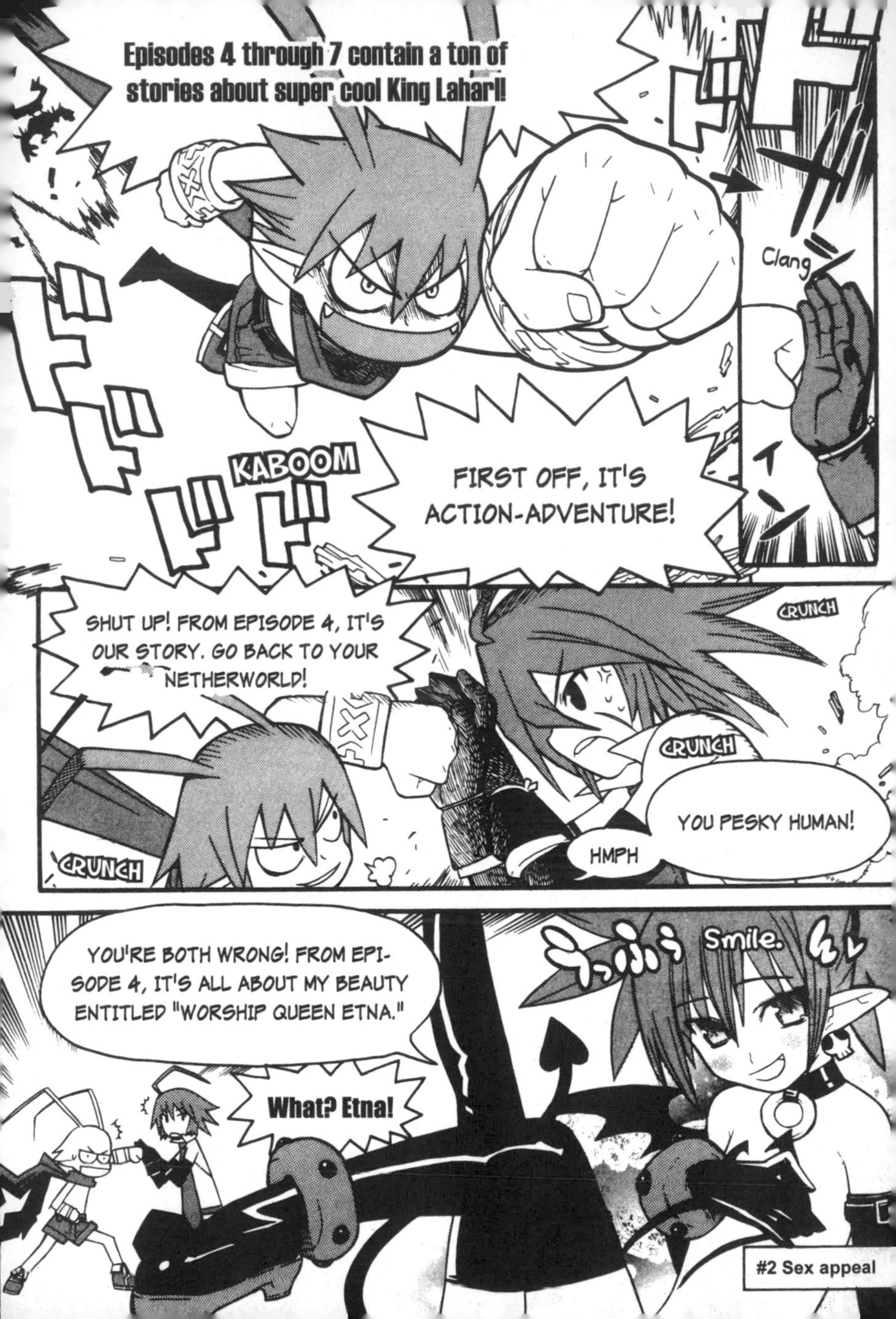

Clang
Episodes 4 through 7 contain a ton of stories about super cool King Laharl!
KABOOM
FIRST OFF, IT'S ACTION-ADVENTURE!
CRUNCH
CRUNCH
YOU PESKY HUMAN!
HMPH
SHUT UP! FROM EPISODE 4, IT'S OUR STORY. GO BACK TO YOUR NETHERWORLD!
CRUNCH
Smile.
YOU'RE BOTH WRONG! FROM EPI-SODE 4, IT'S ALL ABOUT MY BEAUTY ENTITLED "WORSHIP QUEEN ETNA."
What? Etna!
#2 Sex appeal

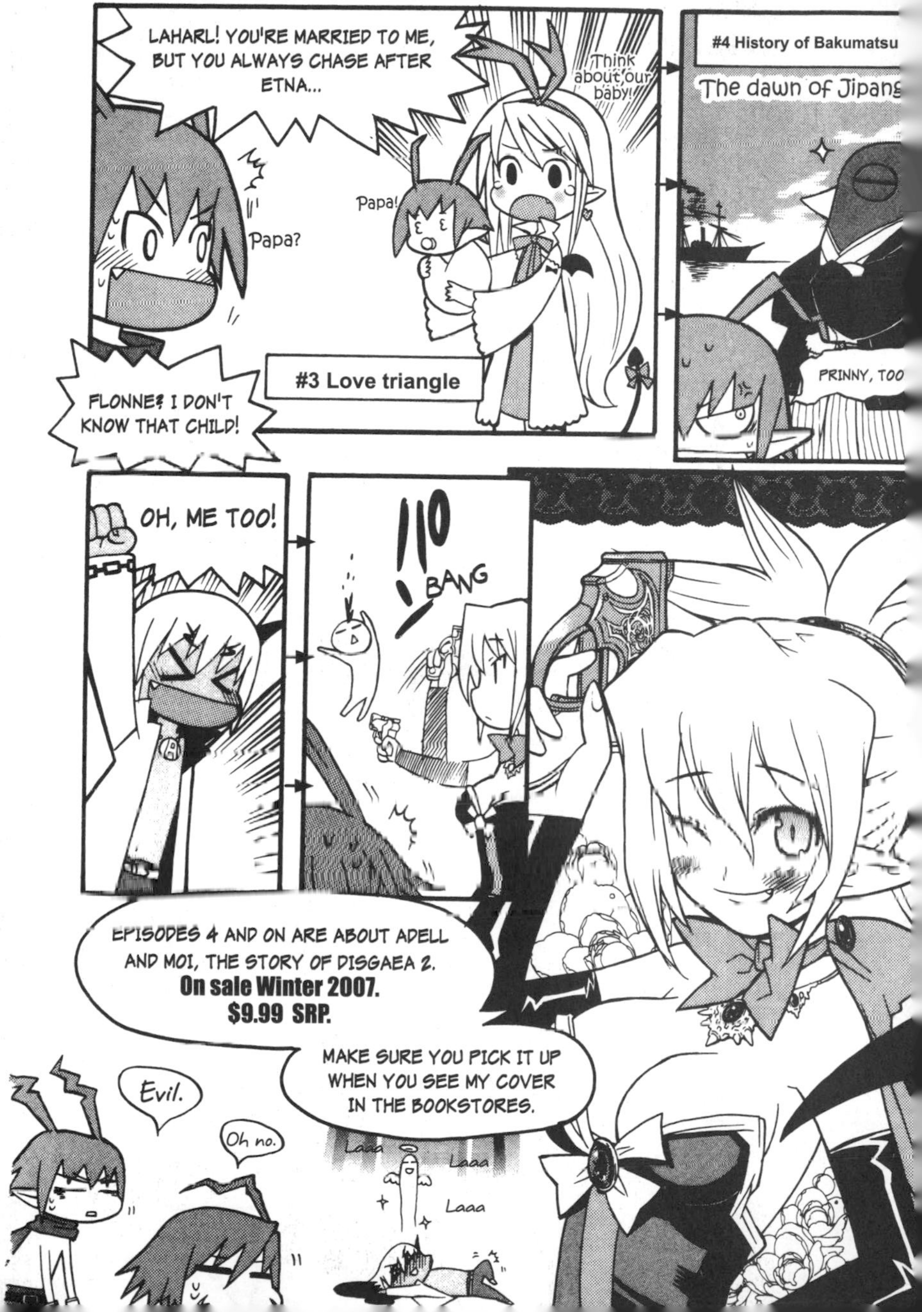
LAHARL! YOU'RE MARRIED TO ME, BUT YOU ALWAYS CHASE AFTER ETNA...
Think about our baby!
Papa!
Papa?
#3 Love triangle
FLONNE?! I DON'T KNOW THAT CHILD!
#4 History of Bakumatsu
The dawn of Jipang
PRINNY, TOO
OH, ME TOO!
BANG
EPISODES 4 AND ON ARE ABOUT ADELL AND MOI, THE STORY OF DISGAEA 2.
On sale Winter 2007.
$9.99 SRP.
MAKE SURE YOU PICK IT UP WHEN YOU SEE MY COVER IN THE BOOKSTORES.
Evil.
Oh no.
Laaa
Laaa
Laaa

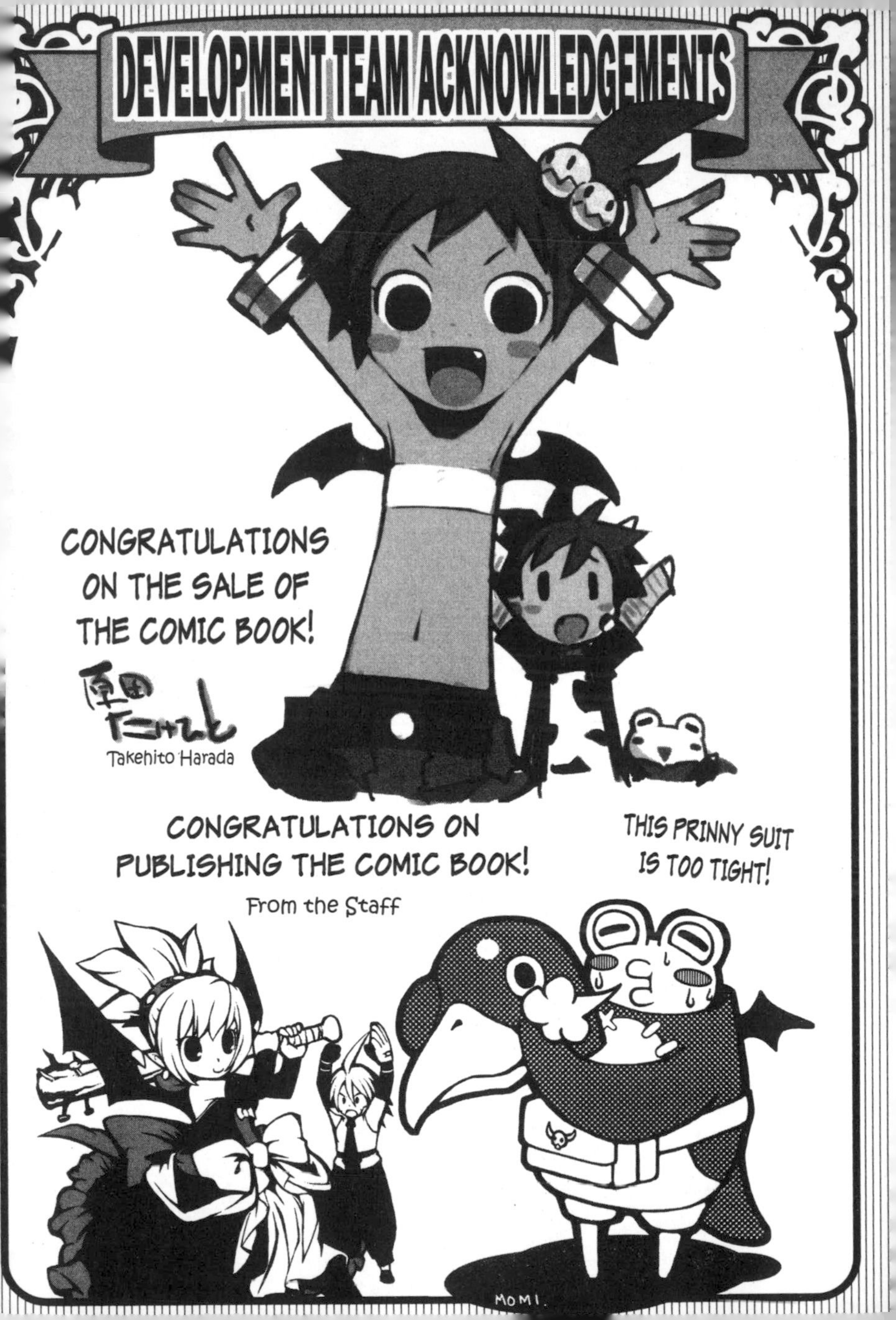
DEVELOPMENT TEAM ACKNOWLEDGEMENTS
CONGRATULATIONS ON THE SALE OF THE COMIC BOOK!
Takehito Harada
CONGRATULATIONS ON PUBLISHING THE COMIC BOOK!
From the Staff
THIS PRINNY SUIT IS TOO TIGHT!
MOMI.

AUTHOR'S NOTE

HOW DID YOU LIKE THE MANGA? IT CONNECTS THE STORY BETWEEN DISGAEA 1 AND 2 AND SHOWS THE START OF DISGAEA 2. I HOPE THOSE WHO PLAYED THE GAMES AS WELL AS THOSE WHO HAVEN'T PLAYED THE GAMES ENJOYED IT.

THERE ISN'T TOO MUCH SPACE, BUT I'D LIKE TO THANK EVERYONE WHO SUPPORTED THIS COMIC!

I WOULD LIKE TO PAY BACK ALL OF THE STAFF OF NIPPON ICHI AND MR. HARADA, THE CHARACTER DESIGNER, FOR THEIR WORDS OF ENCOURAGEMENT BY DRAWING A GOOD COMIC!

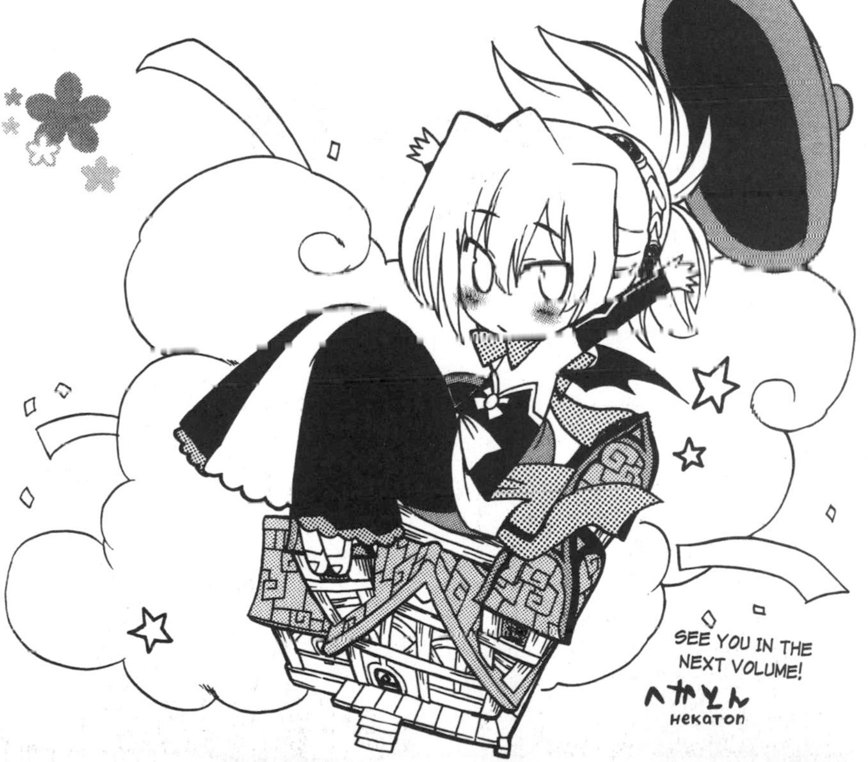
SEE YOU IN THE NEXT VOLUME!
へかとん
Hekaton

TRANSLATION NOTES

Pg. 13

Going around greeting neighbors - In Japan, when you move to a new place, it is customary to go around the neighborhood to pass out gifts (usually snacks) to say hello. Flonne has a sack, which is a furoshiki, a big square cloth used in Japan to wrap up clothes & boxes, and often used as a way to transport carry-ables to your new home.

Pg. 19

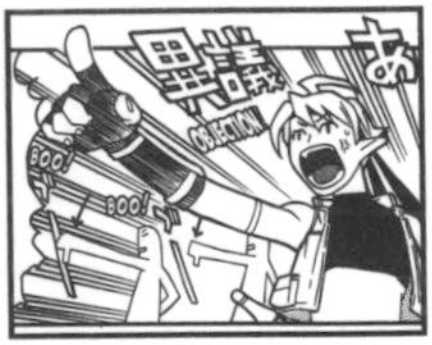
OBJECTION

Objection - A reference to *Gyakuten Saiban*, a video game originally developed by Capcom in 2001 in which the player handles the role of a young defense attorney, Ryuuichi Naruhodou. An American version was released for the Nintendo DS system in 2005 under the title Phoenix Wright: Ace Attorney. In this version, the main character's name was changed to Phoenix Wright (naruhodou translates to "of course"). In the game, the characters point and yell "Objection!" whenever they object to a piece of testimony.

Pg. 25

Sake - Japanese wine brewed from rice.

Pg. 26

Hot springs - The background depicts a Japanese hot springs, and the various food and gifts are those typically sold in and around these resorts. From right to left the items are manjuu (buns on platter), a Japanese bun snack filled with sweet bean paste, a wooden knife, a pennant, and fake fossil. The panel below has Laharl holding a folding fan.

TRANSLATION NOTES

Pg. 30

Yakisoba - A Japanese noodle dish derived from Chinese chow mein. It usually consists of noodles flavored with yakisoba sauce and mixed with pan-fried meat and vegetables. There are instant variations available, that pair instant ramen noodles with flavor packets. It literally translates to "cooked noodles."

Sauce ramen - Instant yakisoba requires boiled water to be poured into the container with the noodles and drained after several minutes. The flavoring sauce is not supposed to be added until after the water is drained. If you add the flavoring sauce before draining the water, you end up with sauce flavored ramen.

Pg. 32

Zhang Fei - A reference to Zhang Fei (167-221CE), a famous Chinese general from the Three Kingdoms period (220-280CE). Along with Guan Yu and Liu Bei, he helped established the Kingdom of Shu. In Japanese, the characters for Zhang Fei's name are pronounced "Yokutoku."

Guan Yu - A reference to Guan Yu (162-219CE), famous Chinese general from the Three Kingdoms period. In Japanese, the characters for Guan Yu's name are pronounced "Uncho."

Netherworld Dynasty Warrior - A reference to the *Dynasty Warriors* series of video games created by Koei. Dynasty Warriors is loosely based around the historical novel, *Romance of Three Kingdoms*, by Luo Guanzhong (circa 1330-1400CE). *Dynasty Warriors* is itself a spin-off

TRANSLATION NOTES

of Koei's popular strategy video game series, *Romance of the Three Kingdoms* based on the novel of the same name.

"The Oath in the Peach Garden" - A reference to the novel, *Romance of Three Kingdoms*. In the novel, Liu Bei, Guan Yu and Zhang Fei swear an oath to be brothers in Zhang Fei's backyard. Together they formed a resistance against the Yellow Turban Rebellion and eventually established the Kingdom of Shu. Presumably, Etna assumes the role of Liu Bei (161-223CE) the first emperor of the Kingdom of Shu ("Gentoku" is the Japanese pronunciation of his name).

Pg. 33

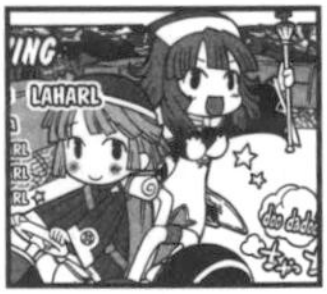
LAHARL

Laharl's video game - Laharl's *Mario Kart*-inspired video game features Prier and Culotte from *La Pucelle*, another strategy RPG created by Nippon Ichi, the company that brought you *Disgaea*.

Pg. 44

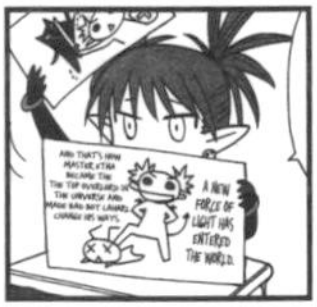
A NEW FORCE OF LIGHT HAS ENTERED THE WORLD.

Etna teaching Prinnies with picture cards - Etna is using kami-shibai (paper play) to teach the Prinnies what her plans are for becoming an overlord. It was a popular form of entertainment for children before television became commonplace.

Pg. 56

Toast in the mouth - A parody of manga/anime high school characters. When high school kids are late for school, they are often depicted running out of the house with a piece of toast in their mouth.

TRANSLATION NOTES

Memorial Netherworld Schoolgirl Etna - A parody of *Tokimeki Memorial*, the popular dating-sim video game series by Konami.

Sempai - The Japanese word for "senior." The direct translation is "you who came first."

Pg. 57

A pheasant won't get shot down if it doesn't cry. - A Japanese saying.

Usagi - "Usagi" is Japanese for "rabbit."

Pg. 67

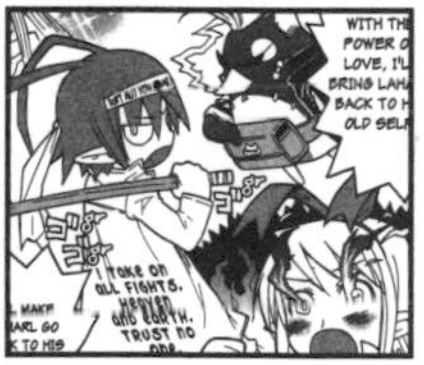
WITH THE POWER OF LOVE, I'LL BRING LAHARL BACK TO HIS OLD SELF
I TAKE ON ALL FIGHTS. HEAVEN AND EARTH. TRUST NO ONE.

Bosozoku Laharl and Prinny - Laharl is dressed as a stereotypical "bosozoku" (Lit. "reckless driving tribe"). Bosozoku are analogous to American biker gangs. Members often wear clothing such as jumpsuits, or in Laharl's case, a long coat with slogans written on it. The Prinny has a dyed pompadour, known in Japan as "Regent," a hairstyle popular amongst bosozoku.

Pg. 81

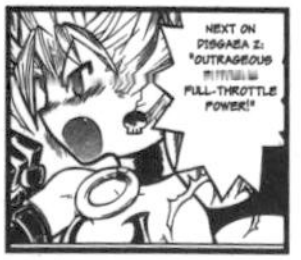
NEXT ON DISGAEA 2: "OUTRAGEOUS FULL-THROTTLE POWER!"

"Outrageous Extreme Full-Throttle Power!" - A parody of the title of the first *Dragon Ball Z* TV ending theme song, "Dete Koi Tobikkiri ZENKAI Power" ("Come Out, Incredible ZENKAI Power").

Pg. 106

Etna's Mask - Parody of the shoujo manga classic *Glass Mask* by Suzue Miuchi. The play title "Blood-Soaked Heavenly Maiden" is a parody of

TRANSLATION NOTES

"Kurenai Tennyo" ("Crimson Heavenly Maiden"), the legendary play for which both Maya Kitajima of *Glass Mask*, and her rival Ayumi Himekawa, are trying to get the title role.

Pg. 124
Mysterious assassin punch of the North Star - A reference to the famous manga and anime, *Fist of the North Star*. The main character, Kenshiro, has a move called "Hokuto Hyakuretsu Ken" ("North Star Hundred Crack Fist") that is capable of causing his opponent's head to explode.

Pg. 156
Cyborg Dark Hero - A parody of the works of Shotaro Ishinomori, creator of *Cyborg 009*, *Kamen Rider*, *8 Man*, and numerous other titles.

Pg. 162
Tea stem - "Tea column" is a term for a tea leaf stem that stands upright in the tea. It is rare occurrence, so when it happens Japanese believe it's a sign of good luck.

Pg. 181
Bakumatsu – Bakumatsu encompasses the period in Japanese history spanning from 1853 to 1867 otherwise known as the late Tokugawa Shogunate. It was during this time that Japan opened itself up to the world ending years of isolationism and while also ushering in a period of political and military modernization.

Jipang – During the 16th century, the English word for Japan was Jipang, which was most likely borrowed from early Mandarin Chinese.

VOLUME 2 PREVIEW

Axel: Dark Hero Axel here, with an exclusive report on volume 2 of Disgaea 2.
Axel: This assignment is full of intrigue and danger at every turn...

Axel: Haa!
Axel: Booby traps around every corner...
Axel: Hiya!

VOLUME 2 PREVIEW

Axel: But!
Axel: Being a Dark Hero, I am not so easily tricked. It will take more than a mere trap to take down a Dark Hero.

Axel: As I journey deeper into the darkness, the sense of doom is intense. Will the Dark Hero be able to get the scoop?
Axel: Nothing will stop the Dark Hero from getting to the story behind the next volume.

VOLUME 2 PREVIEW

Axel: But first, I must dispatch with the assassins that have been sent to silence me.

Axel: Dark Hero Chop!
Axel: Dark Hero Kick!
Axel: Do they think that a few ninja assassins and cyborg killing machines would be able to defeat a Dark Hero such as me? Think again!

VOLUME 2 PREVIEW

Director: Cut! Cut!
Director: Axel, baby. What are you talking about? Ninja assassins and cyborg killing machines? There's nobody here but us. And booby traps? This is an office.

Axel: What about that dangerous stack of papers over there? It could fall over and crush us at any moment.
Director: This is supposed to be a preview, not an action show. Axel, you're supposed to be reporting on volume 2...
Axel: But I'm the Dark Hero. Don't worry, I'm just getting to the story...

VOLUME 2 PREVIEW

Director: Axel, baby, you have to face the facts. You're no longer the Dark Hero that everybody loved.
Axel: What!? Impossible! Everyone knows the Dark Hero Axel!
Director: The report, Axel, what about the report? We've already used up over half the panels and we're almost at the end!

Axel: Okay! Dark Hero Axel delivers on his promises. As stated earlier, here is my ultra exclusive preview.
Director: Finally!

VOLUME 2 PREVIEW

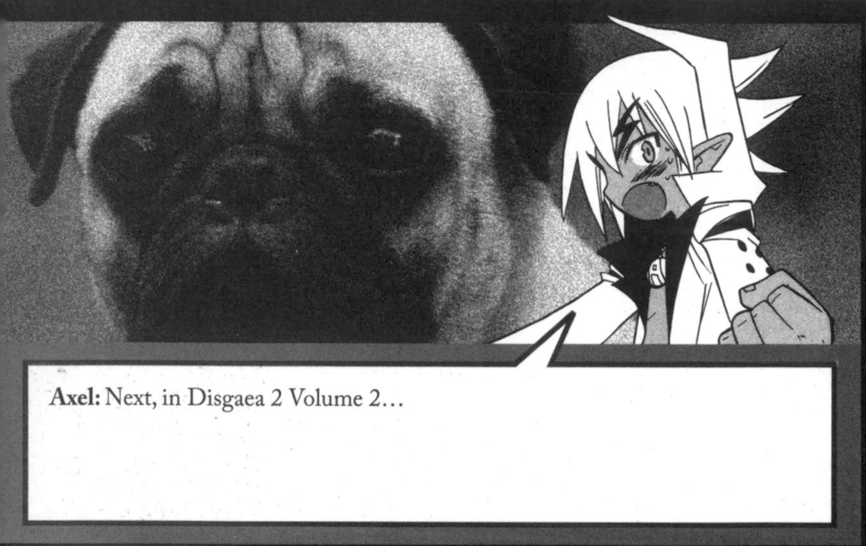
Axel: Next, in Disgaea 2 Volume 2…

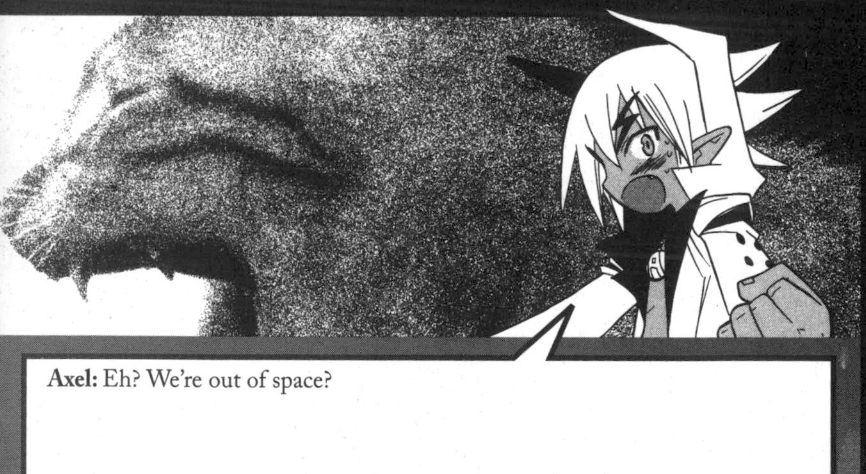
Axel: Eh? We're out of space?

VOLUME 2 PREVIEW

Adell has promised to take Rozalin back to her father, the powerful Lord Zenon. But as they get closer to the mysterious overlord, Rozalin questions what she knows about her father and Adell broods over the fact that he will have to fight against him. The appearances of Beauty Queen Etna and the Dark Hero Axel only ensure that the path to Zenon will be more difficult than they imagined. And Zenon himself is not standing idly by, as his two minions, the mysterious hooded figures, are charged with finding Rozalin and bringing her back.

CHARACTERS: ADELL

Age 17

In order to turn his demon family back into humans, this young man risks his life by standing up against the Overlord Zenon. He is also the only human not affected by Zenon's curse.

He is strong-willed, and when he makes a promise he will risk his life to keep it. He doesn't like lies and girls; he is a hot-blood-ed, straightforward kind of guy.

CHARACTERS: ROZALIN

Age 17

Overlord Zenon's spoiled and sheltered only daughter. She loves and respects her father, who pampers her very much.

She has lived in her mansion her whole life, so she knows nothing of the outside world. Because of this, her common sense and way of thought are different from both humans and demons.

She has no experience in battle, and is Level 1.

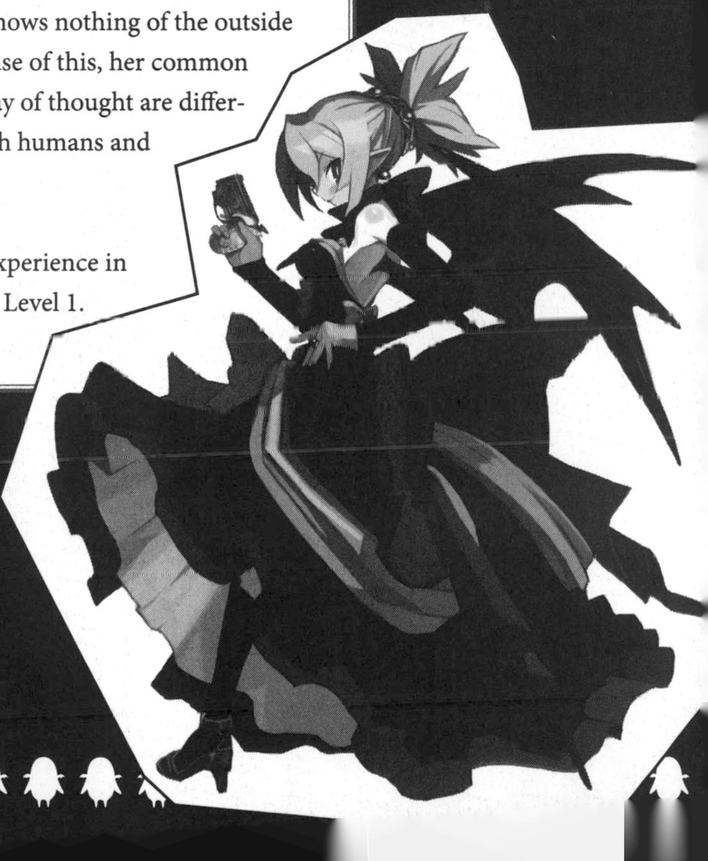

CHARACTERS: HANAKO

Age 9

Adell and Taro's little sister, who is very energetic and a tad precocious. Turned into a demon by Overlord Zenon's curse, she has devil wings on her back. She admires Adell, and her future dream is to become a strong, sexy demon.

Despite her age and looks, her cooking skill is of a professional level.

CHARACTERS: TARO

Age 11

Adell's younger brother, who is timid and a little sarcastic. As a result of Overlord Zenon's curse, he is a demon with horns on his head.

He usually talks in a carefree tone, and is never nervous.

CHARACTERS: ETNA

Age 1473

A Demon Lord who comes to Veldime to defeat the legendary Overlord Zenon in order to obtain the title of Ultimate Overlord. She searches for Overlord Zenon with her servant Prinnies, but because he is nowhere to be found, she has started to get bored. She has very strong powers and it is rumored that her true powers surpass even those of a typical Overlord.

Beware, as she will get very mad if you call her flat-chested.

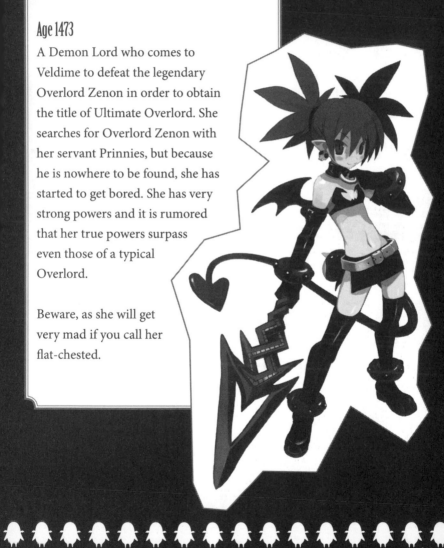

CHARACTERS: LAHARL

Age 1376

The Overlord of a netherworld different from Veldime.

A selfish, egotistical supreme-self believer. He is currently quarreling with his vassal, Etna.

CHARACTERS: FLONNE

Age 1512

A former angel-trainee who is currently a
fallen angel living in Laharl's netherworld.
She is a clutzy little love
maniac who tries to
cover everything
with love.

She also likes hero an-
ime and special effects
movies.

CHARACTERS: ZENON

The father of Rozalin and the conqueror of Veldime, he turned humans into demons. He appeared in Veldime 15 years ago and made a curse that turned the world into a demon world. His curse also saps the memories and consciences from the people of Veldime. He is feared as an overlord who has killed 1,000 other overlords.

CHARACTERS: AXEL

Age 2188

He used to be a popular TV and movie star, but now he works as the host of a local travel show. He still believes he is popular and cannot let go of his past glory. Even though it is a travel show, he tries to force in action scenes. His idiocy always gives his partner director a hard time.

CHARACTERS: PRINNY

Loyal(?) servants hired by Etna.

They are treated poorly by their selfish master on a daily basis, but because of their apathy, it seems that their master-servant relationship is going well.

Inside the Prinnies are actually the souls of humans or demons who have committed crimes during their lifetimes. Supposedly they repent for their sins by doing public service.

CHARACTERS: DAD

Age 41

Adell, Taro and Hanako's slightly meek
father, who, aside from Adell, is the only
other sane person in the family. As a result
of Zenon's curse, he has
turned into a demon zom-
bie, but does not smell. His
real name is Dad.

CHARACTERS: MOM

Age 38

Adell, Taro and Hanako's mother, she was a first-class summoner when she was young. She won't hesitate to do anything in order to get things done, and doesn't care about the details.

She has a third eye in the middle of her forehead because of Zenon's curse.

BROCCOLI BOOKS *FAN QUIZ!*

1. *Until the Full Moon*'s Marlo has the most unfortunate luck. The child of a vampire father and werewolf mother, on nights of the full moon he undergoes a horrific transformation. He turns into a _____.

a) vampire
b) werewolf
c) woman
d) zombie

2. Milfeulle is a good cook, so perhaps it's no surprise that in *Galaxy Angel II*, she ends up selecting Kazuya Shiranami for the new Rune Troupe. Kazuya happens to be a skilled _____ chef.

a) Italian
b) iron
c) pastry
d) Chinese

3. Behold, the return of the Dark Hero in *Disgaea 2*. After a minor dry spell, he's poised to make his return to the limelight. Uh, what's his name again?

a) Adell
b) Axel
c) Vyers
d) Guyver

4. While it may seem like Dejiko from the *Di Gi Charat Theater* series can do whatever she wants (and in fact does) she has someone watching out for her. Is it a balloon, is it a ball? It's just _____.

a) Pat
b) Gema
c) Abarenbou
d) Rod-yan

5. Ashurum, the powerful conglomerate in *E'S*, is often called upon to take care of extremely dangerous criminals. Perhaps it's a good thing then that their agents have _____ powers.

a) political
b) max
c) psychic
d) axis

6. Normad may only appear in the *Galaxy Angel* anime and *Galaxy Angel Party* graphic novels, but he's still an important member of the *Galaxy Angel* family. There's much more to this smart-mouthed plush. What is he really?

a) a lounge singer
b) a standup comedian
c) a missile AI
d) a cappuccino maker

7. Atsuma has been charged with recovering the spirit Okikurumi in *KAMUI*. To aide him in his quest, he is partnered with sword imbued with an immature spirit. What is the spirit's name?

a) Einlanzer
b) Masamune
c) Glamdring
d) Kojomaru

8. Charbroiled dragon, eye of the tiger. In *Disgaea 2* Adell's mom, a former gifted summoner, attempts to summon the powerful Overlord Zenon. Imagine how surprised she is when they summon _____ instead.

a) Rozalin
b) Robin Williams
c) Apollo Creed
d) Laharl

9. Each of the boys in *Aquarian Age – Juvenile Orion* belongs to a different faction. Kaname is a member of the Darklore faction, comprised of vampires, mermaids, demons and fairies. What faction is Tsukasa from?

a) nWo
b) E.G.O.
c) WIZ-DOM
d) ERASER

10. Detective Kosuke Gindaichi isn't the only one following the titular characters of *Yoki Koto Kiku*. A mysterious hooded figure with a scythe is after them as well. Who is this suspicious character?

a) Shinigami
b) Orco
c) the emperor
d) their grandfather

Answers: 1. c, 2. c, 3. b, 4. b, 5. c, 6. c, 7. d, 8. a, 9. d, 10. a

1-2 questions right: Broccoli? Like the producer?
3-4 questions right: It's better than brussel sprouts.
5-7 questions right: I feel like a giant when I eat it.
8-10 questions right: Broccoli's the best!

For more information and the latest news on Broccoli Books, check out the Broccoli Books website:

www.broccolibooks.com

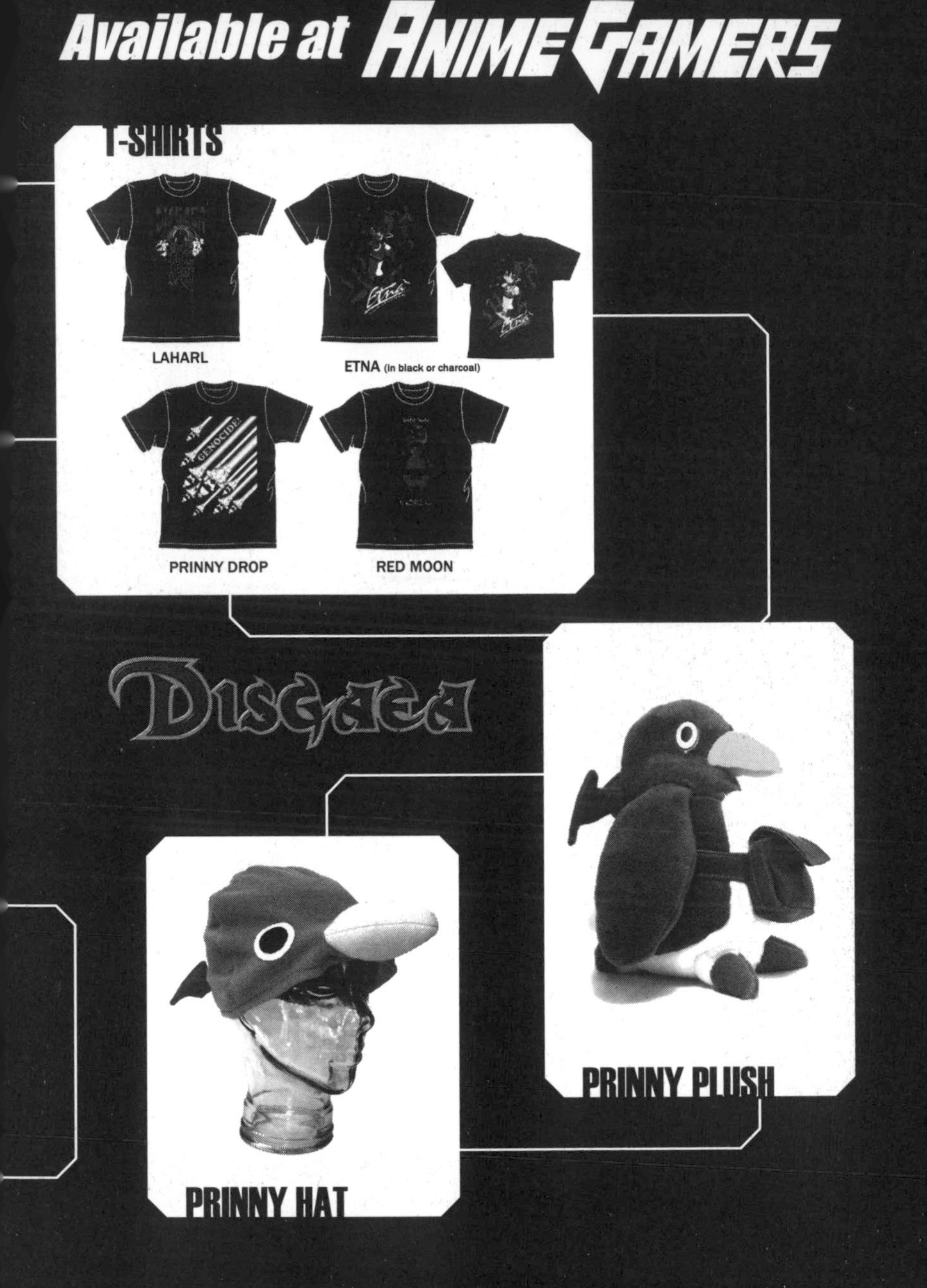
Available at ANIME GAMERS
T-SHIRTS
LAHARL
ETNA (in black or charcoal)
PRINNY DROP
RED MOON
Disgaea
PRINNY PLUSH
PRINNY HAT

PlayStation®2

DISGAEA 2
Cursed Memories

Disgaea®, the definitive SRPG, finally returns!
Get ready for 100+ hours of devilish mayhem!

In Stores Now

TEEN
T
Language
Mild Fantasy Violence
Mild Suggestive Themes
CONTENT RATED BY
ESRB

日本一
SOFTWARE

NIS America
www.NISAmerica.com

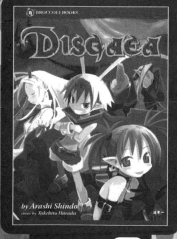

Like Disgaea stuff, but don't know where to get it?
Just order directly from us!

Just photocopy this page, fill out neatly and mail **with money order** for the total amount to the address below:

I Love Disgaea!
c/o Anime Gamers
1728 S. La Cienega Blvd.
Los Angeles, CA 90035

SHIP TO:

NAME:

ADDRESS:

CITY:＿＿＿＿＿＿＿＿ STATE:＿＿＿＿ ZIP:＿＿＿＿＿

EMAIL:

AGE:＿＿＿ GENDER: M / F

Would you like to be added to the mailing list? Yes / No

ITEM	ITEM TYPE	UNIT PRICE	QTY	EXTENDED TOTAL
Prinny fleece cap	APPAREL	$19.95		
Prinny plush	PLUSH	$19.95		
Big Sis Prinny plush	PLUSH	$19.95		
World of Disgaea art book	BOOK	$19.95		
Disgaea 2 Vol. 2 graphic novel	BOOK	$9.95		
Disgaea 2 trading figure set	FIGURE	$79.95		
Trading figure set A: Reigning Overlords	FIGURE	$49.95		
Trading figure set B: Devil May Care	FIGURE	$49.95		
If only BOOKs are ordered, please omit the $10.00 shipping charge from the final total. For Canadian orders, add $3.00 to the first BOOK, and $1.00 for each additional BOOK.			Shipping:	$10.00
			Shipping to Canada:	
			TOTAL:	

Only Money Orders made out in US funds will be accepted using this order form. Make Money Orders out to Anime Gamers. Checks will not be accepted. Credit card payments are accepted, but only for online orders. For domestic shipping, there is a flat rate charge of $10 for all orders except for those only containing BOOKs. Orders that consist of only BOOKs qualify for free shipping, with the exception of Canadian orders. For Canadian orders, add $3.00 for the first BOOK, and $1.00 for each additional BOOK. All shipping is via US Postal Service. This order form is valid for the United States and Canada only. For international orders, please visit: **www.animegamersusa.com**

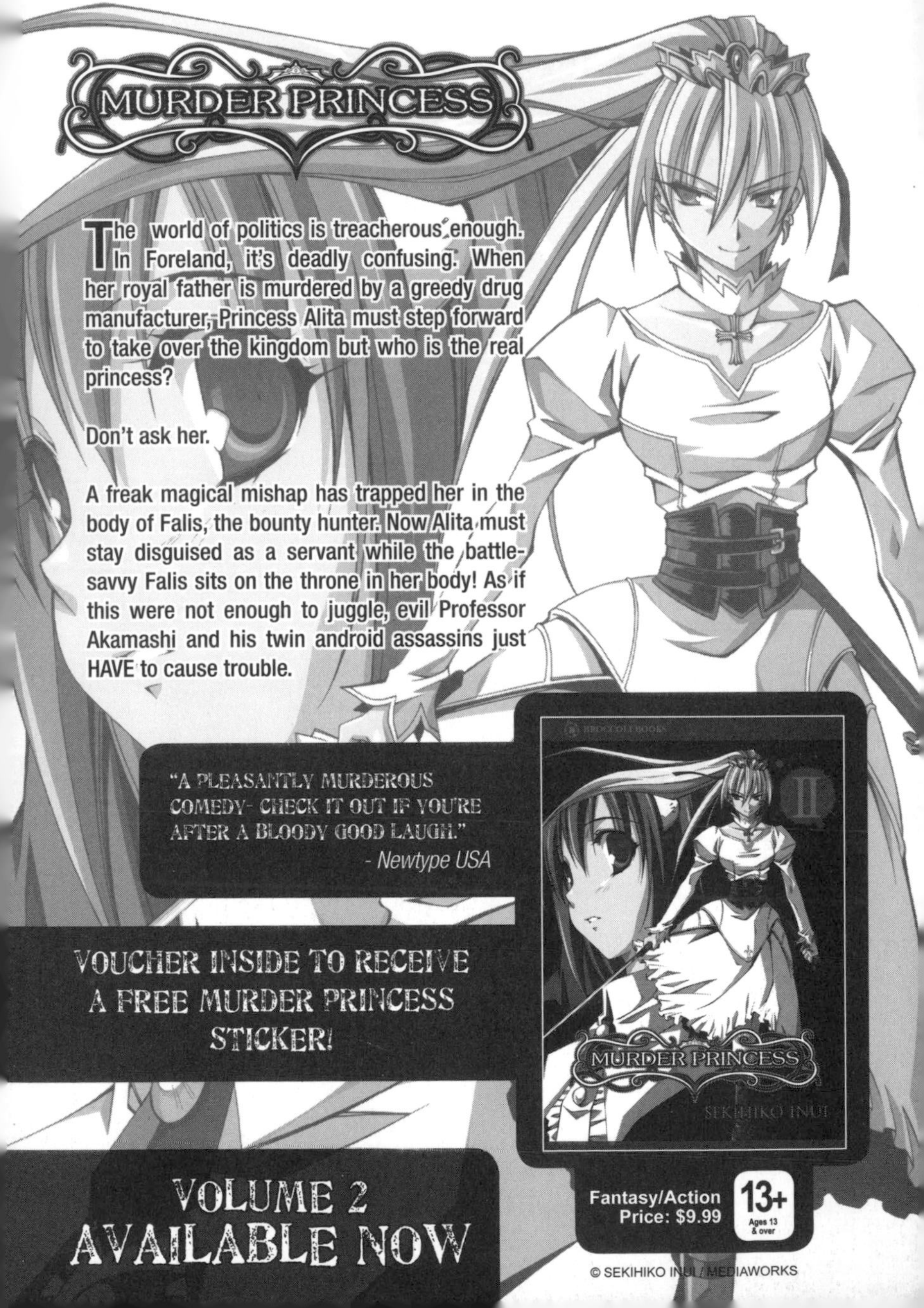
MURDER PRINCESS
The world of politics is treacherous enough. In Foreland, it's deadly confusing. When her royal father is murdered by a greedy drug manufacturer, Princess Alita must step forward to take over the kingdom but who is the real princess?
Don't ask her.
A freak magical mishap has trapped her in the body of Falis, the bounty hunter. Now Alita must stay disguised as a servant while the battle-savvy Falis sits on the throne in her body! As if this were not enough to juggle, evil Professor Akamashi and his twin android assassins just HAVE to cause trouble.
"A PLEASANTLY MURDEROUS COMEDY- CHECK IT OUT IF YOU'RE AFTER A BLOODY GOOD LAUGH."
- Newtype USA
VOUCHER INSIDE TO RECEIVE A FREE MURDER PRINCESS STICKER!
II
MURDER PRINCESS
SEKIHIKO INUI
VOLUME 2 AVAILABLE NOW
Fantasy/Action
Price: $9.99
13+
Ages 13 & over
© SEKIHIKO INUI / MEDIAWORKS

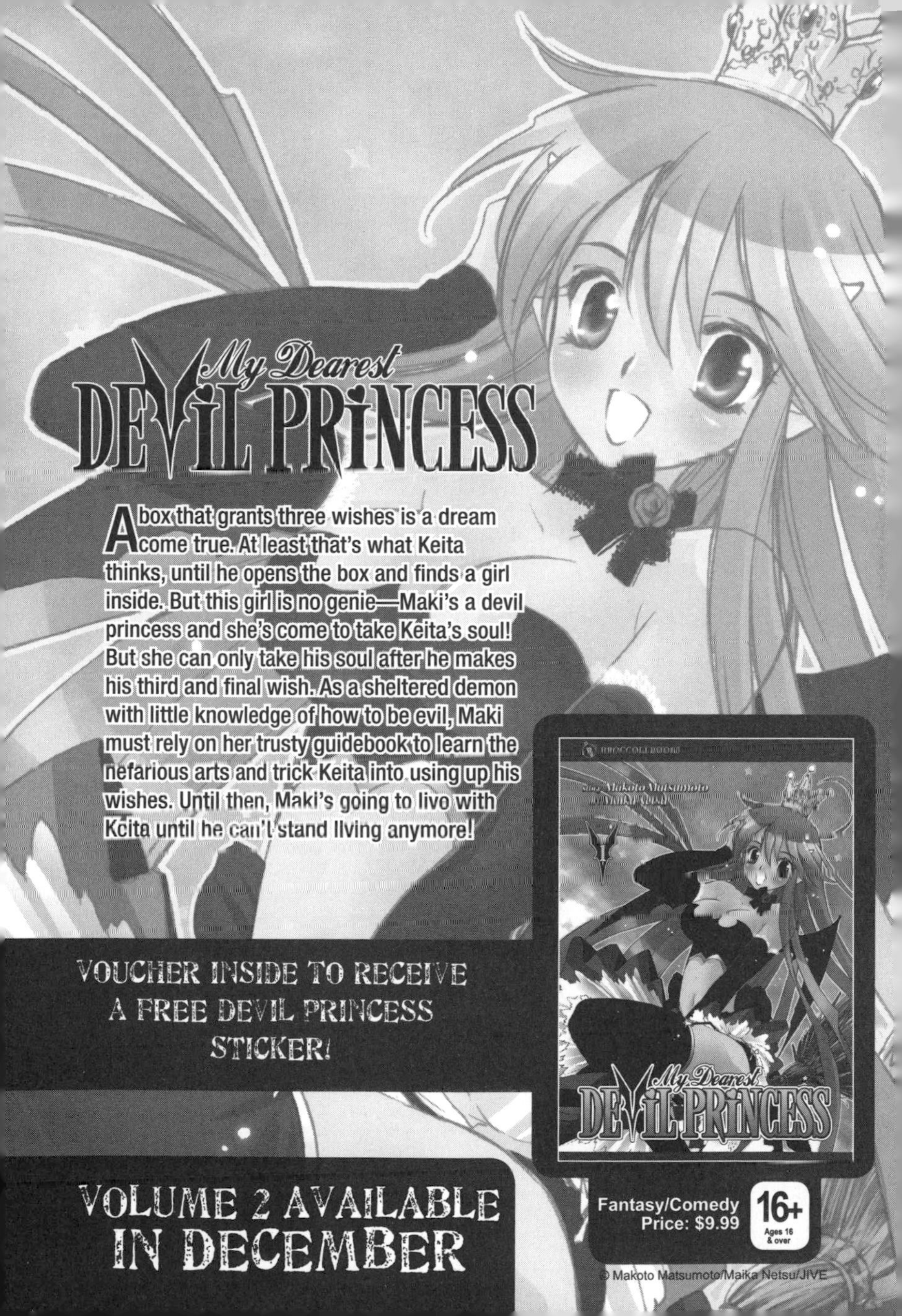
My Dearest
DEVIL PRINCESS
A box that grants three wishes is a dream come true. At least that's what Keita thinks, until he opens the box and finds a girl inside. But this girl is no genie—Maki's a devil princess and she's come to take Keita's soul! But she can only take his soul after he makes his third and final wish. As a sheltered demon with little knowledge of how to be evil, Maki must rely on her trusty guidebook to learn the nefarious arts and trick Keita into using up his wishes. Until then, Maki's going to livo with Kcita until he can't stand living anymore!
VOUCHER INSIDE TO RECEIVE A FREE DEVIL PRINCESS STICKER!
My Dearest
DEVIL PRINCESS
VOLUME 2 AVAILABLE IN DECEMBER
Fantasy/Comedy
Price: $9.99
16+
Ages 16 & over
© Makoto Matsumoto/Maika Netsu/JIVE

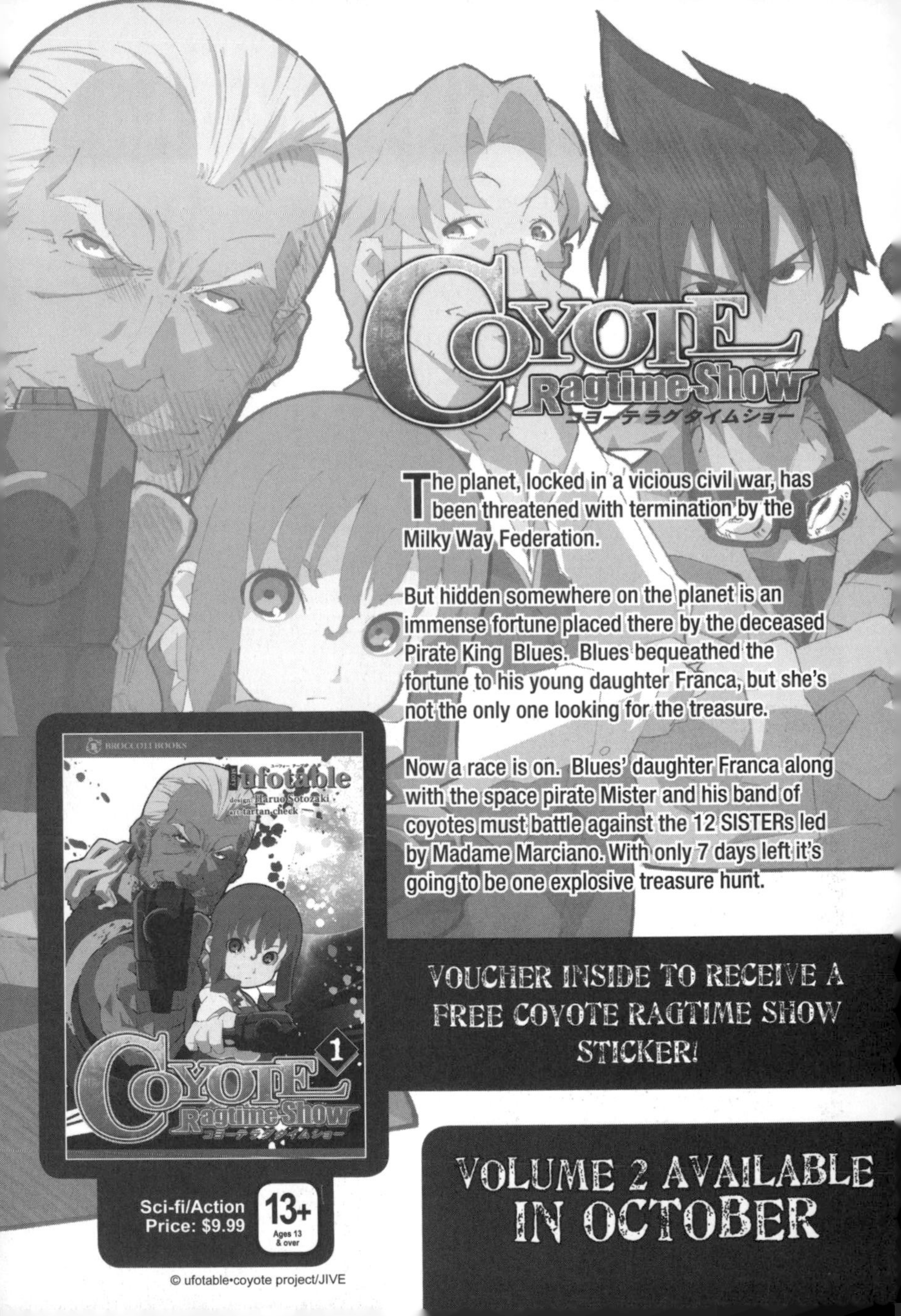
COYOTE Ragtime Show
コヨーテラグタイムショー
The planet, locked in a vicious civil war, has been threatened with termination by the Milky Way Federation.
But hidden somewhere on the planet is an immense fortune placed there by the deceased Pirate King Blues. Blues bequeathed the fortune to his young daughter Franca, but she's not the only one looking for the treasure.
Now a race is on. Blues' daughter Franca along with the space pirate Mister and his band of coyotes must battle against the 12 SISTERs led by Madame Marciano. With only 7 days left it's going to be one explosive treasure hunt.
BROCCOLI BOOKS
ufotable
design Haruo Sotozaki
art tartan check
COYOTE Ragtime Show 1
コヨーテラグタイムショー
VOUCHER INSIDE TO RECEIVE A FREE COYOTE RAGTIME SHOW STICKER!
Sci-fi/Action
Price: $9.99
13+
Ages 13 & over
VOLUME 2 AVAILABLE IN OCTOBER
© ufotable•coyote project/JIVE

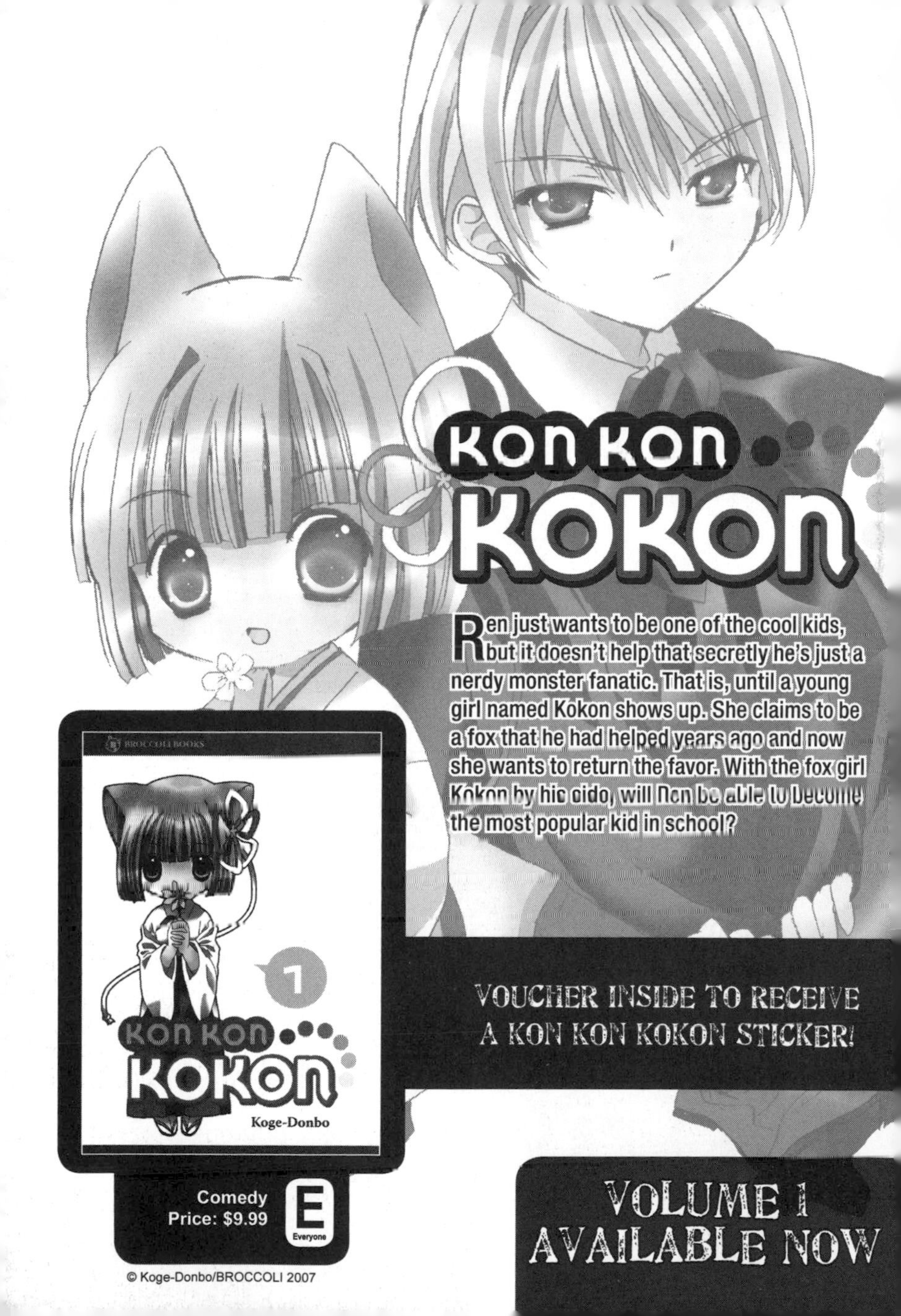
KON KON KOKON
Ren just wants to be one of the cool kids, but it doesn't help that secretly he's just a nerdy monster fanatic. That is, until a young girl named Kokon shows up. She claims to be a fox that he had helped years ago and now she wants to return the favor. With the fox girl Kokon by his side, will Ren be able to become the most popular kid in school?
BROCCOLI BOOKS
1
KON KON KOKON
Koge-Donbo
VOUCHER INSIDE TO RECEIVE A KON KON KOKON STICKER!
Comedy
Price: $9.99
E
Everyone
VOLUME 1 AVAILABLE NOW
© Koge-Donbo/BROCCOLI 2007

GET YOUR BROCCOLI BOOKS AT

ANIME GAMERS

WHEN YOU BUY YOUR BROCCOLI BOOKS
AT ANIMEGAMERSUSA.COM,
THE BONUS ITEM IS ALREADY INCLUDED
PLUS YOU GET FREE SHIPPING!

THAT MEANS NO MORE TEARING OUT THE LAST
PAGE OF YOUR BOOK, NO MORE FILLING OUT THE
QUESTIONNAIRE, AND SENDING IT IN!

VISIT ANIMEGAMERSUSA.COM TODAY!
Also... For the latest deals and promotions, sign up For the Anime Gamers mailing list!

STOP DOOD!
YOU'RE READING THE WRONG WAY!

This is the end of the book! In Japan, manga is generally read from right to left. All reading starts on the upper right corner, and ends on the lower left. American comics are generally read from left to right, starting on the upper left of each page. In order to preserve the true nature of the work, we printed this book in a right to left fashion. Those who are unfamiliar with manga may find this confusing at first, but once you start getting into the story, you will wonder how you ever read manga any other way!

THIS QUESTIONNAIRE IS REDEEMABLE FOR:

Disgaea® 2 Volume 1 Sticker

Broccoli Books Questionnaire

Fill out and return to Broccoli Books to receive your corresponding sticker!*

PLEASE MAIL THE COMPLETE FORM, ALONG WITH UNUSED UNITED STATES POSTAGE
STAMPS WORTH $0.50 ENCLOSED IN THE ENVELOPE TO:**

Broccoli International
Attn: Broccoli Books Sticker Committee
1728 S. La Cienega Blvd
Los Angeles, CA 90035

(Please write legibly)

Name: _____

Address: _____

City, State, Zip: _____

E-mail: _____

Gender: ☐ Male ☐ Female **Age:** _____

(If you are under 13 years old, parental consent is required)

Parent/Guardian signature: _____

Where did you hear about this title?

☐ Magazine   ☐ Convention

☐ Internet   ☐ Club

☐ At a Store   ☐ Other

☐ Word of Mouth

Where was this title purchased? (If known)

_____

Why did you buy this title?

_____

_____

_____

_____

How would you rate the following features of this manga?

	Excellent	Good	Satisfactory	Poor
Translation	☐	☐	☐	☐
Art quality	☐	☐	☐	☐
Cover	☐	☐	☐	☐
Extra/Bonus Material	☐	☐	☐	☐

What would you like to see improved in Broccoli Books manga?

_____

Would you like to join the Broccoli Books Mailing List? ☐ Yes ☐ No

Would you recommend this manga to someone else? ☐ Yes ☐ No

What related products would you be interested in? (Check all that apply)

☐ Apparel ☐ Art Books

☐ Posters ☐ Stationery

☐ Figures ☐ Trinkets

☐ Plushies ☐ Other

Favorite manga style/genre: (Check all that apply)

☐ Shoujo ☐ Anime-based

☐ Shounen ☐ Video game-based

☐ Yaoi

Final comments about this manga:

_____

_____

_____

Thank you!

* While supplies last.
** For residents of Canada, please send an International Reply Coupon (IRC) of $3.00 US made out to "Broccoli International."

All information provided will be used for internal purposes only. We will not sell or otherwise divulge any of the information.

Requests not in compliance with all terms of this form will not be acknowledged or returned. All submissions are subject to verification and become the property of Broccoli International USA. Fraudulent submission, including use of multiple addresses or P.O. boxes to obtain additional Broccoli International USA information or offers may result in prosecution. Broccoli International USA reserves the right to withdraw or modify any terms of this form. Void where prohibited, taxed, or restricted by law. Broccoli International USA will not be liable for lost, misdirected, mutilated, illegible, incomplete, or postage-due mail. Dust jacket offer is only available to residents of the United States and Canada. For updates to the rules and regulations, please see www.broccolibooks.com.